Creative Soccer Training

FABIAN SEEGER | LOÏC FAVÉ

CREATIVE SOCCER TRAINING

350 SMART AND PRACTICAL GAMES
AND DRILLS TO FORM INTELLIGENT PLAYERS-
FOR ADVANCED LEVELS

Meyer & Meyer Sport

Original title: *Kreatives Fußballtraining*, Meyer & Meyer Aachen, 2017

Translated by: AAA Translation, St. Louis, Missouri

British Library Cataloguing in Publication Data

A catalogue record for this book is available from the British Library

Creative Soccer Training

Maidenhead: Meyer & Meyer Sport (UK) Ltd., 2017

ISBN 978-1-78255-120-1

© 2017 by Meyer & Meyer Sport, Aachen, Germany

Auckland, Beirut, Dubai, Hägendorf, Hong Kong, Indianapolis, Cairo, Cape Town, Manila, Maidenhead, New Delhi, Singapore, Sydney, Teheran, Vienna

Member of the World Sport Publishers' Association (WSPA)

www.w-s-p-a.org

Printed by: Print Consult GmbH, Munich, Germany

ISBN 978-1-78255-120-1

Email: info@m-m-sports.com

www.m-m-sports.com

TABLE OF CONTENTS

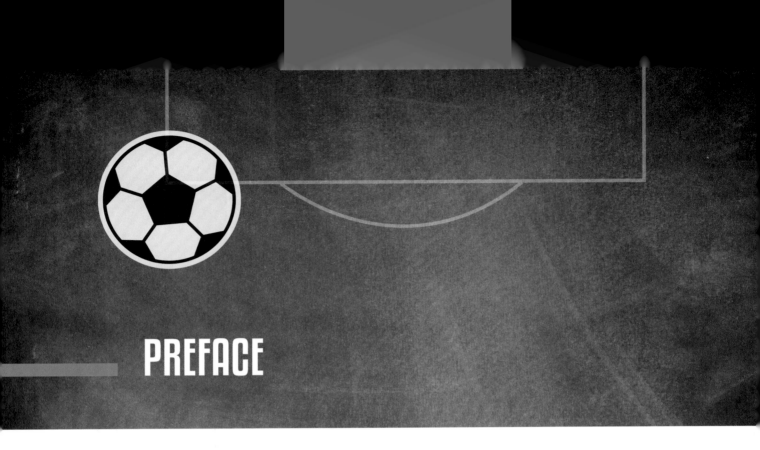

PREFACE

Stephan Kerber

For the past fifteen years I have served in a managerial capacity as the DFB's (German Football Association) base coordinator in Hamburg, Germany, to implement the DFB's talent promotion program at the Hamburg Football Association's six DFB bases. In doing so I have had the pleasure of working with an amazing, enthusiastic coaching team that enjoys developing modern training units for our young up-and-coming soccer players.

This book, with its special creative touch, is a team effort between long-time DFB base coach Fabian Seeger (seven years at the DFB base Sachsenweg) and Loïc Favé, who for the past two years has been working as DFB base coach at the DFB base Mümmelmannsberg.

Both are dedicated to providing attractive, open-ended training exercises to talented up-and-coming players to meet future demands in elite soccer.

In the process, diverse ideas and conversations about the elements of a highly nuanced soccer game resulted in the conception of the many multi-variant exercises intended to specifically develop the players' cognitive capabilities.

Thus this colorful book contains many training exercises such as sport-specific, technically and tactically demanding exercises that are based on geometric shapes, function out of order with simultaneous team actions, take place with and around target areas, promote spatial perceptiveness, and are demanding and thus suitable for an ambitious, ready-to-run, ready-to-work-hard, technically skilled team player.

Symbols, letters, numbers, and colors were used to vividly illustrate playing objectives for the reader in order to facilitate effective learning, particularly with respect to vertical play, chasing the ball, and seeing and recognizing spaces and gaps.

For this I would like to compliment the authors, because next to the motivational and fun training units for the players it will also be challenging for the implementing coach to train with such complexity and to cultivate the joy of playing in his teams.

Since these training exercises have been tested at the DFB bases or with Hamburg Football Association teams (age groups 1999-2005) we have a good idea of how appealing this content is. It results in a greater willingness to run, show more frequent high-intensity actions, help to make quick and accurate decisions, and reveal a high degree of motivation (deep runs, transition behavior in both directions of play). They prompt qualitative technical actions and, adapted to different age groups, generate lots of joy of movement and fun. Many of these exercises teach different elements of elite soccer in an indirect manner and create a myriad of amazing experiences for players, some unforeseeable, making them particularly original and thereby also providing the coach some exciting moments.

As a sequel to Fabian Seeger's first book *The Soccer Games and Drills Compendium*, this book is a continuation of its many ideas and a fantastic interpretation of the demands of today's elite soccer in the form of ambitious training exercises.

My wish for the book's authors and for our combined efforts is that this content may grow wings and be used widely.

Enjoy!

Stephan Kerber

1 INTRODUCTION AND CLASSIFICATION

This book is considered a sequel to the book *The Soccer Games and Drills Compendium. 350 Smart and Practical Games and Drills to Form Intelligent Players—For Advanced Levels*, published in 2016, and its content and quality build on that of its prequel. At the fore in *The Soccer Games and Drills Compendium* is fundamental training content such as passing, dribbling, shots on goal, feints, juggling, and dueling. Additional key subjects are transitioning and reacting, chaos and action, different ways to start a game, active defense, tournaments, tactical exercises, and athletics. This extensive compilation is realistically oriented toward a game-appropriate training approach. The realistic concept is characterized by a very direct representation of actual competitive action and requires the corresponding realistic techniques and tactics. With the book *Creative Soccer Training. 350 Smart and Practical Games and Drills to Form Intelligent Players—For Advanced Levels*, the authors continue their realistic training approach and differentiate the key aspects of basic and classic soccer training. Furthermore, modern, innovative, and new topics of training are cultivated. In addition to the technical-tactical basics in the areas of passing, ball control, shot on goal, tackles, transitioning, chasing the ball, capturing the ball, possession, circulating the ball, and game flow, there is also a focus on creative and imaginative content in the areas of cognition, awareness, pre-orientation, over-the-shoulder glance, color games, playing into the seams, rondos, target areas, action speed, and playing ability. The focus on creativity affects both players and coaches. On the one hand, the bounty of open-ended training activities with lots of options for action and behavior alternatives helps to develop creative players with a high degree of playing ability. On the other hand, the coach's view is directed to innovative training approaches away from the status quo. The training exercises and suggestions introduced here allow the coach to create new possibilities for an appropriately creative and fun training concept.

1.1   EXPLANATION AND USE

This book deliberately forgoes listing rigid field sizes and specific or established distances, and instead emphasizes creativity with respect to implementation on the practice field. The listed number ratios, team sizes, and player numbers are also considered examples and can be interpreted in different ways. Within the scope of implementation with their own training squad, the implementing coach should be given a content framework as a benchmark, without restricting certain organizational freedoms and capabilities. The implementing coach should have the ability to take into account the actual performance capacity, the age-related stage of development, and the current level of his own training squad, and adapt the presented exercises to the specific training situation and organize them in the best possible way. Next to basic training principles a coach's special tools will help to make the individual training exercises simpler or more difficult or adjust the content based on the training squad's current needs. A coach's tools pertain to the use of field size and zone measurements, distances and routes, goal size, team size, number of players and number ratios, verbal and visual coaching signals, and creating rules and standards and specific provocation rules. Next to the immediate effect of the content design of training exercises, the previously outlined coach's tools (i.e., different aspects of training such as intensity and workload, concentration and attentiveness, quality of tasks with respect to overloading or under-loading, transition moments and situations, superior and inferior-number situations, and opponent pressure and pressure of time and space) are impacted and specified. So increasing the field size, for instance, results in more running effort, less opponent pressure, more time for actions, more spread-out play, less ball action, and a corresponding increased focus on endurance while, by contrast, decreasing the field size results in more touches, more tackles, more pressure of time during possession, more pressing, increased intensity, and more fast actions. Increasing the number of goals will prompt more switch of play or initiate aspects such as spatial orientation and peripheral vision. By contrast, using a smaller goal requires more concentration, precision, or detailed techniques. Furthermore, increasing the goal size directly impacts the scoring rate or sense of achievement and has a motivational effect. Another example is the use of different pieces of training equipment to affect anticipation, fear, concentration, ball handling, shooting power, strength, getting-open behavior, or ball control. The deliberate omission of rigid specifications regarding the implementation of the training exercises presented in this book is an attempt to take this creative and varied training approach to the coaching level.

2 TRAINING EXERCISES

Themes in *Training Exercises* include various key subjects and aim to combine different training contents while providing a complex and integrated presentation. In doing so there is also a departure from the classic concept of *practice exercises*. Working on individual training content is replaced by more complex training of multiple elements and advanced content. Hence the term *training exercise* seeks to describe the targeted level of realistic play, heightened complexity, and increased demands. The *training exercises* incorporate elements such as practice, implementation, playing, and competing.

PASSING
BALL CONTROL AWARENESS
SHOT ON GOAL EXPLOITING CHASING
PRE-ORIENTATION CAPTURING THE BALL COGNITION
OVER-THE-SHOULDER GLANCE TACKLES
TRANSITIONS

2.1 PASSING AND BALL CONTROL

Passing and Ball Control contains training exercises to improve passing and ball control techniques. Here the emphasis is on a varied and situation-appropriate technical execution. The passing technique is at the center and ideally should be executed with a firm ankle joint, follow-through movement of the passing leg, and a high degree of body tension. Passes should be played with as much precision as possible, target-oriented, and over various distances. Furthermore, players' awareness is directed toward recognizing passing options and the use of passing gaps. Starting motions that promote a focused receiving posture and an open body position in preparation for receiving a pass are required. Clean trapping and ball control are followed by connecting actions that are geared to position changes as well as starting into and creating space. Next to open passing with action alternatives, these training exercises also include predetermined passing sequences with specific running paths. The aim here is a high number of repetitions and practicing with both feet. Target zones, markers, interfering players, changing the direction of play, and specifying different numbers of touches drive organization, implementation, and variation.

AUTOMATING
ANTICIPATING POSTURE REPETITION
RUNNING PATHS PASSING SEQUENCES
ENGRAIN FEINTS POSTION CHANGE
FOLLOW-UP ACTIONS STARTING MOTIONS
INTERFERING PLAYERS COACH'S SIGNALS
OPEN BODY POSITION PUSH PASSES
PLAYING WITH BOTH FEET FIRST-TOUCH BALL CONTROL
COMMANDS PRECISION

2.1.1   Passing sequence (reacting)

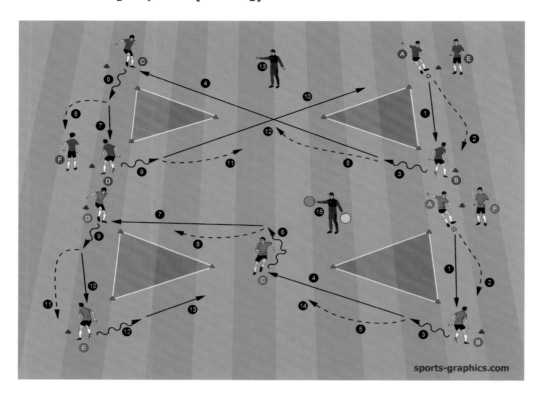

Execution

Below are descriptions of two passing sequences (see BLUE team and RED team). Each group of players circulates one ball around two small fields.

Through pass variation (see BLUE team) and opening up variation (see RED team)

Through pass: Player A passes to player B (see 1) and takes over his position (see 2). Player B controls the ball in the direction of play (see 3) and plays a deep diagonal pass between the two fields to player C (see 4). Subsequently player B runs into the center (see 5) and stops in the middle between the two fields. Player C controls the ball in the direction of play (see 6), passes to D (see 7), and takes over his position (see 8). Player D controls the ball in the direction of play (see 9) and plays a deep diagonal pass between the two fields to player E (see 10). The player who previously ran into the center (player B) lets the ball pass through close to his body (see 10) as a tunnel pass or through pass between his legs to player E, and immediately after the ball passes him runs to this new position C. Player D runs into the center and waits there for the diagonal pass from player A to player B. The coach has the option of changing the direction of play via a predetermined coach's signal (see 12).

Opening up: Player A passes to player B (see 1) and takes over his position (see 2). Player B controls the ball in the direction of play (see 3), plays a diagonal pass to player C positioned in the center (see 4) and takes over his position in the center (see 5). The central player C controls the ball and turns in the direction of play (see 6) to play to player D (see 7) and subsequently takes over his position (see 8). Player D controls the ball in the direction of play (see 9), passes to player E (see 10), and takes over his position (see 11). Player E controls the ball in the direction of play (see 12) and plays (see 13) to player B, who is now positioned in the center (see 14), and continues the passing sequence as described via player F. The coach can use a coach's signal during the passes to the center (see 4 and 13) to specify the side the central player will turn to (see 6).

2.1.2   Passing sequence (looking for position)

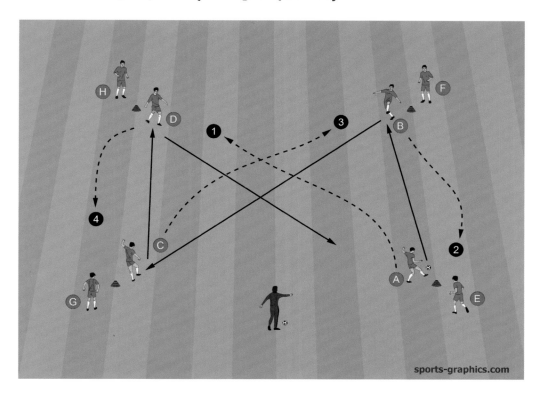

Execution

Players complete a predetermined passing sequence and after each pass have to change to a different position. Position changes take place according to predetermined rules. Players cannot change to positions they passed to. They also cannot change to positions the previous passing player ran to. This means that players are forced to closely follow the passing sequence and be aware of the previously active players' actions in order to accomplish their own position search in accordance with the rules. Player A passes to player B, player B passes to player C, player C passes to player D, and player D passes to player E back at the starting position. The passing sequence continues indefinitely via players E, F, G, and H, and back to the starting position. According to the rules for position changes, player B cannot change to positions G or H (see 2). Player C cannot change to positions H or E (see 3). Player D cannot change to positions E or F (see 4). Starting player A is only restricted from changing to position F, and with his resulting running path (see 1) specifies the follow-up actions of the subsequent pass receivers.

Variations

* Specify playing leg (left/right).
* Specify touches (direct play/two touches).

2.1.3   Passing sequence (opening up)

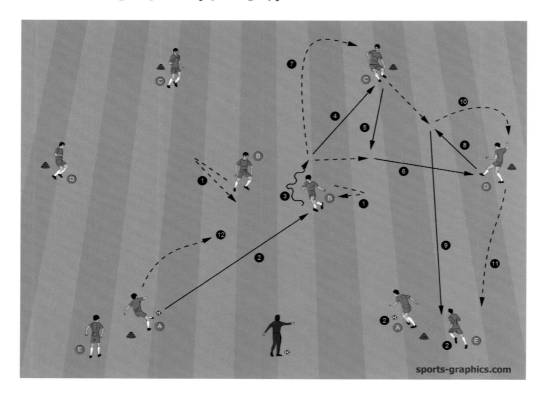

sports-graphics.com

Execution

Players complete a predetermined passing sequence and, after completing their actions, switch to the subsequent position in the passing sequence. In doing so players always position themselves at the cone markers. The starting position is double-manned (see players A and E). There are also two players positioned in the center, even if this position is not marked with a cone. Within the passing sequence, two balls are played simultaneously. Players positioned in the center always begin their actions with a starting movement (see 1). Player A passes the ball to player B in the center (see 2). Player B controls the ball and opens up (see 3) and passes to player C (see 4). Player C plays a back pass to player B (see 5) and player B passes to player D (see 6) before changing to position C (see 7). Player D plays into player C's running path (see 8). Player C plays a deep ball to the starting position E (see 11). After their preliminary pass, players A take over the central position B (see 12). As soon as players E receive the pass (see 9) they start a new action (see 2) to players A now positioned in the center.

Variations

* Specify number of touches (two touches).
* Specify touches (direct play).
* Perform predetermined feints prior to certain passes (see 1 and 9).

2.1.4   Passing sequence (speed dribbling)

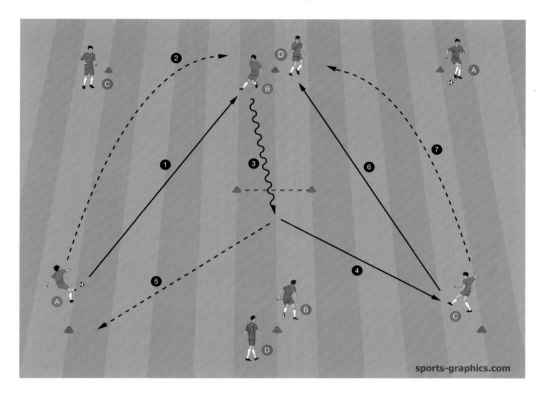

Execution

Players from the GREEN team and players from the RED team simultaneously complete a predetermined passing sequence with the same exercise structure. There are some overlaps in the passing, dribbling, and running paths. This forces the players to keep an eye on the other team and find gaps in order to maintain a smooth flow of passes within their own team. Player A begins with a pass to player B (see 1), follows his pass, and switches to position D (see 2). Player B controls the ball toward the center (see 3) and dribbles through the blue cone goal to play a subsequent pass to player C (see 4), and then changes to position A (see 5). Player C now continues the passing sequence from the other side (see 6 and 7). The RED team trains simultaneously and starts with the identical passing sequence of players A and B.

Variations

* Specify passing leg (left/right).
* Specify position change (double double-pass).
* Perform a feint directly in front of the center cone goal (step-over or fake shot).

2.1.5   Passing sequence (getting open)

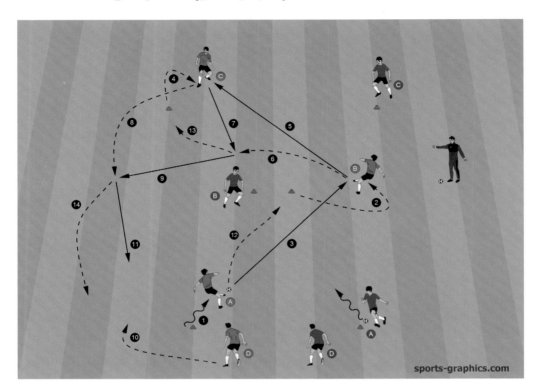

sports-graphics.com

Execution

Players are divided into two teams (see RED team and BLUE team) with a minimum of four players each (see players A, B, C, and D). Each team completes a predetermined passing sequence with its own ball. Due to the configuration of the cones there is some overlap between the two passing sequences (see position B), so the active players must always keep an eye on the other team's disturbing players, make sure their passes are precise, and break away from any possible cover shadows. The two players A each start the preliminary action with a pass. Player A briefly dribbles (see 1). At the same time player B moves from his position into an open playing position (see 2) and receives the pass from player A (see 3). During A's pass (see 3), player C, who is next in the passing order, moves from his position (see 4) and receives the pass from B (see 5). Player B follows his pass (see 6) and receives the back pass from player C (see 7). Player C does a curved run and receives (see 8) the pass into player B's running path (see 9). During player B's pass (see 9), player D moves from the starting position (see 10) and receives the closing pass from player C (see 11). After their final actions the previously active players assume the subsequent starting position within the passing sequence (see 12, 13, and 14) and player D immediately begins a new passing round. The two teams can hold a competition where each team must complete a predetermined number of passing rounds more quickly than the opposing team. Teams regularly change starting positions.

Variations

* Specify receiving and passing leg (left/right, right/left, or alternate).
* Specify touches (direct play/two touches).

2.1.6   Passing sequence (forward play)

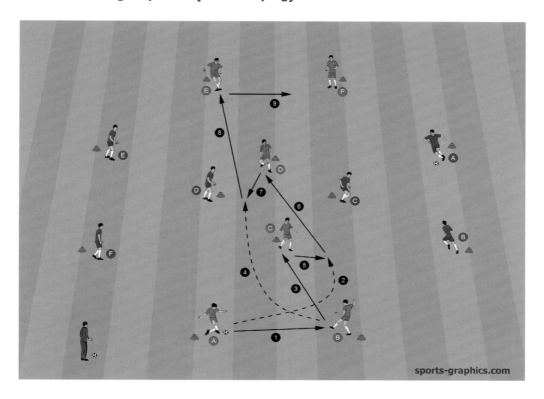

Execution

The RED team and the BLUE team each complete an endless passing sequence. Both teams use the same exercise structure and similar spaces, resulting in an occasional overlap of passing, dribbling, and running paths. This means the players are forced to keep an eye on the other team and find gaps in order to maintain a smooth flow of passes within their own team. On the RED team, player A starts the passing sequence with a pass to player B (see 1). Player A follows his pass on a diagonal (see 4). Player C lets the ball bounce off to player A (see 5). Player A plays a deep pass to player D (see 6). Player D lets the ball bounce off directly to player B (see 7). Player B plays a deep pass to player E (see 8). Next, players A and B assume the positions of players C and D in the center. Players C and D switch to A and B's positions. Player E now starts the described exercise sequence from the opposite side via player F (see 9). The BLUE team simultaneously completes the identical passing sequence (see player A).

Variations

- Specify playing leg (left/right).
- Specify touches (direct play/2 touches).
- Perform feints prior to certain passes (see 1/9 and 8).
- Perform a double double-pass (see 8).

2.1.7   Passing sequence (chaos)

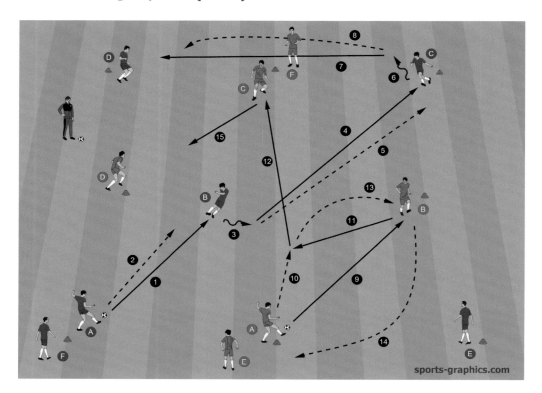

Execution

The RED team and the BLUE team each complete an endless passing sequence. Both teams use the same exercise structure and similar spaces, resulting in an occasional overlap of passing, dribbling, and running paths. This means the players are forced to keep an eye on the other team and find gaps in order to maintain a smooth flow of passes within their own team. The BLUE team positions itself at the blue cone markers and one player (see player B) positions himself in the center of the field. Player A from the BLUE team begins with a pass to player B (see 1). Player A follows his pass and positions himself in the center (see 2). Player B opens up with the ball (see 3) and plays a diagonal pass to player C (see 4) and immediately afterwards takes over his position (see 5). Player C controls the ball (see 6) so he can play the subsequent pass smoothly past RED player C to player D (see 7) and takes over his position (see 8). Player D continues the passing sequence via player A, who is now positioned in the center. The RED team positions itself at the red cone markers. Player A from the RED team begins with a pass to player B (see 9) and follows his pass to the center (see 11) and player A plays a deep back pass to player C (see 12). Players A and B switch positions (see 13 and 14). Player C continues the passing sequence via player D (see 15).

Variations

* Specify playing leg (left/right).
* Perform predetermined feints prior to certain passes (see 4 and 12).
* Perform a double double-pass (see 4 and 12).

2.1.8   Passing sequence (interfering players) (1)

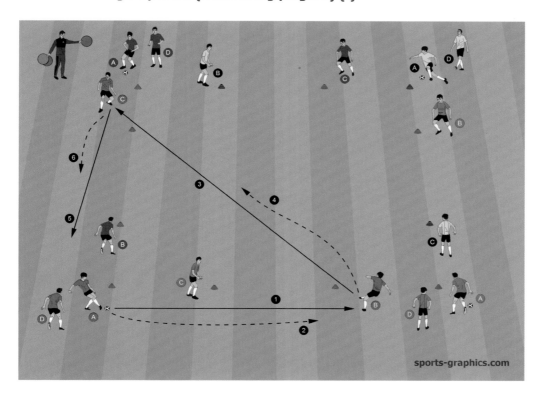

sports-graphics.com

Execution

Players are divided into four teams (see RED team, GREEN team, YELLOW team, and BLUE team) with a minimum of four players each (see players A, B, C, and D). Each team trains on a field marked with cones. The field is triangular and one player is positioned at each cone. The respective starting cone where the group first positions its ball is double-manned (see players A and D). Each group has its own ball and circulates it around their triangle according to a predetermined passing order. The four groups all train simultaneously. Since the four fields are linked, players must always keep an eye on the other teams' disturbing players, play their passes with the necessary precision, and break out of possible cover shadows. Player A plays a pass to player B (see 1) and subsequently takes over his position (see 2). Player B passes to player C (see 3) and takes over his position (see 4). Player C continues the passing sequence via player D (see 5) before assuming the starting position A/D (see 6). The coach can modify technical guidelines via previously agreed on coach's signals (direct play, play with two touches, pass with the left leg, pass with the right leg, or receive with the left/right leg and pass with the right/left), or spontaneously change the direction of play.

Variations

* Complete passing sequence with double double-passes.
* Complete passing sequence with cross-team position changes.
* Modify arrangement of linked diamond-shaped fields.

2.1.9   Passing sequence (interfering players) (2)

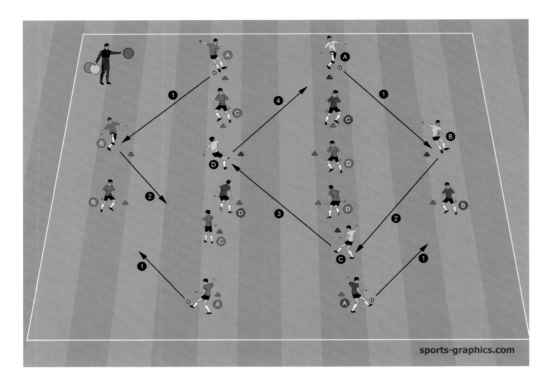

sports-graphics.com

Execution

Players are divided into four teams (see RED team, GREEN team, YELLOW team, and BLUE team) with a minimum of four players each (see players A, B, C, and D). Each team trains on a field marked with cones. The field is diamond-shaped and every player is positioned at a cone marker. Each group has its own ball and circulates it around their field in a predetermined passing order. The four groups train simultaneously. Since the four fields are linked, players must always keep an eye on the other teams' disturbing players, play their passes with the necessary precision, and break out of possible cover shadows. Player A plays a pass to player B (see 1). Player B plays to player C (see 2), and player C passes to player D (see 3). Player D passes back to the starting position to player A (see 4). The coach can modify technical guidelines via previously agreed on coach's signals (direct play, play with two touches, pass with the left leg, pass with the right leg, or receive with the left/right leg and pass with the right/left), or spontaneously change the direction of play. With a fifth player on each team, who would be the second player at each starting position behind player A, the passing players would be able to follow their respective passes and always occupy the subsequent position. The repeated position changes would intensify the disturbance factor. Having the four teams compete against each other to complete a predetermined number of passing rounds as quickly as possible can also intensify the sequences.

Variations

★   Complete the passing sequence with double double-passes.

★   Complete the passing sequence with cross-team position changes.

★   Modify arrangement of linked diamond-shaped fields.

2.1.10   Open passing (slalom course) (1)

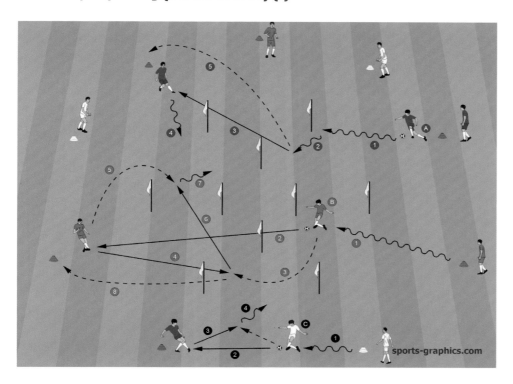

Execution

Players are divided into three teams of four players each. Players position themselves at the cone markers of the same color and each team double-mans one position with ball. There are several poles set up in the center of the field. All three teams train simultaneously. Players are given different instructions for playing on the center. Finally the player in possession has the task of passing to a teammate and taking over his position.

Deep passes variation (see BLUE team)

Player A dribbles toward one of the poles (see 1) and performs a feint (see 2). Next, he plays a deep pass past at least one pole to a waiting teammate (see 3). The teammate controls the ball and starts a new action (see 4). The passing player takes over the now open position (see 5).Variante „Doppelter Doppelpass" (vgl. Team ROT)

Double double-pass variation (see RED team)

Player B dribbles (see 1), passes to a waiting teammate (see 2), gets open (see 3), and receives the back pass (see 4). The teammate gets open (see 5), receives a ball into his running path (see 6), controls the ball, and starts a new action (see 7). The passing player takes over the now open position (see 8).

Include outside players variation (see WHITE team)

Player C dribbles (see 1) and includes a waiting player from another team in a double pass (see 2 and 3) before starting his action in the center (see 4).

2.1.11   Open passing (slalom course) (2)

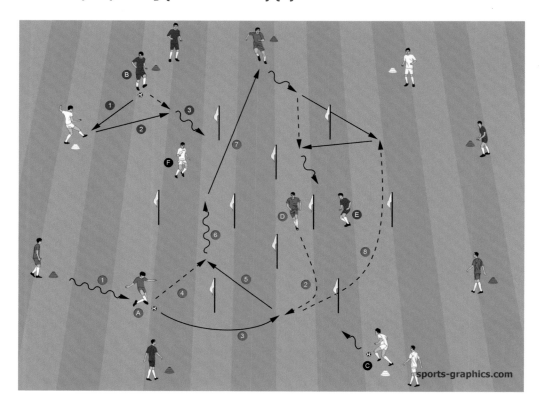

Execution

Players are divided into three teams of five players each. Players position themselves at the cone markers of the same color and each team double-mans one position with a ball. There are several dribbling poles set up in the center of the field. One player from each team positions himself in the center between the poles (see players D, E, and F). All three teams train simultaneously. Players are given different instructions for playing on the center. Finally the player in possession has the task of passing the ball to an outside player and taking over his position.

Simple passing variation (see WHITE team)

Player C dribbles, performs a feint at a pole, and passes to the player in the center. The player in the center controls the ball and passes to a waiting outside player to then take over his position. Player C becomes the player in the center. The center player switches to the outside position.

Double pass variation (see RED team)

Player A dribbles (see 1). The inside player D signals his readiness to receive the ball (see 2) and receives the pass from player A (see 3). After his pass, player A immediately breaks away (see 4) and receives the back pass (see 5). Player A controls the ball (see 6) and now plays to a waiting player (see 7) to then take over his position. Player D reorients himself and creates a new passing station for the player now in possession (see 8).

Include outside players variation (see BLUE team)

Player B dribbles and includes a waiting player from another team in a double pass (see 1 and 2) before starting his action in the center (see 3).

2.1.12   Open passing (commands) (1)

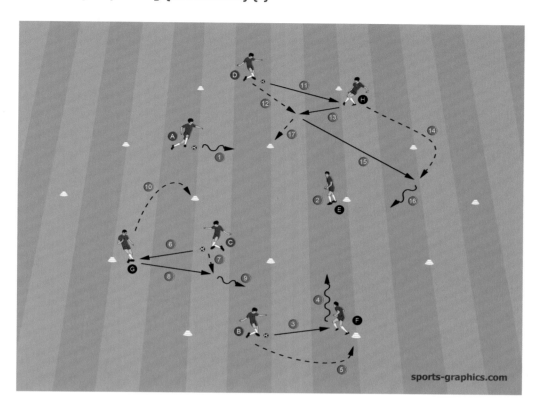

Execution

A number of cone markers are set up on the playing field. Some players have a ball (see players A, B, C, and D) and other players are positioned at the cone markers without a ball (see players E, F, G, and H). The players who have a ball dribble randomly around the field (see player A), perform a feint at the unmanned cones (see 1), and then look for a waiting player without a ball (see 2). Players in possession should involve the waiting players via passes and must issue a command with each pass. The commands prompt predetermined passing sequences and position changes.

Pivot (see player B)

Player B passes to player F (see 3) and issues the command "Pivot" with his pass. Player F reacts, turns, controls the ball, and leaves his position with a dribble (see 4). Player B takes over the position at the cone (see 5).

Bounce (see player C)

Player C passes to player G (see 6) and issues the command "Bounce" with his pass. He immediately breaks away (see 7) and receives a back pass from player G (see 8). Player C traps the ball and dribbles to start a new action (see 9). Player G changes his position and runs to the other cone marker (see 10).

Double (see player D)

Player D passes to player H (see 11) and issues the command "Double" with his pass. He follows his pass (see 12) and receives the back pass (see 13). Player H breaks away around a near cone marker (see 14) and receives a pass into his running path (see 15), and after controlling the ball, starts a new action (see 16). Player D positions himself at an unmanned cone marker (see 17).

2.1.13   Open passing (commands) (2)

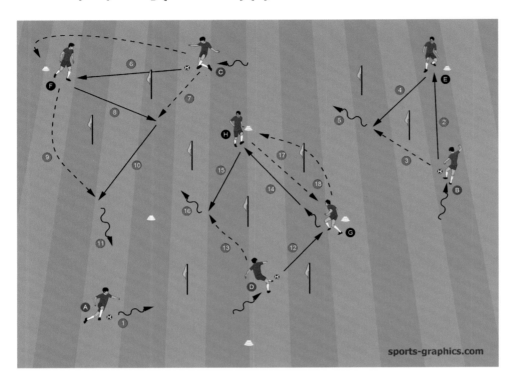

sports-graphics.com

Execution

Several cone markers and dribbling poles are set up on the playing field. Some players have a ball and other players are positioned at a cone marker without a ball (see players E, F, G, and H). The players with a ball dribble randomly around the field (see player A), perform a feint at an unmanned cone (see 1), and then look for a waiting player without a ball. Players in possession should involve the waiting players via passes and must issue a command with each pass.

Bounce (see player B)

Player B passes to player E (see 2), issues the command "Bounce" with his pass, and breaks away (see 3). Player E reacts and plays a back pass to player B (see 4). In doing so, he plays around an imaginary opponent in the form of a dribbling pole. Player B controls the ball and starts his next action (see 5).

Double (see player C)

Player C passes to player F (see 6), issues the command "Bounce" with his pass, and breaks away (see 7). Player F reacts and plays a back pass to player C (see 8), immediately breaks away (see 9), and receives another back pass from player C (see 10), and then starts a new action. Player C takes over the position at the now unmanned cone. Each pass is played around a dribbling pole (see 8 and 10).

Play via player X (see player D)

Player D passes to player G (see 12), issues the command "Play via player X" with his pass (here player H), and breaks away (see 13). Player G controls the ball in direction of the named player and passes to him (see 14). Player H passes to player D (see 15). Player D traps the ball and starts a new action (see 16). Players G and H change positions (see 17 and 18).

2.1.14 Passing in zones (play through the center)

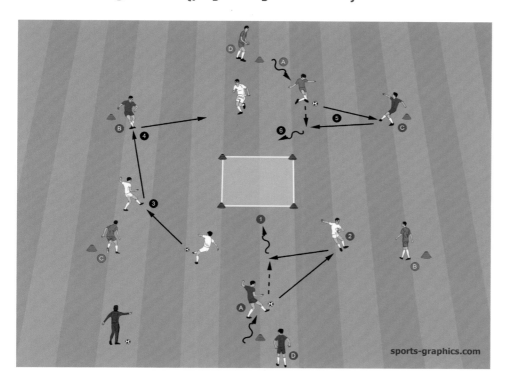

Execution

Players are divided into three teams of four players each. The BLUE team is positioned at the outside blue cone markers and double-mans one station with a ball. The RED team is positioned at the outside red cone markers and double-mans one station with a ball. The WHITE team is positioned in the center with one ball. The BLUE and RED teams each train with one ball. The players A start by dribbling into the field and have specific instructions to ultimately play on the center field YELLOW (see 1) and then pass to a waiting player (see C and B) from their team. The receiving player starts a new action and player A takes over the outside waiting position. The WHITE team circulates a ball via open passing (see 3), and can involve waiting outside players (see 4) as often as possible via a double pass or a third man running. Before playing on the center field, the players A must have played a double pass with a player from the WHITE team (see 2). For added difficulty, player A must first pass to a waiting outside player (see 5) before he can play on the center field via a player from the WHITE team (see 6). Play on the center field can be modified and can be subject to different specifications (see 1).

Variations

* Dribble into the field and pass to the outside to a waiting player.
* Dribble into the field and play a double pass to the outside with a waiting player via the outside player.
* Pass to the outside across two lines of the center field and run through the center field.
* Pass to the outside across two lines of the center field, run through the field and double pass.

2.1.15   Passing in zones (triangles) (1)

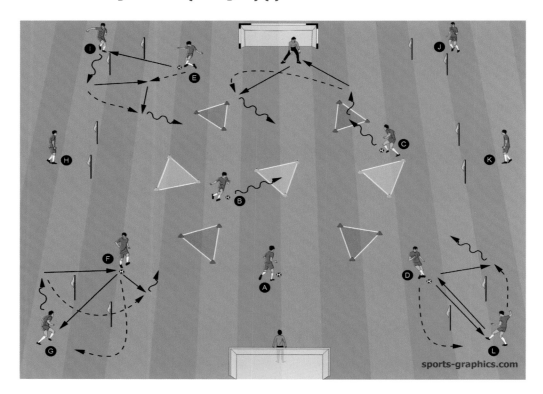

sports-graphics.com

Execution

Several triangles are marked between the two goals in the center of the playing field. In addition there are several passing goals. Each of the players in the center has a ball (see players A, B, C, D, E, and F). The players without a ball are positioned outside, behind the passing goals (see G, H, I, J, K, and L). The players in the center move freely about the field with their ball (see player A), perform feints at the triangles (see player B), have the option of involving the goalkeeper (see player C), and switch positions with the outside players via predetermined passing sequences (see D, E, and F). The goalkeeper can always be included after a feint in a blue triangle (see player C). After involving a goalkeeper, the player gets the ball back via a throw-out by the goalkeeper in an open playing position and dribbles back toward the center for his next action. Position and task changes between inside and outside players can be modified and stepped up.

Double pass (see players D and L)

The passing player receives a back pass straight through the passing goal and plays the ball laterally into the run of the outside player. The outside player controls the ball and starts a new action. The passing player takes over the outside position.

Control the ball (see players E and I)

After receiving the pass, the outside player controls the ball and plays it to the side; the passing player follows and plays the back pass directly into the outside player's running path.

Change direction of play (see players F and G)

The outside player plays the ball to the side and, after the back pass, runs through the center of the passing goal into the field.

2.1.16 Passing in zones (triangles) (2)

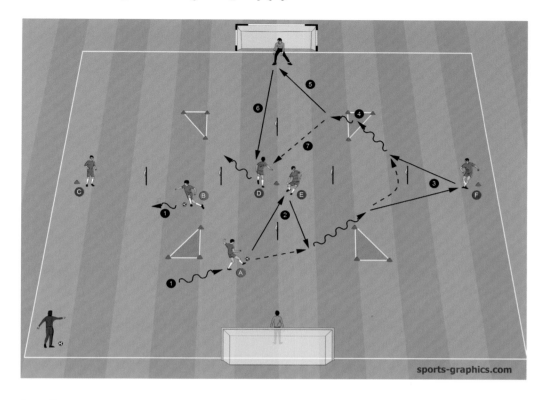

Execution

Several triangles and passing obstacles are marked in the center of the field between the two goals. Two players (see players A and B) are in possession and dribble randomly around the field (see 1). Four players are positioned at the red cone markers without a ball (see players C, D, E, and F). The players in the center complete predetermined passing sequences with the receiving players at the cones, perform feinting movements inside the triangles, and finish on the goal or involve the goalkeeper in passes. Next the tasks are switched and another player takes possession. Players A and B dribble around the field (see 1). Their task is to play a double pass with each of two receiving players, and each time sidestep an imaginary opponent in the form of a marking pole (see 2 and 3). After the second receiving player has been involved, player A must dribble into a triangle and once there, perform a feint (see 4). Immediately after the feint, player A leaves the triangle and finishes on the goal (see 5). Next the goalkeeper throws the ball out to a waiting receiving player (see 6). Player D traps the throw and starts a new action. Player A takes over player D's position (see 7). Adding additional players with and without a ball provides additional options and opportunities. The sequences during position changes after the pass to a goalkeeper can also be modified. The goalkeeper has the option of throwing the ball back to the finishing player, who will look for a new player to pass to and initiates the change.

Variations

* Specify shooting leg (left/right).
* Specify feint (step-over/fake shot/body feint).
* Perform feints prior to certain passes (see 2 and 3).

2.1.17   Passing in zones (looking for position) (1)

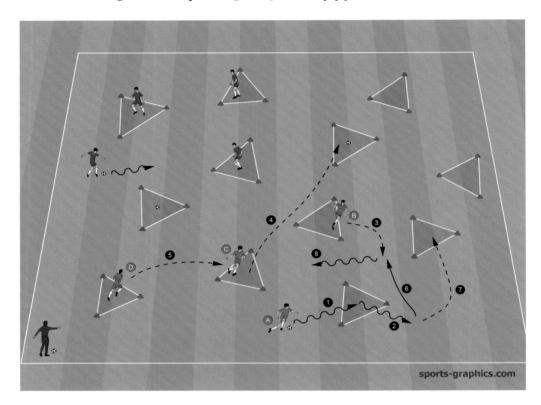

sports-graphics.com

Execution

Several small triangles are marked on the field. Players are divided into teams of four (see BLUE team and RED team). One player from each team has a ball. Each of the other three players is positioned in a triangle (see BLUE team). Additional balls are stored in some of the triangles. Players play the ball along predetermined passing and running paths. Player A dribbles into an unmanned triangle (see 1), performs a feint, and leaves the triangle at a dribble (see 2). He calls a teammate's name (see player B). The player he called leaves his triangle (see 3) for the subsequent pass from the player in possession. Players C and D, who weren't called, switch positions and run into an unmanned triangle (see 7). Player B controls the pass (see 8) and starts a new action.

Variation

★   If a player who wasn't called is in a triangle that houses a ball, he performs the position change in a dribble with the ball at his foot and deposits the ball in the new triangle. The coach can ask the teams via a coach's signal to deposit their own ball in a triangle and to retrieve a new ball from one of the triangles and start the next action with the new ball.

2.1.18 Passing in zones (looking for position) (2)

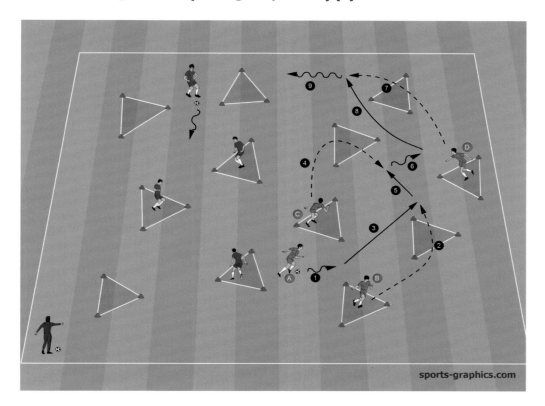

sports-graphics.com

Execution

Several small triangles are marked on the field. Players are divided into teams of four (see BLUE team and RED team). One player from each team has a ball. Each of the other three players is positioned in a triangle (see BLUE team). Additional balls are stored in some of the triangles. Players play the ball along predetermined passing and running paths. Player A always passes to player B, player B always passes to player C, player C always passes to player D, and player D always passes to player A. In addition the respective receiver of the pass always runs through an unmanned triangle prior to receiving the pass (see 2, 4, and 7). After each pass, the players position themselves in an unmanned triangle. The players waiting for the ball always begin their running paths (see 2, 4, and 7) when the respective predecessor and passing player receives and controls the ball (see 6 and 9).

Variations

* Specify playing leg (left/right).
* Specify number of touches (two, three, or four touches).
* Perform feints prior to certain passes (see 3, 5, and 8).
* Change passing order (D to C, C to B, B to A, A to D).
* Change passing order with coach's signal (change from ascending to descending).
* Movement task at a run through a triangle: forward or backward roll (see 2, 4, and 7).

2.1.19   Passing in zones (looking for position) (3)

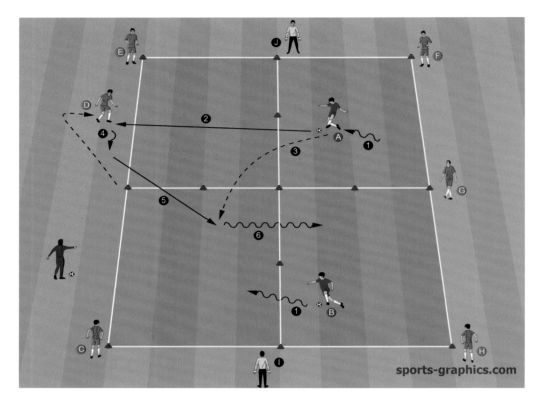

Execution

The playing field is divided into four fields. Two players are on the field with a ball at their feet (see players A and B). Six players without a ball are positioned outside the field (see players C through H). Two goalkeepers may also be positioned at the front edge (see players I and J). Players on the field complete a predetermined passing sequence and pass the ball to a subsequent player in order to take over his outside position. The players initially dribble randomly around the field (see 1) and look for an outside player. Player A passes to outside player D (see 2). After his pass, player A must run to a different field (see 3). Outside player D settles the pass (see 4) and passes back to player A (see 5). Player A controls the ball in the new field and dribbles to a new field for his next action (see 6). The passes must always be played across two lines (see 2 and 5). After player A has completed the specified passing sequence with three different outside players, he switches to an outside position and an outside player with a ball starts a new action.

Variations

★   Specify position change (handoff, simple pass, volley, double double-pass).

★   Position change via goalkeeper (goalkeeper pass, goalkeeper throw-out to an outside player)

★   Involve goalkeepers via a pass to a goalkeeper after each completed action (see 6).

★   Expand passing play (see 5) via a third man running (e.g., player A receives pass from player C).

★   Expand passing play (see 5) via a goalkeeper (e.g., player A receives pass from goalkeeper I).

2.1.20 Passing in zones (include goalkeeper)

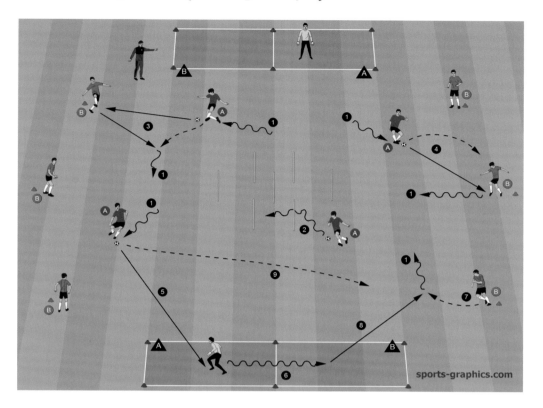

Execution

Six outside positions are marked in the outside areas of the field with one player without a ball positioned at each (see player B). In addition there are two zones in each of the outside areas that are subdivided into two areas (see fields A and B) and each is manned by one goalkeeper. Several slalom poles are set up in the center of the field. Four players are positioned in the center of the field, each with a ball at his foot (see player A). The players in possession dribble around the inner area (see 1). The players A complete independent dribbling and passing tasks. The poles in the center must be negotiated with lots of feints while dribbling (see 1). The outside players can be passed to with the command "Bounce" (see 3), then play a back pass into the field, where the respective player A controls the ball and remains in possession in order to head for another action (see 2). The outside players can be passed to with the command "Change" (see 4) and then move the ball to the center. Next, players switch positions. As a third variation the goalkeeper can be passed to with the command "Switch play" (see 5). The goalkeeper plays the pass sideways (see 6) into the far field (here from zone A to zone B) to subsequently pass to the outside player (see 7) who is breaking away (see 8). The outside player controls the ball and dribbles into the field (see 1) to start a new action. The original passing player (here player A) switches to the now open outside position (see 9).

Variations

* Double pass between passing player and outside player (see 7/9) after switch of play by goalkeeper.
* Command "Double" (see 4) prompts position change with a double double-pass.
* Command "Double" (see 5) prompts back pass from goalkeeper.

2.2   SHOT ON GOAL AND EXPLOITING THE BALL

Shot on Goal and Exploiting the Ball contains training exercises to improve shooting techniques. Here the focus is on the versatile execution of instep shots, inside foot shots, flicks, and volleys. At the center is the shooting technique, which ideally is executed with a firm ankle joint, follow-through with the shooting leg, and with lots of body tension. Shots on goal should be precise, situation-appropriate, and taken from various distances, and should come after dribbling, after settling the ball, and after feints as well as the direct exploitation of passes and crosses. In the course of this process the ability to finish is addressed in a sophisticated manner while also boosting mental strength. Shots on goal are followed by actions which, as downstream action tasks, address transition behavior in the form of running paths, passing sequences, additional shots on goal, and game situations. The training exercises are geared toward lots of repetitions and generate realistic play and a competitive character via pressure situations and a points system. The creative arrangement of the goals provides variety and makes the experience of scoring goals a priority. With its many shots on goal, this training can also serve as goalkeeper training.

PRECISION
ABILITY TO FINISH SHOOTING TECHNIQUE
VOLLEYS INSIDE-FOOT SHOTS
COOLNESS PRESSURE SITUATIONS
VOLLEY TRANSITION BEHAVIOR
CROSSES PLAY WITH BOTH FEET
OUTSIDE-FOOT SHOT LACES KICK
EFFECTIVENESS HEADERS
SHOOTING SEQUENCES OPENING ACTIONS
FOLLOW-UP ACTIONS

2.2.1   Shot on goal with opening on slalom course (feint)

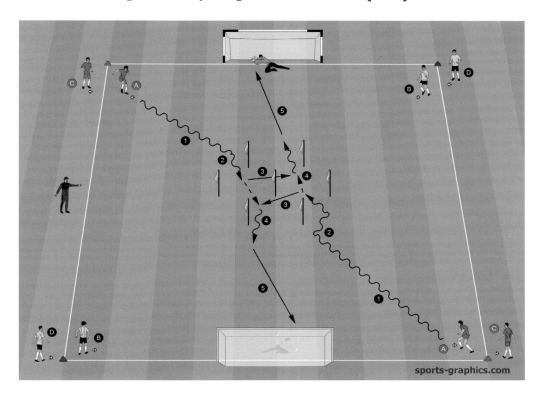

sports-graphics.com

Execution

Players position themselves at four starting positions and start dribbling in pairs from the positions diagonally across from each other toward the center. They perform certain technical sequences at the poles set up in the center, and then each player finishes on the opposite large goal. For the next action the two previously active players line up again at the diagonally opposite position. Players A simultaneously dribble their own ball toward the center (see 1) and perform a feint at the pole of their choice (see 2). Next the players A play a square pass (see 3) and thereby switch balls. The players settle the pass (see 4) toward the goal, perform a feint at another pole, and finish on the large goal (see 5). The first finish by a player A is also the starting signal for the next two players. Both players B begin a new action with the finish of the faster player A.

Variations

* Double pass with the goalkeeper as a starting action (see 1) prior to the first feint.
* Specify passing technique (see 3) for ball change (left foot/right foot).
* Specify passing technique (see 3) for ball change (inside foot/outside foot).
* Specify shooting technique (see 5) for finish on large goals (left foot/right foot).
* Specify shooting technique (see 5) for finish on large goals (laces/inside foot).

2.2.2   Shot on goal with opening on slalom course (double pass)

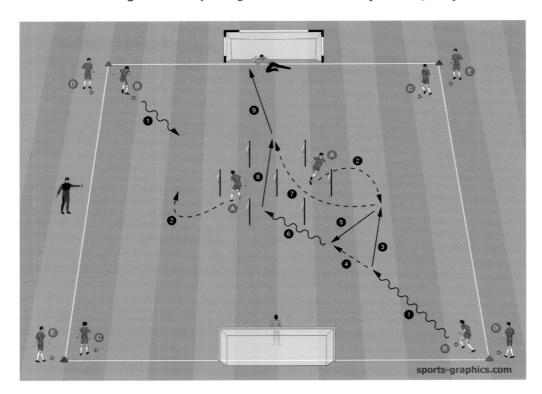

Execution

Players position themselves at four starting positions and start dribbling in pairs from the positions diagonally across from each other toward the center. There are several pole markers set up in the center. Two additional players position themselves among the poles in the center (see players A). The two players B simultaneously dribble their own ball toward the center (see 1). During the dribbling, player A in the center already signals his readiness with a running path outside the grouping of poles (see 2). Player B passes to player A (see 3) and follows his pass toward the center (see 4). Player A passes into B's running path (see 5). Player B settles the ball in the direction of the pole markers (see 6). Player A runs through the center between the poles, toward the large goal (see 7), and receives a pass into his running path (see 8). Player A controls the ball toward the goal and finishes (see 9). The last pole marker is considered the working height. The shooter (see player A) switches to position D with a new ball. The passing player (see player B) takes over the position in the center. The first finish by a player A is also the starting signal for the next two players. With the finish of the faster of the players A, the players C start a new action with the players B, who are now positioned in the center.

Variations

* Double pass with the goalkeeper as a starting action (see 1) prior to the first feint.
* Specify shooting technique (see 9) for finish on large goals (direct finish).
* Perform a feint at a pole marker prior to certain actions (see 6 and 9).
* Specify shooting technique (see 9) for finish on large goals (laces/inside foot).

2.2.3   Shot on goal with opening on slalom course (passing combination)

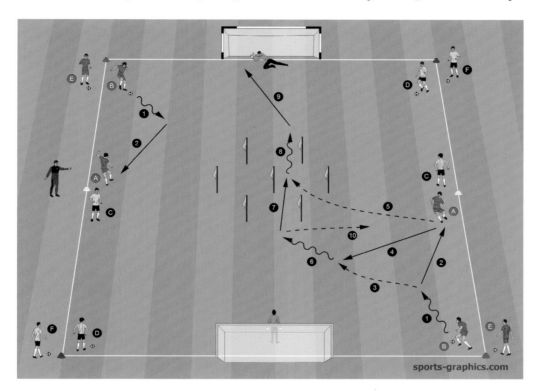

sports-graphics.com

Execution

Players position themselves at six starting positions and start dribbling in pairs from the positions diagonally across from each other toward the center. The players B start simultaneously and dribble toward the center (see 1). Player B passes to player A (see 2) and follows his pass toward the center (see 3). Player A passes back into the running path of player B (see 4) and runs directly toward the center (see 5). Player B controls the ball toward the center (see 6) and plays into the running path of player A (see 7). The last pole marker is considered the working height. Player A settles the pass (see 8) and finishes on the large goal (see 9). The shooter (see player A) switches to A's position in the center (see 10). The first finish by a player A is also the starting signal for the next two players. With the finish of the faster of the players A, both players D start at the centerline with the players positioned to their side (see player C).

Variations

* Perform a feint at a pole marker prior to certain actions (see 7 and 9).
* Specify shooting technique (see 9) for finish on large goals (left foot/right foot).
* Specify shooting technique (see 9) for finish on large goals (laces/inside foot).
* Double pass with goalkeeper as starting action (see 1) prior to first pass (see 2).
* Specify shooting technique (see 9) for finish on large goals (direct finish).
* Specify shooting technique (see 5) for finish on large goals (laces/inside foot).

2.2.4 Shooting sequence (getting open)

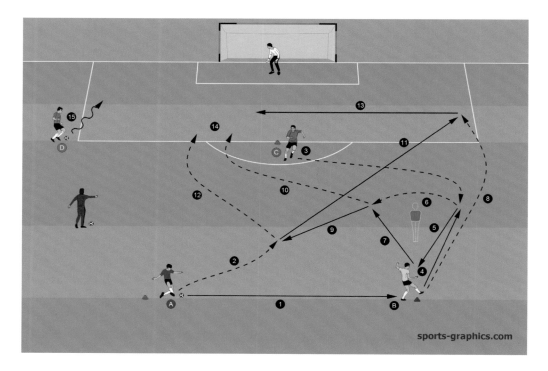

Execution

Players A, B, C, and D each position themselves at a starting position. Players A and D are in possession. Player A begins the sequence, briefly dribbles, plays a pass to player B (see 1), and orients himself to the center (see 2). With the square pass from player A (see 1), player C breaks away from the center with a starting movement (see 3) to the half position in back of the dummy. Player B settles the ball and passes to player C (see 4). Player C plays a back pass (see 5) and immediately signals his readiness to receive a pass behind the dummy (see 6). Player B passes into the running path of player C (see 7) and immediately makes a deep run to an outside position in the direction of the penalty box corner (see 8). Player C passes to player A (see 9) and runs into the center to exploit a cross (see 10). Player A plays a deep diagonal pass to player B (see 11) and also runs into the penalty box (see 12). Player B plays a cross into the center to players A and C (see 13). Players A and C try to exploit the cross (see 14). The outside player D (see 15) briefly dribbles with the finish (see 14). Players A, B, and C transition immediately after the first finish and run once around the center pole marker at starting position C, and then back into the penalty box to exploit the impending cross from player D. Players change to a new starting position for the next round.

Variations

* Specify playing leg (see 5/9) for certain actions (left/right).
* Specify shooting technique (direct finish/header).
* Specify passing technique (see 1, 11, and 13) for certain actions (volley/cross).

2.2.5 Shooting sequence (overlap)

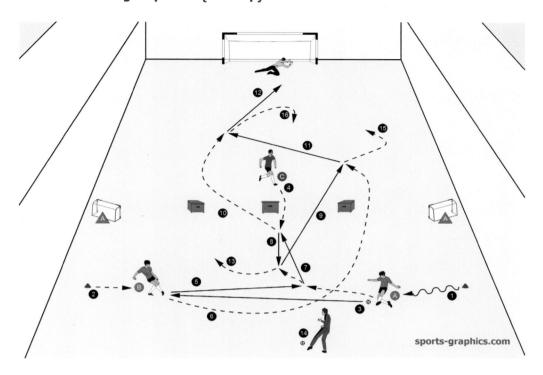

Execution

A predetermined passing sequence with subsequent finish on the large goal manned by a goalkeeper is followed by a 2-on-1-situation on the large goal and the mini goals A. To do so the players position themselves (see players A, B and C) on three start markers. Player C is positioned halfway between the large goal on the one side and the row of vaulting boxes and mini goals on the other side (see mini goals A). Player A is in possession and initiates the sequence with his first touch. Player A briefly dribbles (see 1) and player B starts toward him (see 2). Player A passes to player B (see 3). At the time of the square pass, player C begins to break away for a gap in front of the row of boxes (see 4). Player B passes back to player A (see 5) and continues on a deep run between the row of boxes and mini goal A (see 6). Player A passes to player C (see 7), receives a back pass (see 8), and plays a deep ball to player B (see 9). Immediately after his action, player C runs through a seam (see 10), receives the pass from player B (see 11), and finishes (see 12) on the large goal (one point). After his action, player A orients himself toward the coach (see 13) and receives a pass from the coach (see 14) for the then ensuing 2-on-1-situation. Players A and B (see 15) act as the RED team with superior numbers against player C (see 16) and try to score (one point) on the large goal in 2-on-1. After possibly capturing the ball, player C can counter against the mini goals A (two points). The players move into new starting positions for the next round. Which player is the first to score 10 points?

Variations

* Specify touches (direct passes).
* Specify shooting technique (see 12) for finish (inside foot/outside foot/laces).

2.2.6   Shooting sequence (lay-off)

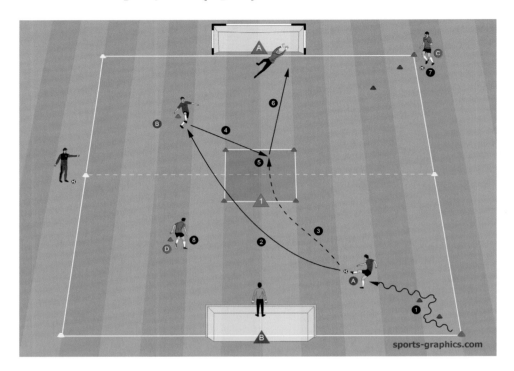

Execution

The BLUE team begins and players A and B start an initial action that ends with a shot on goal A. Player A in possession for the BLUE team begins and dribbles through the cone goal directly in front of the starting position (see 1). Player A then plays a volley to player B (see 2) and runs to the central field (see 3). Player B does a precision lay-off for player A's shot on goal (see 4). The lay-off and subsequent finish must be done from field 1. Player A does a direct finish on goal A (see 5) and tries to score (see 6). The touch by player B is also the starting signal for the RED team. Player C begins the action (see 7) via player D (see 8) with a finish on goal B. The teams compete against each other with the objective of scoring 10 goals as quickly as possible. Each player moves up one position after completing his action. Player A takes over B's position, a third player starts the next action, and player B gets the ball and positions himself at the starting position. Once a team has claimed victory, the exercise is repeated in mirror reverse from the opposite side. Precision can be stepped up by only counting a goal when the finish comes from field 1 into the opposite half (see 5).

Variations

- ★ Specify technique (see 2) for volley (left/right).
- ★ Specify shooting technique (see 6) for finish (inside foot/laces/left/right).
- ★ Specify passing technique (see 4) for lay-off (left/right).
- ★ Modify opening action (see 1/7) by player A/C (double pass with players D/B).

2.2.7   Shooting sequence (passing)

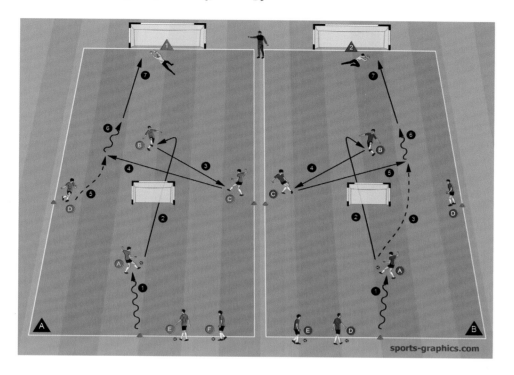

Execution

Below are two shooting sequences (see field A and field B). Players position themselves on four start markers. A goal in the center of the field is an obstacle that players must play over and run around.

Variation 1 (field A)

Player A briefly dribbles (see 1) and plays a volley over the center goal to player B (see 2). Player B lays off to an outside player (here player C) (see 3). Player C plays a diagonal pass into the running path of player D (see 4). Player D moves toward the pass (see 5), controls the ball (see 6), and tries to score on goal 1 (see 7). Next, player B switches to starting position E/F, player D switches to position B, player A switches to position D, and player C remains in his position.

Variation 2 (field B)

Player A briefly dribbles (see 1) and plays a volley over the center goal to player B (see 2). Immediately after, player A runs into the rear half of the field (see 3). Player B lays off to an outside player (here player C) (see 4). Player C plays a diagonal pass into the running path of A (see 5). Player A moves toward the pass, settles the ball (see 6), and tries to score on goal 2 (see 7). Players B, C, and D remain in their positions for the upcoming actions. After a while, all players change positions.

2.2.8   Shooting sequence (crosses)

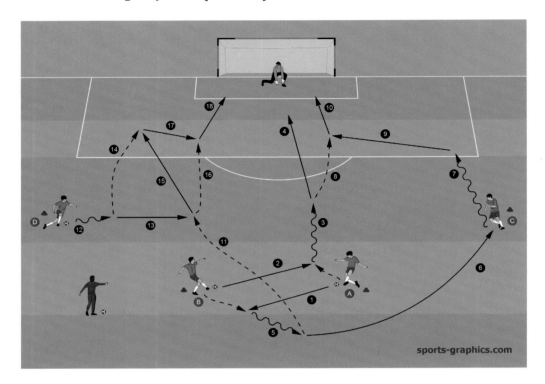

Execution

The four players position themselves in their starting positions (see players A, B, C, and D). Players A, B, and D are in possession. Players A and B initiate the sequence, briefly dribble while maintaining eye contact, and simultaneously pass the ball to each other (see 1 and 2). Player A settles the ball in the direction of the large goal (see 3) and finishes on that goal (see 4). Player B settles the ball in the direction of the centerline (see 5) and plays a long diagonal pass to player C in the outside position (see 6). Player C controls the ball toward the goal (see 7) and plays a cross into the penalty box. Player A, who is already waiting for the ball (see 8), tries to exploit the cross (see 9) with his second finish (see 10). After the pass to the outside position, player B immediately transitions and faces player D (see 11). Player D briefly dribbles (see 12), plays a square pass to player B (see 13), breaks away to his outside position (see 14), and receives a cross (see 17). Player B tries to exploit the cross (see 18). Players move into new starting positions for the next round. After a while, the sequence is completed in mirror reverse from the other side.

Variations

* Organize the activity as a competition (e.g., Which team of four scores the most goals?).
* Specify playing leg (see 9/15/17) for certain actions (right/right/left).
* Specify shooting technique (direct finish/header).
* Specify passing technique (see 6, 9, and 17) for certain actions (volley/cross).

2.2.9   Shooting sequence (wall player) (1)

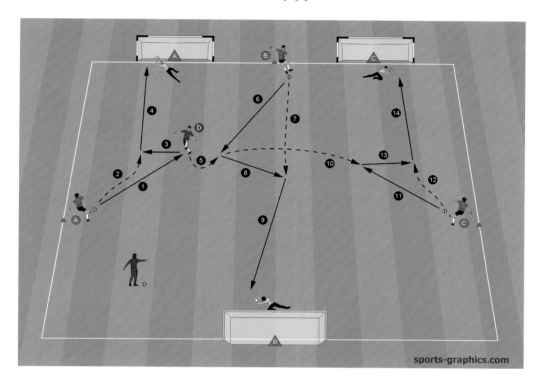

sports-graphics.com

Execution

Players A, B, and C position themselves at the three start markers with a ball. Another player (see player D) positions himself in the center of the field without a ball. Player A begins the action, briefly dribbles, and passes to player D (see 1). Player A follows his pass (see 2), receives a back pass from player D (see 3), and finishes on goal A (see 4). Player D immediately transitions and turns (see 5) toward player B. Player B passes to player D (see 6), follows his pass (see 7), receives a back pass from player D (see 8), and finishes on goal B (see 9). Player D transitions again (see 10) and orients himself toward player C. Player C passes to player D (see 11) and follows his pass (see 12). Player C receives a back pass (see 13) and finishes on goal C (see 14). Players change to the other starting position for the next action.

Variations

* Perform a predetermined feint prior to certain actions (see 1, 4, 6, 9, 11, and 14).
* Specify shooting technique (see 4, 9, and 14) for finish (inside foot/outside foot/laces).
* Specify shooting technique (see 4, 9, and 14) for finish (direct finish/left/right).
* Complete with two goalkeepers (basic manning of goals A and C).

2.2.10 Shooting sequence (wall player) (2)

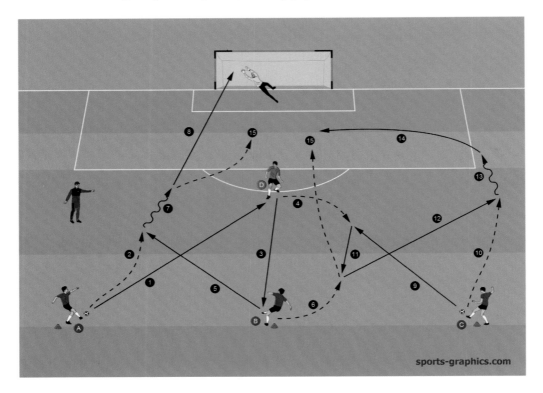

sports-graphics.com

Execution

Players A, B, C, and D position themselves at four starting positions. Players A and C each have a ball. Player A begins the sequence, briefly dribbles, and plays a pass to player D in the center (see 1). Player A follows his pass toward the goal (see 2). Player D passes to player B (see 3), and after his pass orients himself toward player C (see 4). Player B plays into the running path of player A (see 5), and after his pass also orients himself toward player C (see 6). Player A controls the pass toward the goal (see 7) and tries to score on the large goal (see 8). Player C passes to player D (see 9) as soon as player D has transitioned and is ready to receive the pass (see 4). After his pass, player C runs to the outside position (see 10). Player D passes to player B (see 11). Player B plays into the running path of C (see 12), and after his action immediately runs toward the goal. Player C controls the ball (see 13) and plays a cross in front of the goal (see 14). Players A and B are facing the center and try to convert the cross (see 15). Players change to new starting positions for the next round.

Variations

* Mirror reverse sequence from the other side (play with both feet).
* Play out a 2-on-1-situation in the center after the cross (player A acts as defender).
* Specify shooting technique (see 15) after the cross (direct finish).
* Specify shooting technique (see 15) after the cross (header).
* Perform predetermined feint prior to select passes (see 1, 5, and 14).
* Specify shooting technique (see 8) for player A (low/high/laces/inside foot).

2.2.11 Shooting sequence (seam) (1)

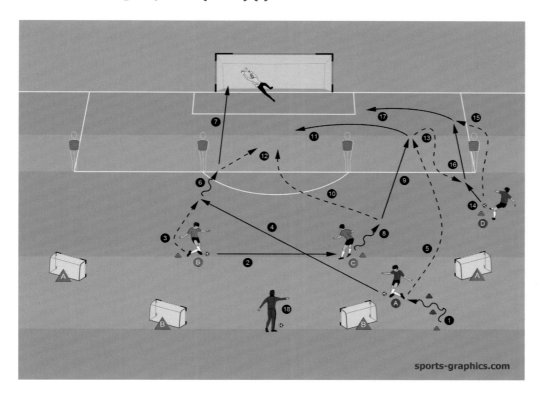

sports-graphics.com

Execution

Players position themselves in the four starting positions. Players A, B, and D are all in possession. Player A initiates the sequence with his first touch and briefly dribbles (see 1). Player B immediately reacts and plays a pass to player C (see 2) and right after breaks away toward the large goal (see 3). Player A plays a diagonal pass into the running path of player B (see 4) and immediately makes a deep run close behind player C (see 5). Player B settles the ball toward the goal (see 6), performs a feint in front of the dummy, and takes a shot (see 7) on the large goal (one point). Player C dribbles toward the penalty box, waits for the overlap, plays a pass into the seam into the running path of player A (see 9), and then immediately runs to the center in front of the goal (see 10). Player A plays a cross to players B and C in front of the goal (see 11). Players B and C try to exploit the cross (see 12) and score on the large goal (two points). Player A, who played the cross, immediately transitions after his pass (see 13) and runs from the offside position back to the zone in front of the dummies outside the penalty box. Player D plays a pass to player A (see 14) and immediately after runs from the outside into the penalty box, close behind the dummies (see 15). Player A settles the ball and plays into the seam and deep into the running path of player D (see 16) while observing the offside rule. After their first finish (see 12), players B and C run around a dummy of their choice and look for the impending cross from player D (see 17). Players B and C try to exploit the cross (two points). After their last actions (see 16 and 17), players A and D run around the outside of the outermost dummy and receive another ball from the coach (see 18). Player A and D now work together as the BLUE team and try to score on the large goal (one point) in the subsequent 2-on-2. Players B and C transition after their last action and now work together as the RED team. They try to prevent the other team from scoring and, after possibly capturing the ball, try to launch a counterattack on the mini goals.

2.2.12 Shooting sequence (seam) (2)

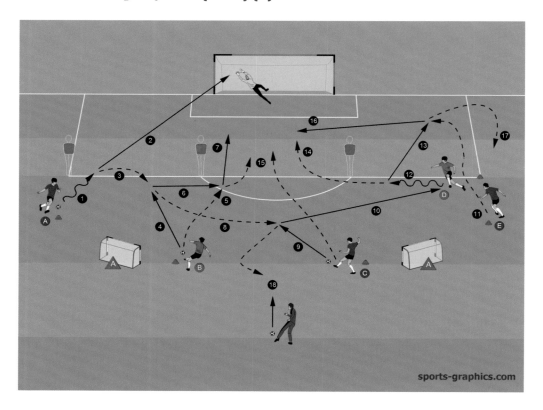

Execution

The players (see players A, B, C, D, and E) spread out on the starting positions. Players A, B, and C are in possession. Player A initiates the sequence, briefly dribbles (see 1), performs a feint at the dummy, and takes a shot on the large goal (see 2). After his shot, player A immediately transitions (see 3) and receives a pass from player B (see 4). After his pass, player B runs toward the center (see 5), receives a back pass from player A (see 6), and finishes on the large goal (see 7). After his second action (see 6), player A runs straight to the center (see 8) and receives a pass from player C (see 9), which he passes directly on to player D (see 10). With the pass from player A (see 10), player E starts a deep run close behind player D (see 11). Player D settles the pass parallel to the penalty box (see 12) and, while observing the offside rule, plays a pass to player E (see 13) and immediately runs to the center (see 14). Player E crosses the ball in front of the goal (see 16). Players B, C, and D try to convert the cross and score (see 14 and 15). After the service, (see 16), player E immediately transitions for the ensuing 3-on-2-situation (see 17). Simultaneous with the third shot, player A receives the pass from the coach (see 18) for the 3-on-2-situation. Players A, C, and E now work together as the BLUE team in possession with superior numbers, and try to score on the large goal. Players B and D are now the RED team and try to prevent the other team from scoring, and, after possibly winning the ball, try to score on the mini goals.

Variations

* During the cross (see 16) player C acts as the defender against attackers B and D.
* During the cross (see 16) players B and D act as defenders against attacker C.

2.2.13 Shooting sequence (transitioning)

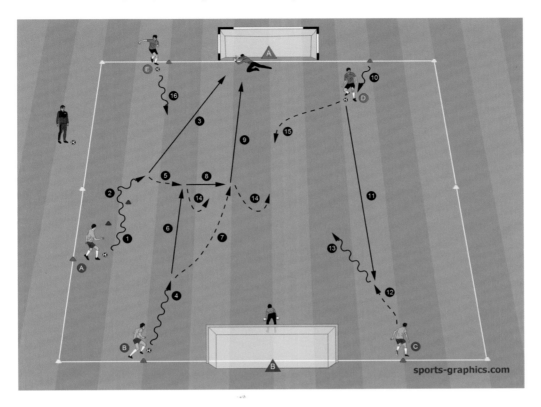

sports-graphics.com

Execution

The five players (see players A, B, C, D, and E) spread out in the starting positions. Players A, B, D, and E are in possession. Player A initiates the sequence, briefly dribbles (see 1), and takes his ball through the cone slalom in front of him (see 2). After the slalom, player A takes a shot on the large goal A (see 3). Player B begins to dribble (see 4) during A's finish. After his shot on goal, player A immediately transitions (see 5) and receives the pass from player B (see 6). Player B follows his pass toward the goal (see 7), receives a square pass (see 8), and finishes on the large goal A (see 9). Player D briefly dribbles during B's finish (see 10) and plays a pass to player C (see 11). Player C moves toward the pass (see 12) and settles the ball in the direction of goal A (see 13). Players A and B transition after their previous situations and now get into offensive mode for the subsequent 3-on-1-situation. Players A, B, and C try to score on goal A (see 13 and 14). Player D follows his pass (see 15) and tries to prevent a goal, and, after possibly capturing the ball, tries to score on goal B. After the 3-on-1-situation, player E dribbles into the field (see 16) and, together with player D, tries to score on goal B. In doing so, players D and E work together as the RED team against all the players from the BLUE team who had previously scored (see 3, 9, and 13/14). The teams' starting positions and tasks change regularly.

Variations

* Organize the activity as a competition (e.g., Which team scores the most goals?).
* Modify the defenders (player A always defends/player B/C depending on scored goal).
* Modify the technical tasks for BLUE team (slalom/feints/specify playing leg).

2.2.14 Shooting sequence (competition)

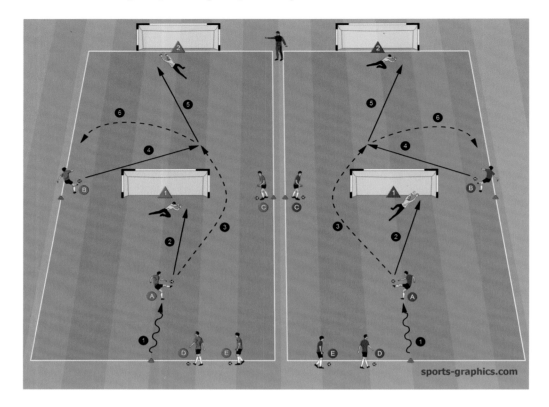

Execution

The RED team competes against the BLUE team. The teams complete a shooting sequence with two goals, one behind the other (see goals 1 and 2), in their own fields, with two shots each. Player A briefly dribbles (see 1) and finishes on goal 1 (see 2). Immediately after, he runs around the center goal 1 (see 3) and into the rear half of the field. Here player A receives a well-timed pass (see 4) from the outside player on the weak side of the field (here player B). Player A exploits the pass and takes a shot on goal 2 (see 5). After his second finish (see 5), the shooter (here player A) takes over the position of the passer (see 6). An appropriate number of extra balls should be kept at positions B and C. After his action (see 4), the passing player (here player B) switches to the starting position (see player D/E). With the second finish, another player (here player D) can begin a new action. He always chooses for his running path into the rear half of the field (see 3) the path not previously taken and receives the pass from the previously inactive outside player (here player C). As part of the competition, the teams try to score more goals than the opposing team.

Variations

★ Perform a predetermined feint prior to certain actions (see 2, 4, and 5).

★ Modify running path (see 3) for second finish (run backwards and turn at a level with the goal).

★ Specify shooting technique (see 2) for finish (inside foot/outside foot/laces).

★ Specify shooting technique (see 5) for finish (direct finish/left/right).

2.2.15 Shooting sequence with follow-up action (1-on-1) (1)

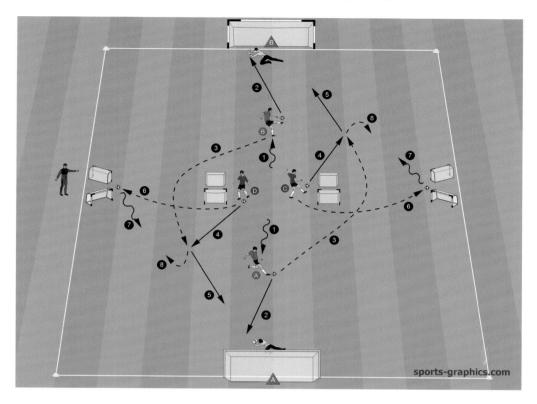

Execution

Four players are positioned in the center of the field, each with a ball at his foot (see RED team and BLUE team). Eight mini goals are set up along the centerline and an additional ball is positioned at each of the two outermost mini goals. The two players from the RED team (see players A and B) simultaneously begin their action and briefly dribble (see 1). Player A finishes on goal A and player B finishes on goal B (see 2). Players A and B quickly transition and run into the opposite half (see 3). Player A receives a pass into his running path from player C (see 4) and finishes on goal B (see 5). After their passes, the two passing players (see players C and D) immediately run to the outside to the two balls positioned at the mini goals (see 6) and dribble toward the large goals (see 7). Players A and B immediately transition after their two shots (see 5) and get into defensive mode for the subsequent 1-on-1 (see 8). Player C attacks goal B against player A, and player D attacks goal A against player B. After successfully winning the ball, players A and B can counterattack on the mini goals. Players change to new starting positions for the next action.

Variations

★ Perform a predetermined feint prior to certain actions (see 2 and 5).

★ Modify running path (see 3) for the second finish (run backwards and turn at a level with the goal).

★ Specify shooting technique (see 2) for finish (inside foot/outside foot/laces).

★ Specify shooting technique (see 5) for finish (direct finish/left/right).

2.2.16   Shooting sequence with follow-up action (1-on-1) (2)

Execution

One player with a ball is positioned at each of two start markers (see players A and B). After a signal from the coach, players A and B simultaneously start their actions, briefly dribble (see 1), and try to score (one point) on goals A and B (see 2). After their shots, players A and B immediately transition and run into the other half of the field (see 3) for 1-on-1 against goal C. The goalkeeper in goal C throws out the ball to one of the two players (here player B) (see 4). Player B controls the ball (see 5) and tries to score a goal C (two points). Player A tries to prevent player B from scoring (see 6) and, after successfully capturing the ball, tries to launch a counterattack on mini goals 1 and 2 (three points). In doing so, player A is allowed to involve the goalkeepers in goals A and B as neutral players. The goalkeepers are allowed to move freely and, depending on the game situation, can signal their availability between mini goal 1 and goals A and B (see 7) or between goals A and B. Players change to new starting positions for the next action.

Variations

- ★ Modify starting movement (see 1) of players A and B (perform predetermined feint).
- ★ Specify shooting technique (see 2) of players A and B (laces/inside foot/left/right).
- ★ Modify starting movement (see 4) of goalkeeper C (throw-out/roll/punt/laces kick).
- ★ Modify running path (see 3) for 1-on-1 (running path outside around goals A and B).

2.2.17 Shooting sequence with follow-up action (2-on-1) (1)

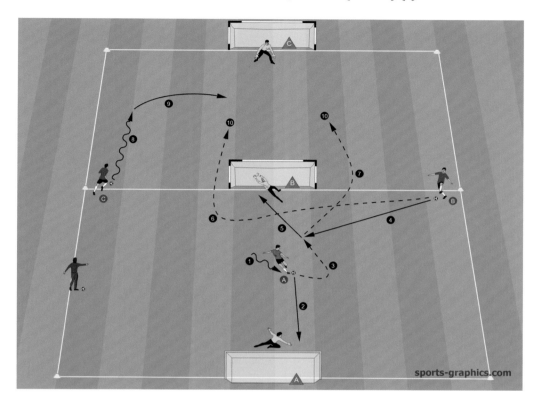

Execution

One player with a ball is positioned at each of three pole markers (see players A, B, and C). After a starting signal from the coach, player A begins his action, briefly dribbles (see 1), and tries to score on goal A (see 2). After the shot, player A immediately transitions (see 3) and receives a pass from player B (see 4). Player A tries to convert the pass into goal B (see 5). After the pass, the passing player (see player B) runs around the goal (see 6) and into the opposing half. After his second finish, player A also runs into the other half (see 7). With the second shot from player A (see 5), player C begins his action, briefly dribbles (see 8), and plays a cross in front of the goal (see 9). Players A and B try to exploit the cross (see 10). Players change to new starting positions for the next action.

Variations

* Modify starting movement (see 1) of player A (double pass with goalkeeper in goal B).
* Modify starting movement (see 4) of player B (pass from goalkeeper in goal C).
* Specify shooting technique (see 2) of player A (laces/inside foot/left/right).
* Specify shooting technique (see 5/10) of certain finishes (direct finish/header).
* Modify running path (see 6 and 7) for cross (crossing/overlapping).
* Modify 1-on-1 after the cross from player C (player A becomes the defender).
* Modify 1-on-1 after the cross from player C (player B becomes the defender).
* Coach passes a ball for 2-on-1 after the cross (players B/C on goal A against player A on goal B).

2.2.18 Shooting sequence with follow-up action (2-on-1) (2)

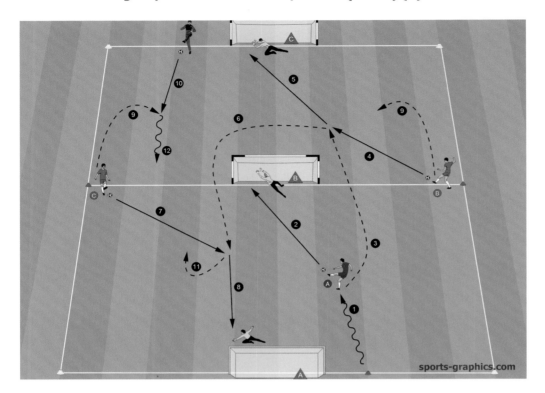

Execution

One player with a ball is positioned at each of three start markers (see players A, B, and C). Player A starts the action and briefly dribbles (see 1). Next, player A finishes on goal B and tries to score (see 2). After his shot, player A immediately runs into the other half of the field (see 3) to receive a pass into his running path from player B (see 4). Player A exploits the pass and finishes on goal C (see 5). Right after his shot, player A runs back into the other half of the field (see 6), receives a pass into his running path from player C (see 7), and tries to also exploit this pass and score on goal A (see 8). After their passes, the two passing players (see players B and C) transition and move into an open playing position for a pass from the coach (see 9). In the ensuing 2-on-1-situation, players B and C now work together as the RED team against player A. The coach puts the ball into play to one of the two RED team players (here player C) (see 10). Player A immediately transitions after his last shot (see 8) and goes into defensive mode (see 11). The RED team (see players B and C) tries to score on goal A (one point) from the 2-on-1-situation. After successfully capturing the ball, player A has the option of a counterattack on goal B (one point) or goal C (two points). Players change to new starting positions for the next action.

Variations

∗   Modify opening action (see 1) of player A (feint/double pass with goalkeeper in goal A).

∗   Perform predetermined feints prior to certain actions (see 2, 5, and 8).

∗   Specify shooting technique (see 2, 5, and 8) for finish (direct finish/left/right).

∗   Modify running path (see 3 and 6) of player A (running path around center goal on weak side).

2.2.19 Shooting sequence with follow-up action (2-on-1) (3)

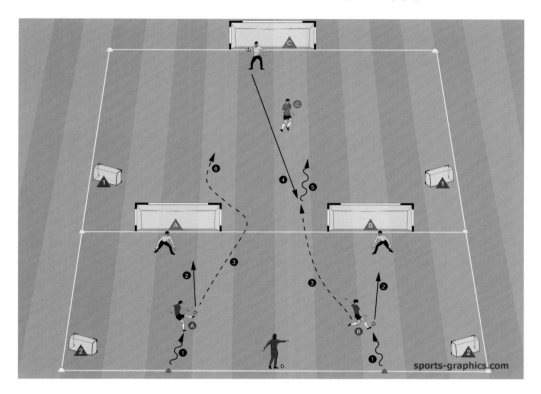

Execution

One player is positioned at each of three start markers (see players A, B, and C). Players A and B each have a ball and after a starting signal from the coach, start their actions, briefly dribble (see 1), and try to score (one point) on goals A and B (see 2). After their shots, players A and B immediately transition and run into the other half of the field (see 3). Player C is positioned in the other half as a defender without a ball. The goalkeeper C throws out the ball to one of the two players (here B) (see 4). Player B settles the ball (see 5) and together with player A (see 6) tries to score on goal C in 2-on-1 against player C (one point). After he successfully captures the ball, player C can launch a counterattack on mini goal 1 (one point) and mini goal 2 (2 points). In doing so, player C can involve the goalkeepers in goals A and B as neutral players. The goalkeepers can move freely and, depending on the game situation, can signal their availability between mini goal 1 and goals A and B, or between goals A and B. Players change to new starting positions for the next action.

Variations

★ Modify starting action (see 1) of players A and B (perform predetermined feint).

★ Specify shooting technique (see 2) of players A and B (laces/inside foot/left/right).

★ Modify starting action (see 4) of goalkeeper C (throw-out/roll/punt/laces kick).

★ Modify running path (see 3) for 2-on-1 (running paths outside around goals A and B).

★ Modify running path (see 3) for 2-on-1 (cross/overlap).

★ Coach passes a ball for 1-on-1 in starting field (player A on goals A/B and player B on mini goal 2).

2.2.20 Shooting sequence with follow-up action (2-on-2) (1)

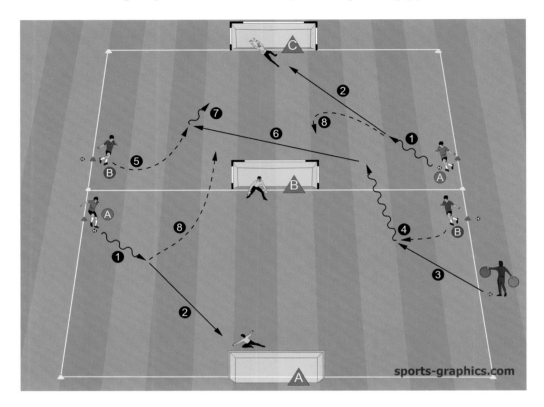

Execution

One player with a ball is positioned at each of four start markers (see players A and B). With a signal, the coach designates one pair of players (here the RED players). After a starting signal from the coach, players A and B from the RED team simultaneously start their actions, briefly dribble (see 1), and try to score on goals A and B (one point) (see 2). As the RED team players A and B take their shots, the coach brings a ball into the game to one of the players from the BLUE team (here player B) (see 3). The BLUE team players do not need their balls and leave them at the starting marker. Player B controls the pass (see 4) and player B runs into the center without a ball (see 5). Players A and B from the BLUE team try to score on the far goal (here goal C) (see 7) with other passing options (see 6). After their shots (see 2), players A and B from the RED team transition and in 2-on-2 try to prevent the opposing team from scoring (see 8), and, after successfully capturing the ball, can counterattack on goal A. In doing so, players A and B from the RED team can involve the goalkeeper in goal B as a neutral player. The goalkeeper can move freely and, depending on the game situation, can make himself available on the left or right next to his goal. Players change to new starting positions for the next action.

Variations

* Modify starting action (see 1) of player A/B (double pass with players from BLUE team).
* Modify starting action (see 1) of player A/B (perform a predetermined feint).
* Specify shooting technique (see 2) of player A/B (laces/inside foot/left/right).
* Modify opening action (see 5/6) of BLUE team (pass in front of goal B).

2.2.21 Shooting sequence with follow-up action (2-on-2) (2)

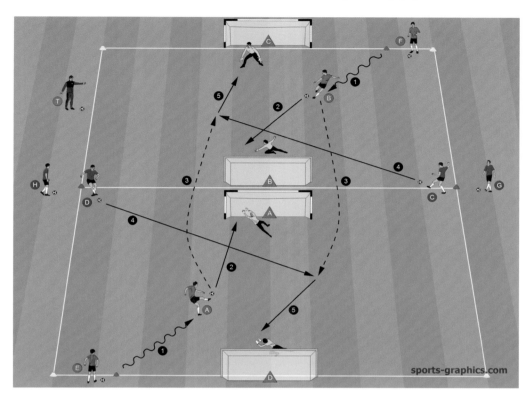

Execution

One player with a ball is positioned at each of four start markers (see players A, B, C, and D). Players A and B start the action and briefly dribble (see 1). Player A finishes on goal A and player B finishes on goal B (see 2). After their finish, players A and B run into the opposite half of the field (see 2). Players A and B each receive a pass into their running path from players C and D, who are positioned outside (see 4). Player A does a direct finish on goal C and player B does a direct finish on goal D (see 5). Next, the coach brings a ball into play for a closing 2-on-2-situation. He plays the ball to one of the players from the BLUE team (see player D or C). After their finish (see 5), players A and B transition to defense. In the ensuing play, the BLUE team attacks goals C and D, and the RED team attacks goals A and B. For the next round players A, B, C, and D move to new starting positions. Players E, F, G, and H will complete the following round.

Variations

* Modify running path (see 3) of players A and B (running path around center goal on strong side).
* Specify shooting technique (see 2) for finish (inside foot/laces/left/right).
* Modify opening action (see 1) of player A/B (perform predetermined feint).
* Specify passing technique (see 4) for certain passes (volley).

2.2.22 Shooting sequence with follow-up action (2-on-2) (3)

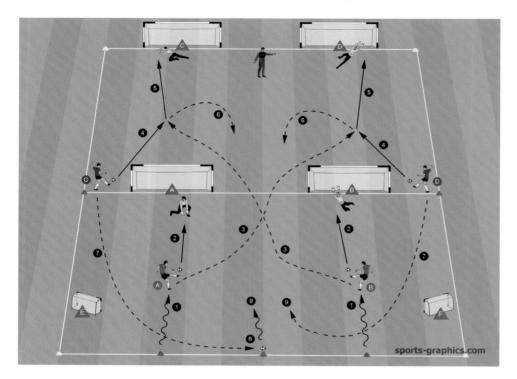

Execution

One player with a ball is positioned at each of four start markers (see players A, B, C, and D). Players A and B (see RED team) start the action and briefly dribble (see 1). Next, player A finishes on goal A and player B finishes on goal B as they try to score (see 2). After their shots, players A and B run into the opposite half of the field and cross running paths (see 3). Players A and B each receive a pass into their running path (see 4) from players C and D (see BLUE team). Player A exploits the pass with a direct shot on goal D, and player B takes a shot on goal C (see 5). After the shots, players A and B immediately transition and play 2-on-2 as the RED team (see 6). Players C and D also transition after their passes, and run toward the ball positioned between the start markers (see 7). The BLUE team picks up the ball (see 8) and acts as the attacking team in possession (see 9). During the 2-on-2, the BLUE team attacks goals A and B (one point) and C and D (two points). The RED team defends the goals and, after successfully capturing the ball, can launch a counterattack on mini goals E and F (two points). Players change to new starting positions for the next action.

Variations

* Modify starting action (see 1) of players A and B (perform a feint).
* Modify starting action (see 1/2) of players A and B (finish on goal diagonally across).
* Specify shooting technique (see 2) for finish (inside foot/outside foot/laces).
* Specify shooting technique (see 5) for finish (direct finish/left/right).
* Modify running path of outside players (running path via outside/outside player in center).

2.3   TACKLING AND TRANSITIONING

Tackling and Transitioning includes training exercises to improve tackling skills. Here the emphasis is on multi-variant implementation of 1-on-1 situations. The primary focus is on the individual tactics of tackling play and includes offensive and defensive actions. At the center of individual tactics in offensive play are specific, fast-paced, and opponent-vanquishing solutions, with prepared running feints prior to receiving the ball and promising use of feints during possession. Within the scope of individual tactics in defensive play, the primary focus is on timing in decreasing the distance to the opponent, situation-appropriate pressing, getting into a sideways stance with a low center of gravity, controlling, running down, and forcing the player in possession off the ball, as well as ultimately winning the ball. The challenges of positional play are stepped up largely via transitions with ensuing and successive game situations as well as target-oriented follow-up actions after winning the ball. The training exercises include side and front tackles that are executed in the center, on the wing, and with various distances between players. A variety of number ratios are used that result in game situations with superior and inferior numbers and touch on aspects of group tactics. Constant opponent and time pressure as well as the organization of a points system emphasize the realistic play and competitive character.

CAPTURING THE BALL
INFERIOR-NUMBER SITUATIONS TIME PRESSURE
TRANSITIONING SKILLS FINISHES
OPPONENT PRESSURE
TECHNIQUES DEFENSIVE ACTIONS
TACKLES TEMPO
SUPERIOR-NUMBER SITUATIONS
OFFENSIVE ACTIONS POINTS SYSTEM
USE OF FEINTS ORIENTATION

2.3.1 From 1-on-1 to 2-on-1

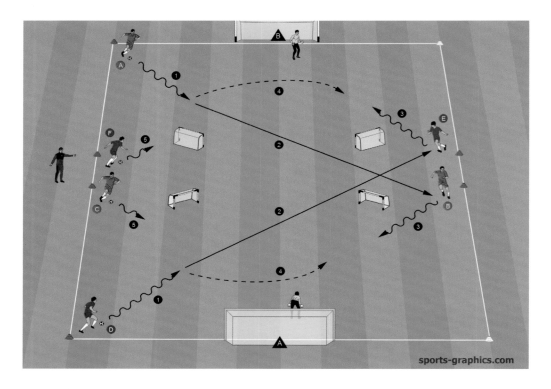

sports-graphics.com

Execution

After an opening technique in the form of a diagonal pass and controlling the ball, various game situations ensue. Here the RED players B and C always attack goal A and the RED player A always attacks the mini goals in the upper half of the field. BLUE players E and F always attack goal B and the BLUE player D always attacks the mini goals in the lower half of the field. After a pass has been played into the other half of the field (see 2), the game situations in the upper and lower half of the field proceed separately. With a signal from the coach, the players A and D simultaneously start the opening techniques and dribble, each with his own ball, into the field (see 1). They pass the ball diagonally to a player marked with the same color (see 2). Player A passes to player B and player D passes to player E. Players B and E control the passes (see 3) and then try to score on the large goals in 1-on-1 play against the opposing passers. After their passes (see 2), the passing players immediately transition and switch to defensive play (see 4). After possibly capturing the ball, they can counter on the mini goals. After a goal is scored from the 1-on-1 or the ball has left the field, a third player (see players C and F) starts into the field with his own ball for the subsequent 2-on-1-situation (see 5). For a new round, players regularly change to new starting positions.

Points system

★ Goal scored in 1-on-1 on large goal (1 point)/goal scored in 1-on-1 on mini goal (2 points).

★ Goal scored in 2-on-1 superior number (1 point)/goal scored 2-on-1 inferior number (2 points).

2.3.2   From 1-on-1 to 2-on-2

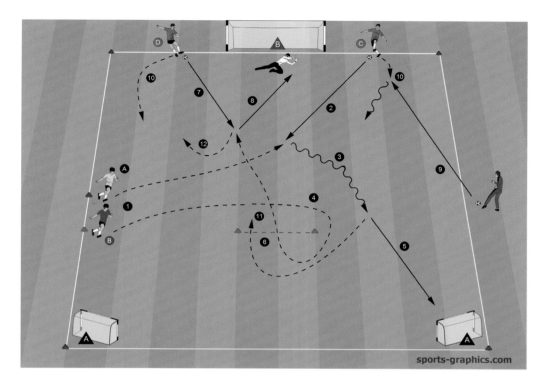

sports-graphics.com

Execution

After two consecutive 1-on-1 situations between players A and B, a 2-on-2-situation ensues between the RED team and players A and B. At a starting signal, players A and B run into the field without a ball (see 1). Player C brings the ball into the game to player A (see 2). Player A tries to break away from the opponent at his back (see player B), settles the pass (see 3), pivots, and tries to score on the mini goals A (see 5). Player B tries to prevent the goal (see 4), and, after possibly capturing the ball, tries to score on the large goal B. After a goal is scored from 1-on-1, either on a mini goal or a large goal, both players A and B immediately transition and run through the center cone goal from the back (see 6). The faster player (here player B) receives a pass from player D (see 7). Player B controls the ball and finishes on the large goal B (see 8). With B's finish, the coach brings a ball into the game for the ensuing 2-on-2 (see 9). Players C and D start toward the coach's ball (see 10) and work as a team against players A (see 11) and B (see 12). The RED team (see players C and D) attacks the mini goals and, after possibly capturing the ball, players A and B attack the large goal.

Variations

* Optional play against all goals after dribbling through cone goal in 1-on-1.
* Optional play against all goals after dribbling through cone goal in 2-on-2.
* Another 1-on-1-situation after pass from player D (see 7).

2.3.3 From 1-on-1 to 3-on-3

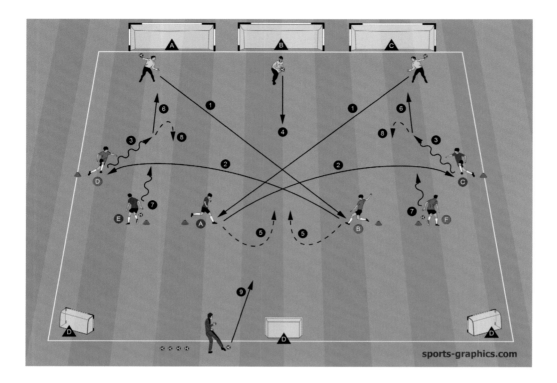

sports-graphics.com

Execution

After an opening technique with subsequent shots on goal, three 1-on-1 situations ensue and finally the teams play 3-on-3 on the large and mini goals. Players are divided into two teams (see BLUE team and RED team) and position themselves at the starting positions in the center of the field. The field is framed by three large goals (see goals A, B, and C) and three mini goals D on the opposite side. Three goalkeepers, each holding a ball, are positioned in the large goals. Players E and F are also in possession of a ball. The sequence begins with an opening action by goalkeeper A and C. With a signal from the coach the two goalkeepers simultaneously throw out their ball to players A and B (see 1). Players A and B settle their ball and play a diagonal pass to their teammates C and D (see 2). Players C and D settle the pass toward the large goals (see 3). With C or D's first touch, goalkeeper B throws out the ball to one of the players A or B (see 4). Players A and B now prepare for a subsequent 1-on-1 (see 5). The receiver of the pass (see player A or B) attacks the large goal B and, after possibly capturing the ball, his opponent tries to launch a counterattack on the mini goals D. Players C and D finish on goals A and C (see 6). With the finish of the respective players, the players E and F start additional 1-on-1 situations with their own ball. Player E attacks the large goal A against player D, and player F attacks the large goal C against player C. After possibly capturing the ball, players C and D try to launch a counterattack on the mini goals D (see 8). The three 1-on-1 situations take place simultaneously. As soon as one 1-on-1 situation ends with a goal, the two players can support their teammates. After all three balls are out of the game and all game situations have ended, the coach brings a ball into the game for a closing 3-on-3 (see 9). Players change to new starting positions for the next round.

2.3.4 From 1-on-2 to 3-on-3

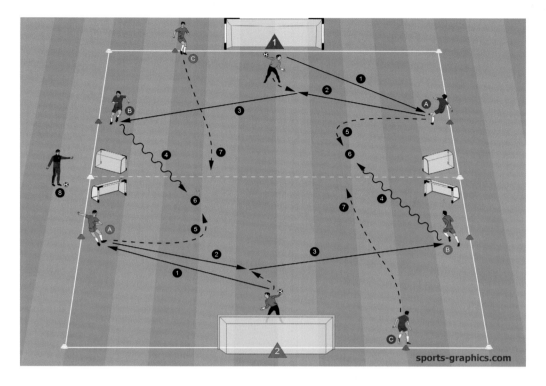

Execution

After an opening technique in the form of a predetermined passing sequence, two 1-on-1 situations against the two large goals ensue simultaneously with the delayed advance of another defender for a 1-on-2. The players (see players A, B, and C) position themselves in the starting positions and both goalkeepers are in possession. The players from the RED team always attack goal 1 and the players from the BLUE team always attack goal 2. The goalkeepers simultaneously throw out their balls to the players A (see 1). Players A pass their ball back to the goalkeeper (see 2). The goalkeeper sends the back pass to the other side (see 3). The receiving player B settles the pass (see 4) and dribbles into the opposing half. After their passes, the players A transition and move into defensive mode (see 5). Now the 1-on-1 situations between players B and A ensue on both sides (see 6). The players B in possession try to score on the large goal. The players A try to prevent an opposing goal and, after successfully capturing the ball, try to launch a counterattack on the mini goals. After the respective attacker (see player B) dribbles across the centerline (see 4), one other defender (see player C) is allowed to move up (see 7). This creates a superior-number situation for the defense and builds up time pressure on the attacker. After both 1-on-2 situations end via a goal on a large or mini goal, the coach brings a final ball into the game for a closing 3-on-3 situation against both large goals (see 9). Players regularly switch their starting positions.

Variation

* Specify passes (see 3) for players A (volley).

2.3.5   From 2-on-2 to 4-on-4

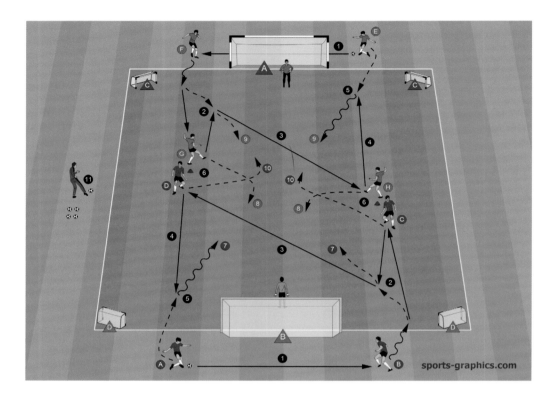

Execution

After an opening technique in the form of a passing sequence, two simultaneous 2-on-2 situations ensue against the large goals A and B and the mini goals C and D. Next are two transition actions into 4-on-4. Players A/B and E/F position themselves behind the large goals, each with a ball. Players C/D and G/H position themselves in a staggered formation in the center of the field at the cone markers. After a signal from the coach, players A and E simultaneously begin their actions. Player A/E plays to player B/F behind the goal (see 1). Player B/F controls the ball into the field and plays a double pass with player C/G (see 2). Player B/F plays a diagonal ball to player D/H (see 3). Player D/H lets the ball bounce off to player A/E (see 4). Player A/E runs toward the pass and controls the ball toward the center (see 5). After their actions, the players in the center transition to defense for the ensuing 2-on-2 situation (see 6). Players A and B now work as the team in possession (see 7) and try to score on the large goal A. Players G and H are the opponents (see 8) and try to prevent a goal, and, after successfully capturing the ball, try to launch a counterattack on the mini goals D. At the same time, players E and F are also a team in possession (see 9) and try to score on the large goal B. Players C and D are the opponents (see 10) and try to prevent a goal, and, after successfully winning the ball, try to launch a counterattack on the mini goals C. After the first 2-on-2 situation ends with a goal, the players get involved in the other still ongoing 2-on-2 situation and play 4-on-4. The designations for the large and mini goals from the previous 2-on-2 play are still in effect here. After the second 2-on-2 situation also ends with a goal, the coach brings another ball into the game (see 11). The teams now play 4-on-4 and try to score on the large goals A and B. Afterwards the coach has the option of adding another ball to the game for another 4-on-4 situation. The teams now play against the mini goals and can involve the goalkeeper for 4-on-4-plus-2.

2.3.6   Different player ratios (from 1-on-0 to 3-on-3)

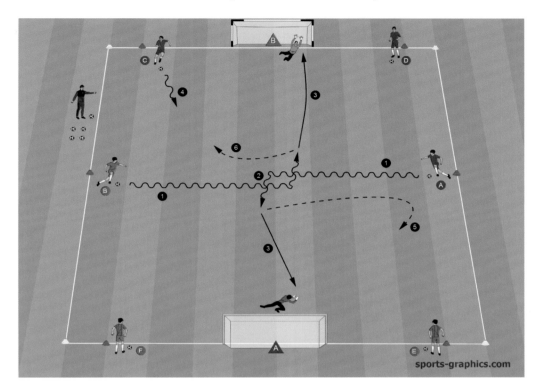

Execution

After an opening technique in the form of dribbling and a shot on goal, the different game situations begin. The BLUE team always attacks goal A and the RED team always attacks goal B. Players A and B simultaneously start the opening technique and, after a signal from the coach, dribble toward each other (see 1). Players A and B dribble past each other (see 2), turn left toward the respective opposing goal, and both finish on that goal (see 3). Next, the coach chooses one of the four players positioned outside with a ball (see players C, D, E, and F). The player who was called first (here player C) dribbles his ball into the field for the subsequent 2-on-1 against goal A. After their shots, players A and B transition to offense (see 5) and defense (see 6) for the subsequent 2-on-1. After a goal has been scored from the 2-on-1 or the ball has left the field, the coach chooses the next player who immediately dribbles into the field with his own ball. By choosing the subsequent player, the coach brings about a balanced (see subsequent activation of player F or E) or heightened superior number ratio (see subsequent activation of player D). One by one, the coach calls all waiting players until finally a 3-on-3-situation is created. The coach has the option of bringing additional balls into the game for more 3-on-3 situations.

Points system

* Goal scored after shot on goal (see 3) during opening technique (1 point)
* Goal scored with superior numbers (2 points)/goal scored with inferior numbers (3 points)
* Goal scored after winning the ball with inferior numbers (4 points)

2.3.7 Increasing player ratio (from 1-on-0 to 3-on-3)

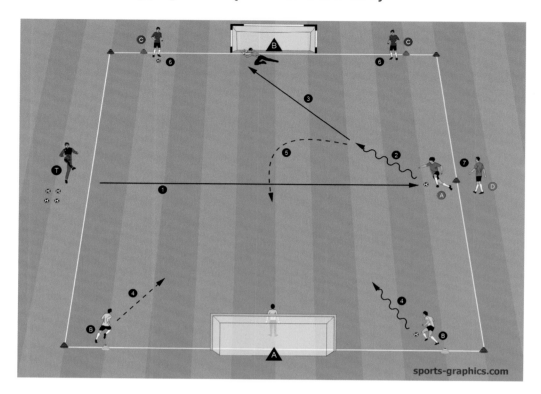

sports-graphics.com

Execution

After an opening technique in the form of controlling the ball and a shot on goal, the different game situations begin. The BLUE team always attacks goal A and the YELLOW team always attacks goal B. Players A and D offer variable support to the teams based on a decision by player A during the opening technique. The coach starts with a ball and passes to player A (see 1). Player A can choose either goal, controls the ball (see 2), and takes a shot on the chosen goal (see 3). The subsequent game situations are determined by player A's choice of either goal A or B (here goal B). With the shot on goal, the team of two positioned on the opposite side (here player B) starts into the field with a ball (see 4) and plays against goal B. After his shot, player A immediately transitions, goes into defensive mode (see 5), and, after possibly capturing the ball, can launch a counterattack on goal A. After a goal is scored or the ball leaves the field, the players C start into the field with a ball (see 6) and together with player A engage in 3-on-2 on goal A. After this 3-on-2 situation the coach brings the final ball into the game and passes to player D. Player D settles the ball and dribbles into the field (see 7). Together with the BLUE team (see player C), player D plays 3-on-3 against the YELLOW team and player A. Players change to new starting positions for the next round.

Points system

* Goal scored after shot (see 3) during opening technique (1 point)
* Goal scored during possession with superior number (2 points)/goal scored after capturing the ball with inferior number (3 points)
* Goal scored from 3-on-3 (1 point)

2.3.8   Increasing player ratio (from 1-on-0 to 4-on-3)

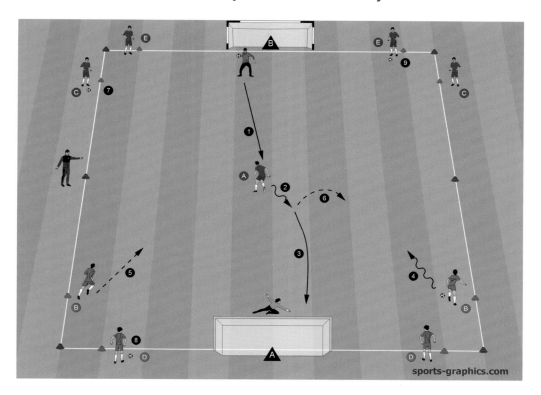

Execution

After an opening technique in the form of a throw-out from the goalkeeper and a shot on goal, the different game situations begin. The BLUE team always attacks goal A and the RED team always attacks goal B. The goalkeeper in goal B starts and throws out his ball to player A positioned in the center (see 1). Player A controls the ball, opens up (see 2), and finishes on goal A (see 3). While player A takes his shot, two players from the RED team are activated (see players B). The player in possession dribbles into the field (see 4). His partner starts into the field without a ball (see 5) for the ensuing 2-on-2 situation. After his shot on goal, player A transitions and goes into defensive mode (see 6). After a goal is scored in the 2-on-1 or the ball leaves the field, the players C start for the 3-on-2 (see 7). The previously active players transition and always participate in the subsequent game situations (here players A and B). Subsequently the players D start for the 4-on-3 (see 8), and afterwards the players E start for the 5-on-4 (see 9). Players change to new starting positions for the next round.

Points system

* Goal scored after shot on goal (see 3) during opening technique (1 point)
* Goal scored with superior numbers (2 points)/goal scored with inferior numbers (3 points)
* Goal scored after winning the ball with inferior numbers (4 points)

2.3.9   Increasing player ratio (from 1-on-1 to 4-on-4)

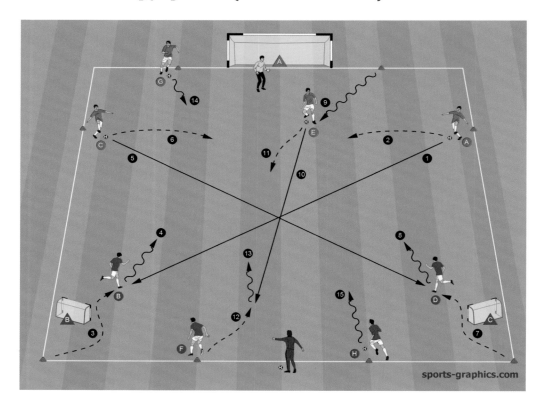

sports-graphics.com

Execution

After brief opening techniques, 1-on-1, 2-on-2, and 3-on-3 situations begin. After that, the players engage in 4-on-3 and finally 4-on-4 play. To do so, the players from the two teams (see RED and BLUE) position themselves at the different starting positions. Players A, C, E, G, and H each have a ball. Players B and D start without a ball from a cone marker behind mini goals B and C. The sequence begins with player A. Player A passes to player B (see 1) and runs to the center (see 2). Player B runs around the mini goal B toward the pass (see 3) and attacks the large goal A in 1-on-1 (see 3). After possibly capturing the ball, player A can launch a counterattack against the mini goals B and C. After a goal has been scored, player C passes to player D (see 5) and runs to the center (see 6). Player D runs toward the pass (see 7), controls the ball, and engages in 2-on-2 play between players A/C and B/D (see 8). After the 2-on-2 situation ends with a goal, player E briefly dribbles (see 9), passes to player F (see 10), and runs to the center (see 11). Player F runs toward the pass (see 12) and engages in a 3-on-3 situation between players A/C/E and B/D/F (see 13). After the 3-on-3 situation ends, player G dribbles into the field and a 4-on-3 situation ensues between players A/C/E/G and B/D/F (see 14). After the 4-on-3 situation ends, player H dribbles into the field and a 4-on-4 situation between players A/C/E/G and B/D/F/H ensues (see 15). Next, the coach has the option of bringing another ball into the game for another 4-on-4 situation. Players A/C/E/G can be tasked with an enhanced opening technique in the form of a double pass with the goalkeeper A (see 1, 5, 10, and 14), provided the previous goal on a mini goal has been scored and the goalkeeper is ready to play. Players change to new starting positions for the next round. After a certain amount of time, the teams change tasks.

2.3.10 Increasing player ratio (from 1-on-0 to 5-on-4)

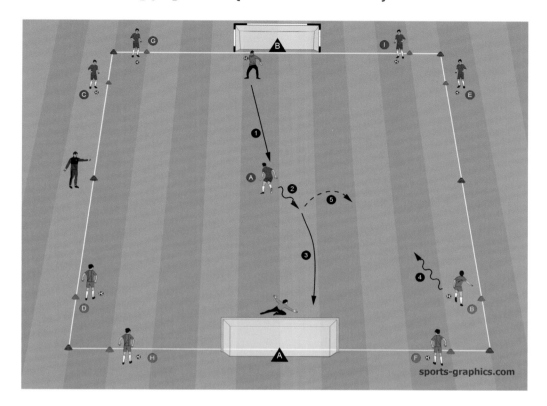

Execution

After a brief opening technique in the form of a throw-out by the goalkeeper and a shot on goal, the different game situations begin. Team BLUE always attacks goal A and team RED always attacks goal B. The goalkeeper in goal B begins and throws out a ball to player A positioned in the center (see 1). Player A controls the ball, opens up (see 2), and finishes on goal A (see 3). At the same time as player A's shot on goal, one of the players from the RED team (see player B) starts into the game for the subsequent 1-on-1 situation (see 4). After his shot on goal, player A immediately transitions and goes into defensive mode (see 5). After a goal is scored from the 2-on-1 or the ball has left the field, a new player from the BLUE team (see C) and a new player from the RED team (see D) in turn start into the field. One after another all of the players positioned outside with a ball start into the field (see players E, F, G, H, and I). The previously active players transition and always participate in the subsequent game situations (here players A and B). So the first 1-on-1 is always followed by other game situations with superior and inferior numbers. Next, after all outside players have been activated, the teams play in a 5-on-4 situation. Players change to new starting positions for the next round.

Points system

⋆ Goal scored after shot on goal (see 3) during opening technique (1 point)
⋆ Goal scored in possession with equal numbers (1 point)/goal scored
    after winning the ball with equal numbers (2 points)
⋆ Goal scored in possession with superior numbers (1 point)/after winning
    the ball with inferior numbers (3 points)

2.3.11 Increasing player ratio (from 1-on-1 to 5-on-5)

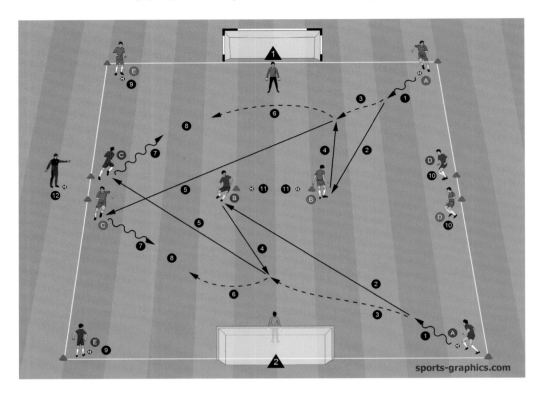

Execution

After completing one opening technique each in the form of predetermined passing sequences, two parallel 1-on-1, 2-on-2, and 3-on-2 situations begin. The players from the BLUE team always attack goal 1 and the players from the RED team always attack goal 2. After successfully capturing the ball, the respective defending team must play a pass off the field. At the beginning of the sequence, the players position themselves in different outside positions. Players A, B, and E have a ball. The sequence begins simultaneously with a brief dribble by player A (see 1). The players A pass into the center to players B (see 2), follow their pass (see 3), receive the back pass (see 4), and play a closing pass into the other half to players C (see 5). The players A immediately go into defensive mode (see 6) while the players C control the pass (see 7) and, in the 1-on-1 situation (see 8), try to score on their respective large goal. After finishing or clearing the ball, the players E in possession (see 9) immediately start with a diagonal pass to opposing players D. The opposing players D control the ball (see 10) and together with their teammates (see players C) play 2-on-2 against players A and E. After the 2-on-2 situation has also ended, the coach brings a final ball (see 12) into the game for the closing 5-on-5 on both goals. Players regularly change starting positions.

Variations

- Modify the opening technique via a double pass with the goalkeeper (see 1).
- Specify passes (see 9) for players E (volley).

2.3.12   Increasing player ratio (from 1-on-1 to 8-on-8)

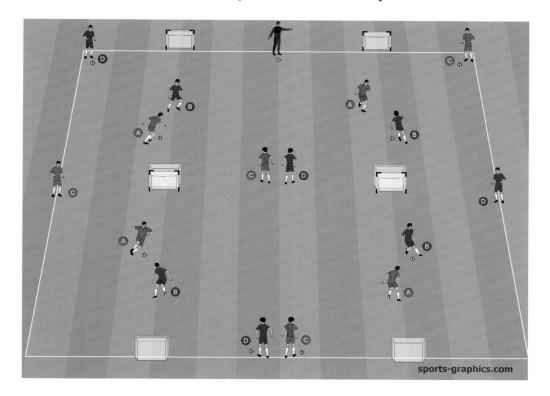

Execution

The RED team and the BLUE team consist of eight players each. The teams initially play four 1-on-1 situations, then four 2-on-2 situations, and finally 8-on-8 against each other. The field is divided into four playing fields with two mini goals on each field. One player from each team positions himself in one of the four fields for the 1-on-1 (see players A and B). After a starting signal, the four 1-on-1 situations begin. The players have only 10 seconds to get off a shot on goal and hopefully score. After the four 2-on-1 situations, the coach gives a starting signal after 10 seconds for the ensuing 2-on-2 situations, and the waiting players dribble with their ball or run without a ball into the field for the 2-on-2. Again the teams have 10 seconds to score a goal. After 10 seconds, the coach brings a final ball into the game for the closing 8-on-8 against all eight mini goals. Players change to new starting positions for the next round.

Variations

* Vary the time limit (12/14 seconds).
* Players support their teammates on other fields after their own 2-on-2.
* Vary starting action for 2-on-2 (player in possession plays against player without ball).
* Enforce a prerequisite for shot on goal in 8-on-8 (4 passes in own ranks).
* Specify shooting technique in 8-on-8 (direct finish).
* Use restrictions for 8-on-8 (play against specific mini goals inside/outside).

2.3.13 Different player ratios (from 1-on-1 to 4-on-4)

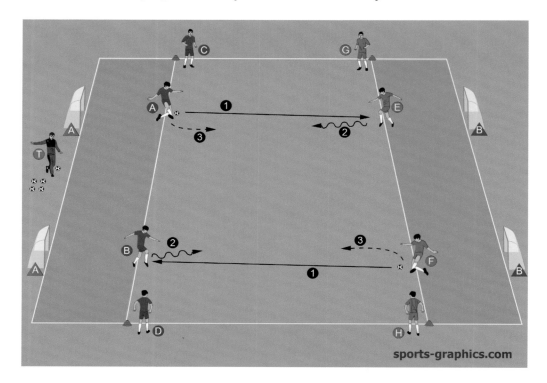

Execution

After completing an opening technique in the form of a pass and controlling the ball, two 1-on-1-situaitons and subsequent superior and inferior-number situations against the mini goals begin. The RED players always attack the two mini goals A and the BLUE players always attack the two mini goals B. At a signal from the coach, the player pairs positioned in the field (see players A/E and B/F) start their respective 1-on-1 situations. The players A and F in possession pass their balls to their respective opposites (see 1). Players B and E control the passes (see 2) and try to score on the predetermined mini goals. Players A and F try to prevent an opposing goal and, after possibly capturing the ball, try to launch a counterattack against the predetermined mini goals. After a goal is scored from a 1-on-1 situation or the ball has left the field, both players transition and support their respective team partners in the 2-on-2. After both 1-on-1 situations or the 2-on-2 situation have ended, the coach plays four successive additional balls into the game. After each game situation, he plays a pass specifically to one of the four players positioned outside (see players C, D, G, and H). The respective receiver settles the coach's ball and together with the previously active players plays against the predetermined mini goals. The active players transition and go into defensive and offensive mode. Players change to new starting positions for the next round.

Variations

★ Activate two players via the coach's ball (pass receiver and opposing player).

★ Use additional coach's balls for more consecutive 4-on-4 situations.

2.3.14 Different player ratios (from 2-on-2 to 4-on-4)

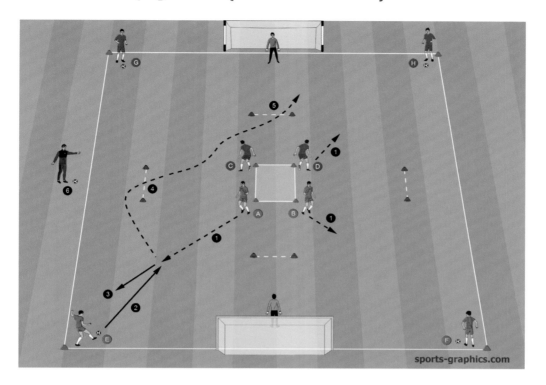

Execution

After completing an opening technique in the form of a running task, a 2-on-2 situation begins. Two players from each team position themselves in the center at the cone markers of the same color (see players A/B and C/D). Two additional players, each with a ball, position themselves next to their own large goals manned with a goalkeeper (see players E/F and G/H). At a signal from the coach, the four players in the center simultaneously start the opening technique and run. Players A, B, C, and D begin with a run toward an outside teammate (see 3). Next, they run through two cone goals of their choice (see 4 and 5). The coach brings a ball into the game (see 6). Right after their runs, the center players A/B play 2-on-2 against C/D on the two large goals. After the 2-on-2, more superior and inferior-number situations against the two large goals follow. To do so, the coach successively chooses one of the four outside players (see players E, F, G, and H). Each chosen player dribbles into the field and tries to score a goal with the previously active players. After the last player is chosen, the concluding 4-on-4 begins. Players change to new starting positions for the next round.

Variations

* Modify movement task (run backwards).
* Modify opening technique (second double pass with an outside player after the running task).
* Modify opening technique (dribble through two cone goals plus back pass to outside player).

2.3.15 Different player ratios (from 1-on-0 to 5-on-5)

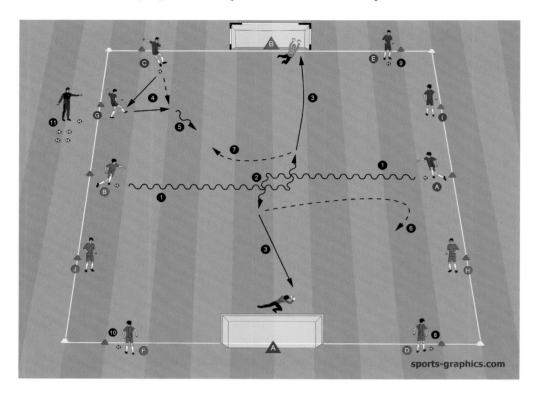

sports-graphics.com

Execution

After completing an opening technique in the form of a dribble and a shot on goal, the different game situations begin. The BLUE team always attacks goal A and the RED team always attacks goal B. Players A and B simultaneously start the opening technique and, after a signal from the coach, dribble toward each other (see 1). Players A and B dribble past each other (see 2), turn left toward the respective opposing goal, and both finish on that goal (see 3). Next, the coach chooses one of the four players waiting outside with a ball, one at a time (see players D, E, and F). After completing a predetermined passing sequence (see 4), the first player chosen (here player C) moves into the field in possession (see 5) for the subsequent 2-on-1 on goal A. The outside players C, D, E, and F each get involved via a double pass with the outside players G, H, I, and J (see 4 and 5) positioned in front of them. After their shots on goal, the players A and B immediately transition and get into offensive (see 6) and defensive (see 7) mode for the next 2-on-1. After a goal is scored from the 2-on-1 or the ball has left the field, the coach chooses the next player to immediately dribble into the field via the predetermined passing sequence. One by one, the coach calls up the outside players C, D, E, and F, creating corresponding superior and inferior-number situations. After he has activated these four players he plays a pass to one of the four remaining outside players G, H, I, and J. The player receiving the pass settles the ball and dribbles into the field. The three remaining players also start into the field. A closing 5-on-5 situation ensues.

Points system

* Goal scored during opening technique (1 point)/goal scored with superior number (2 points)/goal scored with inferior number (3 points)

2.4   CHASING AND CAPTURING

Chasing and Capturing includes training exercises to improve individual and group tactical defensive behavior with the goal of winning the ball, and with offensive transition actions. Here emphasis is placed on facilitating a basic attitude and mentality. This basic active defensive attitude includes the permanent chasing and confronting of the opponent, applying constant pressure on the player in possession, and finally the objective of touching the ball and getting it under one's own control. Players must have passion, dedication, assertiveness, and toughness in tackles. Beyond that players should act as a group, coordinate with each other, and use intensive pressing as the situation demands. Mutual assistance via coaching and communication as to the start of pressing must be clearly defined and can depend on the opponents and correspondingly designated pressing victims, bad ball handling, or closed body position. A successful ball capture is followed by follow-up actions like dribbling, passing, or shots on goal and corresponding transitions to create scoring opportunities on offense, or safeguarding the ball within their own ranks on defense. The training exercises include versatile games of catch and ball-capturing games with different superior and inferior number ratios. This requires fleet-footed running movements with intensive sprinting, different directional changes, and situation-appropriate running feints. Within the scope of these catching and capturing games, winning the ball is further organized based on opening techniques in the form of passing combinations, dribbling, finishing, and provoked turnovers.

TRANSITION ACTIONS
COUNTERPRESSING SUPERIOR NUMBER
SPRINTING BALL ORIENTATION
GAMES OF CATCH PRESSURE SITUATIONS
TACKLES
BODY CONTACT TIME PRESSURE
PHYSICAL PLAY INFERIOR NUMBER
TACKLES

2.4.1   Opponent chase in groups of two (2-on-4)

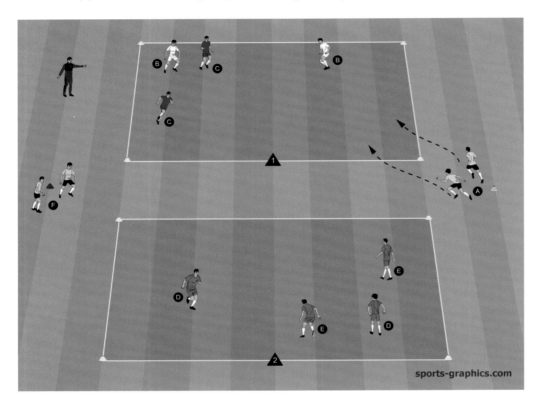

Execution

Players are divided into multiple teams of two players each. Initially there are two teams (see team B/C and team D/E) on each of the fields 1 and 2. Two additional teams are positioned outside at the starting positions (see teams A and F). The players on the two fields have the task of running away from the respective catchers cleverly and by using lots of feints, without being touched by a respective catcher's hand. At a signal from the coach, team A begins with the run onto field 1 to touch three players there. After team A has touched three players, team A remains on the field and the players from the team that was touched most often (see team B or team C) switch to the starting position, and during the next round act as the catchers. Immediately after team A has touched three players, team F starts onto field 2 to touch three players there.

Variations

★ Complete exercise with ball at foot (dribble/win ball).

★ Complete exercise with one ball per field (player in possession cannot be touched).

★ Complete exercise with ball in hand of catchers (touch opponents with the ball).

★ Complete exercise as game of catch by capturing bibs.

2.4.2   Opponent chase in groups of three (3-on-6)

sports-graphics.com

Execution

Players are divided into three teams (see WHITE, BLUE, and GREEN teams). Two teams (see WHITE and GREEN) spread out on the two fields. The third team (here the BLUE team) plays with an inferior number and positions itself outside between the two fields. The players from the WHITE team and GREEN team move around their fields without a ball. The BLUE team players play in a group of three with an inferior number and chase the opposing players, trying to touch one of them by hand (see 1 and 2). The chasing team has 10 seconds to do so. If the chasing team (here the BLUE team) manages to touch a player within the allotted amount of time, the tasks switch. This means three players from the touched player's team must chase on the other field. The team that was previously able to touch a player remains on the played-on field. If the other chasing team (here the BLUE team) is unable to tag a player, three new players from the BLUE team sprint onto the other field and there try to catch a player within the allotted amount of time (see 3). The three previously active players take over the waiting position and must chase again.

Points system

★ Surviving the 10 seconds without getting tagged by the opponent (1 point)

★ Tagging an opponent within the 10 seconds (1 point)

Variation

★ Vary the intensity (change of field sizes, timing, and time limits).

2.4.3   Opponent chase competition (passing combinations)

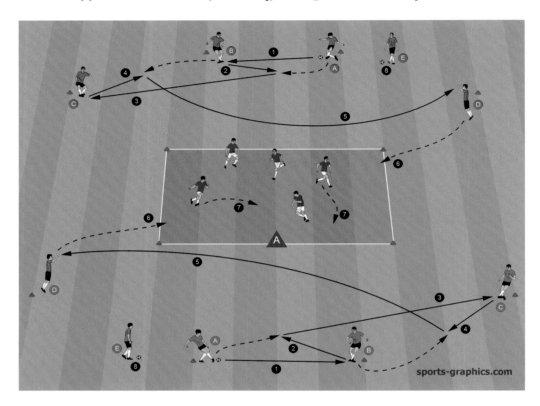

sports-graphics.com

Execution

Players are divided into three teams (see GREEN, BLUE, and RED teams). Two teams position themselves outside, each at four cone markers (see GREEN team and RED team). The third team (here the BLUE team) positions itself on a center field (see field A). The GREEN and RED teams compete against each other and one player from each team (see player D) tries to chase a player from the BLUE team on the center field according to a predetermined passing sequence. After a signal from the coach, the players A from both teams simultaneously begin the passing sequence. Player A passes to player B (see 1), follows his pass, and receives a back pass (see 2) from player B. Player A plays a long pass to player C (see 3). Player B pivots and receives the back pass from player C (see 4). Player B settles the ball and plays a volley to the far player D (see 5). Player D catches the ball and sprints with the ball in hand to the center field (see 6). The players D from the GREEN and RED teams now try as quickly as possible, and in front of their respective opposing catcher, to chase a player from the BLUE team and touch him with their own ball (see 6). The BUE team players try to escape the catchers via running paths filled with feints (see 7). The first catcher to tag a player from the BLUE team scores one point for his own team. As soon as a player from the BLUE team has been tagged both players E begin a new action (see 8). The previously active players A, B, and C now move up one position for the next round. After a chasing team has tagged a predetermined number of players, the tasks switch and another team positions itself on field A.

Variation

✳ Compete while dribbling with ball at foot (player D and player from BLUE team with own ball).

2.4.4   Ball chase in groups of two (2-on-2)

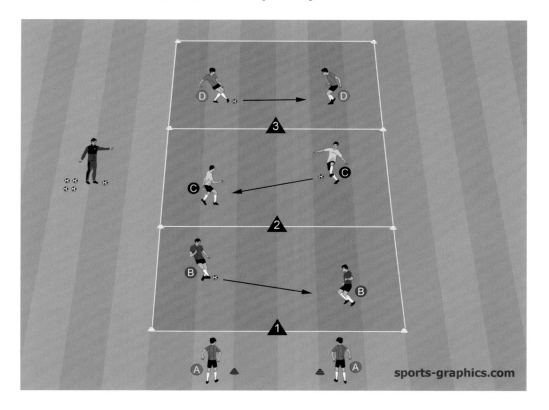

sports-graphics.com

Execution

Players are divided into multiple teams of two players each (see teams A, B, C, and D). The two players from team A are positioned off the fields at the starting position. There is a team with a ball positioned on each of fields 1, 2, and 3 (see team B, C, and D). The teams on the fields circulate the ball in their own ranks and try to prevent the opposing teams from scoring a goal. After a signal from the coach, team A starts into field 1 and tries to capture the ball and clear it off the field. After successfully winning the ball, team A remains on field 1 and is immediately given a new ball by the coach. After the turnover, the team that lost the ball (here team B) immediately starts into field 2 to capture team C's ball. After successfully winning the ball from team B on field 2, the team that lost the ball (team C) runs into field 3 in order to capture the ball from team D. Finally, after team D has lost its own ball to team C, team D immediately runs outside and around all the fields, back to the starting position, and immediately starts a new action to win the ball from team A on field 1. After each turnover the coach plays a new ball onto the field, so that a pass is always played on each field.

Variations

★   Successful ball capture may occur only after a pass within their own ranks (opportunity for counterpressing).

★   Complete the exercise without a ball as a game of catch (tagging both players results in field change).

★   Add neutral players (2-on-2 plus 1).

2.4.5   Ball chase in groups of two (2-on-4) (1)

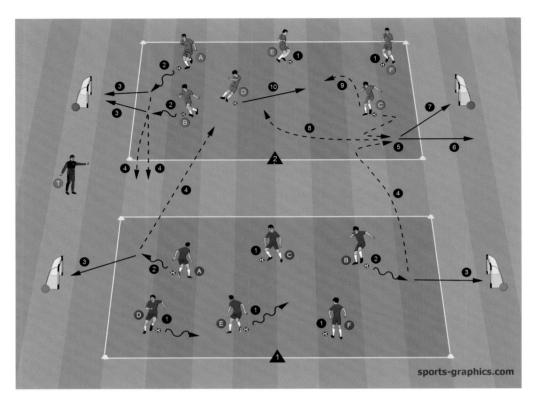

Execution

The players spread out on the two fields 1 and 2, each with a ball. Next to each field are two goals marked with the team's colors. All players dribble with their own ball (see 1). The coach calls up two players (here player A and player B), who run into the opposing field to capture balls. The call for two players applies to both teams, meaning two players (see players A and B) from each team always start into the opposing field and four players always remain on their own field with their ball (see players C, D, E, and F). The called-up players dribble toward the mini goals (see 2) and put their own ball in the back of the mini goal of their choice (see 3). Immediately after the players run into the opposing field (see 4) to try to capture balls there. The players (see player B from BLUE team) try to capture an opponent's ball (see 5) and after successfully winning a ball, play it off the field (see 6) or put it in the back of a mini goal (see 7). The two players must capture all three remaining balls, one by one, and after winning the first ball (see 8) immediately transition to pressure the next player (see player D from RED team). Players can work together to do so (see BLUE team and 4/8). The players from the two opposing teams who have already lost their own ball (see player C from RED team) can then support the players in possession (see 9), signal their readiness, and receive passes so that the players who are being pressured (see player D from RED team) can get out of pressure situations during possession play (see 10). If the two players (see players A and B) work together, multiple successive superior and inferior-number situations develop, from 2-on-1 to 2-on-2, to 2-on-3, and finally 2-on-4. During 2-on-4 play, touches can be limited for the team in possession. The sequence can be completed in competition format with the goal of accomplishing the four ball captures in the least amount of time possible.

2.4.6   Ball chase in groups of two (2-on-4) (2)

sports-graphics.com

Execution

Players are divided into two teams of four players each (see RED and YELLOW teams). There are four players from the RED team on field A. The players from the YELLOW team are divided between field A and B. On field A, the RED team is in possession and plays against the players from the YELLOW team (see players A and B). Players A and B from the YELLOW team try to capture the ball. They have a limited amount of time to do so. As soon as the RED team has played 10 passes amongst themselves and the YELLOW team has not captured the ball, the RED team is awarded a point. After the RED team successfully completes 10 passes, the coach brings a new ball onto field B. The superior number changes. Four players from field A switch to field B. Now the YELLOW team plays 4-on-4 on field B with all four players against two players from the RED team. As soon as the YELLOW team has played ten passes, the scoring and field changes are repeated. As soon as an inferior-number team wins a ball, it immediately scores and the coach brings a new ball into the opposite field.

Variations

★   Specify touches for the superior-number team (2 touches/direct passes).
★   Point scored for inferior-number team winning the ball only after a pass in own ranks.

2.4.7 Ball chase in groups of two (2-on-4) (3)

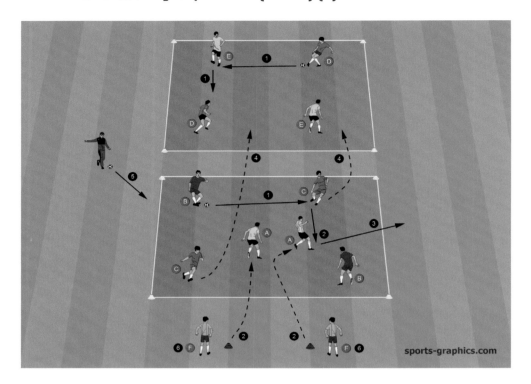

sports-graphics.com

Execution

Players are divided into multiple teams of two players each. There are two teams playing 4-on-2 on each of the two fields (see teams C/B and D/E). The players on each field circulate a ball (see 1) and try to prevent a turnover via the respective defending players (see team A). Teams A and F are positioned at the starting positions outside the first field. The first team (see team A) starts the first action and both players run onto the first field without a ball (see 2) to intercept a pass (see 2) and to play the captured ball off the field. After a successful capture, team A has fulfilled its task and remains on the first field for a subsequent action. The team that loses the ball (here team C) switches to defense and runs from the first to the second field (see 4) to try to win the ball from teams D and E in possession on the second field. Meanwhile the coach brings a new ball onto the first field and teams A and B begin to circulate the new coach's ball in their own ranks without an opponent. After team C has won the ball on the new field (see 4), a new team F (see 6) starts from the starting position to capture the ball from teams A and B on the first field. After team C captures the ball, the team losing possession on the second field (see team D or E) leaves the field and takes over starting position F. Team C remains on the second field with the team in possession (see team D or E). Right away the coach also brings a new ball into the game on the second field.

Variation

* After ten successful passes in 4-on-2 without the opposing team touching the ball (see team A on the first field or team C on the second field), the team not in possession (see team A or C) must change to the other field without a ball to try to capture the ball there.

2.4.8 Ball chase in groups of two (2-on-4) (4)

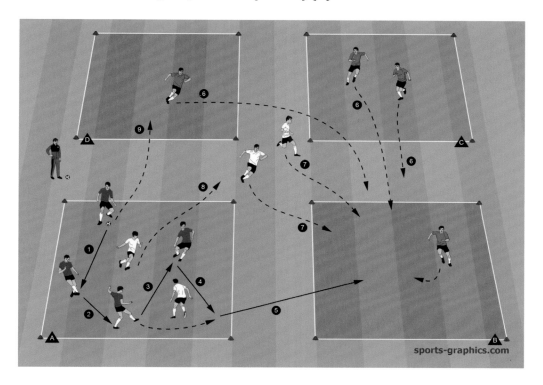

Execution

Players are divided into three teams (see BLUE, WHITE, and RED team) and play on a total of four fields (see fields A, B, C, and D) as well as the spaces between the fields. The team in possession plays with superior numbers against a chasing team and can prompt a switch of play with an opening pass. Play for possession begins on field A. The team in possession (here the BLUE team) tries in 4-on-2 to circulate the ball within their own ranks without the opponent capturing the ball (see 1, 2, 3, and 4). The inferior number players (here the WHITE team) chase the ball and try to capture it. In doing so, the chasing WHITE team is divided and the two additional players are at the waiting positions in the center between the fields. The third team (here the RED team) is positioned in a staggered formation so the fields on the strong side (here field B and D) have one player and the diagonally opposed field (here field C) has two players. After a predetermined number of passes, the team in possession (here the BLUE team) tries to pass into another field (here field B) (see 5). As soon as a successful liberating pass into another field is played (see 5), the teammates of the player receiving the ball must quickly establish a superior number on the played-on field (see 6). The players from the center run into the played-on field as the chasers (see 7). The previously active players switch to the center (see 8) and the team that accomplished the switch of play (see 5) divides up between the three currently not played-on fields (here fields A, C, and D) (see 9). If the WHITE team captures the ball with inferior numbers on field A, the WHITE team must play the ball onto any field (here fields B, C, and D). In this case the BLUE team becomes the chasing team with inferior numbers and the WHITE team divides up between the three not played-on fields. This reorientation also takes place when the ball goes into touch and leaves the field. Achieving the predetermined number of passes and the switch of play is worth one point. Capturing the ball and a switch of play is also worth one point.

2.4.9 Ball chase in groups of two (2-plus-2 against 4)

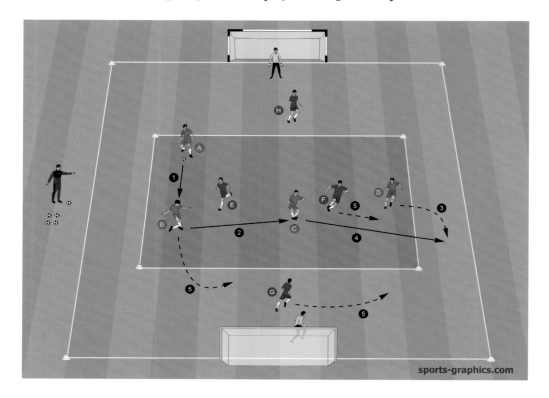

sports-graphics.com

Execution

The RED team plays the BLUE team in 4-on-2 plus 2. To do so, four players from the RED team are positioned in the center field (see players A, B, C, and D). Two players from the BLUE team position themselves in the center field and initially play against the ball with inferior numbers (see players E and F). Two additional players from the BLUE team (see players G and H) position themselves centrally outside the center playing field in front of the large goals (see players G and H). The team in position (here the RED team) initially plays for possession and tries to complete a predetermined number of passes without losing possession (see 1 and 2). After the predetermined number of passes, one player from the team in possession can move sideways off the field (see 3) and receive a pass (see 4). The 4-on-4 game against the large goals begins with a successful pass to one of the players running out of the field (here player D). To do so, all players transition to offense and defense (see 5). The game is now played on the large field between the large goals. After the BLUE team successfully wins the ball in 4-on-4, the BLUE team can also attack the large goals. If the BLUE team captures the ball before the predetermined number of passes (see 1 and 2), a pass can be played to one of the outside players (see players G and H). After a predetermined number of passes in 4-on-4 the BLUE team can attack the large goals. If a ball leaves the field or a team scores, the coach has the option of bringing a new ball into the game. Positions of individual teams and players switch regularly.

Variations

★ Points are awarded after scoring on a large goal (one point).

★ The weak-side outside player is not allowed to engage (here player H).

2.4.10   Ball chase in groups of three (3-plus-2 against 5) (1)

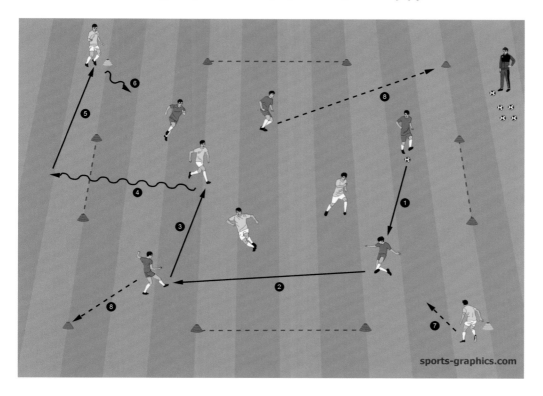

Execution

The RED team plays against the YELLOW team. The team in possession (here the RED team) plays for ball holding and tries to keep the ball within their own ranks for as long as possible without a turnover (see 1 and 2). The opposing team (here the YELLOW) team defends with three players. Two players from the YELLOW team stand at the outside positions marked with the same color. The YELLOW team tries to capture the ball with inferior numbers (see 4). Immediately after successfully capturing the ball (see 3), one player tries to dribble through one of the four marked outside cone goals (see 4) and subsequently plays a pass to one of the two outside players (see 5). The tasks change with a successful pass to one of the outside players (see 5) and the player receiving the pass dribbles into the field (see 6). The outside player who did not receive a pass runs into the field at the same time (see 7) for 5-on-3. Two players from the team that lost the ball (here the RED team) man the outside positions marked with the same colors (see 8) and the remaining players become the inferior-number team. The game continues with changing tasks, as previously described. If a ball leaves the field, the coach has the option of bringing a new ball into the game.

Points system

* Ten consecutive passes for the team in possession (1 point)
* Capturing the ball and forced change of tasks (1 point)
* Twenty consecutive passes for the team in possession (2 points)
* Capturing the ball without the opponents winning a point and forced change of tasks (2 points)

2.4.11   Ball chase in groups of three (3-plus-2 against 5) (2)

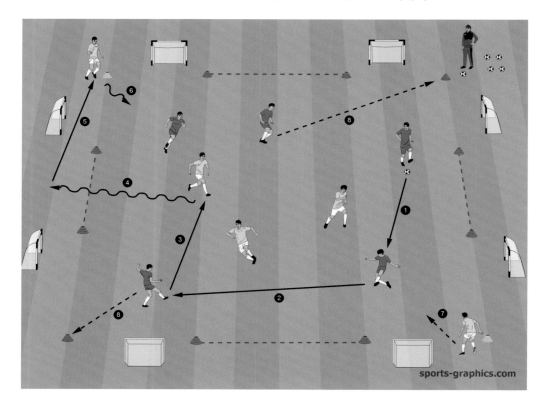

Execution

The RED team plays against the YELLOW team. The team in possession (here the RED team) plays for ball holding, tries to keep the ball within their own ranks for as long as possible without a turnover (see 1 and 2), and, after six consecutive passes without the opponent touching the ball, has the option of finishing on the mini goals positioned outside, scoring one point. The opposing team (here the YELLOW team) defends with three players. Two of the players stand on the outside positions marked with the same color. The YELLOW team tries to capture the ball with an inferior number (see 4). Immediately after successfully winning the ball (see 3), one of the players tries to dribble through one of the four outside cone goals (see 4) and plays a subsequent pass to one of the two outside players (see 5). Tasks change with a successful pass to one of the outside players (see 5) and the receiving player dribbles onto the field (see 6). The player who did not receive the pass (see 7) runs into the field at the same time for 5-on-3 play. Two of the players from the team losing possession (here the RED team) man the outside positions marked with the same colors (see 8) and the remaining players become the inferior-number team. The game continues with changing tasks, as previously described. If a ball leaves the field or a team scores on the mini goals, the coach has the option of bringing a new ball into the game.

Variations

* Limit touches for superior-number team in possession.
* Establish minimum number of touches for superior-number team in possession.
* Specify shooting technique (direct finish/left/right).

2.4.12   Ball chase in groups of three (3-plus-2 against 5) (3)

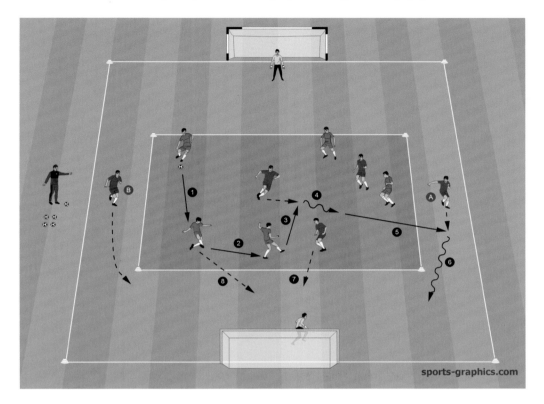

Execution

The RED team plays 5-on-3 against the BLUE team. Five RED team players position themselves in the center field. Three BLUE team players position themselves in the center field and initially work against the ball with an inferior number. Two additional BLUE team players (see players A and B) position themselves to the side and outside the center field. The team in possession (here the RED team) plays for ball holding and tries to keep the ball within their own ranks for as long as possible without the opposing team touching the ball (see 1 and 2). The BLUE team tries to intercept a pass (see 3) and, after successfully capturing the ball (see 4), tries to pass to one of the two outside players (here player A) (see 5). After a successful pass to an outside player, that player moves the ball toward a large goal (see 6) and the BLUE team tries to score on the large goal. All of the BLUE team players transition to offense (see 7) and all of the RED team players transition to defense (see 7). The game is now played on the large field between the large goals. As soon as the RED team wins back the ball, it again tries to play pass combinations on the center field. As soon as the ball is back in the RED team's ranks and being passed in the center field, two players from the BLUE team again position themselves in the outside positions and do not participate in the game until the next turnover. If a ball leaves the field or a team scores, the coach has the option of bringing a new ball into the game. Individual teams and players regularly switch positions.

Variations

- Points awarded to team in possession after ten successful passes (see 1 and 2) (1 point)
- Points awarded after scoring on large goal (1 point)
- The outside player on the weak side cannot be engaged (here player B) in 5-on-4.

2.4.13 Ball chase in groups of three (3-on-6)

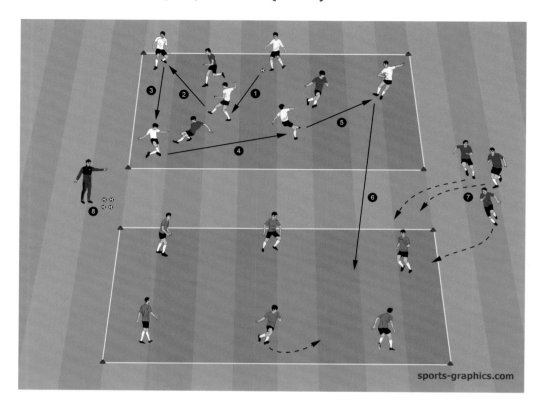

sports-graphics.com

Execution

Players are divided into three teams (see WHITE team, BLUE team, and GREEN team). Two teams spread out on the two fields. The third team (here the BLUE team) plays with an inferior number and positions itself outside between the two fields. The WHITE and GREEN teams work together. The players in possession (here the WHITE team) let the ball circulate within their own ranks, ideally without the opposing team capturing the ball (see 1, 2, 3, 4, and 5). After a predetermined number of passes, the ball can be played into the other field (see 6). Players from the BLUE team work as a team of three with an inferior number and try to capture the ball. After capturing the ball, the inferior-number team can activate the waiting players via a pass into the other field (see 7). After a switch of play by the team in possession (see 6), a waiting BLUE team threesome is also activated and becomes the chasing team on the other field (see 7). After the field change, the three previously active BLUE team players take over the outside waiting positions until the next field change. After a predetermined period of time, the tasks switch. A passing sequence (six passes) without a touch by the opposing team and subsequent switch of play is worth two points; without switch of play, it is worth one point. The inferior-number team is also rewarded if it captures the ball (one point) and if it captures the ball with a switch of play (two points).

Variations

* Specify number of passes (2/3/4 passes) for the possible switch of play.
* Vary the number of players (4 chasing players/4 waiting players).
* Vary the intensity (increase/decrease field size).

2.4.14   Ball chase in groups of four (4-on-8)

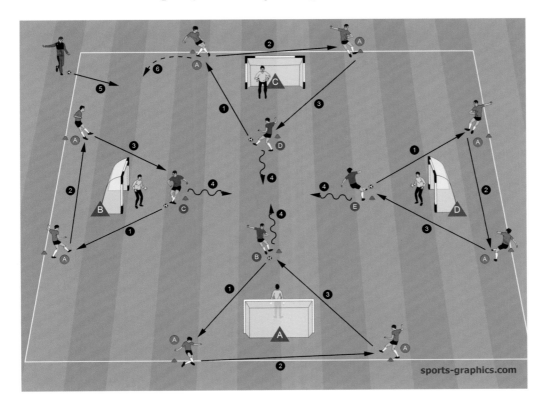

Execution

A total of 12 players are positioned at the 12 start markers. Two players are positioned behind each of the large goals (see goals A, B, C, and D) (see player A). In the center another player is positioned in front of each goal (see players B, C, D, and E). Each large goal is surrounded by a group of three players who play passes to each other around the goal (see 1, 2, and 3). At a signal from the coach, the four balls are quickly passed to the BLUE players (see 2 and 3). The BLUE players (see players B, C, D, and E) control the passes to the rear (see 4) and finish on the goals behind them. Player B finishes on the large goal C, player C finishes on the large goal D, player D finishes on the large goal A, and player E finishes on the large goal B. With his signal, the coach brings another ball into the game. All RED team players transition in the direction of the coach and let the new ball circulate within their own ranks. After their shots, the four BLUE team players also transition, work together as the inferior-number team, and try to win back the ball. After successfully winning the ball, the BLUE team can immediately attack the large goals. To start a new action, the players change to new starting positions and change the direction of play during the opening passes.

Variations

* Optional play against the large goals after ten consecutive passes by the RED team.
* Specify touches for the superior-number team (2 touches/direct passes).
* Specify passing technique during opening passes (direct passes/2 (3) touches).

2.4.15 Ball chase in groups of four (increasing number of opponents)

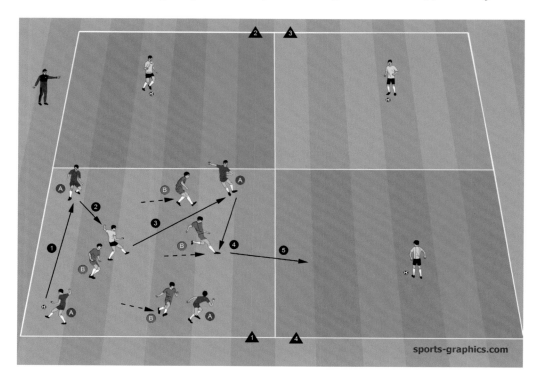

sports-graphics.com

Execution

The BLUE team (see player A) plays in possession with the neutral YELLOW players against the RED team (see player B). The game begins on field 1. After the RED team captures the ball, the fields are played on consecutively. There is one neutral player with a ball on each field. The BLUE team tries to keep the ball in its own ranks for as long as possible (see 1) without the RED team capturing the ball. The BLUE team can involve the neutral players in the passing sequence in 4-on-1 play (see 2 and 3). The RED team tries to intercept a pass (see 4) and after successfully capturing the ball, plays it outside the field (see 5). Immediately after the RED team captures the ball, all players switch to field 2. On the next field the BLUE team again plays for ball holding with a neutral player and the RED team again tries to capture the ball. After the RED team wins the ball again in 4-on-4-plus-2 play, the teams switch to 4-on-4 plus 3 on field 3, and finally play 4-on-4 plus 4 on field 4. After all four fields have been played on, the tasks change so that team A switches to the neutral positions, team B is in possession, and the neutral players try to capture the ball. The sequence can be completed in competition format with the goal of winning the ball four times in the shortest amount of time.

Variations

* Play 4-on-4 plus 1 on all fields (no field changes for neutral players).
* Specify touches for neutral players (direct play).
* Specify touches for the team in possession (direct passes).

2.4.16 Ball chase (from 1-on-4 to 2-on-4 to 2-on-6)

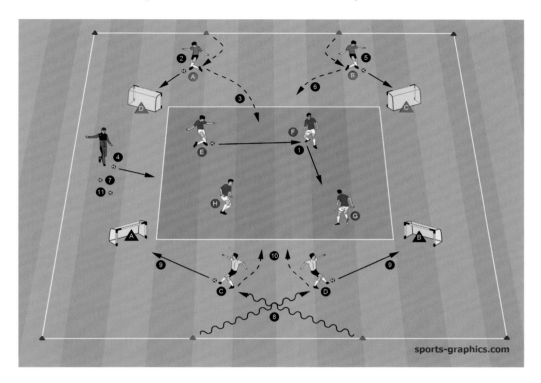

sports-graphics.com

Execution

Players are divided into three teams (see RED, BLUE, and YELLOW teams). The RED and YELLOW teams consist of two players each (see players A/B and C/D) and position themselves with a ball at the outside start markers around a large field. A smaller field is marked off in the center, which is framed by four mini goals open to the outside (see mini goals A, B, C, and D). The BLUE team players are positioned in the center field (see players E, F, G, and H) with a ball. The BLUE team circulates a ball within their ranks (see 1) and tries to prevent the chasing players from capturing the ball. Player A begins the first action, briefly dribbles, shoots his ball into mini goal D (see 2), and runs to the center field and tries to capture the ball there (see 3). As soon as player A has touched the ball, the coach plays a new ball to one of the BLUE team players (see 4). The BLUE team players try to also keep the new ball in their ranks for as long as possible without the opposing team capturing it. Player A continues the chase and player B begins a new action with the coach's ball (see 4). Player B shoots his ball into mini goal C (see 5) and runs to the center field to support player A in 2-on-4 (see 6). As soon as the second ball (see 4) has been touched by one of the chasing players (see players A and B), players C and D simultaneously start a new action (see 8) and the coach brings a third ball into the game (see 7). With the third coach's ball, the BLUE team works together with the previously chasing RED team and lets the new coach's ball circulate within their ranks. Players C and D put their balls in the back of mini goals A and B (see 9) and run to the center field for the 2-on-6 (see 10). As soon as players C and D have touched the third ball, the coach brings a final ball into the game (see 11). The final coach's ball is played in 4-on-4. Here the BLUE team plays against the RED and YELLOW teams. With the final coach's ball, the teams play 4-on-4 and play against the mini goals A, B, C, and D.

2.5   COGNITION AND PERCEPTION

Cognition and Perception includes training exercises to improve action speed and optimize cognitive processes. Here the emphasis is on focused, refined, and quick observation, cognition, information processing, and orientation combined with situation-appropriate decision making and implementing quick-response follow-up actions. In the area of perception, lifting the eyes from the ball as well as using peripheral vision are fostered and the ability to transition between technical processes with the ball and multi-dimensional cognitive and movement tasks are appealed to. Along with individual tasks, the training exercises also include more complex training elements in small groups for mutual awareness and coordinated playing actions. Reacting to auditory and visual signals is combined with follow-up actions in the form of running paths, passes, dribbling, and finishing. Training exercises are intensified and enhanced by organizing competitions with corresponding cognition under time and opponent pressure. Additional training games use color signals and commands to prompt changes in the direction of play and to facilitate targeted finishes.

TRANSITION ACTIONS
IMITATING COMMANDS
COLOR SIGNALS COACH'S SIGNALS
DECISION MAKING RELAYS
COMPETITIONS
REACTING

2.5.1   Simple game of catch (1-on-3)

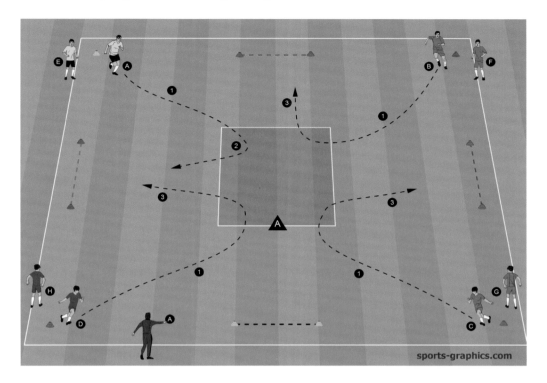

Execution

One player from each of the YELLOW, GREEN, RED, and BLUE teams compete against each other. A field is marked off in the center (see zone A). Several colored cone goals are set up to the sides of the center field. Players A, B, C, and D start the first action and simultaneously run toward the center field without a ball (see 1). While the four players are running toward the center (see 1), the coach designates one of the four players (here player A). Player A immediately becomes the catcher and tries to tag one of the other three players with his hand (see 2). The three players who weren't designated (see players B, C, and D) try to run through one of the four cone goals without first getting tagged by the catcher (see 3). After a signal from the coach, all four players must run through the center field A. The four players E, F, G, and H start in the next round. Any player who reaches a cone goal without getting tagged is awarded one point. A catcher who tags an opponent with his hand is awarded three points.

Variations

* Vary running style (see 1) until coach's signal (hobble/skip left/right).
* Vary running style (see 1) until coach's signal (skip forward/backwards).
* Vary running style (see 1) until coach's signal (run backwards/skip/forward roll).
* Specify running path (run through the cone goal of own team's color).
* Specify running path (run through the cone goal opposite the goal of own team's color).
* Specify running path (run through cone goal to the right of goal of own team's color).
* Specify running path (run through cone goal to the left of goal of own team's color).
* Complete at a dribble with ball at foot (catcher positions his own ball in center).

2.5.2   Complex game of catch (1-on-1 against 1)

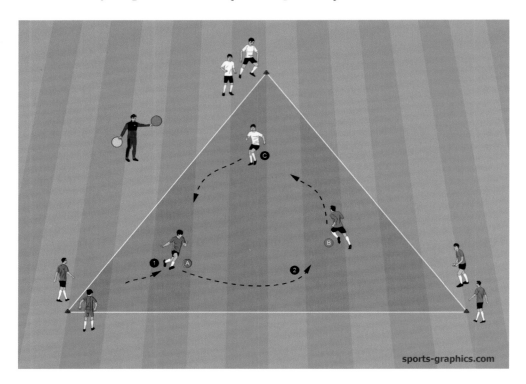

Execution

Players are divided into three teams (see RED, GREEN, and WHITE teams) and position themselves at the corners of the triangular center field. One player from each team starts onto the field (see 1). Each player now tries to catch the player running to his right and tag him by hand (see 2) without getting tagged by the player on the left. The first player to tag another player is awarded one point for his team.

Variations

★   Complete as a competition (Which team scores the most points?).

★   Complete as a competition (Which player scores the most points?).

★   Vary the starting command via a visual coach's signal (BLUE/left and YELLOW/right).

★   Vary the catching direction via an auditory starting command (left/right).

★   Vary the catching direction (even number/left or uneven number/right).

★   Vary the catching direction (arithmetic problem).

2.5.3 Simple running competition (1-on-1)

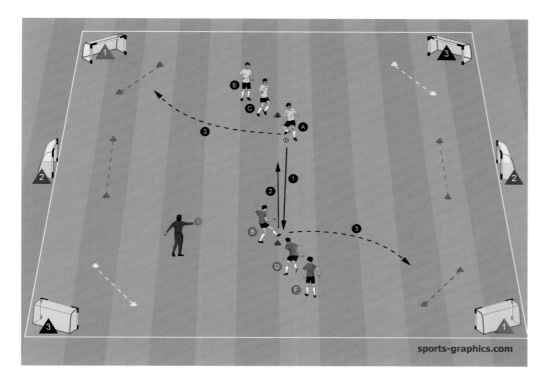

sports-graphics.com

Execution

One player from the YELLOW team and one player from the RED team compete against each other. Each team consists of several players (see players A/C/E and B/D/F). Teams position themselves at two start markers in the center. Positioned to the side of the teams are several colored cone goals. The field is framed by six mini goals (see mini goals 1, 2, and 3). Players A and B begin and play direct passes back and forth (see 1 and 2). Player A always passes to player B (see 1) and player B always passes to player A (see 2). The direct passes continue until a signal from the coach. With a starting signal the coach designates one of the colored cone goals (here the BLUE cone goal). Players immediately run toward the designated cone goal (see 3). The first player to run through the designated cone goal is awarded one point for his team. The two subsequent players continue the passing sequence (here players C and D) until the next coach's signal.

Variations

★ Each pair of players (see players A/B, C/D, and E/F) completes the passing sequence with their own ball. At a signal from the coach a 1-on-1 situation against a color-designated cone goal begins, which the player in possession at the time of the coach's signal must dribble through. The opposing player is the catcher and tries to tag the player in possession by hand before he is able to move through the goal.

★ Each pair of players (see players A/B, C/D, and E/F) completes the passing sequence with their own ball. At a signal from the coach a 1-on-1 situation begins against a color-designated mini goal on which the player in possession at the time of the coach's signal tries to finish. The opposing player is the catcher and tries to tag the player in possession by hand before he is able to finish.

2.5.4   Complex running competition (2-on-2 against 2)

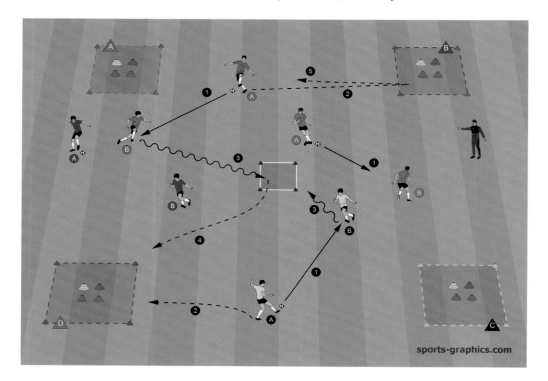

Execution

Players are divided into four teams (see RED, BLUE, YELLOW, and GREEN teams). For each team a field of the same color is marked off in the corners of the playing field (see fields A, B, C, and D). Marking cones in the four corresponding team colors are positioned on the outer fields. A small neutral field is marked off in the center. Each team has a ball and passes their own ball within their own ranks (see 1). After a coach's signal, the running competition begins. Players must try to retrieve designated cones from other fields (see 2) and bring them to their own fields (see 5). Prior to that their own ball must be dribbled into the center field by the current player in possession (see 3) and deposited there. Only then can both players run to the remaining cones on other fields (see 4). Each player can hold only one cone at a time. To prevent the opponent from succeeding, it might be wise to pay attention to the opponent's approach by making it a priority to target cones that are crucial to the opponent. The competition ends when one team has brought the designated cones to their own field.

Variations

* Coach's signal specifies to collect four cones of their own team's color.
* Coach's signal specifies to collect any four cones of the same color.
* Coach's signal specifies to collect one cone of each color.
* Complete while dribbling (each player with ball at foot).

2.5.5   Simple ball competition (1-on-1)

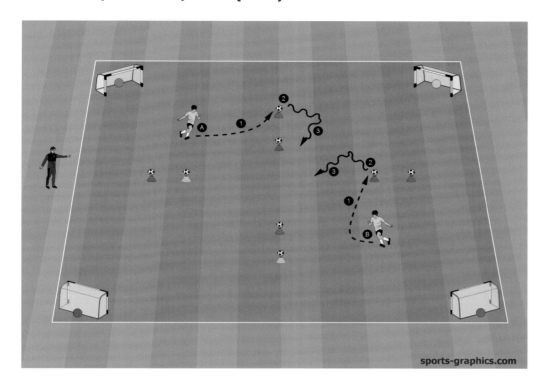

Execution

Two cones of four different colors (a total of eight cones) are positioned in the center of the field with a ball on each cone. There is one mini goal of each color in the corners of the field. Players A and B play against each other. Players run to a cone (see 1), use their foot to take the ball off that cone, control it (see 2), shoot it in a mini goal (see 2), and run to the next cone marker.

Variations

* At the beginning the coach names four different cone colors. Players shoot the balls in the order named, one after the other, into the mini goals of their choice.

* At the beginning the coach names four different cone colors. Players shoot the balls in the order named, one after the other, into the mini goals of the same color.

* At the beginning the coach names four different cone colors. Players shoot the balls in the order named, one after the other, into the opposite color mini goals.

* The coach names a player. The named player takes four shots in a row from four different-colored cones into the mini goals of his choice. The second player imitates the previous player's sequence, retrieves the balls from the cones in the same order, and finishes on the mini goals of his choice.

* The coach names a player. The named player shoots four balls in a row from different-colored cones into the mini goals of his choice. The second player imitates the named player's sequence, retrieves the balls from the cones in the same order, and finishes on the same mini goals.

2.5.6   Individual awareness (controlling the ball)

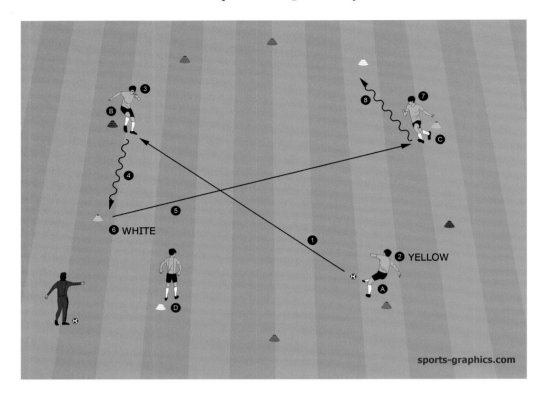

sports-graphics.com

Execution

Several different-colored cone markers are set up in a circle. Four players (see players A, B, C, and D) are positioned inside the circle, each in front of a cone. One player (see player A) has a ball and starts the passing play. Player A passes the ball to a player of his choice (here player B). As he passes the ball, he calls out the color of one of the cones to the right or left of the pass receiver (here BLUE or YELLOW). Player A (see 2) calls out a color with this pass (see 1) (here YELLOW). Player B must turn toward the designated color (see 3) and play the ball toward the cone marker of that color (see 4). Player B continues the passing sequence from that cone. With his subsequent pass (see 5), player B (see 6) calls out a new color (here WHITE). The next pass receiver again turns toward the designated color (see 7) and continues the action of controlling and passing the ball (see 8).

Variations

★   Perform a feint after controlling the ball with first touch (see 4 and 8).

★   Limit touches for pass receiver (2/3 touches).

★   A third player designates the signal (see player D).

★   Add more signals via a third player (e.g., DIRECT [pass receiver continues sequence with direct pass]).

★   Add more signals (e.g., NAME [pass receiver plays direct pass to named player]).

★   Add more signals (e.g., COLOR plus RECEIVING LEG [heightened objective]).

★   Add more signals (e.g., COLOR plus RECEIVING LEG plus PLAYING LEG [heightened objective]).

2.5.7   Individual awareness (opening up)

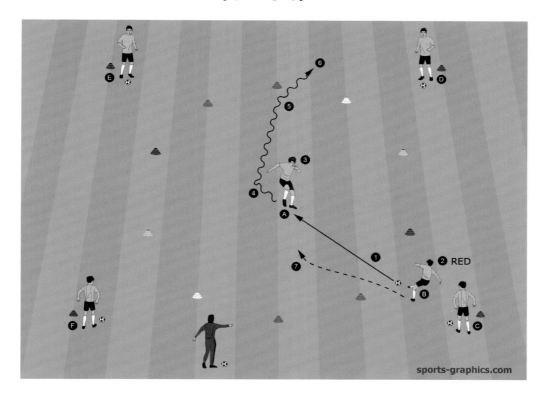

Execution

Several cone markers are set up in a circle. One player is positioned in the center of the circle (see player A). The other players are positioned at the four starting positions outside the circle (see players B, C, D, E, and F), each with a ball. The starting position with a ball is double-manned (see players B and C). Player B passes the ball to player A (see 1). With his pass, the passing player (here player B) calls out the color (see 2) of one of the cone markers (here RED). The pass receiver in the center (here player A) turns toward the designated color (see 3), controls the ball with his first touch in the direction of the designated color (see 4), dribbles toward that cone marker (see 5), and out of the circle (see 6). After his pass, the passing player (here player B) immediately runs to the center (see 7) to start a new action, to ask for a pass, and to receive a pass along with a command from one of the outside players. Player A dribbles to the subsequently open starting position (see 6). To do so, the player can and should dribble through the center as a disturbance factor to elicit heightened awareness from the respective pass receiver by distracting him.

Variations

* Perform a feint in front of the cone after controlling the ball with one touch (see 5).
* Designate two colors (first color is the direction of controlling the ball and the second color is the direction of dribble).
* Designate signal via a third player (see players C, D, E, or F).

2.5.8 Team competition (simple dribbling)

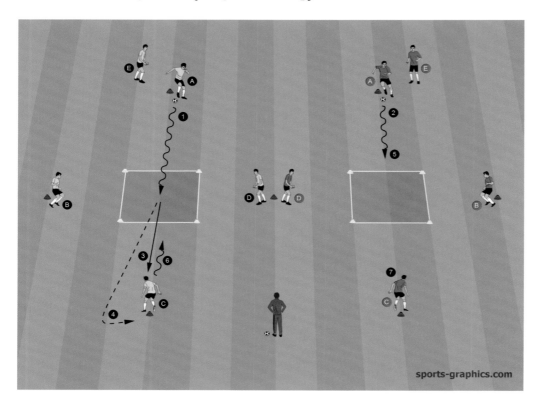

Execution

The YELLOW team competes against the RED team. Each team consists of at least five players (see players A, B, C, D, and E). Each of the two teams plays on one field. Players position themselves on four starting positions that are evenly spread out around their own field. One player in possession (see player A) and another player (see player E) are positioned at each of the starting positions. The first player at the starting position dribbles into the center field, passes his ball to the outside player, and then takes over his position. The coach designates a team (here the YELLOW team). The designated YELLOW team does not have a predetermined passing sequence. The first player from the YELLOW team (see player A) begins and dribbles toward the center field (see 1). The opposing player A from the RED team starts at the same time (see 2). Player A dribbles into the field and plays a pass to an outside player of his choice (see 3) and then takes over the pass receiver's position (see 4). The opposing player A from the RED team imitates the passing sequence (see 5), dribbles into the field, and also plays to player C from his own team. Player A has chosen to pass to player C (see 3). The pass receiver (here player C) starts a new action (see 6). On the opposing field, the pass receiver also starts, and in his subsequent action (see 7) imitates the passing direction predetermined by the opponent. As soon as the imitating team makes a mistake, the specifying team is awarded one point. The imitating team will again specify the passing sequence during the next round. After 20 correct sequences by the imitating team, the tasks change, and the imitating team is awarded one point.

2.5.9   Team competition (simple passing)

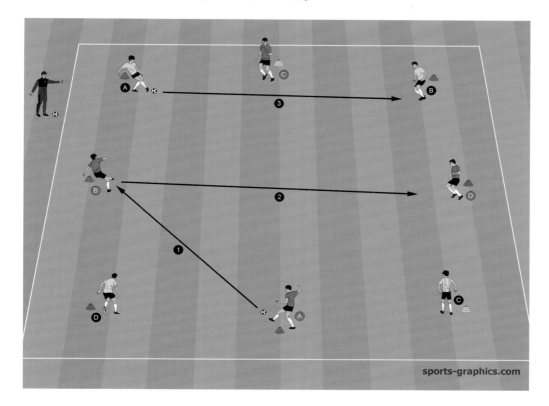

sports-graphics.com

Execution

The RED team competes against the YELLOW team. Each team consists of four players (see players A, B, C, and D). Each player positions himself at a colored cone marker. The four cones have four different colors. The four colors are the same for each team. Both teams have a ball and circulate it within their ranks with two touches per player. The coach designates one team (here the RED team) which will not have a mandatory passing sequence. The player in possession can therefore pass to the receiver of his choice. Player A chooses player B and passes to player B (see 1). Player B chooses player D and passes to player D (see 2). The passing sequence continues indefinitely. The YELLOW team begins with the first pass from the Red team (see 1) and tries to imitate the RED team's passing sequence. Player A must therefore pass the ball to the red cone marker to player B (see 3) and player B must pass the ball to the green cone marker to player D. The designated team (here the RED team) now tries to circulate the ball as quickly as possible until the YELLOW team makes a mistake or is no longer able to follow the passing sequence. The RED team is awarded one point. The players can help each other by giving commands. Next the tasks and teams switch and the YELLOW team dictates the passing sequence via their own passes.

Variations

* Specify passing technique (direct play).
* Specify passing technique (receive left/pass right).
* Specify passing technique (receive right/pass left).
* Add one player per team (switch to position of pass receiver).

2.5.10   Team competition (open dribbling)

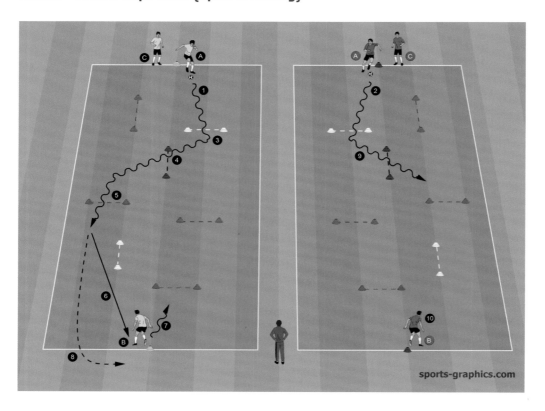

Execution

The YELLOW team competes against the RED team. Each team consists of three players (see players A, B, and C). Each of the teams plays on its own field. Several different-colored cone goals are positioned on each field. Starting positions are located at the narrow sides of the field. Each team has one ball at the beginning of the sequence. First, the players complete a dribbling task and then pass the ball to their partner on the opposite end, and then switch to the position of pass receiver. The coach designates one team (here the YELLOW team) which does not have a mandatory sequence for playing on the cone goals during their dribbling task. The first player from the YELLOW team (see player A) begins and dribbles into the field to then dribble through three cone goals of his choice (see 1). The opposing player A from the RED team starts at the same time (see 2). Player A from the YELLOW team dribbles through a white goal (see 2), through a black goal (see 4), and finally through a red goal (see 5). Next he plays a pass to his partner at the opposite end (see 6). The pass receiver immediately begins his next action (see 7). The passing player (see player A) takes over the pass receiver's position (see 8). The opposing player from the RED team imitates the YELLOW team player's dribbling task sequence (see 9). After receiving the pass, the RED team's receiving player also imitates the dribbling sequence specified by the second YELLOW team player (see 10). As soon as the imitating team makes a mistake, the specifying team is awarded one point. The imitating team will again specify the dribbling sequence during the next round. After 10 correct sequences by the imitating team, the tasks switch, and the imitating team is awarded one point.

2.5.11 Team competition (open passing)

Execution

The RED team competes against the YELLOW team. Each team plays on its own field. There are a total of eight different-colored cone goals positioned on each field. Each field is also framed by three mini goals. Each team has one ball at the beginning of the sequence. Four more balls are positioned on the corner marker of each field. Each team plays on two cone goals with each of the five balls and finishes on one mini goal. The coach designates one team (here the RED team) which does not have a mandatory passing sequence. The RED team begins and first plays on a black cone goal (see 1). Next, the RED team plays on a red cone goal (see 2) and finishes on the center mini goal (see 3). Next, the RED team starts another action with a new ball (see 4). The RED team completes the predetermined sequences with all five balls. The YELLOW team starts at the same time and imitates the RED team's sequences. Accordingly, the YELLOW team also plays first on the black cone goal (see 5 and 6). For the next action the YELLOW team always uses the ball positioned diagonally opposite in the own field. After all five balls are out of the game, the tasks change. The YELLOW team can now choose freely and the RED team imitates the sequences on their own field.

Points system

* Mistake by imitating team (1 point for specifying team)
* Imitating team stops play (2 points for specifying team)
* Faultless sequence by imitating team (1 point for imitating team)

2.5.12 Team competition (complex passing)

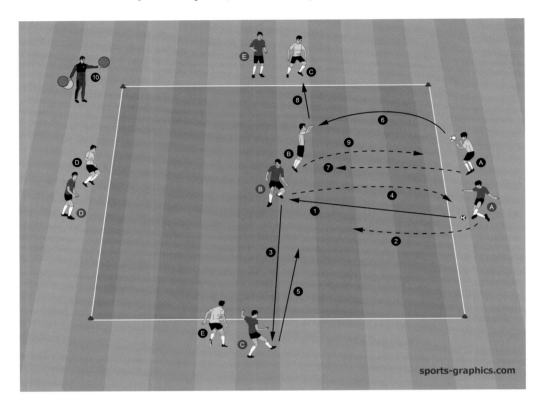

Execution

Two teams circulate a ball within their own ranks on one field. To do so, two of the four players from each team position themselves at the narrow ends of the center field. Players have guidelines for passing techniques, direction of play, and position changes. The BLUE team players circulate their ball clockwise. Player A from the BLUE team passes the ball to player B in the center (see 1) and follows his pass to take over the position in the center (see 2). Player B passes the ball clockwise to the next player C (see 3) and takes over the previous passer's position (here player A) (see 4). Player D plays the ball into the center (see 5) and the passing sequence continues via player A to player D with corresponding position changes. Player A from the YELLOW team throws the ball into the center to player B (see 6) and takes over the center position (see 7). Player B throws the ball counterclockwise to the next player C (see 8) and takes over the previous passer's position (here player A) (see 9). The passing sequence continues via player C to player A with corresponding position changes. The coach designates a color (see 10) and with a coach's signal modifies individual sequence parameters. The teams compete against each other and are awarded a point any time the opposing team makes a mistake.

Coach's signals

- Coach's signal RED cone marker (change direction of play)
- Coach's signal GREEN cone marker (change passing technique/switch from foot to hand)
- Coach's signal YELLOW cone marker (teams switch balls)
- One whistle (direct passes)
- Two whistles (pass with 2 touches/throw after one bounce)

2.5.13 Game (2-on-3)

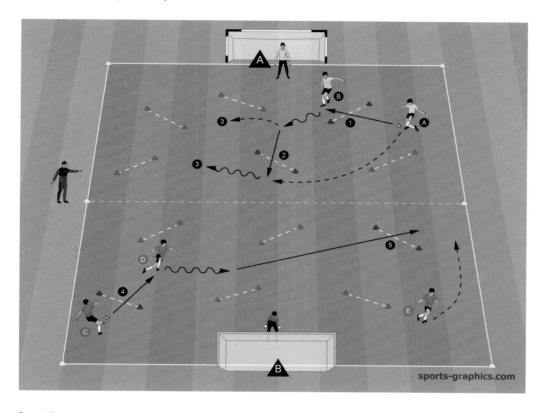

Execution

After an opening technique, a 2-on-3 game situation ensues. The field is divided into two halves and framed by two large goals (see large goals A and B). There are six colored cones in each of the two halves. The cones positioned in each half are the same color and are arranged asymmetrically. The YELLOW team consists of two players (see players A and B) and the GREEN team consists of three players (see players C, D, and E). Each team has a ball and is positioned in their own half. The inferior-number team (see the GREEN team) begins the opening technique and plays on four cone goals, one after the other. The team can freely choose the order of the cone goals. The YELLOW team plays on the first cone goal (see 1), passes through the second cone goal (see 2), and continues the predetermined sequence at another cone goal (see 3) until they have played on four cone goals. The GREEN team starts at the same time and imitates the sequence. The GREEN team reacts and plays (see 4 and 5) on the cone goals in their own half that correspond to the YELLOW team's sequence. After the YELLOW team has played on four cone goals, a 2-on-3-situation immediately follows and the YELLOW team tries to score on the large goal B with the own ball. After the GREEN team has imitated the sequence and has also played on four cone goals, the player in possession passes the previously used ball to the coach and the GREEN team defends the large goal B to subsequently attack the large goal A after successfully winning the ball. The coach has the option of bringing the ball previously used by the superior-number team into the game for another 2-on-3 situation. Players regularly change to new starting positions.

Variation

* Play on cone goals (see 1) at a dribble (dribble through cone goals).

2.5.14 Game (5-on-5)

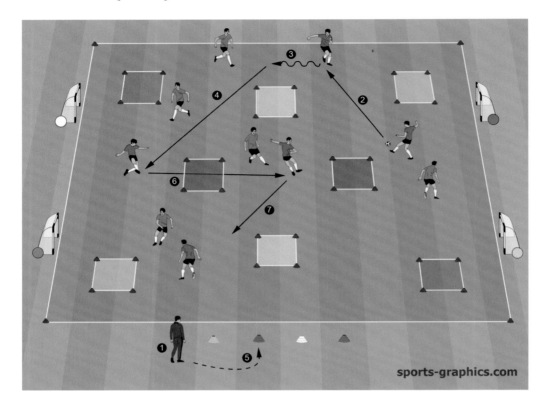

Execution

The RED team plays 5-on-5 against the GREEN team. There are several different-colored fields marked on the playing field. The mini goals are also color-coded. Four cones that match the colors of the fields and mini goals are set up off the field. As long as the coach stands next to the cones (see 1), the team in possession (here the RED team) circulates the ball within their own ranks (see 2, 3, and 4). The GREEN team tries to capture and then keep the ball within their own ranks. During the game for ball holding, the teams must constantly keep an eye on the coach. As soon as the coach changes his position (see 5) and stands behind one of the cones (here GREEN), targeted play on the marked fields begins. The teams now try to play on the fields designated by the coach's position (here the GREEN fields) (see 6). After a field has been successfully played on, a new game for possession begins (see 7) until the coach designates the next fields by changing his position.

Variations

* Play on fields by dribbling (dribble across two lines of a field).
* Play on fields with a feint (feint on the field with subsequent pass).
* Play on fields with third man running (redirect off the field).
* Optional play on the four mini goals after successful play on fields.
* Optional play on mini goal of same color after successful play on fields.
* Coach's position directly generates play on color-coded mini goals.

2.6 PRE-ORIENTATION AND OVER-THE-SHOULDER GLANCE

Pre-Orientation and Over-the-Shoulder Glance includes training exercises to improve play in complex game situations with time and opponent pressure from different directions. Here the emphasis is on early assessment of the game situation, timely recognition of dangers and opportunities, and situation-appropriate decision making for promising actions. Orientation prior to receiving the ball by eliminating one-dimensional ball focusing, by looking over both shoulders, and by using peripheral vision plays an important role here. A further requirement is players coaching each other with clear commands and supporting each other. Improved pre-orientation via anticipatory playing will enable the player to stay calm in spite of confusing playing actions and a fast pace, and will make decision making in appropriate game situations and promising follow-up actions easier. Training exercises include isolated exercises to sensitize players to the over-the-shoulder glance and to provide practice in a protected space. Players must recognize visual and auditory signals, process them, and accomplish specified follow-up actions. Application is further enhanced in combination with open passing and in complex game situations with opponent and time pressure.

PERCEPTION
OPPONENT PRESSURE PIVOTS
DECISION MAKING PRESSURE SITUATIONS
COLOR SIGNALS FOLLOW-UP ACTIONS
TIME PRESSURE REACTING
PERIPHERAL VISION
COMMANDS ORIENTING
OBSERVING ANTICIPATING THE BALL

2.6.1   Decision making after over-the-shoulder glance (passing and ball control)

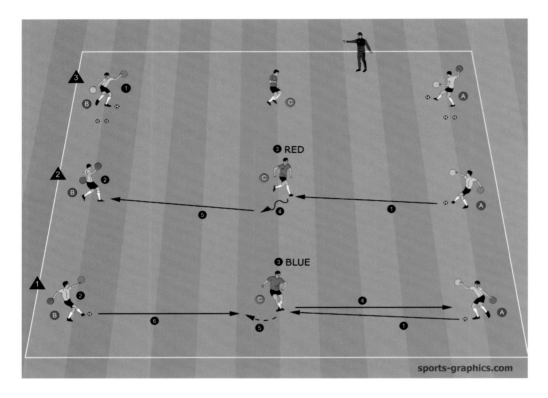

Execution

Each training squad consists of three players (see players A, B, and C). Two players position themselves in outside positions (see players A and B). Players A and B carry different-colored cone markers and alternate flashing different colors. A third player (see player C) is positioned in the center between the two receivers and works on his awareness with over-the-shoulder glances and by watching for signals behind his back. Players switch tasks in regular intervals. As a variation, the arm used by players A and B to flash the designated color (left/right) can also communicate other action demands (e.g., in which direction to open up) to the center player. In **the back pass variation** (see build-up 1) the weak-side player (here player B) flashes a color (here BLUE) (see 2) with each pass to the center (see 1). The center player tries to pick up on these signals with over-the-shoulder glances, designate them (see 3), and then play the direct back pass (see 4). Next, player C pivots (see 5), receives the next pass from player B (see 6), and tries to designate the color signaled by player A. In the **opening up variation** (see build-up 2), player C tries to pick up on the color signal behind his back (see 2) with an over-the-shoulder glance and quickly designate it before receiving the pass (see 3). Player C continues the passing sequence by opening up (see 4), passes to player B (see 5), and then, during the back pass from player B, designates the color signal from player A. In the **decision-making variation** (see 3), the center player, according to previously determined colors signaled behind his back, must either play a direct back pass (see build-up 1) or open up (see build-up 2).

2.6.2   Decision making after over-the-shoulder glance (soccer tennis)

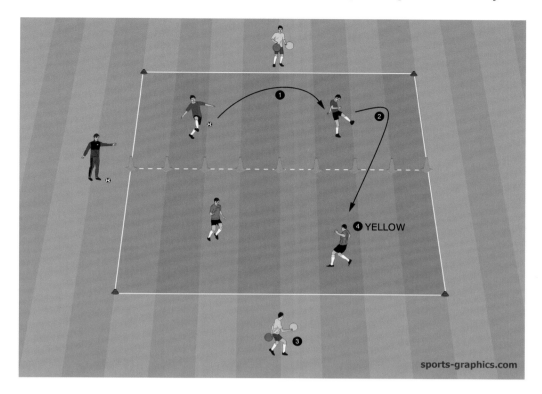

Execution

The BLUE team plays 2-on-2 against the RED team. The teams play soccer tennis over a net, which here is shown as a row of cone markers. A third player is positioned behind the halves and holds several different-colored cone markers. The players on the field can pass the ball to each other (see 1) without the ball touching the ground. Next, they try to play the ball over the net into the opposing half (see 2). As soon as a pass is played over the net (see 2), the outside player behind the pass receiver raises a cone (here YELLOW). By glancing over this shoulder, the pass receiver tries to see and designate the color signal before his first touch (see 4). After a pass over the net (see 2), the ball can touch the ground once. The game continues even if the pass receiver was unable to recognize the color or designated it incorrectly.

Points system

* Opponent is awarded one point if there is contact with the net or the ball goes into touch (see 2).
* Opponent is awarded one point if the ball touches the ground twice in own field.
* Own team is awarded one point for each correctly designated color (see 3).

Variations

* Vary number of players (3/4/5 players per team).
* Designate requirements for playing over the net (1/2/3 passes [see 1]) with own team.
* Vary touches for individual players (2/3/4 mandatory touches/direct play).
* Signal color (see 3) with left hand (pass over net with right leg).
* Signal color (see 3) with right hand (pass over net with left leg).

2.6.3   Decision making after over-the-shoulder glance (simple passing sequence)

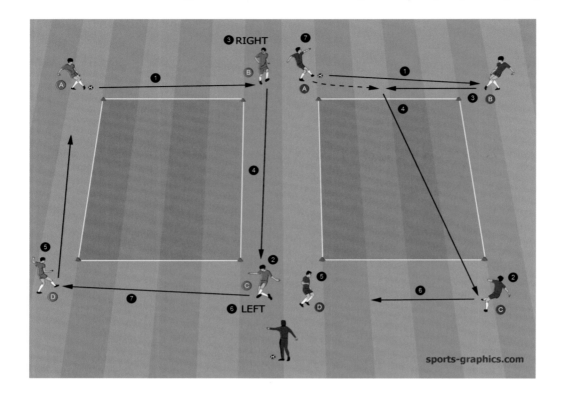

Execution

Players complete a predetermined passing sequence around a central rectangle. The ball always moves from player A to player B and from player C to player D. After their pass, the players remain in their positions. Pass receivers must always keep an eye on the next player in line with an over-the-shoulder glance so they are able to see his hand signals and complete the corresponding tasks. As a variation, passing sequences can be completed as a competition with several groups. The fastest team to accurately complete a predetermined number of actions is the winner.

Perception variation (see RED team)

With each pass (see 1), the player next in line after the pass receiver (here player C) raises an arm (see 2). The respective pass receiver (here player B) must notice the raised arm by glancing over his shoulder and try to correctly designate it left/right before he controls the ball (see 3). The passing sequence continues (see 4 and 7) and with each subsequent pass (see 4) a hand signal is given (see 5) and designated by the pass receiver (see 6).

Decision-making variation (see BLUE team)

With each pass (see 1) the player next in line after the pass receiver (here player C) raises an arm (see 2). Depending on which arm is raised, the player anticipating the pass (here player B) must decide how to continue the passing sequence (see 3). If the left arm is raised the passing sequence continues in ascending order (see RED team). As soon as a right arm is raised the passing sequence continues via a direct back pass and a diagonal pass (see 4). Each subsequent pass to the next position (see 4 and 6) is accompanied by a new hand signal (see 5 and 7).

2.6.4 Decision making after over-the-shoulder glance (complex passing sequence)

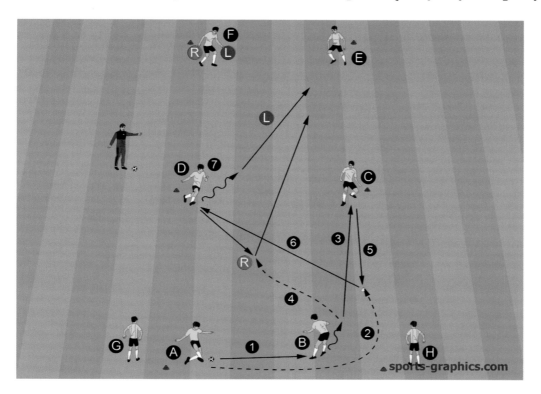

Execution

Players complete a predetermined passing sequence and position themselves in six starting positions. Positions A and B are double-manned (see players G and H). The players in the center (see starting positions D and C) practice pre-orientation with over-the-shoulder glances according to the commands by a player positioned behind them (see player F). Player A begins the passing sequence, plays to player B (see 1), and overlaps (see 2). Player B controls the ball, passes to player C (see 3), and then drops away to the center (see 4). Player C plays to player A (see 5). Player A passes to player D (see 6). At the time of player A's pass (see 6), the player (see player F) positioned behind the pass receiver (see player D) gives a command and raises his right arm (see R) or left arm (see L). While the pass (see 6) is played, the pass receiver (here player D) must notice and recognize the command by glancing over his shoulder (see 7). Player D must complete his next action according to the command. A left arm raised means that player D must open up with a subsequent pass (see L) and a right arm raised signifies a back pass to player B (see R). In this case player B plays a pass to the receiver (see player E). After glancing over his shoulder and recognizing the signal, player D either decides to continue his own game (see L) or play a back pass (see R). Player E starts a new action from the opposite side. After the final pass, players switch starting positions always in pairs for a new round (see L or R). Players A and B take over C and D's positions and are active in the center. Players C and D take over E and F's positions. Players E and F start the next round and players G and H remain in their starting positions to receive the final pass of the new round. Players A/D/F/G and B/C/E/H should independently alternate between the left and right side to practice playing with both feet and especially to regularly practice the over-the-shoulder glance in position D.

2.6.5   Decision making after over-the-shoulder glance (double passing sequence)

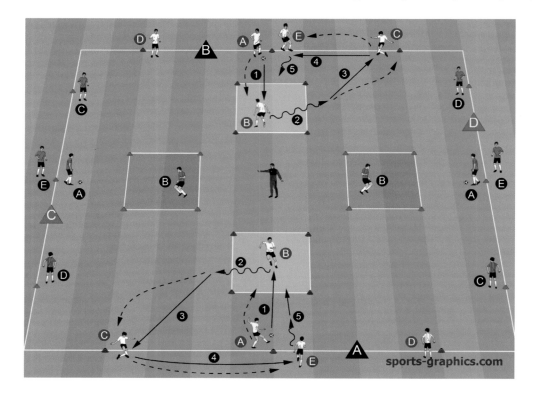

sports-graphics.com

Execution

All players are divided into two teams (see WHITE and RED teams). Each team positions itself at two stations with at least five players at each station (see groups A, B, C, and D). The five players within each group spread out at a starting position (see players A and E), on a field in front of the starting position (see player B), and to the side along the baseline (see players C and D). Group A completes a passing sequence in which player B can choose to continue play to the left or the right. Group B imitates this passing sequence and in the process is forced to look over their shoulder to see the process on the opposite side. Group A begins the sequence. Player A passes to player B (see 1). Player B chooses to continue play (see 2) to the left or the right (here to the right) and dribbles off the field. Player B passes to player C (see 3), player C passes to player E (see 4), and player E starts a new action (see 5). After their actions, all players move up one position. Group B imitates group A's sequence. After looking over his shoulder, the imitating player B must also decide whether to continue play to the left or right. The RED team practices at the same time, whereby group C makes the decision for continued play and group D must imitate accordingly. Tasks change at regular intervals.

Variations

* Complete as competition (Which team is the first to correctly imitate 20 play continuations?).
* Modify the passing sequence (expand certain passes [see 1 and 3] to double double-passes).
* Modify the decision-making process (play in the opposite direction).

2.6.6 Decision making after over-the-shoulder glance (open passing)

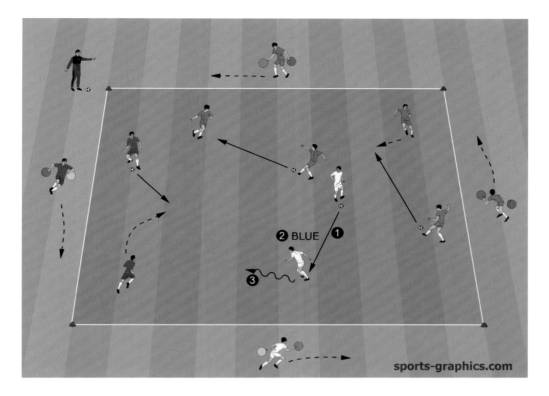

sports-graphics.com

Execution

Players are divided into multiple teams of three (see WHITE, GREEN, RED, and BLUE). The two players on the field have a ball and pass to each other (see 1). The player off the field has two different-colored cone markers and continually runs around the field. Prior to each pass, the pass receiver takes his cue from the outside player and before controlling the ball, names the color of the cone held up by the outside player (see 2). After controlling the ball, the player in possession slows down the game with his partner with a brief dribble (see 3) and then passes back to the teammate.

Basic idea

In many game situations high-speed modern soccer puts a lot of time and opponent pressure on players. A pass receiver's early awareness and orientation prior to controlling the ball is extremely important. A player anticipating the ball makes decisions for sensible and situation-appropriate follow-up actions through pre-orientation and early awareness of open and occupied spaces, possible passing options, or approaching opponents. Players are called upon to already pay attention to the positions of outside players while passing and to constantly focus on pre-orientation.

Variations

* Modify the decision-making process (specify side for ball control or playing leg).
* Complete as competition (Which team is the first to play 10/20 passes with at least four touches?).
* Complete with teams of four (group of three on the center field).

2.6.7   Decision making after over-the-shoulder glance (open passing along lines)

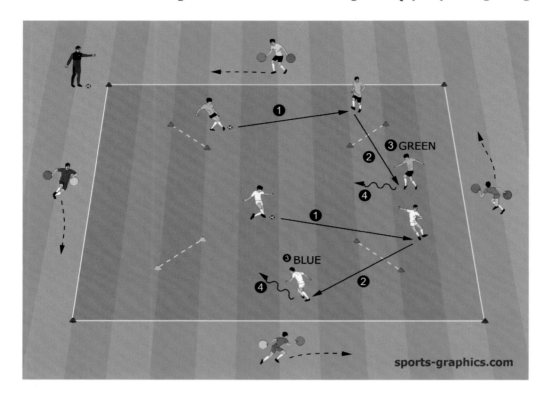

sports-graphics.com

Execution

Players form two groups of three players each (see BLUE team and WHITE team). Four additional players stand off the field. There are different-colored cone goals positioned on the field. The outside players wear colored bibs that match the colors of the cone goals, and also carry a colored cone marker in each hand. The outside players continuously run around the outside of the field and alternately hold up one of the two colored cones as a signal for the players on the field. Each of the teams on the field has a ball and lets the ball circulate within their own ranks (see 1 and 2). As they do so, they play passes through the cone goals (see 2). Each player receiving a pass through a cone goal (see 2) tries to see which color cone the outside player is holding up behind him by glancing over his shoulder prior to controlling the ball. The pass receiver must loudly name the color of the raised cone (see 3). The passing sequence continues and the next cone goal is played on. As a variation, players must always name the color of the cone that matches the color of the outside player who played on the previously played-on cone goal. The sequence can also be completed as a competition with the objective of playing through ten cone goals as quickly as possible and correctly naming all of the respective colors.

2.6.8   Decision making after over-the-shoulder glance (open passing on zones)

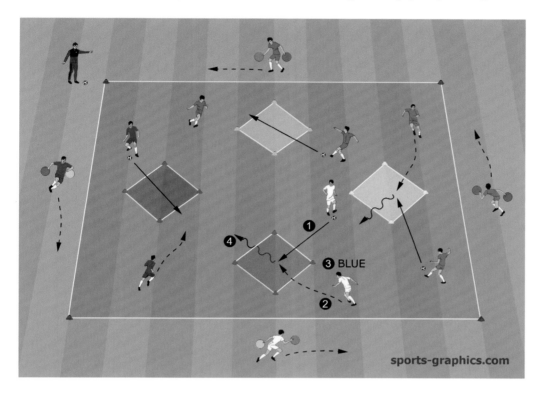

sports-graphics.com

Execution

Players are divided into several teams of three (see WHITE team, GREEN team, RED team, and BLUE team). Three players from each team are positioned on the center field and one player outside the field. The three players on the field have a ball and pass it back and forth (see 1). The player outside the field has two different-colored cones and continuously runs around the field. The teams on the center field play into the fields marked with four different colors by playing a pass across two lines (see GREEN and YELLOW field), or chase (see 2) a pass played into one of the fields (see 1) and then leave the field at a dribble (see 4). While playing into the fields, prior to receiving a pass the pass receiver must look to his team's outside player and name the color he holds up (see 3). Afterwards open passing and the subsequent play into a field continue (see 4).

Variations

* Complete as a competition (Which team is the first to play 10/20 passes with at least four touches?).
* Complete with teams of four (group of three on the center field).

2.6.9   Game (double 1-on-1)

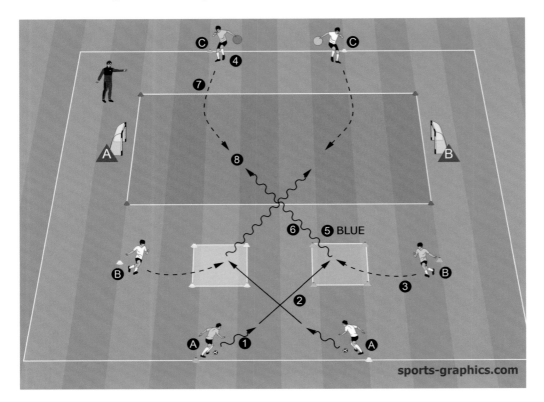

Execution

Players are divided into two teams of three players each (see YELLOW team and WHITE team). The three players position themselves at three different starting positions. The players B stand outside in front of an action field (see YELLOW and WHITE field). The players C position themselves behind the field with the mini goals (see BLUE field) and each holds two different-colored cone markers. The players A start simultaneously and both groups complete a passing sequence with subsequent tackles. Player A briefly dribbles (see 1) and passes the ball into the diagonally opposite field (see 2), which player B moves into (see 3) to control the pass toward the BLUE field. During the pass into the field (see 2) player C holds up a colored cone (see 4). Player B tries to catch the signal by glancing over his shoulder and naming the color shown (see 5). Next, player B dribbles into the BLUE field (see 6) and players B and C (see 7) try to score on mini goals A and B from 1-on-1 play (see 8). The sequence can be completed as a competition. The teams try to score as many goals as possible on the mini goals.

2.6.10   Game (3-on-3)

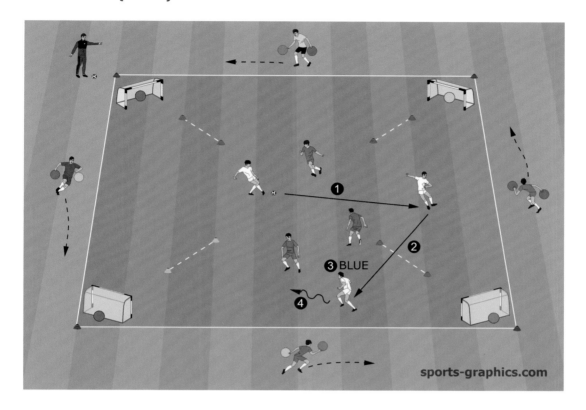

Execution

The WHITE team plays 3-on-3 against the RED team. There are four additional players standing outside the field. Different-colored cone goals are set up on the field. The outside players wear bibs that match the colors of the cone goals and each holds two cone markers. The outside players are continuously running around the field and alternately raising one of the colored cone markers as a signal for the players on the field. The two teams on the field initially play for ball holding (see 1, 2, and 4). In doing so, the team in possession (here the WHITE team) tries to play a pass through one of the cone goals (see 2). With each successful pass through a cone goal, the pass receiver tries to name the color (here RED) of the cone held up by the outside player behind him, before trapping the ball (see 3). If he is able to name the color before controlling the ball, his team is awarded one point. The game immediately continues (see 4). As a variation the players can try to name the cone color that matches the outside player whose color matches the previously played on cone goal. The successful team could also be allowed to play on one of the four mini goals as a follow-up action.

2.6.11   Game (3-on-3 plus 3)

sports-graphics.com

Execution

Players are divided into three teams of three players each (see BLUE team, RED team, and GRAY team) and play 3-on-3 plus 3 against each other. To do so, one team (here the GRAY team) is positioned at the narrow ends of the YELLOW and BLUE fields as neutral receivers (see players A and C) and in the center between the two fields (see player B). The team not in possession (here the RED team) always has one player without a ball positioned on the weak-side field (see player A). The team in possession (here the BLUE team) plays 4-on-2 together with outside player A against two players from the RED team (see players A and C) on the YELLOW field (see 1, 2, and 3). After successfully involving the outside player (see 2 and 3) and the subsequent pass to the center player B (see 4), the BLUE team scores a point and switches play to the BLUE field. With each pass into the center (see 4), the opposite outside player (here player C) raises a colored cone (see 5). The center player B tries to see the color shown by glancing over his shoulder and calls it out before controlling the ball (see 6). Player B continues the game with a pass to player C (see 7). The teams switch to the opposite field (see 8). One player from the BLUE team (here player C) remains on the YELLOW field (see 9). The game continues on the BLUE field. The RED team plays with players A, B, and C against the BLUE team with players A and B. By involving player C, the RED team tries to switch play back to the YELLOW field via the center player B.

Points system

★   BLUE team: Successful involvement of receiver (see 2 and 3) and switch of play (see 4) (1 point).

★   RED team: Winning the ball and direct switch of play to weak-side teammate (see player A) (1 point).

★   GRAY team: Player B calls color correctly (see 5) before controlling the ball (1 point).

2.6.12 Game (4-on-4)

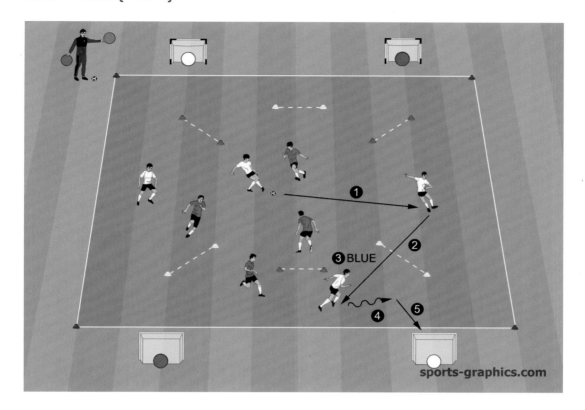

Execution

The WHITE team plays 4-on-4 against the RED team. Several cone goals are set up on a marked field. The field is framed by four mini goals. The cone goals are marked with the same colors as the mini goals, WHITE and RED. The two teams initially play for ball holding (see 1) and try to keep the ball within their own ranks without the opposing team capturing the ball. The teams also try to play on the cone goals and to play a pass through a cone goal to a teammate (see 2). With each successful pass through a cone goal, the pass receiver tries to call out the color (see 3) of the cone the coach is holding up (here BLUE), before trapping the ball. If he is able to call out the correct color before controlling the ball, the team can attack the mini goals of the same color.

Variations

* Coach continuously moves around the field and changes positions.
* Specify play on cone goals (alternate playing on RED and WHITE goals).

2.6.13 Game (4-on-4 plus 2) (1)

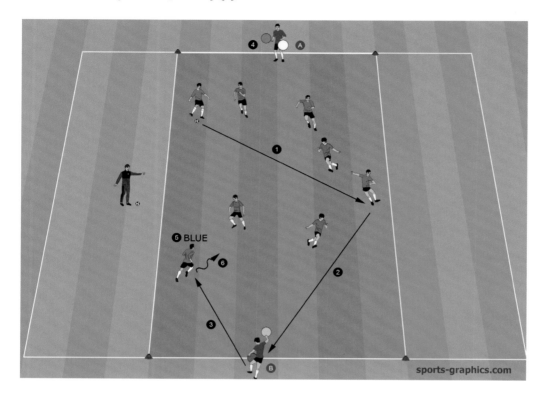

Execution

The GREEN team plays 4-on-4 plus 2 against the RED team. To do so, two neutral outside players position themselves at the two narrow sides of the field (see players A and B). Players A and B hold several different-colored cone markers and always hold up one cone. The raised cone always changes. In addition, the players A and B act as neutral teammates for the team in possession and can be passed to any time. The respective team in possession (here the GREEN team) tries to keep possession for as long as possible without the opposing team winning the ball (see 1) and to frequently involve the outside players in the passing sequence (see 2 and 3). After a pass from outside (see 3), the respective pass receiver tries to call out the color (see 4) of the cone currently held up by the player opposite him before controlling the ball (see 5). The game continues directly (see 6). As a variation the outside players can wait to hold up a cone (see 4) until a pass to the outside is played (see 2). A team is awarded one point for each correctly called color (see 5). Outside players change at regular intervals.

2.6.14 Game (4-on-4 plus 2) (2)

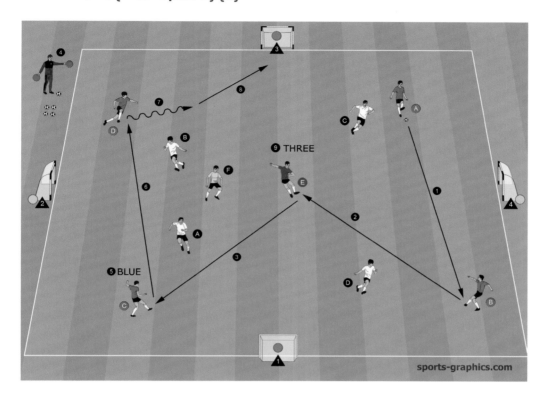

sports-graphics.com

Execution

The RED team plays 4-on-4 plus 2 against the WHITE team. Two neutral players wearing two different-colored bibs (see BLUE and YELLOW bibs) are active on the field (see player E and F). The field is framed by four mini goals, which are also marked blue and yellow. The respective team in possession (here the RED team) initially plays for ball holding (see 1) and tries to involve the neutral players in the passing sequence (see 2 and 3). As soon as a neutral player has been involved (see 2 and 3), the team can finish on two mini goals. In doing so, only the mini goals (see BLUE mini goals) that match the color of the neutral player who received the previous pass (here player E) can be played on. As soon as both neutral players have been involved one after another in the passing sequence, the team in possession can finish on all four mini goals. In addition to scoring on a mini goal the team in possession can also score additional points. To do so, the coach alternately holds up different-colored cone markers. As soon as a player from the team in possession (here player C), who receives a pass from a neutral player (see 3), correctly names the cone color prior to his first touch (see 5), the team is awarded an additional point.

Variations

★ Neutral player designates goals to be played on via signal (see 9).

★ Increase awareness via coach's constant position changes (see 4).

★ Add a requirement for play on mini goals (double involvement of neutral players).

★ Add a requirement for passing to a neutral player (3 passes within own ranks).

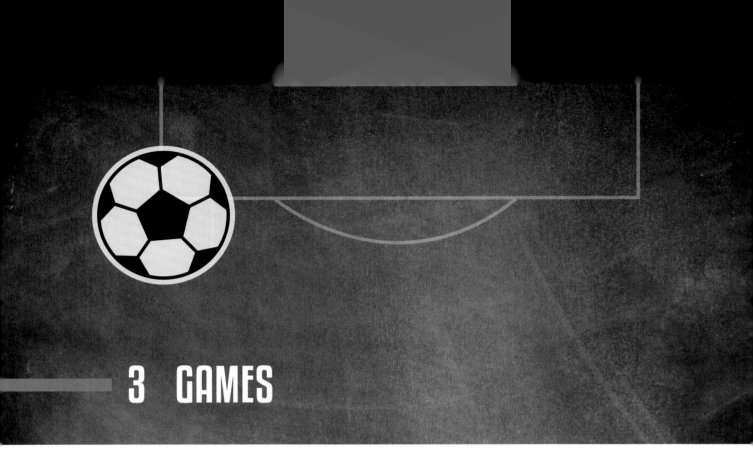

3 GAMES

Games focuses on making games and competitions realistic. Within the scope of these games, classic elements such as operating within the team, playing against an opponent, playing on goals, and scoring points are combined and elaborated on with modern elements like playing on geometric fields, defined target zones, kick-off variations via openings to techniques and competitions, or the use of color signals.

POSSESSION TARGET SPACES
FIELDS TARGET ZONES KICK-OFF
PLAYING ABILITY SEAMS
ACTION SPEED RONDOS
ZONE RULES VERTICAL PLAY
POSSESSION PLAYING LEG BALL CIRCULATION
OPENING TECHNIQUE RULE VARIATIONS
ADVERSARY GAMES GAME IDEAS COLOR GAMES

3.1 OPENING TECHNIQUES AND DIFFERENT WAYS TO START A SOCCER GAME

Opening Techniques and Different Ways to Start a Soccer Game includes games with creative opening variations as alternatives to the classic kick-off with two organized teams that start from their own goals. Starting situations begin in motion with staggered and random team positioning and nonspecific team and position assignments. Opening techniques require transitioning after technical tasks like dribbling, passing combinations, and shots on goal, and their competitive format determines possession in subsequent game situations. Here alternating between practicing and engraining techniques is directly linked to playing and adapting. It is imperative to quickly re-orient and provide structure within the acting team at the beginning of the game situation while simultaneously concentrating on resulting directions of play and goal array. Games are played with small teams as 2-on-2, 3-on-3, or 4-on-4.

SEARCHING FOR POSITION
SCORING OPPORTUNITIES FINDING POSITION
SPATIAL BEHAVIOR INFERIOR NUMBER
GOALKEEPER INVOLVEMENT DRIBBLING TASKS
COUNTERING TIME PRESSURE SUPERIOR NUMBER
RUNNING PATHS GAME SITUATIONS
CHANGE IN DIRECTION OF PLAY CREATIVITY
FINISHES PASSING COMBINATIONS
PASSING SEQUENCES TECHNICAL TASKS
DISORDER

3.1.1   Double 2-on-1 after passing combination (1)

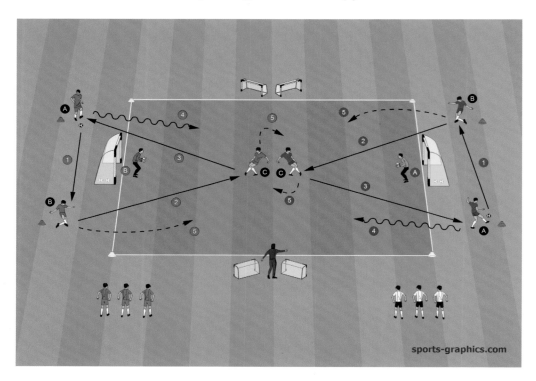

Execution

Two 2-on-1 situations ensue after a predetermined passing sequence. Players A and B are on offense and play against player C. The passing sequence begins with player A behind the goal. Player A passes to player B (see 1). Player B passes the ball into the field to player C (see 2). Player C passes to player A (see 3). Player A controls the ball in the direction of the field (see 4). Next, all players transition for the two subsequent 2-on-1 situations (see 5). Players A and B from the RED team are in possession against player C from the BLUE team and attack the goal of goalkeeper A. Players A and B from the BLUE team are in possession against player C from the RED team and attack the goal of goalkeeper B. After capturing the ball, the inferior number player (see player C) has the choice of countering on the two mini goals. The teams switch after each round (see GREEN team and WHITE team). The individual players independently change starting positions within their teams.

Points system

* Goal scored on large goal (1 point)
* Capturing the ball and scoring on a mini goal (2 points)

Variations

* Specify touches (3 touches/2 touches/direct play).
* Goalkeeper starts passing sequence with throw-out (waist-high/high).

3.1.2   Double 2-on-1 after passing combination (2)

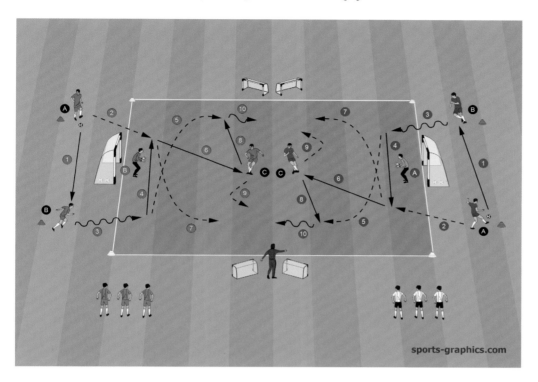

sports-graphics.com

Execution

Two 2-on-1 situations ensue after a predetermined passing sequence. Players A and B are on offense and play against player C. The passing sequence begins with player A behind the goal. Player A passes to player B (see 1) and runs into the field (see 2). Player B controls the ball toward the field (see 3) and plays a square pass to player A (see 4). Player B crosses A's running and passing paths (see 5). Player A passes the ball into the center to player C (see 6) and overlaps player B (see 7). Player C plays a square pass to player B (see 8), pivots, and goes into defensive mode for the subsequent 2-on-1 situation (see 9). Player B controls the ball offensively and together with player A goes into offensive mode for the subsequent 2-on-1 situation. Players A and B from the RED team play in possession against player C from the BLUE team and attack the goal of goalkeeper A. Players A and B from the BLUE team play in possession against player C from the RED team and attack the goal of goalkeeper B. After winning the ball, the inferior number player (see player C) has the opportunity to counter on the two mini goals. The teams switch after each round (see GREEN team and WHITE team). The individual players independently change starting positions within their teams.

Points system

* Goal scored on large goal (1 point)
* Capturing the ball and scoring on a mini goal (2 points)

3.1.3   Double 2-on-1 and 3-on-3 after passing combination and shot on goal

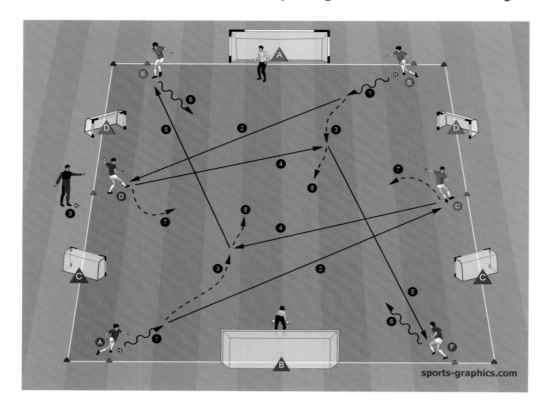

sports-graphics.com

Execution

After a predetermined passing sequence, two 2-on-1 situations ensue on the large goals A and B and the four mini goals C and D. Players spread out in staggered playing positions. After a signal from the coach, players A and B start the sequence, each with his own ball. Players A/B briefly dribble (see 1), play a square pass to players C/D (see 2), and then run into the center (see 3). Players C/D play a back pass (see 4). Players A/B pass the ball to players E/F (see 5). Players E/F dribble into the field for the subsequent 2-on-1 situations (see 6). Players C/D transition to offense (see 7) and players A/B transition to defense (see 8). Players C/E play 2-on-1 against player A. In doing so, players C/E attack the large goal B and player A counters on the mini goals D. Players D/F play 2-on-1 against player B. in doing so, players D/F attack the large goal A and player B counters on the mini goals C. After the two 2-on-1 situations end, the coach plays a ball into the game and the teams play 3-on-3 on the mini goals. The BLUE team is allowed to involve their own goalkeeper B in the game and attacks the mini goals D. The RED team is allowed to involve their own goalkeeper A and attacks the mini goals C. After a goal is scored on the mini goals, the coach brings the next ball into the game for another 3-on-3 situation (see 9). The direction of play changes with the new ball and the teams play on the large goals. The BLUE team now attacks the large goal B and the RED team attacks the large goal A. Players change starting positions for a new sequence.

Points system

* Goal scored in 2-on-1 (1 point)/goal scored in 1-on-2 after capturing the ball (2 points)
* Goals cored on a mini goal in 3-on-3 (1 point)/goal scored on a large goal in 3-on-3 (2 points)

3.1.4   2-on-2 after passing and first-touch ball control

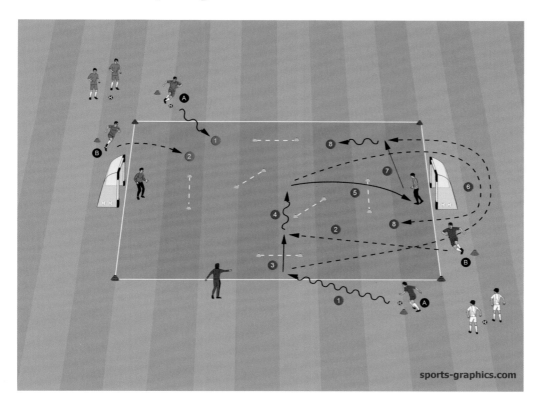

sports-graphics.com

Execution

The BLUE team initially competes for speed against the RED team and plays against the cone goals marked in the center of the field. Next is a 2-on-2 situation. The teams of two position themselves at the starting positions, each with a ball (see players A and B). At a signal from the coach, a technique-oriented competition begins and the BLUE team and the RED team start simultaneously (see 1 and 2). The pairs must play on the cone goals in the center with one pass. Player A dribbles the ball into the field (see 1). Player B runs into position (see 2) to receive a pass through one of the cone goals (see 3). He controls the ball (see 4) and passes the ball to their own goalkeeper (see 5). Both players now run around the own goal, crossing running paths (see 6). The coach names the faster team (here the BLUE team). The goalkeeper from the designated faster team passes the ball to a teammate (see 7). The opposing goalkeeper passes the ball off the field to the coach. Now the teams play 2-on-2 against the large goals until a goal is scored or the ball leaves the field. The BLUE team is in possession (see 8). Subsequently the coach has the option of bringing a second ball into the game for another 2-on-2 situation. Teams switch after each round (see GREEN team and WHITE team). The individual players independently change starting positions within their teams.

Variations

★ Play on multiple cone goals in a row prior to running task/pass to goalkeeper (see 3).

★ Goalkeeper starts 2-on-2 play with a throw-out (waist-high/high).

★ Change direction of play with the second ball from the coach.

3.1.5   2-on-2 after dribbling and passing

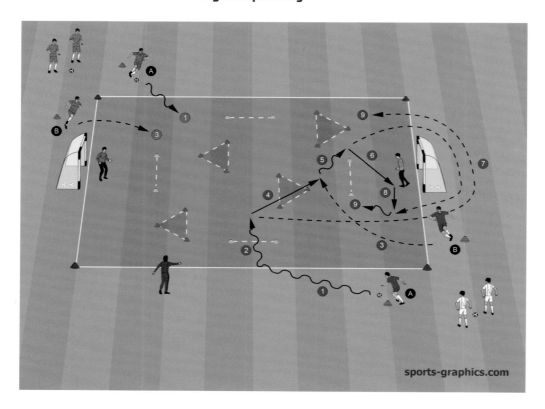

sports-graphics.com

Execution

The BLUE team competes for speed against the RED team and plays on the cone goals and passing triangles marked in the center of the field. Next is a 2-on-2 situation. The teams of two position themselves at the starting positions, each with a ball (see players A and B). At a signal from the coach, a technique-oriented competition begins and the BLUE team and the RED team start simultaneously (see 1 and 3). The pairs must play on the cone goals and passing triangles in the center. The players begin with a cone goal, dribble through the goal, and then play a pass through one of the passing triangles. Players must alternate between playing on cone goals and dribble triangles. Player A dribbles the ball into the field (see 1) and dribbles through a cone goal (see 2). Player B gets in position (see 3) to receive a pass across two lines of a passing triangle (see 4). He controls the ball (see 5) and passes to their own goalkeeper (see 6). Now both players must run around the own goal, crossing running paths (see 7). The coach names the faster team (here the BLUE team). The goalkeeper from the designated faster team passes the ball to a teammate (see 8). The opposing goalkeeper passes off the field to the coach. Now the teams play 2-on-2 on the large goals until a goal is scored or the ball leaves the field. The BLUE team is in possession (see 9). Subsequently the coach has the option of bringing a second ball into the game for another 2-on-2 situation. Teams switch after each round (see GREEN team and WHITE team). The individual players independently change starting positions within their teams.

Variations

* Play on multiple cone goals/passing triangles in a row prior to pass to goalkeeper (see 2 and 4).
* Change direction of play with the coach's second ball.

3.1.6   2-on-2 after dribbling and finish

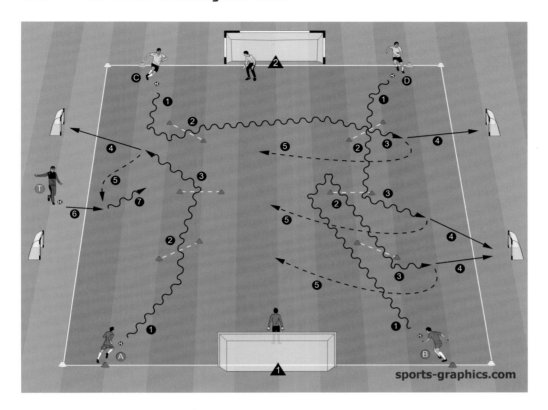

Execution

After an opening technique in the form of dribbling and subsequent finish, the RED team (see players A and B) plays 2-on-2 against the YELLOW team (see players C and D). After a signal from the coach, all four players start dribbling into the field from their starting positions with the ball at their foot (see 1). On the field are multiple marked cone goals. Each player must choose two cone goals to dribble through (see 2 and 3) and afterwards put his own ball in the back of the mini goal of his choice (see 4). After finishing on the mini goals (see 4), all players transition for the subsequent 2-on-2 (see 5). The coach brings a new ball into the game for the 2-on-2 (see 6). One player gets the pass from the coach (here player A) and starts into the 2-on-2 with the ball at his foot (see 7). The YELLOW team attacks goal 1 and the RED team attacks goal 2.

Variations

* Modify the technical task (feints at cone goal).
* Ramp up technical task (dribble through 3/4 cone goals).
* Specify finish (see 4) on mini goals (finish with weak leg).
* Specify finish (see 4) on mini goals (shoot from weak side of field).
* Complete opening technique without ball (run forward/backward through cone goals).
* Complete specific feint prior to finish (see 4) on mini goals.
* Opportunity to finish on all four mini goals in 2-on-2 after 10 passes in a row.

3.1.7   2-on-2 after shooting sequence

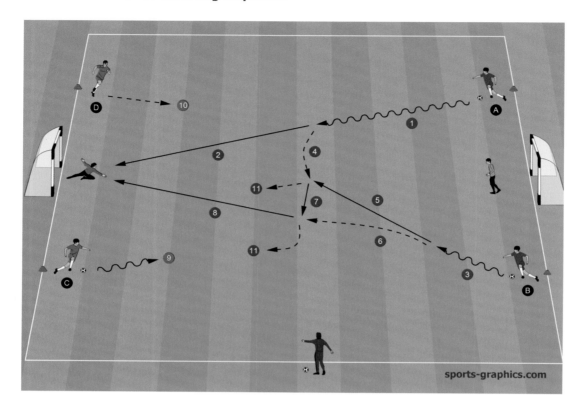

Execution

Players A and B each take a shot on goal. Next a 2-on-2 situation between the RED team and the BLUE team ensues. Player A briefly dribbles (see 1) and finishes on the large goal (see 2). While player A takes his shot, player B briefly dribbles (see 3). After his first shot, player A turns (see 4) and receives a pass from player B (see 5). Player B follows his pass toward the goal (see 6) and receives a square pass from player A (see 7). Player B finishes on the large goal (see 8). While player B takes his shot, player C from the RED team starts dribbling into the field with the ball at his foot (see 9). At the same time, player D starts onto the field without a ball (see 10). The two RED team players now try to score a goal in 2-on-2 play. Players A and B transition to defense (see 11). After successfully capturing the ball, the BLUE team can counter on the other large goal. The teams now play 2-on-2 on the two large goals until a goal is scored or the ball leaves the field. Subsequently the coach has the option of bringing a second ball into the game for another 2-on-2 situation. After each round the individual players independently change starting positions within their teams.

Variations

★   Player C begins with a square pass to player D (see 9).

★   Player C already starts with the square pass from player A (see 7).

★   Player B can participate in 2-on-2 only if he scores a goal (see 8).

★   Players A and B must perform a feint prior to their shot on goal (see 2 and 8).

★   Players A and B finish with a specified shooting technique (see 2 and 8).

★   Player B must take a direct shot on goal (see 8).

3.1.8   2-on-2 after passing combination and shot on goal (1)

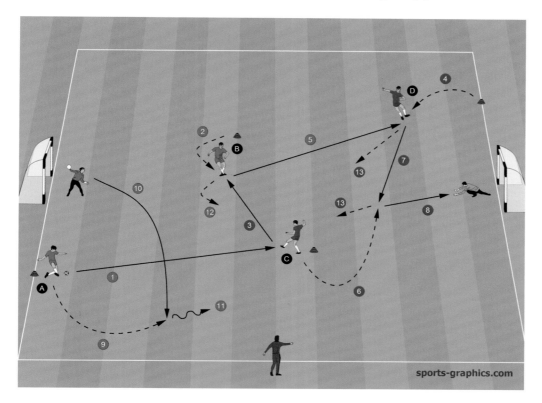

Execution

A 2-on-2 situation between the RED team and the BLUE team ensues after a predetermined passing sequence with subsequent shot on goal. The passing sequence begins with player A. Player A briefly dribbles and plays a pass to player C (see 1). With the first pass, player B peels away in open playing position (see 2) and receives a pass from player C (see 3). With the second pass, player D peels away from his starting cone (see 4) and receives a pass from player B (see 5). Player C turns (see 6) and receives a square pass from player D (see 7). Player C takes a shot on goal (see 8). With the shot by player C, player A in open playing position (see 9) signals his readiness for the goalkeeper's throw-out (see 10). Player A controls the throw-out and dribbles into the field for the subsequent 2-on-2 (see 11). Player B gets into offensive mode for the 2-on-2 (see 12). Players C and D get into defensive mode (see 13). The teams now play 2-on-2 on both large goals until a goal is scored or the ball leaves the field.

Points system

* BLUE team scores after passing sequence and shot by player C (1 point).
* RED team scores during 2-on-2 (2 points).
* RED team scores after winning the ball during 2-on-2 (3 points).

Variation

* Second ball from coach (after throw-out by BLUE team goalkeeper).

3.1.9   2-on-2 after passing combination and shot on goal (2)

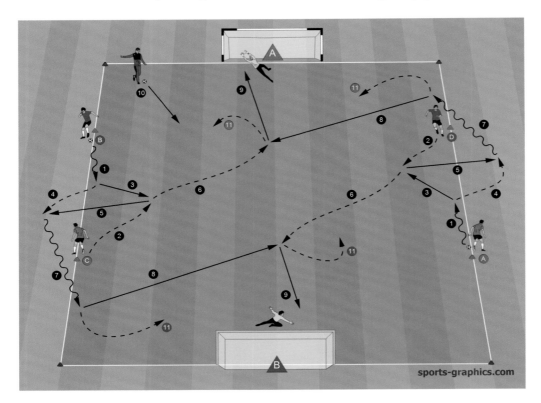

Execution

After simultaneous double passes, crosses, and shots on goal, a 2-on-2 situation ensues between the RED team and the BLUE team. The passing sequence begins at the outside positions, and after a signal from the coach, players A, B, C, and D start simultaneously. Players A/B briefly dribble (see 1). At the same time, players C/D signal their readiness toward the center (see 2). Players A/B pass into the center (see 3) and break away to the outside (see 4). Players C/D play a back pass (see 5) and run to the center to receive the cross (see 6). Players A/B control the pass toward the large goals A and B (see 7) and cross into the center (see 8). Players C/D try to exploit the cross and score (see 9). After the first cross, the coach brings a ball into the game for the subsequent 2-on-2 (see 10). All of the players transition (see 11). Players A and C play with goalkeeper A against players B and D plus goalkeeper B. Players switch starting positions within their team for a subsequent round. After a while this exercise should be played in mirror-reverse so players will also have to cross with the left leg.

Points system

* Goal scored after cross (see 9) during opening technique (1 point)
* Goal scored during 2-on-2 (1 point)/winning the ball and scoring during 2-on-2 (2 points)

Variation

* Specify shooting technique (direct finish/header/inside foot/left/right).

3.1.10   2-on-2 after passing combination and shot on goal (3)

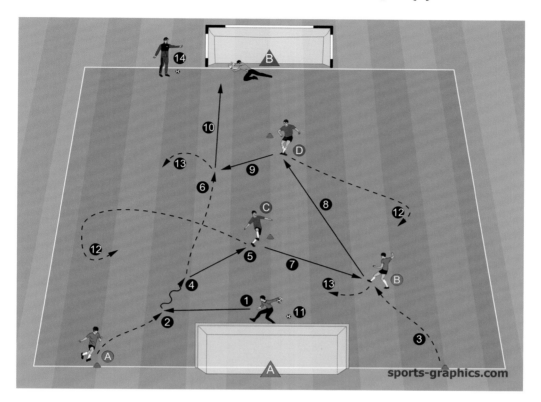

Execution

After a passing combination with a shot on goal B, a 2-on-2 situation ensues between the RED team and the BLUE team. Players position themselves at different start markers. Goalkeeper A holds a ball in his hands and has a second ball on the ground next to him. Goalkeeper A starts the action and rolls the ball into the running path of player A (see 1). Players A and B run into the field (see 2 and 3). Player A controls the ball (see 4), passes to player C (see 5), and runs toward the goal (see 6). Player C lays off to player B (see 7). Player B plays a long ball to player D (see 8). Player D lays off to player A (see 9). Player A finishes on goal B (see 10). After their actions, all of the players transition for the immediately following 2-on-2 situation (see 12 and 13) that starts with goalkeeper A (see 11). Goalkeeper A brings the second ball into the game. Afterwards the coach has the option of bringing another ball into the game for the next 2-on-2 situation (see 14). The RED team plays on goal B and the BLUE team plays on goal A. Players switch change positions for a new action.

Variations

* Goalkeeper's choice (see 1) between player A or B.
* Change direction of play after second ball from goalkeeper A (see 11).
* Change direction of play with each ball from the coach (see 14).
* Right to possession depends on successful shot on goal (see 10).

3.1.11   2-on-2 after passing combination and shot on goal (4)

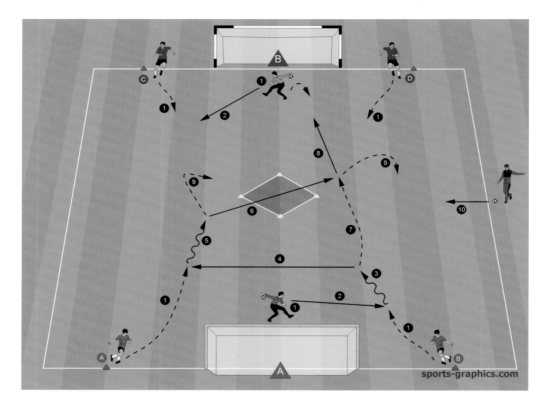

Execution

After two simultaneous passing combinations, each accompanied by a finish, a 2-on-2 situation ensues between the RED team and the BLUE team. Players position themselves at different start markers. Both goalkeepers have a ball and simultaneously initiate the opening technique. With a signal from the coach, the players A/C and B/D start into the field (see 1). The goalkeepers A/B roll their balls to one of the two players (here players B and C). The pass receivers control the ball toward the center (see 3), the teams play a pass in front of the center diamond (see 4), and a second pass through the diamond (see 5 and 6). The respective pass receiver (here players B and C) takes a shot on goal B/A (see 8). After their actions, all of the players transition for the now imminent 2-on-2 situation (see 9). The coach brings a ball into the game (see 10). The RED team plays on goal A and the BLUE team plays on goal B. Players change starting positions for a new action.

Variations

* Goalkeeper's choice (see 1) between player A or B.
* Right to possession depends on success and speed of shot on goal (see 8).
* Specify (see 8) shot on goal (direct finish/inside foot/outside foot/left/right).
* Specify passing technique (direct pass) for certain passes (see 4 and 6).

3.1.12 3-on-3 after passing combination (1)

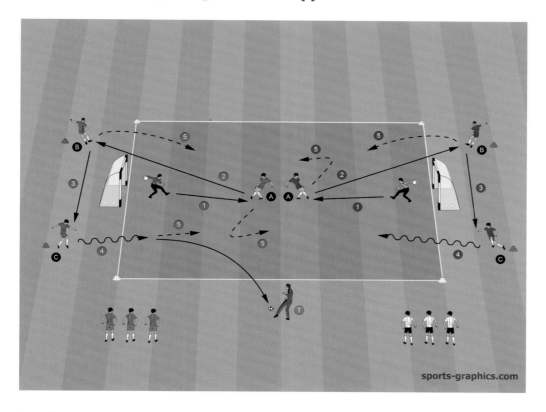

sports-graphics.com

Execution

After a predetermined passing sequence, the RED team and the BLUE team play 3-on-3. The passing sequence begins with the goalkeeper and both teams start simultaneously after a signal from the coach. The goalkeeper rolls the ball (see 1) to the field player (here player A). Player A plays a diagonal pass to player B (see 2). Player B passes the ball behind the goal to player C (see 3). Player C controls the ball toward the field and dribbles the ball into the center (see 4). The passing sequence is a speed contest. Teams must get the ball to player C as quickly as possible via combination passes. The faster team remains in possession for the subsequent game. The coach names the faster team (here the BLUE team). Player C from the BLUE team dribbles into the field (see 4). Players B and C transition for 3-on-3 play (see 5) and get into offensive mode. The slower team (here the RED team) must pass their own ball to the coach (see player C). The RED team transitions for 3-on-3 play (see 5) and goes into defensive mode. The teams now play 3-on-3 on the large goals until a goal is scored or the ball leaves the field. Afterwards the coach has the option of bringing a second ball into the game for another 3-on-3 (see coach T). Teams switch after each round (see the GREEN team and the WHITE team). The individual players independently change starting positions within their teams.

Variation

★ The coach names the faster team (here the BLUE team). The slower team plays their own ball not to the coach, but rather the player in possession (see player C), who finishes on the opposite goal in 1-on-0. The 3-on-2 situation with the superior number BLUE team begins simultaneously. After his finish, player C from the RED team can transition and complete the RED team for 3-on-3.

3.1.13   3-on-3 after passing combination (2)

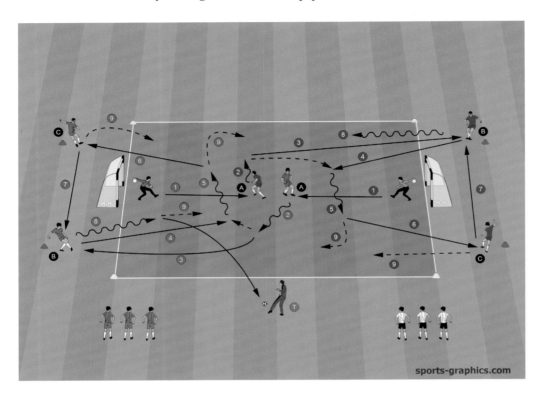

sports-graphics.com

Execution

After a predetermined passing sequence, the RED team and the BLUE team play 3-on-3. The passing sequence begins with the goalkeeper and after a signal from the coach, both teams start simultaneously. The goalkeeper rolls the ball (see 1) to the field player (here player A). Player A controls the ball, opens up (see 2), and plays a diagonal pass to player B (see 3). Player B plays a back pass to player A (see 4). Player A controls the ball (see 5), and then passes to player C (see 6). Player C passes the ball behind the goal to player B (see 7). Player B controls the ball and dribbles into the field (see 8). The passing sequence is a speed contest. The teams must get the ball to player B as quickly as possible via passing combinations. The faster team remains in possession for the subsequent game. The coach names the faster team (here the BLUE team). Player B from the BLUE team dribbles into the field (see 8). Players A and C transition for the 3-on-3 (see 9) and get into offensive mode. The slower team (here the RED team) must pass their own ball to the coach (see player B). The RED team transitions for the 3-on-3 (see 9) and gets into defensive mode. Now the teams play 3-on-3 on the large goals until a goal is scored or the ball leaves the field. Afterwards the coach has the option of bringing a second ball into the game for another 3-on-3 situation (see coach T). Teams switch after each round (see GREEN team and WHITE team). The individual players independently change starting positions within their teams.

Variations

* Specify touches (3 touches/2 touches/direct play).
* Goalkeeper starts the passing sequence with a throw-out (waist-high/high).

3.1.14   3-on-3 after dribbling and passing

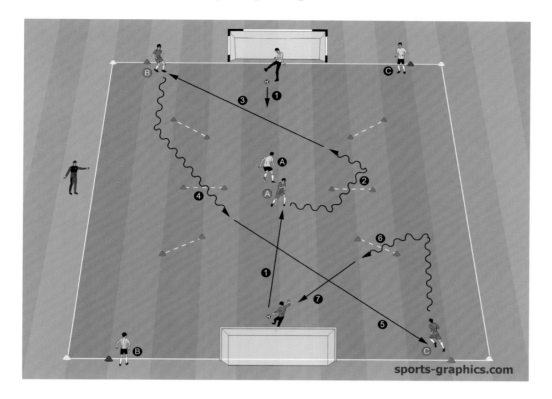

sports-graphics.com

Execution

After a signal from the coach and subsequent throw-outs by the goalkeeper, the players from the RED and YELLOW teams simultaneously complete a dribbling and passing task with final back passes to their own goalkeeper. All three players (see players A, B, and C) participate in the passing task. Immediately after, a 3-on-3 game on both large goals begins. After the coach's opening signal, the goalkeepers roll their balls to player A positioned in the center (see 1). Player A dribbles through a cone goal of his choice (see 2) and passes (see 3) to an outside player of his choice from his own team (here player B). The pass receiver (here player B) controls the ball and also dribbles through a cone goal of his choice (see 4) and passes (see 5) to the third teammate (here player C). The third player also dribbles through a cone goal of his choice (see 6) and passes the ball back to their own goalkeeper (see 7). Now the subsequent 3-on-3 game begins, starting with the goalkeeper. The faster team, named by the coach, remains in possession. After the final pass, the goalkeeper from the slower team plays his ball to the coach. The players from the faster team get into offensive mode and the players from the slower team get into defensive mode. The 3-on-3 game continues until a team scores a goal or the ball leaves the field. Immediately after, the coach brings a second ball into the game for another 3-on-3 situation.

Variations

* Ramp up technical task (2 dribbles per player through cone goals).
* Modify technical task (pass to outside player [see 2 and 5] through a cone goal).
* Modify return (see 7) to goalkeeper (cross from opposing half).

3.1.15   3-on-3 after shooting sequence (1)

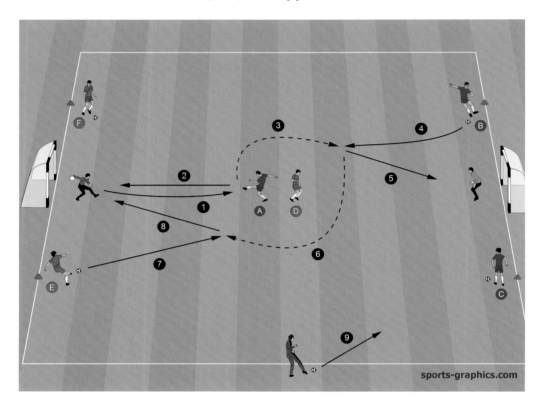

Execution

Players A and D each take three shots on goal. Next a 3-on-3 situation ensues between the RED and BLUE teams. The outside players (see players B, C, E, and F) each have a ball and pass their balls, one after the other, to the respective shooters A and D. The goalkeeper rolls the ball to player A (see 1). Player A takes a shot on goal (see 2), pivots (see 3), and receives a pass from player B (see 4) to shoot on the opposite goal (see 5). Player A pivots again (see 6), and now receives a pass from player E (see 7) to take a final shot (see 8). After a signal from the coach, the passing and shooting sequence begins with both goalkeepers. Players A and D are active at the same time and complete their shots. After all of the outside players have passed their balls to the shooters and the first shooter (see player A or B) has taken his third shot, the coach plays a ball into the game for 3-on-3 play (see 9). To do so, the coach passes the ball to one of the four outside players (here player C). The teams now play 3-on-3 on both large goals until a goal is scored or the ball leaves the field. The coach has the option of bringing more balls into the game for new 3-on-3 situations. After each round the individual players independently change starting positions within their teams.

Variations

* The coach brings the ball into the game via the goalkeeper for 3-on-3 play.
* Specify shooting technique (direct finish/inside foot/laces).
* Specify passing leg for outside players (left/right).
* Change direction of play with each new coach's ball.

3.1.16   3-on-3 after shooting sequence (2)

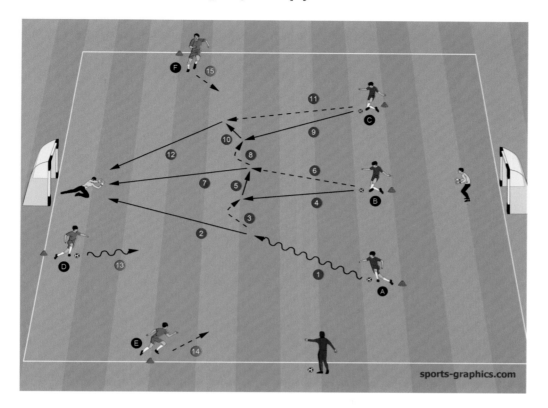

Execution

Each of the BLUE team players takes a shot on goal. Afterwards, a 3-on-3 situation between the RED and BLUE teams ensues. Player A briefly dribbles (see 1) and finishes on the goal (see 2). After his shot he turns (see 3), receives a pass from player B (see 4), and does an immediate lay-off (see 5). Player B follows his pass (see 6) and also finishes on the goal (see 7). After his shot he turns (see 8), receives a pass from player C (see 9), and does an immediate lay-off (see 10). Player C follows his pass (see 11) and is the last BLUE team player to finish (see 12). Player D from the RED team (see 13) starts with the shot by player C (see 12) and dribbles into the field with the ball at this foot for the subsequent 3-on-3 game. Players E and F run into the field for the 3-on-3 (see 14 and 15) and get into offensive mode. After their actions, all three players from the BLUE team transition and get into defensive mode for the 3-on-3. The teams now play 3-on-3 on both large goals until a goal is scored or the ball leaves the field. Afterwards the coach has the option of bringing a second ball into the game for a new 3-on-3 game. After each round, the individual players independently change starting positions within their teams.

Variations

* The BLUE team defends in 3-on-3 play only with the players who scored a goal.
* Possession during 3-on-3 play for the BLUE team if all players scored.
* Specify shooting technique (laces/inside foot/weak foot/direct finish).
* Player D from the RED team begins with a pass to player E or F (see 13).
* Change direction of play with each new coach's ball.

3.1.17   3-on-3 after passing combination and shot on goal (1)

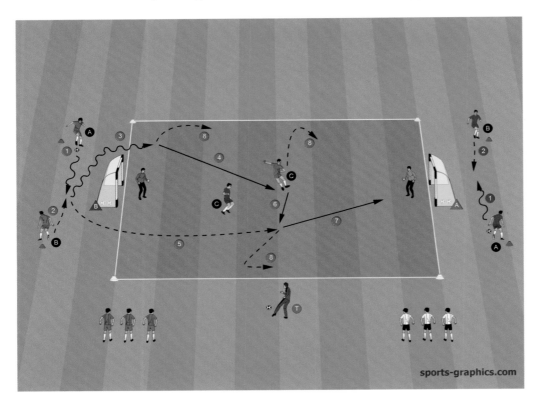

Execution

After a predetermined passing sequence, 3-on-3 play ensues between the RED and BLUE teams. The passing sequence begins behind the large goals A and B, and after a signal from the coach, both teams start simultaneously. Player A briefly dribbles (see 1) and player B runs toward the player in possession (see 2). The players surrender and accept the ball and cross their running paths. Player B dribbles into the field (see 3) and plays a pass to player C positioned in the center. After surrendering the ball, player A runs into the field (see 5), receives the pass from player C (see 6), and finishes on the opposite goal (see goal A). The BLUE team's simultaneous and identical sequence ends with a shot by player C on goal B. After the finishes, all players immediately transition and prepare for the subsequent 3-on-3 situation. The RED team attacks goal A and the BLUE team attacks goal B. The coach's pass can vary and the coach also has the option of playing several balls in a row into the game to generate additional transitions and 3-on-3 situations. Teams switch after each round (see GREEN and WHITE teams). The individual players independently change starting positions within their teams.

Variations

* Specify touches (3 touches/2 touches/direct play).
* Specify shooting technique (direct finish/inside foot/laces/left/right).

3.1.18 3-on-3 after passing combination and shot on goal (2)

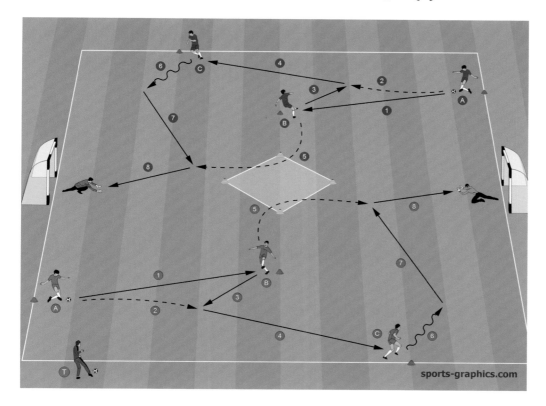

sports-graphics.com

Execution

After a signal from the coach, the players from the RED team and the players from the BLUE team simultaneously complete a predetermined passing sequence that ends with shots on goal. Next, a 3-on-3 situation follows after a ball from the coach. The players A start the passing sequence at the same time. Player A passes to player B (see 1) and follows his pass (see 2). Player B passes the ball into the running path of player A (see 3). Player A plays a deep pass to player C (see 4). After his action, player B transitions and runs into the center through the diamond (see 5) and to a finishing position centered in front of the goal. Player C controls the ball toward the goal (see 6), looks up, and passes into the running path of player B (see 7). Player B finishes on the goal (see 8). With the square pass from player C (see 7), the coach brings a ball into the game for the subsequent 3-on-3 situation (see T). The coach varies his passes and passes the ball to one of the players A. All six players now play 3-on-3 on both large goals until a goal is scored or the ball leaves the field. After the 3-on-3, the coach has the option of again bringing another ball into the game for another 3-on-3 situation. After each round the individual players independently change starting positions within their teams.

Variations

★ After playing on the diamond (dribble/pass) the team in possession can attack both goals.

★ Specify shooting technique (laces/inside foot/weak foot/direct finish).

★ Specify passing technique during passing sequence (direct play/2 touches).

★ Perform predetermined feints prior to certain passes (see 4 and 7).

3.1.19   3-on-3 after passing combination and shot on goal (3)

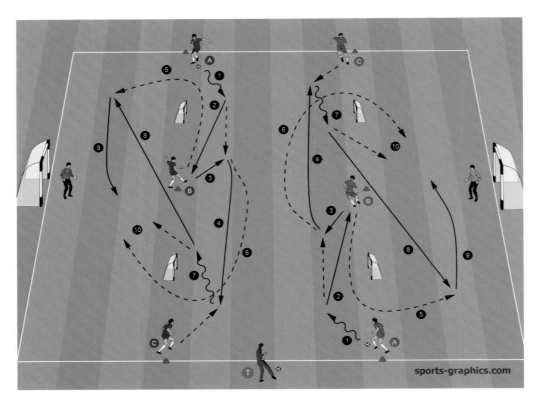

Execution

After a signal from the coach, the players from the RED team and the players from the BLUE team simultaneously complete a predetermined passing sequence that ends with shots on goal. After a ball from the coach, a 3-plus-1 against 3-plus-1-situation on two mini goals each follows, and finally a 3-on-3 situation on the large goals. The players A simultaneously start the passing sequence. Player A briefly dribbles (see 1) and passes to player B (see 2). Player B plays a back pass to player A (see 3) and player A plays a long ball to player C (see 4). Player B runs around the mini goal to the outside position (see 5). Player A runs around the far mini goal (see 6). Player C controls the ball in the center (see 7) and plays to player B on the outside position (see 8). Player B plays the ball to the center for a shot on goal (see 9). Players A and C run to a finishing position in front of the goal (10) and try to exploit the pass from player B. Afterwards the coach brings a new ball into the game for the subsequent 3-plus-1 against 3-plus-1 situation. The team that finishes first gets the ball and the goalkeepers move between the mini goals as deep receivers for their team. The 3-on-3 situation continues until a goal is scored or the ball leaves the field. In this case the coach brings a second ball into the game for 3-on-3 play.

Variations

- ★ Specify player B's ball into the box (direct play/low pass/square pass).
- ★ Specify running paths (see 10) prior to conversion (cross paths).
- ★ Specify touches for goalkeeper in 3-plus-1 against 3-plus-1 (direct play).
- ★ Play on large goals also possible after six consecutive passes in 3-on-3.
- ★ Requirement for finish in 3-plus-1 against 3-plus-1 (involve goalkeeper/6 passes).
- ★ Perform predetermined feints prior to certain passes (see 4, 8, and 9).

3.1.20 4-on-3 and 4-on-4 after shooting sequence

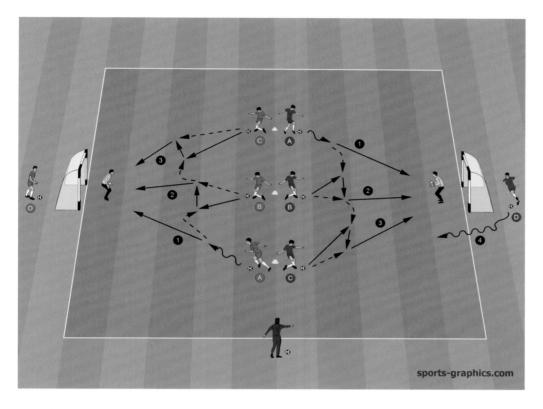

sports-graphics.com

Execution

Three players from the RED team and three players from the BLUE team (see players A, B, and C) each take a shot on goal. One other player from each team is positioned behind the goals (see player D) with a ball at his foot. After the passing and shooting sequence, the players D intervene in the game for 4-on-3 and 4-on-4 play. After a signal from the coach, the two players A start simultaneously, briefly dribble, and take a shot on goal (see 1). After the shot, the players A transition, receive a pass from the players B and provide an assist for the players B (see 2). Afterwards, the players B transition and provide another assist for the players' C shots on goal (see 3). The coach names the faster team (here the BLUE team) and the fourth player from the named team dribbles into the field for the 4-on-3 superior-number situation (see 4). The teams now play 4-on-3 on the two large goals until a goal is scored or the ball leaves the field. In these instances, player D from the inferior-number team (here RED) participates in the following 4-on-4 and dribbles into the field. After the 4-on-4, the coach has the option of bringing another ball into the game for a new 4-on-4 situation. After each round the individual players independently change starting positions within their teams.

Variations

* Only the players who scored participate in the game (see players A, B, and C).
* Specify shooting technique (laces/inside foot/weak foot/direct finish).
* Change direction of play with each new coach's ball.

3.1.21   4-on-4 after passing combination and shot on goal

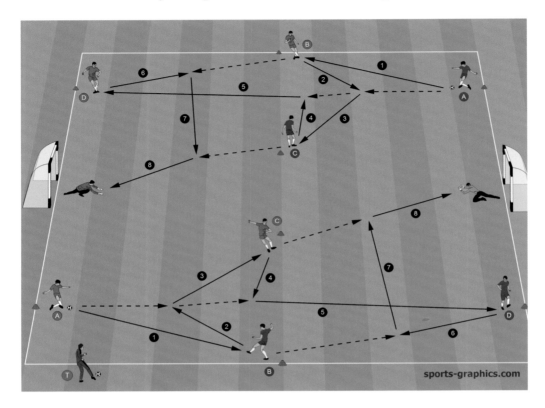

Execution

After a signal from the coach, all players from the RED and BLUE teams simultaneously complete two identical passing sequences with two closing shots on goal. Next, after a ball from the coach, a 4-on-4 situation follows. The players A start the passing sequence at the same time. Player A passes to player B (see 1), follows his pass, and receives a back pass from player B (see 2). Player A passes to player C (see 3) and again follows his pass. Player A plays the back pass from player C (see 4) deep to player D (see 5). Player D lays off to the outside into the running path of player B (see 6). Player B plays a square pass (see 7) to player C, who is running into the center. Player C finishes on the goal (see 8). With the square pass from player B (see 7), the coach brings a ball into the game for the subsequent 4-on-4 situation (see T). The coach varies his passes and passes the ball to players A or B. All eight players transition and, depending on the coach's pass, get into defensive or offensive mode. The teams now play 4-on-4 on the two large goals until a goal is scored or the ball leaves the field. After the 4-on-4, the coach has the option of bringing another ball into the game for a new 4-on-4 situation. After each round, the individual players switch starting positions independently within their teams.

Variations

* The players C only participate in the subsequent game after scoring a goal (see 8).
* Specify shooting technique (laces/inside foot/weak foot/direct finish).
* Specify passing technique (direct play/2 touches).
* Perform predetermined feints prior to certain passes (see 5 and 7).

3.1.22 4-on-4 after passing and first-touch ball control

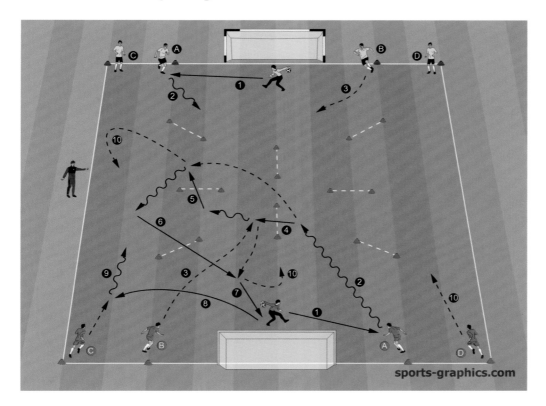

sports-graphics.com

Execution

After a signal from the coach with subsequent throw-outs by the goalkeeper, the players from the RED and YELLOW teams simultaneously complete a passing task with closing back passes to their own goalkeeper. Initially only two players (see players A and B) are involved in the passing task. Immediately after, a 4-on-4 game on the two large goals begins. After the opening signal from the coach, the goalkeepers roll their ball to one of the players (here player A) next to the goal (see 1). The pass receiver (here player A) dribbles into the field (see 2) and his partner (here player B) runs into the field without a ball (see 3). The two players now have the task of playing as quickly as possible on three different cone goals in a row with a pass across the line (see 4, 5, and 6), and then pass the ball to their own goalkeeper (see7). The faster team named by the coach (see the RED team) remains in possession for the subsequent 4-on-4 game. Here the coach plays the ball into the game (see 8) to one of the outside players C or D (here player C). The pass receiver (here player C) dribbles into the field (see 9) while player D, who is still waiting at the cone, runs into the field without a ball, and the previously active field players A and B transition to offense (see 10). The slower team (here the YELLOW team) plays the ball to the coach and transitions to defense for the 4-on-4 game. The subsequent 4-on-4 game continues until a team scores a goal or the ball leaves the field. Immediately afterwards, the coach brings a second ball into the game for another 4-on-4 situation.

Variations

* Ramp up technical task (4/5 passes through cone goals).
* Modify technical task (dribble through cone goals).
* Modify technical task (combination of dribbles and passes through cone goals).

3.1.23 4-on-4 after passing combination and shot on goal

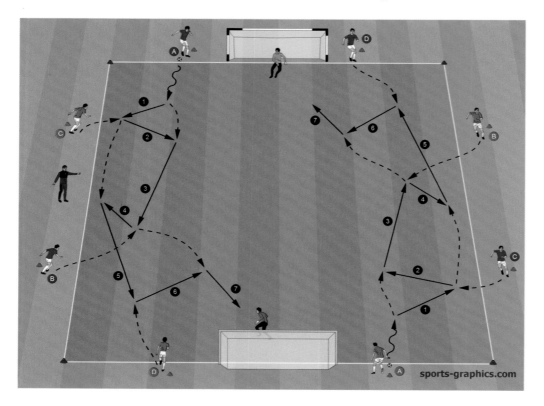

Execution

After a predetermined passing sequence, the RED team plays 4-on-4 on the two large goals against the BLUE team. The RED team always plays with the RED goalkeeper. The BLUE team always plays with the BLUE goalkeeper. Both players A have a ball and simultaneously start the passing sequence. Player A briefly dribbles and plays to the approaching player C (see 1). Player A follows his pass to the center and receives the back pass from player C (see 2). Player A plays a long ball to player B, who is starting toward him (see 3). Player B lets the ball bounce off to player C (see 4). Player C plays a long ball to player D, who is starting toward him (see 5). Player D lets the ball bounce off to player B (see 6). Finally, player B plays the ball to the goalkeeper (see 7). Once the players have finished their own actions on the ball during the passing sequence they can already move into strategically appropriate positions for the subsequent game. While the pass is played to the goalkeeper (see 7), the coach names a team by calling out the respective team color. The named team is in possession for the subsequent 4-on-4 game. The goalkeeper of the named team can bring his own ball directly into the game. The goalkeeper of the team that wasn't named passes the own ball to the coach. The teams now play 4-on-4 on the two large goals until a goal is scored or the ball leaves the field. Afterwards the coach has the option of bringing a second ball into the game for another 4-on-4 situation. After each round, the individual players independently change starting positions within their teams.

Variations

* Change direction of play with the coach's second ball.
* Perform predetermined feints prior to certain passes (see 3, 5, and 7).
* Goalkeeper starts 2-on-2-game with a throw-out (waist high/high).

3.1.24 3-on-3 after passing combination and shot on goal

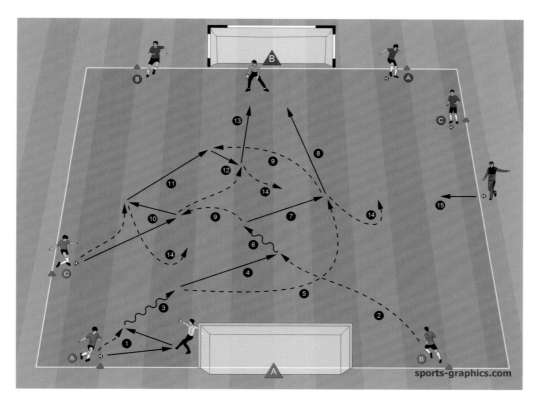

Execution

A 3-on-3 situation between the RED and BLUE teams ensues after a simultaneous passing combination with two shots on goal. Players position themselves at different starting positions. Players A and C each have a ball. After a signal from the coach, both teams simultaneously start the predetermined opening techniques. The RED team finishes on goal B and the BLUE team finishes on goal A. Player A briefly dribbles and plays a double pass with the own goalkeeper (see 1). Player B starts into the field (see 2). Player A controls the pass, dribbles into the center (see 3), plays a pass to player B (see 4), and overlaps the pass receiver (see 5). Player B controls the pass (see 6) and plays a square pass to player A (see 7). Player A takes a shot on goal (see 8). After their actions, players A and B immediately transition and face player C (see 9). Player C plays a double pass with player B (see 10). Player C plays a long ball to player A (see 11). Player B turns, receives the pass from A (see 12), and takes a shot on goal (see 13). Right after their actions all of the players transition for the subsequent 3-on-3 situation (see 14). The coach brings a ball into the game (see 15) and the teams try to score during 3-on-3 play.

Variations

★ Possession goes to faster team to complete opening technique.

★ Goalkeeper receives coach's ball (see 15).

★ Change direction of play with coach's ball (see 15).

3.1.25 5-on-5 after open passing combination

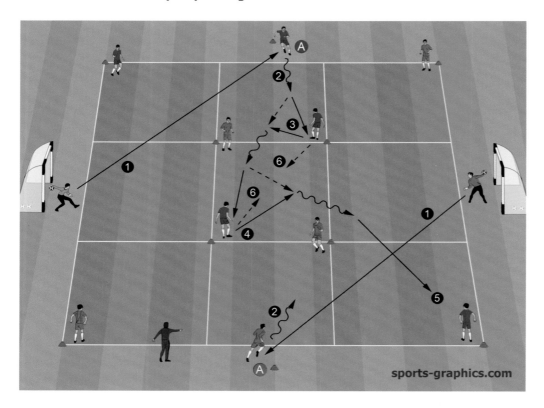

sports-graphics.com

Execution

After a signal from the coach with subsequent throw-outs by the goalkeepers, the RED and BLUE teams simultaneously complete a dribbling, passing, and running task with final back passes to the own goalkeeper. One by one, all players from both teams get involved in the passing sequence, followed by a 5-on-5 game. At a signal from the coach, the goalkeeper throw their balls to the players A, positioned outside (see 1). Player A dribbles into the field (see 2) and now has the task of playing a double pass to all four teammates (see 3, 4, and 5). Player A can freely choose the order. After their first action, the receiving players must high-five the next receiver in line (see 6). After all four players have been involved in the passing sequences, player A passes the ball to their own goalkeeper. The coach names the faster team, which remains in possession for the subsequent 5-on-5 game. The slower team plays their own ball to the coach and transitions to defense. The 5-on-5 game continues until a team scores a goal or the ball leaves the field. Immediately afterwards, the coach brings a second ball into the game for an additional 5-on-5 situation. All players change starting positions for another round.

Variation

★ After passing back to the goalkeeper, the players A go back to their starting positions off the playing field. The game with the faster team's ball is 4-on-4. The coach's second ball goes to a player A and is used for a 5-on-5 situation.

3.2   RONDOS AND POSSESSION

Rondos and Possession includes games on small fields with a superior number possession team against an inferior number defending team. Here the term *rondo* refers to possession games known as superior number games or warm-up games that are characterized by passing combinations with few touches against inferior-number blocking and chasing defenders. The starting point is a 4-on-2 situation that becomes progressively more complex and intensive via additional playing objectives and expanding team sizes. The superior number facilitates passing play and creates a competitive feel because players who lose possession switch to defensive positions after passing errors and turnovers. The players in possession practice passing and ball holding with safe combinations and try to form triangle and diamond formations, create permanent open players, and try to get open in gaps and get in open playing positions. Players without a ball practice joint defense with the goal of capturing the ball or disrupting passing combinations, and work to block passing lanes, cover each other, recognize pressing triggers, and create double-team situations. Games are augmented by advanced playing objectives, field changes via switch of play, increased team sizes, and playing on predetermined zones and follow-up actions on goals.

INFERIOR NUMBER
PRESSING DOUBLE TEAMING
FIELD CHANGES SPATIAL BEHAVIOR
FOLLOW-UP ACTIONS LINE PASSING
PASSING COMBINATIONS SUPERIOR NUMBER
TRIANGLES GETTING OPEN
CAPTURING THE BALL INTERFERING PLAYERS
OPEN PLAYING POSITION PASSING RELAYS
POSSESSION SPATIAL PRESSURE
SWITCH OF PLAY OPPONENT PRESSURE

3.2.1 Simple field change

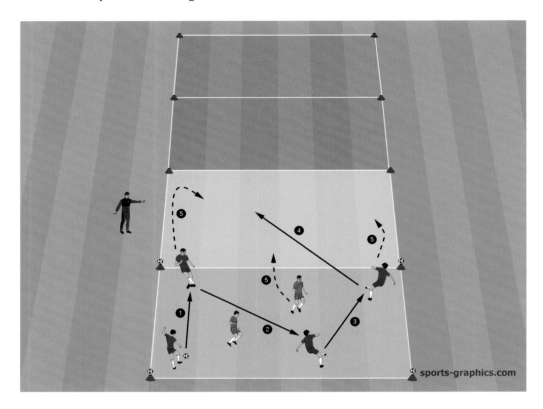

Execution

The BLUE team is in possession and plays 4-on-2 against the RED team. The BLUE team initially tries to play three passes in the YELLOW field without opposing touches (see 1, 2, and 3). The RED team tries to prevent these passes and to play the ball out of the field. After three successful passes, the BLUE team tries to switch to the adjacent WHITE field with a pass (see 4). After a pass into the next field, all players follow (see 5). Next, the BLUE team tries to play three consecutive passes on the WHITE field and then switch to the GREEN field, and finally to the BLUE field. If the RED team takes a ball out of the game, the BLUE team starts back into the YELLOW field with one of the balls positioned in the corners of the YELLOW field.

Points system

★ BLUE team: switch to next field (1 point) and 3 passes in BLUE field (2 points).

★ RED team: capture the ball and pass out of field (1 point).

★ RED team: capture the ball, pass to teammate, and pass out of field (2 points).

Variations

★ Field change specification: players can start into next field before the pass (see 4).

★ Field change specification: players must start into next field after/with the pass.

★ Field change specification: dribble/direct pass/pass with weak foot (see 4).

★ Specify maximum number of touches per player (4 touches/3 touches/2 touches/direct play).

★ Specify required number of passes prior to field change (4 passes/3 passes/2 passes/open play).

★ Position mini goal as final target behind the BLUE field.

3.2.2   Simple field change (running paths)

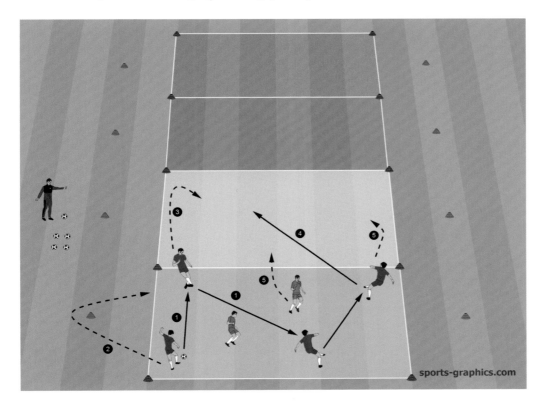

sports-graphics.com

Execution

The BLUE team is in possession and plays 4-on-2 against the RED team. The BLUE team tries to remain in possession in the YELLOW field without any opposing touches (see 1). The RED team tries to capture the ball and play it out of the field. The BLUE team has the objective of switching to the adjacent WHITE field (see 5) with a pass (see 4). First, a player from the BLUE team must run around an outside cone marker (see 2). Only when this player is back in the YELLOW field can the team switch to the WHITE field (see 3, 4, and 5). After a pass into an adjacent field, all six players follow (see 5). Next the BLUE team tries to keep possession in the WHITE field, run around a cone marker, and reach the BLUE field via the GREEN field. If the RED team takes a ball out of the game, the coach brings a new ball into the game for the BLUE team. Finally, the BLUE team has the objective of running around a cone marker next to the BLUE field. How long will it take the BLUE team to run around a cone next to the BLUE field? How many balls does the RED team capture before the BLUE team has run around a cone next to the BLUE field?

Variations

* Modify coach's ball: coach's ball always in YELLOW field or coach's ball always in field currently played on.
* Field change specification: players can start into next field before the pass (see 4).
* Field change specification: players must start into next field after/with the pass (see 4).
* Field change specification: dribble/direct pass/pass with weak foot (see 4).
* Specify maximum number of touches per player (4 touches/3 touches/2 touches/direct play).
* Requirement for field change: run around both cones (left and right) next to the field).
* Requirement for field change: each BLUE team player must run around a cone marker.

3.2.3 Simple field change (competition)

sports-graphics.com

Execution

Players are divided into pairs (see BLUE team, GREEN team, and RED team) and initially play 4-on-2 for possession. Two groups always work together (see BLUE team and GREEN team) against one defending team (see RED team), which tries to capture the ball. After successfully capturing the ball, the pair that made the critical error that caused the turnover switches to defense. The team in possession (see BLUE team and GREEN team) first tries to remain in possession in the YELLOW field. Meanwhile, one player tries to run around a center cone marker and return to the respective playing field. As soon as this player has returned to the field the team can switch to the next adjacent field (see WHITE field). The sequences continue, so in the end the team in possession has the objective of switching to the BLUE target field via the GREEN field. The BLUE team's final goal is to run around the cone marker next to the BLUE field. After a successful ball capture, the teams switch tasks as described above, and the game starts up again in the YELLOW field. The double structure creates a competition with six player pairs. After one of the groups of four successfully runs around a cone marker next to the BLUE field, a new round begins and all teams start out again in the YELLOW field. The team in possession can score one point if it runs around the cone marker next to the BLUE field. The team that plays defense scores a point after capturing the ball.

Variations

* Field change specification: dribble/direct pass/pass with weak foot.
* Specify maximum number of touches per player (4 touches/3 touches/2 touches/direct play).
* Position a mini goal as final target behind BLUE target field.

3.2.4   Simple field change (wing player)

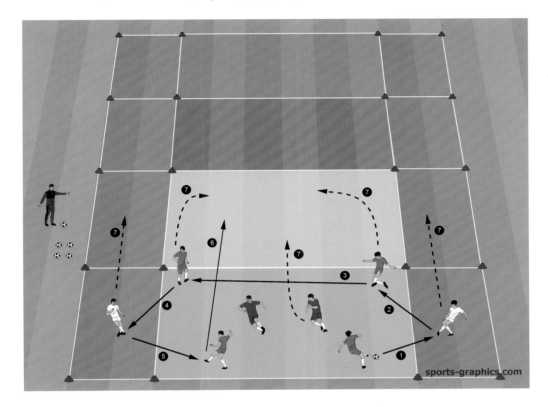

Execution

The RED team is in possession and plays 4-on-2 against the BLUE team. The RED team in possession also works with two additional players (see WHITE team) in 4-plus-2 against 2. The RED team initially plays for possession in the YELLOW field and tries to pass to both of the WHITE team players (see 1 and 4). The WHITE team players always pass the ball back into the field (see 2 and 5). After play has been successfully shifted via both players, a pass can be played into the adjacent WHITE field (see 6). After a pass into the next field, all eight players follow (see 7). Next, the RED team tries to switch play in the WHITE field via both players in order to finally switch via the GREEN field to the BLUE field, and finish there by again having passed to both WHITE team players. If the BLUE team takes a ball out of the game, the coach brings a new ball for the RED team into the currently played-on field.

Points system

* How long does it take the RED team to play on the BLUE target field?
* How many balls does the RED team need to play on the BLUE target field?
* How many balls does the BLUE team capture before the BLUE target field is played on?

Variations

* Field change specification: dribble/direct pass/pass with weak foot (see 6).
* Specify maximum number of touches per player (4 touches/3 touches/2 touches/direct play).
* Specify maximum number of touches for WHITE team (2 touches/direct play).
* Opportunity for field change without involving WHITE team after 8 consecutive passes.

3.2.5 Complex field change (chaos)

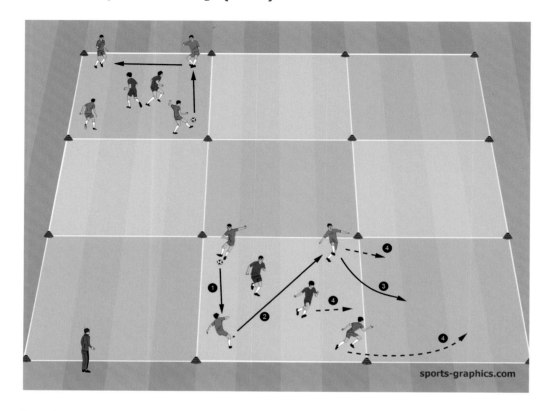

sports-graphics.com

Execution

Players are divided into pairs (see BLUE team, GREEN team, and RED team) and play 4-on-2 initially for possession (see 1 and 2). Two groups always work together (see RED team and GREEN team) against one defensive team (see BLUE team), which tries to capture the ball. After successfully capturing the ball, the pair that made the critical error that caused the turnover switches to defense. The teams in possession have the objective of switching to a neighboring field with a pass (see 3). After a pass into a neighboring field, all six players follow (see 4). Since multiple groups of six are active within the same field structure, it is feasible that at times they will play in the same field, resulting in intentional interfering from players and teams ideally having to keep an eye on the other groups of six to switch to an open field if possible.

Points system

* Teams in possession: switch to a neighboring field and complete a pass in the new field (1 point).
* Team playing defense: capture ball/touch on ball (1 point)

Variations

* Field change specification: players can start into next field before the pass (see 3).
* Field change specification: players must start into next field after/with the pass (see 3).
* Field change specification: dribble/direct pass/pass with weak foot (see 3).
* Specify maximum number of touches per player (4 touches/3 touches/2 touches/direct play).
* Specify required number of passes before a field change (3 passes/2 passes/open play [see 1 and 2]).

3.2.6 Complex field change (competition)

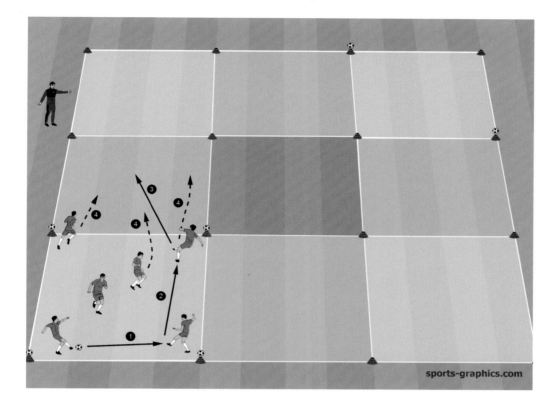

sports-graphics.com

Execution

The RED team is in possession and plays 4-on-2 against the GREEN team. The RED team initially tries to play two passes in the starting field at the bottom left (see 1 and 2) without any opposing touches. The GREEN team tries to prevent the passes and tries to play the ball out off the field. After three successful passes, the RED team tries to switch to the adjacent YELLOW field with a pass (see 3). After a pass into an adjacent field, all players follow (see 4). Next, the RED team tries to play three consecutive passes in the YELLOW field and then switch to an adjacent field, and finally, after playing in all WHITE and YELLOW fields, switch to the BLUE target field (see image center). If the GREEN team takes a ball out of the game, the RED team starts again with one of the balls positioned in the corners of the YELLOW starting field. As soon as all five balls have been played, the GREEN players switch to the team in possession.

Points system

* Teams in possession: switch to a neighboring field (1 point)
* Teams in possession: switch to BLUE target field (5 points)
* Teams playing defense: capture ball/touch on ball (1 point)
* Teams playing defense: capture ball in YELLOW starting field (2 points)

Variations

* Specify direction of play (clockwise [see image]/counterclockwise).
* Choice of direction of play (clockwise [see image]/counterclockwise).
* Field change specification: dribble/direct pass/pass with weak foot (see 3).
* Specify maximum number of touches per player (4 touches/3 touches/2 touches/direct play).
* Specify required number of passes before a field change (3 passes/2 passes/open play [see1 and 2]).

3.2.7   2-on-4 ball chase

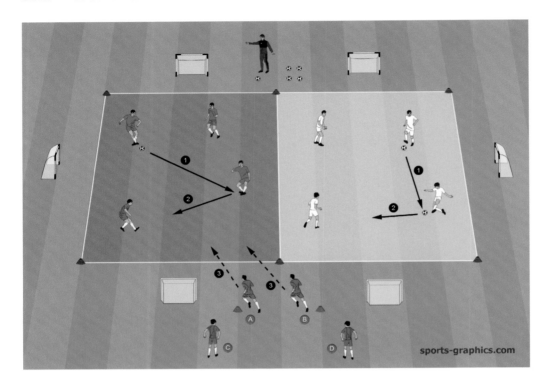

Execution

Four players are positioned on each the GREEN field and the WHITE field (see GREEN team and WHITE team). Players are circulating a ball in each field (see 1 and 2). Another team, the RED team, is initially positioned outside the field (see players A, B, C, and D). Two players from the RED team (see players A and B) start into a field with the goal of capturing the ball (see 3). Once there, the two players try to touch the ball. After they touch the ball in the GREEN field they immediately switch to the WHITE field to try to capture the WHITE team's ball. The coach brings a new ball into the game for the GREEN team. After players A and B capture the ball in the WHITE field, they immediately return to their starting position and activate players C and D. Players C and D start a new action and begin to capture the ball in the GREEN field. After a certain amount of time or a predetermined number of balls, tasks change and the RED team players switch with a team in possession.

Points system

* Team in possession: 10 consecutive passes without RED team capturing the ball (1 point)
* Team playing defense: RED team captures the ball (1 point)

Variations

* Opportunity to finish on a mini goal after 10 successful passes (2 points)
* Opportunity to finish on a mini goal after capturing the ball (2 points)
* Requirement for players A and B to switch (capturing the ball 4 times in a row)
* Juggle the ball for as long as players A and B are active in the opposite field (see WHITE team).

3.2.8   2-plus-2 against 2 zone play (hexagon)

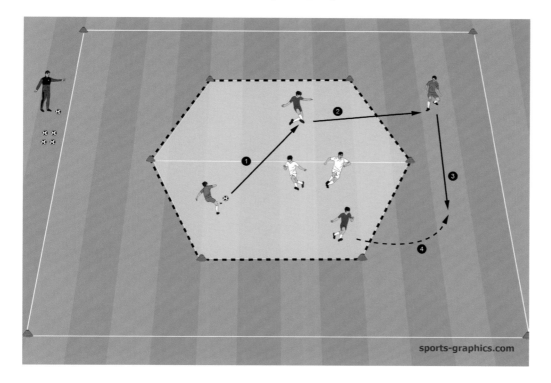

Execution

Players are divided into pairs (see RED team, BLUE team, and WHITE team) and play 4-on-2 for possession. Two groups always work together (see RED team and BLUE team) against one defensive team (see WHITE team), which tries to capture the ball. After successfully capturing the ball, the team that made the critical error that caused the turnover switches to defense, and the coach brings a new ball into the game. In the center of the field is a hexagon, which all players are allowed to enter. The teams in possession (see RED team and BLUE team) try to play passes amongst each other (see 1) without the WHITE team touching the ball. They also have the goal of playing combination passes across the lines of the hexagon (see 2). To do so, they can position themselves outside the hexagon at any time or break away from inside the hexagon to receive a pass (see 4). After a successful pass across one of the hexagon's lines (see 2), the game immediately continues (see 3) and the teams in possession try to play across another one of the hexagon's lines.

Points system

* Team in possession: 4 (8) successful consecutive passes across the hexagon's lines (1 point)
* Team playing defense: captures the ball/touches the ball before 4 (8) successful passes (1 point)

Variations

* Specify for play across lines: players can run across lines before the pass (see 2).
* Specify for play across lines: players must run across lines after /with the pass (see 2).
* Specify for play across lines: dribble/direct pass/ pass with weak foot (see 2).
* Specify maximum number of touches per player (4 touches/3 touches/2 touches/direct play).

3.2.9   4-on-2 zone play (for points)

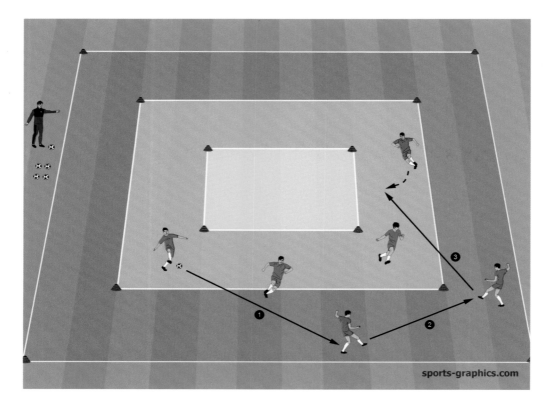

sports-graphics.com

Execution

The RED team is in possession and plays 4-on-2 against the GREEN team. The RED team tries to keep possession for as long as possible without a player from the GREEN team touching the ball (see 1, 2, and 3). The field is divided into three zones (see BLUE zone, YELLOW zone, and WHITE zone). All players can enter and play in all of the zones at any time. After each touch by the GREEN team, the coach brings a new ball into the game for the RED team. Teams play freely without touch limits.

Points system

* Team in possession: 3 consecutive passes in BLUE field (1 point)
* Team in possession: 5 consecutive one-touch ball control in BLUE field (2 points)
* Team in possession: pass across two lines of YELLOW field (3 points)
* Team in possession: dribble across two lines of YELLOW field (4 points)
* Team playing defense: Touch on ball in WHITE field (1 point)
* Team playing defense: Touch on ball in YELLOW field (2 points)
* Team playing defense: Touch on ball in BLUE field (3 points)
* Team playing defense: two consecutive touches without points scored by team in possession (4 points)

Variations

* Specify maximum number of touches for team in possession (3 touches/2 touches/direct play).
* Position mini goals outside playing field for transition after ball is captured.
* Position mini goals outside playing field for a follow-up action by possession team.

3.2.10 4-on-2 zone play (play via wing player)

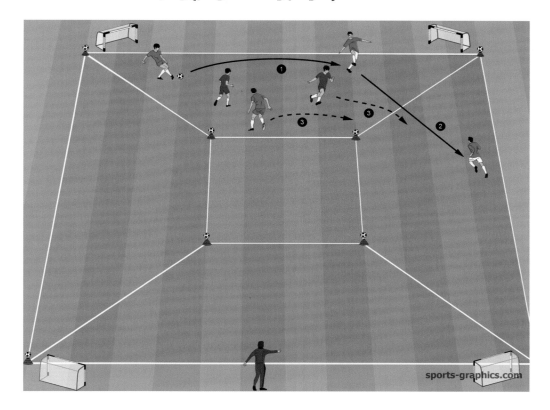

Execution

The RED team is in possession and plays 4-on-2 against the BLUE team. The RED team tries to keep position for as long as possible without one of the BLUE team players touching the ball (see 1). In the center of the field is a marked rectangular zone, which initially no player is allowed to enter or play into with a pass. The RED team in possession has the goal of playing across as many of the diagonal lines as possible with a pass to the teammate (see 2). After a pass into another field (see 2), all players switch (see 3) into the played-on field. Only when all four players from the team in possession are in the next field can this field be left again via a pass across a next line. If a player from the BLUE team captures the ball and takes it out of the game, the RED team can immediately use one of the balls positioned on the cone markers to immediately continue the game. After all nine balls have been in the game, the tasks change and the BLUE team players get possession. The team in possession is awarded one point for each field change. The inferior-number team is awarded one point for each ball capture.

Variations

* BLUE team scores on a mini goal after capturing the ball (2 points)
* RED team scores on a mini goal after successfully playing across three lines (2 points)
* BLUE team scores on a mini goal after capturing the ball and a successful pass (3 points)
* RED team scores two consecutive goals on a mini goal without the BLUE team capturing the ball (3 points)
* BLUE team scores on a mini goal after capturing the ball and playing on the center field (4 points)
* RED team scores on a mini goal after playing across three lines and playing on the field (4 points)

3.2.11   4-on-2 zone play (through the center)

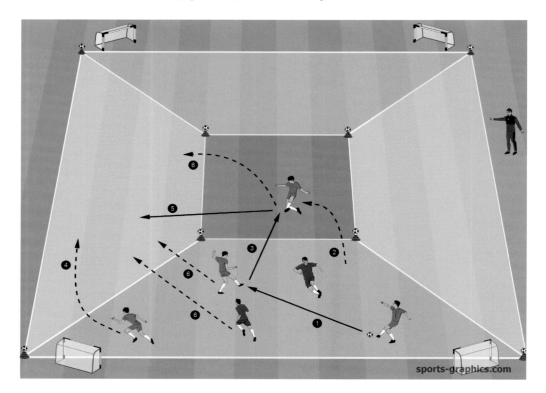

Execution

The RED team is in possession and plays 4-on-2 against the BLUE team. The RED team tries to keep possession for as long as possible without a BLUE team player touching the ball (see 1). In the center of the field is a marked rectangular zone. The RED team in possession has the goal of making a field change to an adjacent field (see WHITE field) and to do so must first play in the BLUE field. One player breaks away into the central BLUE field (see 2) and there receives a pass (see 3). As soon as this pass has taken place, the players can move into an adjacent field to create a passing opportunity there (see 4). After a successful pass into an adjacent field (see 5), all players switch to the new field to be played in (see 6). If a player from the BLUE team captures the ball and takes it out of the game, the RED team can immediately use one of the balls positioned on the cone markers to continue the game. After all nine balls have been in the game, the tasks change and the BLUE team players get possession.

Points system

* Team in possession: switch to an adjacent field (1 point)
* Team playing defense: capture ball/touch on ball (1 point)
* BLUE team scores on a mini goal after capturing the ball (2 points)
* RED team scores on a mini goal after playing on the central field three times (2 points)
* BLUE team scores on a mini goal after capturing the ball and a successful pass (3 points)
* RED team scores two consecutive goals on a mini goal without the BLUE team capturing the ball (3 points)

Variation

* Specify maximum number of touches for RED team (3 touches/2 touches/direct play).

3.2.12 4-on-2 zone play (switch play)

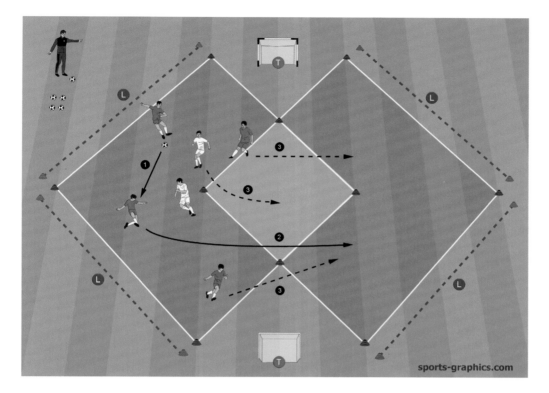

sports-graphics.com

Execution

The RED team is in possession and plays 4-on-2 against the WHITE team. The RED team tries to keep possession for as long as possible without a WHITE team player touching the ball (see 1). The playing field is divided into two fields (see GREEN fields) that are linked by a central zone (see YELLOW field). All players can run and play in all zones at any time (see 2 and 3). After each touch by the WHITE team, the coach brings a new ball into the game for the RED team. The team in possession tries to achieve a field change via the YELLOW field. To do so they must play a pass through the YELLOW field (see 2). After a successful pass through the YELLOW field, all six players switch to the opposite side (see 3). The field change is complete when the team in possession has played two follow-up passes in the new field. In continued play, another field change back to the starting field is an option.

Points system

* Team in possession: ten consecutive passes without turnover in GREEN field (1 point)
* Team in possession: switch via a pass through the YELLOW field (2 points)
* Team in possession: switch by dribbling through the YELLOW field (3 points)
* Team playing defense: touch on ball in GREEN field (1 point)
* Team playing defense: capture ball and dribble across an outside (see L) dribble line (2 points)
* Team playing defense: capture ball and score (see G) on a mini goal (3 points)

Variations

* Specify field change (players can run across lines before the pass [see 2]).
* Specify field change (players must run across lines after/with the pass [see 2]).
* Specify field change (dribble/direct pass/pass [see 2] with weak foot).

3.2.13 Alternating 4-on-2 zone play (switch play)

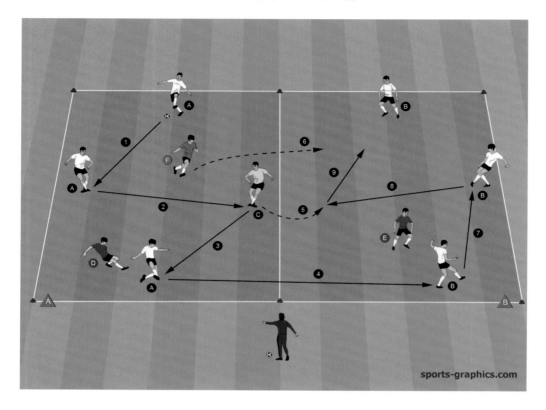

sports-graphics.com

Execution

Players are identified via different-colored bibs. The WHITE players (see players A and B) work with the YELLOW player (see player C) as the team in possession. The BLUE players (see D and E) work with the RED player (see player F) as the chasing and ball-capturing team. Some of the players are permanently positioned on the two fields and cannot leave them (see players A/B and D/E). Players A and D man field A, and players B and E man field B. Players C and F can change fields and support their respective teams on both fields. As long as the ball is in field A, the players A and C play 4-on-2 against players D and F (see 1, 2, and 3). After a successful pass into the opposite field (see 4), only players C and F can switch to field B (see 5 and 6). Now the game for possession continues on field B (see 7 and 8). Here players B and C play 4-on-2 against players E and F. Players D, E, and F try to capture the ball and clear it off the field (1 point). The players in possession try to achieve a switch of play and involve player C in the adjacent field (see 8 and 9) in a passing sequence (1 point). The inferior number players must capture a predetermined number of balls. Next, the players' tasks change.

Variations

* Specify maximum number of touches per player (3 touches/2 touches/direct play).
* Requirement for switch of play (2/3/4 passes within their own ranks).
* Requirement for switch of play (direct passes).

3.2.14 4-on-2-plus-2 zone play (through the center)

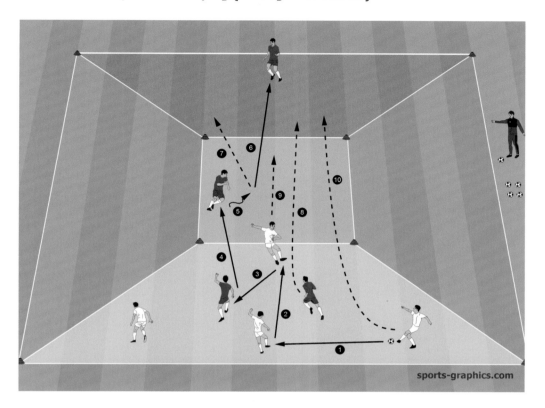

sports-graphics.com

Execution

Players are divided into two teams of four players each (see WHITE team and BLUE team). The WHITE team begins in possession and positions all four of its players in the WHITE field. The BLUE team positions two of its players in the WHITE field, one player in the central YELLOW field, and one player in the BLUE field. The WHITE team in possession plays to keep possession for as long as possible in the WHITE field (see 1 and 2). The two BLUE team players try to capture the ball (see 3) and play it into the BLUE field. This requires passing to the central player in the YELLOW field (see 4). This player opens up and passes the ball into the BLUE field (see 5 and 6). After a successful pass into the BLUE field, all four BLUE team players switch to the BLUE field (see 7 and 8) to play 4-on-2 for possession. To do so, two players from the WHITE team also switch to the BLUE field (see 9 and 10). The two remaining WHITE team players man the central YELLOW field and the WHITE field in case one of the WHITE team players captures the ball and a subsequent change back to the WHITE field results. Ten successful passes during 4-on-2 without a touch by the opposing team is worth one point. A successful ball capture or a field change is also worth one point.

Variations

* Specify maximum number of touches in YELLOW field (direct play [see 5 and 6]).
* Specify maximum number of touches by team in possession (3 touches/2 touches/direct play).
* Specify pass into central field (direct pass/pass with weak foot [see 4]).
* Opportunity to immediately counter-press and prevent field change after turnover.

3.2.15   4-on-2-plus-2 zone play (transition)

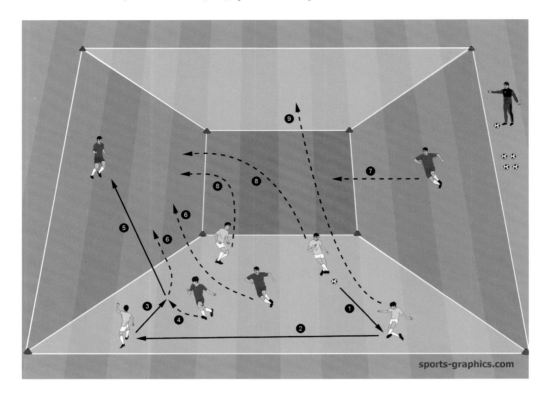

sports-graphics.com

Execution

Players are divided into two teams of four players each (see YELLOW team and BLUE team). The YELLOW team begins in possession and positions all four of its players in the YELLOW starting field. The BLUE team positions two of its players in the YELLOW field, and one player in each of the two BLUE side fields. The YELLOW team in possession plays to keep possession for as long as possible in the YELLOW field (see 1 and 2). The two BLUE team players try to capture the ball (see 3 and 4) and pass it to one of the two players in the side fields (see 5). After a successful pass into the BLUE field, all four BLUE team players switch to the BLUE field (see 6 and 7) to play 4-on-2 for possession. The two YELLOW team players also switch to the BLUE field for the 4-on-2 (see 8). To do so, the two YELLOW team players must run through the central field (see 8). The two remaining YELLOW team players now man the two YELLOW fields (see 9) in case a YELLOW team player captures the ball and another field change to one of the YELLOW fields results.

Points system

* Ten successful passes during 4-on-2 without a touch by the opposing team (1 point)
* Twenty successful passes during 4-on-2 without a touch by the opposing team (2 points)
* Successful ball capture and field change (1 point)

Variations

* Specify maximum number of touches for team in possession (3 touches/2 touches/direct play).
* Opportunity to immediately counter-press and prevent field change after turnover.

3.2.16 4-on-2 plus 2 (forward play)

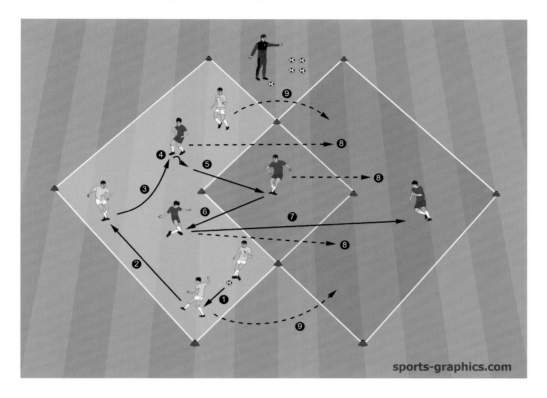

Execution

Players are divided into two teams of four players each (see YELLOW team and BLUE team). The YELLOW team begins in possession and positions all four of its players in the YELLOW field. The BLUE team positions two of its players in the YELLOW field, one player in the central field, and one in the BLUE field. The YELLOW team in possession plays to keep possession for as long as possible in the YELLOW field (see 1 and 2). The two BLUE team players try to capture the ball (see 4) and switch to the BLUE field via the central field. This requires involving the central player (see 5) and a third man running (see 6). Next, a field change to the BLUE field via a pass is possible (see 7). After a successful pass into the BLUE field (see 7), all four BLUE team players switch to the BLUE field (see 8) to play 4-on-2 for possession. To do so, two of the YELLOW team players also switch to the BLUE field (see 9). The two YELLOW team players are not allowed to run through the central field to get there (see 9). The remaining two YELLOW team players now man the YELLOW field and the central field in case one of the YELLOW team players captures the ball, resulting in another field change into the YELLOW starting field.

Points system

* Ten successful passes during 4-on-2 without a touch by the opposing team (1 point)
* Twenty successful passes during 4-on-2 without a touch by the opposing team (2 points)
* Successful ball capture and field change (2 points)

Variations

* Specify field change (after ball capture players can run directly into BLUE field).
* Specify maximum number of touches per player (4 touches/3 touches/2 touches/direct play).
* Specify maximum number of touches (see 6) in central field (2 touches/direct play).

3.2.17   4-on-2 plus 2 against 4 (seams)

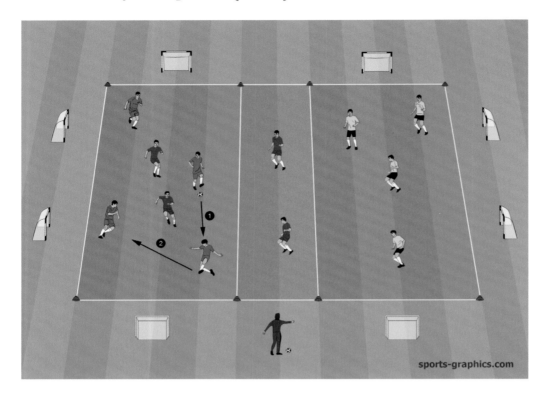

sports-graphics.com

Execution

The RED team plays 4-on-2 against the BLUE team. The team in possession (here the RED team) tries to keep the ball within their own ranks (see 1 and 2) without the opposing team capturing the ball. Beyond that the RED team tries to pass the ball to the YELLOW team in the field on the opposite side. To do so the ball must be passed through the central zone. The BLUE team tries to capture the ball and two other BLUE team players try to intercept the switching pass. As soon as the RED team can play a successful switching pass to the YELLOW team, the game immediately continues in the opposite field. There the YELLOW team plays for possession against two players from the BLUE team who were previously positioned in the center. Two players from the BLUE team now man the two center positions. The YELLOW team in possession now plays for possession and tries to exploit a gap in the ranks of the BLUE team for another switch of play. After the BLUE team successfully captures the ball, the BLUE team plays 4-on-8 on the mini goals against the RED team and the YELLOW team. After a successful finish, the BLUE team gets possession and switches to an outside field. The team that lost the ball switches to an inferior number and into the central zone. A successful switch of play by a team in possession (one point) or a successful switch of play via a direct pass by a team in possession (two points) is rewarded. The inferior-number team can score points by winning the ball (one point) or winning the ball and scoring on a mini goal (two points).

Variations

* Specify maximum number of touches per player (4 touches/3 touches/2 touches/direct play).
* Prerequisite for finish on mini goal after capturing the ball (1/2/3 passes within own ranks).

3.2.18 4-on-2-plus-2-against-4 zone play with outside players (seams)

sports-graphics.com

Execution

The RED team plays 4-on-2 against the BLUE team. The team in possession (here the RED team) tries to keep the ball within their own ranks without the opposing team capturing the ball (see 1 and 2). Beyond that, the RED team tries to pass the ball to the YELLOW team in the field on the opposite side. To do so, the ball must be passed through the central zone. The BLUE team tries to capture the ball and two other players from the BLUE team try to intercept the switching pass. After six consecutive successful passes without the opposing team capturing the ball, the RED team also has the option of switching play to the opposite field via one of the goalkeepers (see players A and B). As soon as the RED team plays a successful switching pass to the YELLOW team, the game immediately continues in the opposite field. The YELLOW team then plays for possession against two players from the BLUE team who were previously positioned in the center. The two center positions are now manned by the two BLUE team players who were previously active in the outside field. The YELLOW team now in possession continues to play for possession and tries to exploit a gap in the ranks of the BLUE team for another switch of play. After the BLUE team successfully wins the ball, the BLUE team plays 4-plus-2 against 8 on the mini goals against the RED and YELLOW teams. Here the BLUE team can involve the two goalkeepers. After a successful finish, the BLUE team gets possession and switches to an outside field. The team that lost the ball switches to the inferior number and into the central zone.

Points system

* Capturing the ball and scoring on a mini goal (1 point)
* Capturing the ball and direct finish on mini goal A or B after pass from a goalkeeper (3 points)
* Switch of play through the center (1 point) or after switch of play via a goalkeeper (2 points)

3.2.19 4-on-2 plus 2 against 4 (disrupting player[s])

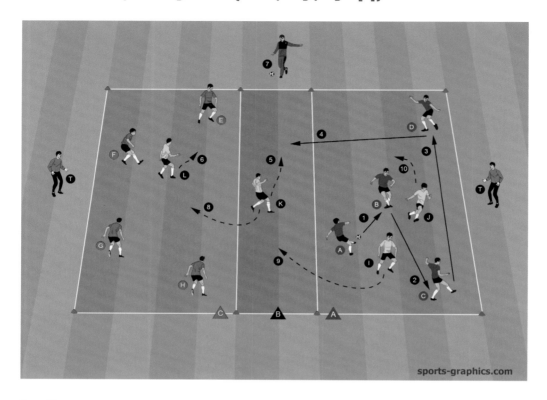

Execution

Players are divided into three teams of four players each. The field is divided into three sections. A team is positioned in each of the two outside fields A and C (here the BLUE and RED teams). The third team (here the YELLOW team) is spread out across all three fields, whereby two players are always active in the field where the ball is currently located (see players I and J in field A), one player is in the central field (see player K), and one player is in the far field C (see player L). Two additional players are positioned at the narrow ends of fields A and C (see goalkeeper GP) as outside players. The BLUE and RED teams work together and try to keep the ball within their own ranks without the opposing team capturing the ball. The BLUE team plays 4-on-2 in field A (see 1, 2, and 3) and has the option of involving the outside player (see player GP) in 4-plus-1 against 2. After three successful passes (see 1, 2, and 3), the BLUE team can attempt a switch of play to field C (see 4). Players K and L can try to prevent this switch of play in their respective zones by blocking the passing lanes (see 5 and 6) and clearing the ball. Correspondingly, the RED team players (see players E, F, G, and H) must always be ready in the gaps to facilitate a switch of play. As soon as a switch of play (see 4) takes place, the game immediately continues in field C, and the RED team plays with the goalkeeper in 4-plus-1 against 2. If player K or L prevents the switch of play (see 5 and 6) the coach brings a new ball into the game for the RED team (see 7) and thereby forces a switch of play. The YELLOW team players transition and split up for the new game situation. Player L remains in field C and immediately begins to try to capture the ball. Player K in the center switches to field C (see 8). Player I switches to zone B (see 9) and player J remains in zone A (see 10). After a predetermined period of time or a number of required ball captures, the teams change tasks. A successful switch of play or a successful ball capture is worth 1 point. A switch of play via a direct pass or preventing a switch of play is worth 2 points for the respective team.

3.2.20 4-on-2 via 2-on-2 (forward play)

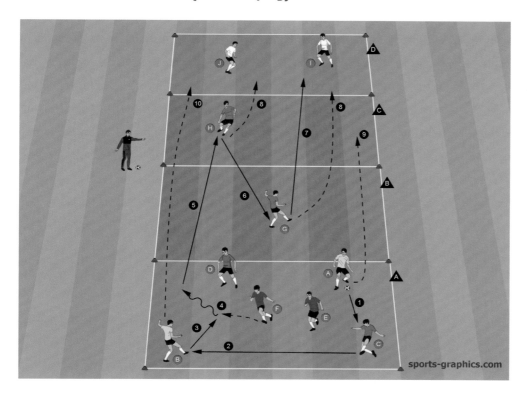

Execution

Players are divided into five teams (see YELLOW, RED, BLUE, GREEN, and WHITE teams) of two players each. The field is divided into four sections (see fields A, B, C, and D). The game begins with possession in field A. Two teams always work together in possession (here the YELLOW and RED teams) against one chasing team (here the BLUE team). The remaining two teams (here GREEN and WHITE) spread out in the other fields. The GREEN team positions one player in each of the fields B and C, and the WHITE team positions itself in field D. The players in possession (see players A, B, C, and D) try to keep the ball within their own ranks for as long as possible without the opponents capturing the ball (see 1 and 2). The chasing players (see players E and F) try to intercept (see 4) a pass (see 3) and pass it out of the field (see 5). In doing so, the ball is played to players I and J (see 7) via players G and H (see 5 and 6) in field D. After each ball capture and corresponding switch of play, the players change positions for the subsequent corresponding 4-on-2 situation in the far field (here field D) with the appropriate positioning for a switch of play to the central fields B and C. The team in the center moves up (see 8) and works with the WHITE team in possession. The team that previously lost the ball (see 4) (here the YELLOW team) takes over the chasing position (see 9 and 10). The team that previously won the ball (here the BLUE team) remains in the previously played in field (here field A) and the team previously in possession, which was not directly involved in the turnover (here the RED team), switches to the center and mans fields B and C in a staggered formation.

Variation

* Passing sequence with five consecutive passes (1 point)/ball capture and switch of play (1 point)

3.3   BALL CIRCULATION AND PLAYING FOOT

Ball Circulation and Playing Foot includes games with an emphasis on situation-appropriate behavior signaling readiness, and getting open as well as confident combination play. Here the focus is on versatile games of ball holding. This involves elements of decision making under opponent pressure, maintaining confidence when playing at high speed, and the use of practiced content in complex situations. The games involve different team sizes and number ratios. Passing play is initially made easier by using neutral passing opportunities or superior-number situations, and is enforced via provocation rules. Integrating sub-goals with passing tasks that facilitate shots on goal as follow-up actions further enhances these games. Moreover, players are constrained by zone affiliation within the scope of possession play that makes combinations more difficult and raises group tactical demands.

GETTING OPEN
DOUBLE PASS POSSESSION
BREAKING AWAY THIRD MAN RUNNING
SUPERIOR NUMBER PASSING OPPORTUNITIES
BALL HOLDING PASSING OPTIONS
INFERIOR NUMBER   FOLLOW-UP ACTIONS
TRIANGLES PASSING RELAYS
PASSING COMBINATIONS GROUP TACTICS
POSITION CHANGES

3.3.1   3-on-3 plus 4 (include center players)

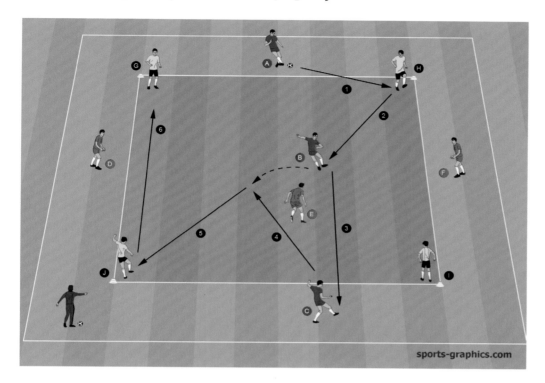

sports-graphics.com

Execution

The BLUE team plays 3-on-4 against the RED team. To do so, four neutral players are positioned in the corners (see players G, H, I, and J). The BLUE and RED teams each have one player positioned in the center (see players B and E) and two players in the outside receiving positions (see players A/C and D/F). The team in possession (here the BLUE team) tries to keep the ball within their own ranks for as long as possible without the opponents capturing the ball, and is allowed to include the neutral receivers in the passing sequence. Here it is possible for an outside player to pass to a neutral player (see 1) or for a pass to be played directly between two neutral players (see 6). The game's objective is to pass to the respective team in possession's center player (here player B) (see 2) and afterwards accomplish a continuation of play. All outside players and all neutral players are limited to no more than one touch. The opposing team tries to capture the ball to prompt a task change. The goal of the team in possession is to include the center player as often as possible. The opposing team primarily tries to take the center player out of the game via player E.

Points system

* Neutral player receives pass/continue play to a neutral player (1 point)
* Neutral player receives pass/continue play to an outside player (2 points)
* Outside player receives pass/continue play to a neutral player (3 points)
* Outside player receives pass/continue play to the other outside player (4 points)
* Double pass with neutral player (5 points)/double pass with outside player (6 points)

3.3.2 3-plus-4 against 3-plus-4 (outside player position change)

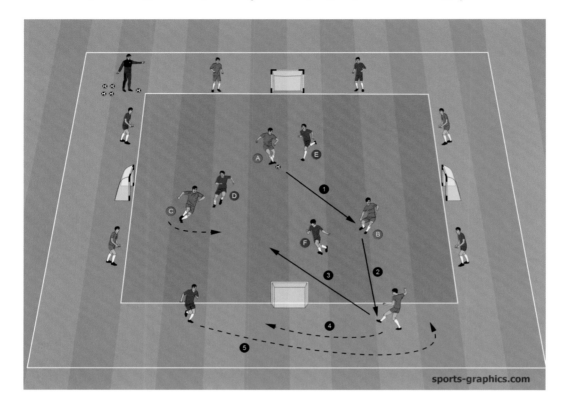

Execution

The RED team plays 3-plus-4 against 3-plus-4, initially for ball holding, against the BLUE team. Three players from each team are on the field (see players A/B/C and D/E/F). Four outside players per team are positioned between the four mini goals outside the field. The team in possession tries to keep possession (see 1) without an opposing player capturing the ball. The team in possession also has the task of including one of the four outside players in the passing sequence (see 2 and 3). Meanwhile the opposing outside players are not allowed to intervene in the game. As soon as an outside player has been involved, he switches outside positions with his counterpart on the other side of the mini goal (see 4 and 5). After the outside player's involvement, the game continues and other outside players can be included in the passing sequence. The opposing team tries to capture the ball to then play for ball holding with their own outside players. After a team has involved two outside players in a row without the opposing team capturing the ball, they can finish on the four mini goals. If a ball leaves the field or a team scores on the mini goals, the coach has the option of bringing a new ball into the game. The teams and individual players regularly change positions.

Variations

* Specify passing technique (see 3) for all outside players (direct passes).
* Opportunity for direct passes between two neutral players.
* Specify shooting technique (direct finish/left/right).
* Prerequisite for playing on mini goals (include 3/4 outside players).

3.3.3   4-plus-2 against 4-plus-2 (goalkeeper in center)

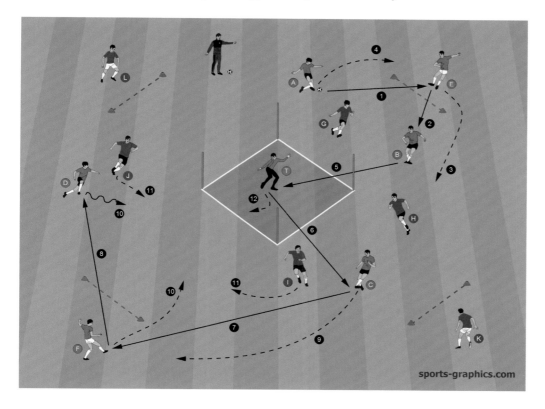

Execution

The RED team plays 4-on-4 against the BLUE team. In the center of the field is a marked off field manned by a goalkeeper (see goalkeeper GP). There are two red and two blue cone goals set up in the four corners. Positioned behind each dribble goal is one outside player (see players E/F and K/L). The team in possession (here the RED team) initially plays for ball holding and tries to keep the opponent from capturing the ball. The goalkeeper can be included as a neutral player (see 5 and 6). The team in possession also tries to play combinations between outside players and play through the cone goals (see 1 and 8). Cone goals can be played on from the inside (see 1) and the outside (see 8). The outside players and the goalkeeper can play a direct back pass to the passing players or to a third player. As soon as an outside player has been passed to, he immediately switches to a field position (see 3 and 10). The respective passing player (see players A and C) immediately takes over the outside position (see 4 and 9). As soon as both outside players have been included without an intermittent touch by the opponent, play on the center field begins. The central field becomes a goal and the goalkeeper transitions accordingly (see 12). The RED team in possession tries to score (see 10). The BLUE team tries to prevent a goal from being scored (see 11).

Variations

★ Positioning of remaining and neutral outside players (4 against 4-plus-4).

★ Opportunity for playing on center field as a goal after predetermined number of passes (6/8/10 passes).

3.3.4   5-on-5 (goalkeeper in center)

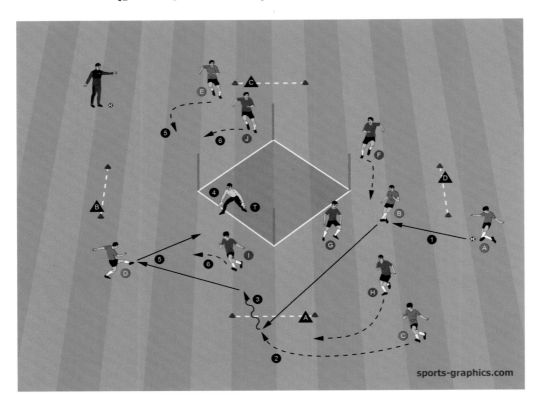

sports-graphics.com

Execution

The RED team plays 5-on-5 against the BLUE team. In the center of the field is a marked off field manned by a goalkeeper (see goalkeeper GP). Four cone goals are set up in the outer area (see cone goals A, B, C, and D). The team in possession (here the RED team) initially plays for ball holding (see 1) and tries to prevent the opponents from scoring a goal. The goalkeeper can be included as a neutral player. The team in possession also tries to play on the cone goals. A cone goal has been correctly played on when a player (see player C) runs up to a cone goal from the outside (see 2) and dribbles through it (see 3). As soon as a cone goal has been correctly played on, play on the central field begins. The center field becomes a goal and the goalkeeper transitions accordingly (see 4). The RED team in possession tries to score a goal (see 5). The BLUE team tries to prevent a goal from being scored (see 6). After a ball leaves the game, the coach brings in a new one.

Variations

* Prerequisite for playing on cone goals (2/3/4 passes in own ranks).
* Prerequisite for playing on center goal (play on several cone goals).
* Modify play on cone goals (basic passes/dribbling/double pass).
* Open different sides of the field via cone goals A, B, C, or D.

3.3.5   2-on-2 plus 4 (outside player finishes)

Execution

The RED team plays 2-on-2 plus 4 against the YELLOW team. The RED team in possession (see players A and B) plays for ball holding in the center field (see 3) and can include the four BLUE outside players (see players E) in the passing sequences (see 1 and 2). The two opposing players in the center (see players C and D) try to capture the ball to prompt a task change and, once in possession, immediately work with the four outside players. The team in possession has the option of scoring on one of the four mini goals under specific guidelines. If a ball leaves the field or a team scores on the mini goals, the coach has the option of bringing a new ball into the game.

Variations

* No direct passes between outside players/limited touches for outside players.
* Specify shooting technique for playing on mini goals (direct finish/left/right).

Prerequisites for playing on mini goals

* Include two outside players without opponents capturing the ball.
* Include two outside players in direct play without opponents capturing the ball.
* Include one outside player in third man running.
* Direct pass from outside player to outside player.

3.3.6   2-plus-2 against 2-plus-2 (outside player finishes)

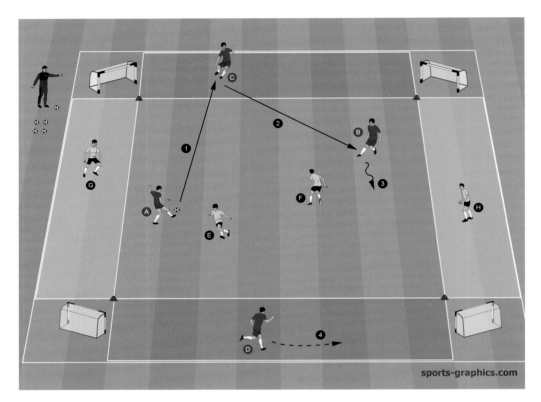

Execution

The BLUE team plays 2-plus-2 against 2-plus-2 against the YELLOW team. Two players from each team are positioned in the center (see players A/B and E/F). The remaining four players spread out in the outer zones marked with the same colors (see players C/D and G/H). The team in possession plays for ball holding (see 1 and 3) in the center field (see players A and B) and can involve their own outside players (here players C and D) in the passing sequence (see 1 and 2). The two opposing team players positioned in the center (here players E and F) try to capture the ball to, immediately afterwards, play for possession with their own outside players (here G and H). The team in possession has the option of scoring on the four mini goals under specific guidelines. If a ball leaves the field or a team scores a goal on the mini goals, the coach has the option of bringing a new ball into the game.

Prerequisites for playing on mini goals

★   Involve both of own outside players without opponents capturing the ball.

★   Involve both of own outside players in direct play without opponents capturing the ball.

★   Double involvement of both of own outside players without opponents capturing the ball.

★   Double involvement of own outside players in direct play without opponents capturing the ball.

★   Involve one outside player in third man running.

★   Involve both outside players in third man running.

★   Direct pass from outside player to outside player.

3.3.7   3-plus-4 against 3-plus-4 (outside player finishes)

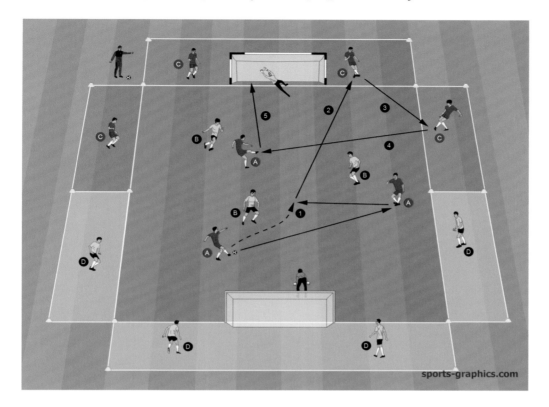

Execution

The BLUE team (see players A and C) plays 3-plus-4 against 3-plus-4 against the YELLOW team (see players B and D). There a several marked off zones around the central field. Four players from each team (see players C and D) are positioned in the zones next to the opposing half. The teams play 3-on-3 on the two large goals in the center field (see 1). The outside players can be included in the game at any time (see 2). In doing so, the outside players are allowed to play passes amongst themselves (see 3). The outside players can also play passes behind the large goals. The players in the field can use no more than two touches per action. The outside players must play direct passes. The BLUE and YELOW teams try to score as many goals as possible (see 5) and remain in possession after scoring. The own goalkeeper immediately brings a new ball into the game. Players in the outside zones change regularly.

Variations

* Modify specifications for passes (open play).
* Prerequisite for finish (see 4) on large goals (direct pass).
* Prerequisite for finish (see 5) on large goals (direct finish).
* Prerequisite for pass (see 2) into zone next to goal (direct pass).

3.3.8   4-on-4 plus 4 (wall player finishes)

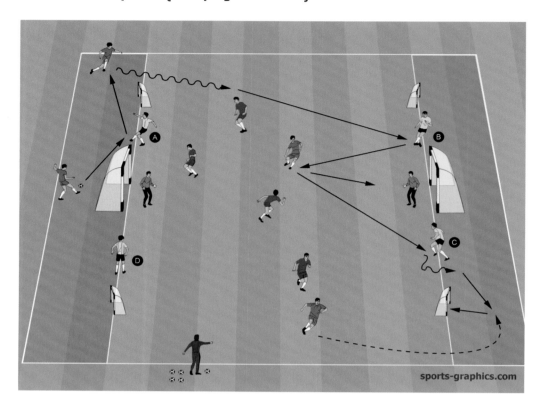

sports-graphics.com

Execution

The RED team plays 4-on-4 plus 4 against the BLUE team. The inside field is framed by two large goals and four mini goals that are open at an angle. All players can run and play any time on the playing zone behind the goals. Four neutral players (see players A, B, C, and D) are positioned between the large goals and the mini goals. The two teams initially play on the field for ball holding. The team in possession (here the RED team) can include the neutral players (see player A) in the passing sequence in 4-on-4 plus 4. After successfully passing via the neutral player, play on the large and mini goals can begin. To do so, the neutral players can continue to act as receivers (see player B). The neutral players can also control a pass, open up, and play on the playing zone behind the goals with a pass (see player C). After the BLUE team captures the ball, the tasks change. After a goal is scored or the ball leaves the field, the coach has the option of bringing a new ball into the game.

Variations

* Goalkeepers support defensive players (block a neutral player).
* Prerequisite for finish (see play via player B) on large goals (direct finish).
* Limit touches for turn by neutral player (2 touches).
* Opportunity for passing to goalkeepers prior to first pass to a neutral player.

3.3.9 4-on-4 plus 2 against 4 (zone play with finish)

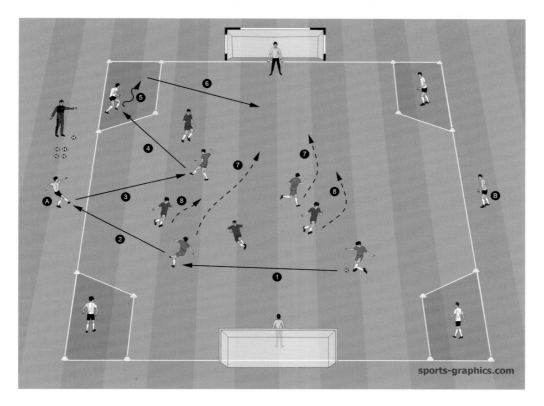

sports-graphics.com

Execution

The RED team plays 4-on-4 plus 2 against 4 against the BLUE team. Each of the RED and BLUE teams has four players in the center field. Two neutral players are positioned in the outside positions at the sides (see players A and B), and additional neutral receivers are positioned in the four corner fields. The team in possession (here the RED team) initially plays for ball holding (see 1). The team in possession also has the objective of including one of the two receivers (here players A and B) in the passing sequence (see 2 and 3). After one of the outside players (here player A) has been included in the game and one of the four central players is back in possession (see 3), play on the four large goals can begin. To score a goal, the team in possession must first pass to one of the four outside players in the corner fields (see 4). The respective pass receiver can control the ball in his zone without opponent pressure (see 5) and places a pass for the finish (see 6). After a successful pass to an outside player, the team in possession transitions toward the goal it must now play on (see 7) and gets into offensive mode. The opposing players get into defensive mode (see 8). The opposing team tries to capture the ball to, immediately afterwards, initiate play on the large goals via the two neutral players (see players A and B). If a ball leaves the field or a team scores a goal, the coach has the option of bringing a new ball into the game. The teams and individual players regularly switch positions.

Variations

* Prerequisite for playing on large goals (include both outside players A and B).
* Quick change after scoring (immediate change of 4 outside players into the field).

3.3.10 Staggered 4-on-4 plus 4 (zone play for ball holding)

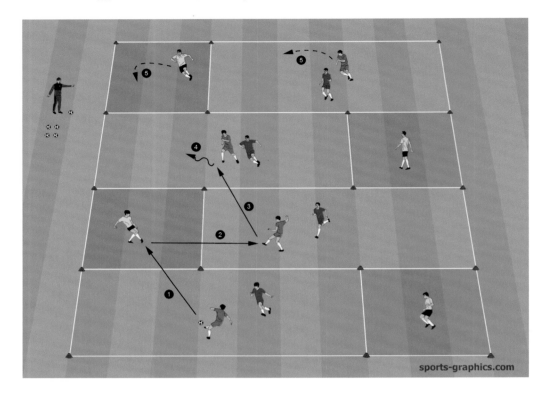

sports-graphics.com

Execution

The RED team plays 4-on-4 plus 4 for ball holding against the BLUE team. To do so, players are positioned in specific zones and cannot leave them. The playing field is divided into four large fields, each manned with one player from each team (see RED team and BLUE team). In addition there are four small fields, each manned with one neutral player (see YELLOW team). The players in possession try to keep the ball within their own ranks for as long as possible without the opponents capturing the ball. The team in possession can involve the neutral outside players (see 1 and 2) and play direct passes amongst themselves (see 3). All players in possession must break away in open playing position and move away from the potential opponent (see 5). After a turnover, the tasks change and the game continues directly. If a ball leaves the field, the coach has the option of bringing a new ball into the game. Teams and individual players change positions regularly.

Variations

★ Optional direct passes between two neutral players.

★ Limit touches for neutral players (see YELLOW team).

★ No volleys/allow volleys.

★ Specify minimum number of touches for players in large fields (see 4).

3.3.11   Staggered 5-on-5 (zone play for ball holding)

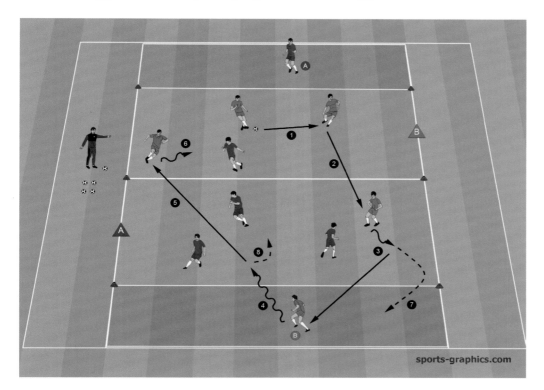

Execution

The GREEN team plays 5-on-5 for ball holding against the BLUE team. Players are positioned in specific zones and initially cannot leave them. The field is divided into two outer zones (see GREEN zone and BLUE zone) and two center fields (see fields A and B). Three players from the BLUE team and one player from the GREEN team are positioned in field A (see field A). Three players from the GREEN team and one player from the BLUE team are positioned in field B (see field B). One BLUE team player is positioned in the BLUE outside zone (see player A) and one player from the GREEN team is positioned in the GREEN outside zone (see player B). The teams try to stay in possession for as long as possible without the opposing team capturing the ball (see 1 and 2). The team in possession (here the GREEN team) must bring the player in their own outside zone (see player B) into the game (see 3). Next the outside player (see player B) must pass the ball back to field B (see 5). As soon as an outside player has been passed to (see 3), the passer (see 7) and the receiver (see 8) switch positions and fields. A long pass from the far zone (here zone B) directly to the outside player is also an option. A back pass to zone B without passing to the outside player is also a possibility. After a turnover, the tasks change.

Variations

* Limit touches for superior number players (see zones A and B).
* Specify passing technique (see 2) for certain passes (direct passes).
* No volleys/allow volleys after 5 consecutive passes in field A/B.

3.3.12   Staggered 6-on-6 (zone play for ball holding)

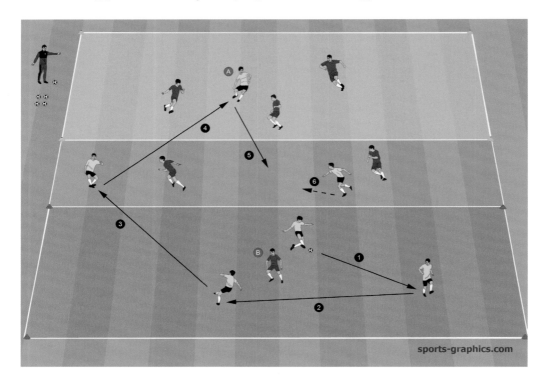

Execution

The YELLOW team plays 6-on-6 for ball holding against the BLUE team. Players are positioned in specific zones and cannot leave them. The field is divided into two outside zones (see YELLOW zone and BLUE zone) and a center field. Two players from each team are positioned in the center field. Three players from the BLUE team and a target player (see player A) from the YELLOW team are positioned in the YELLOW field. Three players from the YELLOW team and one target player from the BLUE team (see player B) are positioned in the BLUE field. The teams try to keep possession for as long as possible without the opposing team capturing the ball (see 1, 2, and 3). The team in possession (here the YELLOW team) has the task of including their own target player (see player A) in the passing sequences (see 4 and 5). A long pass from the far zone (here the BLUE zone) directly to the target player is an option here. A back pass to the BLUE zone without having passed to the outside player is also a possibility. If a ball leaves the field, the coach has the option of bringing a new ball into the field. After a turnover, the tasks change and the game continues directly.

Variations

★   Limit touches for superior number players (see BLUE zone and YELLOW zone).

★   Specify passing technique (see 4) for certain passes (direct passes).

★   No volleys/allow volleys after five consecutive passes in BLUE/YELLOW field.

★   Facilitate advance of one player from center zone.

★   Add a target player to BLUE and YELLOW zones.

3.4 COLOR GAMES AND ADVERSARY GAMES

Color Games and Adversary Games incudes games played with multiple teams with an emphasis on possession. The teams are identified by different colors and bibs. At the center are different number ratios and team affiliations that change during the game during offense and defense. The players' awareness is directed toward quickly recognizing and differentiating changing team affiliations that are combined with frequent transitions. The basic concept of ball holding is ramped up with the different possible playing directions and subsequent follow-up actions with scoring opportunities on mini goals after meeting additional playing objectives. Moreover these games generate basic elements of group tactical attacking and defending behavior.

COLOR SIGNALS
THIRD MAN RUNNING DEFENSIVE UNIT
GETTING OPEN SPATIAL BEHAVIOR
COMMANDS TRIANGLES
ACTION SPEED
INTERFERING PLAYERS NEUTRAL PLAYERS
CAPTURING THE BALL ORIENTING
SUPERIOR NUMBER TOUCH RHYTHM FIELD ZONES
COACH'S SIGNALS SPACING
ALERTNESS INFERIOR NUMBER COACHING
POSITION CHANGES TRANSITIONS
SWITCH OF PLAY

3.4.1   2-plus-4 against 4 (getting open)

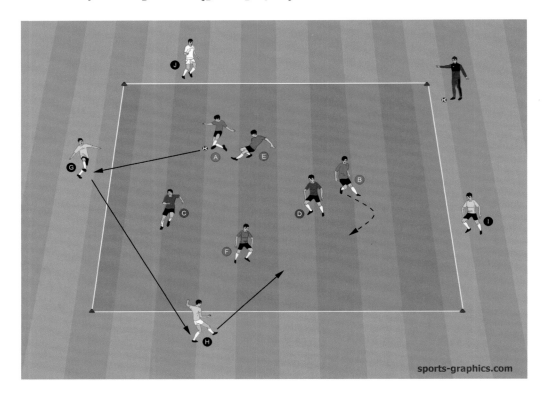

Execution

Players are divided into multiple teams of two players each (see GREEN, BLUE, RED, YELLOW, and GRAY teams). Three teams position themselves inside the central field (see GREEN, BLUE, and RED teams). Two teams spread out evenly, each team with one outside player, at one side of the central field (see YELLOW and GRAY teams). The four outside players always play 2-plus-4 against 4 with just one team (here the GREEN team) against the two other teams (here the BLUE and RED teams). The teams in possession try to keep the ball within their own ranks for as long as possible without the opponents capturing the ball. The outside players (see players G, H, I, and J) can also play passes amongst themselves. The goal of the team in possession is to involve the respective teammates in the field (here players A and B). After the ball is captured, the game immediately continues. The team previously in possession (here the GREEN team) immediately becomes the inferior-number team and the team that won the ball (here the BLUE team) can immediately initiate their own ball holding with the four outside players.

Variations

* Modify changeover after turnover (two-man GREEN team switches to outside positions).
* Specify touches (2 touches per player).
* Specify passing technique for neutral goalkeeper (direct passes).
* Complete as a competition (e.g., Which team plays the most passes?).

3.4.2 Double 3-on-3 (goal hunt)

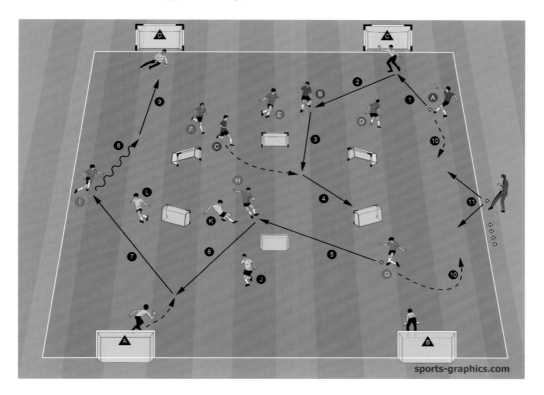

sports-graphics.com

Execution

Players are divided into multiple teams of three players each (see BLUE, RED, GREEN, and WHITE teams). Each of the four large goals (see goals A, B, C, and D) is manned with one goalkeeper. In the center of the field are several mini goals that open to the inside. Two teams always play 3-on-3 against each other. The BLUE team plays the RED team and the GREEN team plays the WHITE team. Both 3-on-3 situations are played with their own ball and proceed simultaneously. All teams and players can move freely around the entire field. In order to take a shot on goal, the teams must play three consecutive passes within their own ranks without the opposing team capturing the ball. The teams in possession can involve the goalkeepers as neutral receivers (see 1, 2, and 3) or play on the center (see 5, 6, and 7). After the three passes, the team in possession can play on a mini goal (see 4) or a large goal (see 8) and try to score (see 9). After a goal has been scored or the ball is out of the game, all six previously active players reorient themselves (see 10) to receive the next ball from the coach (see 11). For each goal scored the shooter's team is awarded one point. Which team will score the most points?

Variations

* Goal scored on a mini goal (1 point)/goal scored on a large goal (2 points)
* Specify shooting technique (direct finish).
* Specify touches (2 touches per player).
* Specify passing technique for neutral goalkeeper (direct passes).
* Assign large goals to just one team.

3.4.3   Double 3-on-3 plus 4 (chaos)

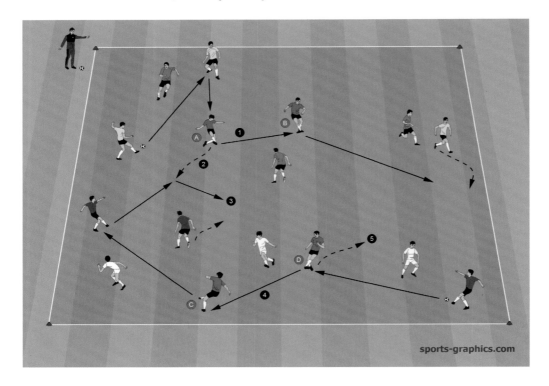

Execution

Players are divided into multiple teams (see YELLOW, GREEN, BLUE, and WHITE teams). Two games are being played simultaneously on the field. All teams play for ball holding and strive for long possession phases without their opponents capturing the ball. Both game situations are completed with their own ball so two balls are on the field at the same time. All teams in possession can pass to the neutral players (see RED team) (see players A, B, C, and D). The YELLOW team plays against the GREEN team and has the option of passing to the RED team players (here players A and B) in 3-on-3-plus-4 play (see 1). At the same time, the BLUE team plays against the WHITE team and also has the option of involving the RED team players (here players C, D, and A) in 3-on-3 plus 4 (see 4). The neutral players can intervene in both game situations. Player A is initially involved in the game between the YELLOW and GREEN teams (see 1) and, right after his pass, transitions toward the other game situation (see 2) and participates in the game between the BLUE and WHITE teams (see 3). After his pass (see 4), player C also transitions (see 5) and is ready to participate in a follow-up action by the YELLOW team players. All teams can use the entire field so that the other game situation produces interfering players who activate the players' alertness and cognition. After a certain amount of time the neutral players change. The game situations can be completed as a competition. The team in possession is awarded one point for six consecutive passes. Which team has more points after two minutes?

Variations

* Specify touches (2 touches per player).
* Specify passing technique for neutral players (direct passes).
* Permanent assignment of neutral players for 3-on-3-plus-2 situations.

3.4.4   From double 3-on-3 to 6-on-6 (transition and orientation)

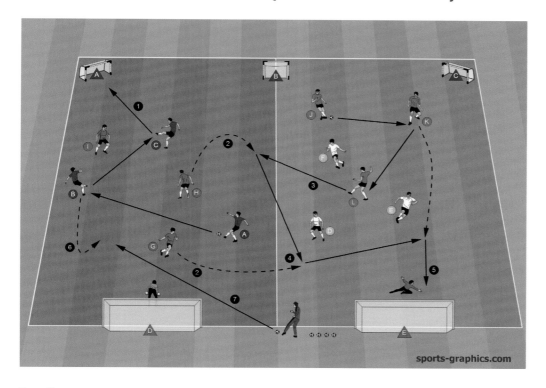

Execution

Players are divided into multiple teams of three players each (see BLUE, RED, WHITE, and GREEN teams). The playing field is framed by three mini goals (see mini goals A, B, and C) and by two large goals (see goals E and D) manned by two goalkeepers, and is divided into two halves. On the left side of the field, the BLUE team plays against the RED team. In doing so, the BLUE team attacks the mini goals A and B and the RED team attacks the large goal D. In the right field, half the WHITE team plays against the GREEN team. The WHITE team attacks the mini goals B and C and the GREEN team attacks the large goal E. The two 3-on-3 situations begin with possession by the BLUE and WHITE teams at their own large goals. The two 3-on-3 situations initially run independently and simultaneously side-by-side and all teams try to score a goal. As soon as a team has scored a goal (see 1), a 6-on-6-situation that involves all players starts with the ball in the other half. In keeping with the previous orientation, the BLUE and WHITE teams play on mini goals A, B, and C against the RED and GREEN teams on the entire field. The players transition accordingly (see 2) and are included in the 6-on-6 (see 3 and 4) to score a goal (see 5). After the second ball has also left the field, all players transition for a new ball from the coach and a final 6-on-6 situation (see 6). The coach brings a new ball into the game (see 7). For the next round, the players change starting positions clockwise so they'll attack the mini goals and large goals with equal frequency.

Variations

* Specify shooting technique (direct finish).
* Complete as competition (e.g., Which team scores the most goals?).

3.4.5   4-on-4 plus 4 (third man running)

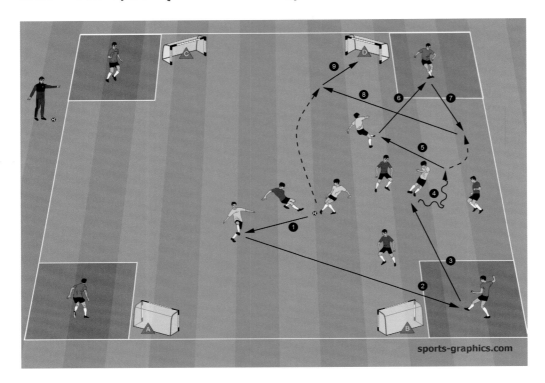

Execution

Players are divided into three teams (see YELLOW, BLUE, and RED teams). Two teams always play in the center field (see YELLOW and BLUE teams). The center field is framed by four mini goals (see mini goals A, B, C, and D) and has four marked off fields in the corners, each manned by a player from a third team (see RED team). The outside players (see RED team) cannot leave their fields. The team in possession (here the YELLOW team) tries to keep the ball within their own ranks without it getting captured by the opposing team (see 1), and also tries to involve the outside players in the passing sequence as a third man running. To do so, a pass is played to an outside player (see 2), and the outside player plays the back pass into the field to another pass receiver (see 3). Immediately after (see 4 and 5), the team in possession tries to involve another outside player in third man running (see 6 and 7). After two outside players have been successfully involved, play on the mini goals (see 8 and 9) begins. As soon as a goal is scored, the coach brings a new ball into the game, the outside players switch to the center as a team, and the team that was scored on switches to the outside positions. Two teams in possession always play together with superior numbers (see YELLOW and RED teams) against one inferior number, chasing team (see BLUE team). After capturing the ball, the inferior-number team (see BLUE team) can finish on the mini goals.

Variations

* Limit touches for superior number players (2/3 touches/1-2-1-2-rhythm).
* Limit touches for outside players (direct play).
* Prerequisite for playing on mini goals (play via 3/4 outside players).
* Play on the far mini goals (here mini goals A and C) after involving outside players.
* Complete as competition (e.g., Which team is the first to score 5 goals?).

3.4.6   4-on-4 plus 4 (goalkeeper in center)

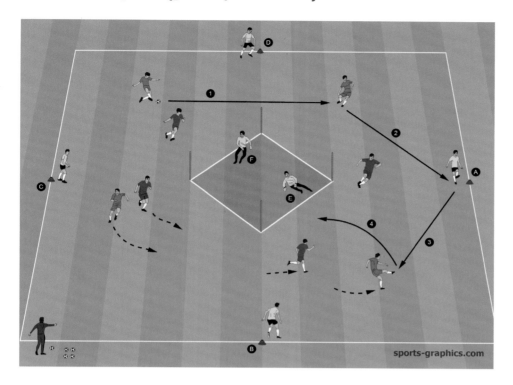

Execution

The RED team plays 4-on-4 against the BLUE team. The two teams initially play for ball holding (see 1) without playing on the center diamond or running through it. Two goalkeepers are positioned in the center diamond (see players E and F). Four neutral players are positioned in four outside positions (see players A, B, C, and D), and can be included by the team in possession (here the RED team) in their own passing sequences (see 2 and 3). The opposing team (here the BLUE team) tries to disrupt the passing sequence and capture the ball to subsequently team up with the neutral outside players while in possession. After an outside player (here player A) has been successfully included in the passing sequence (see 2 and 3), the team in possession can finish on the central diamond field (see 4). The two goalkeepers try to prevent goals on all four sides of the diamond. If a ball leaves the field or a team scores a goal, the coach has the option of bringing a new ball into the game. The teams and individual players regularly change positions.

Variations

* Position a single goalkeeper in the central diamond field.
* Optional involvement of both goalkeepers as neutral players in 4-on-4 plus 6.
* Prerequisite for finishing on diamond field (involve 2/3/4 outside players).
* Specify finish (see 4) on diamond field (direct finish).
* Quick change after a goal (four outside players immediately switch to the field).

3.4.7   4-on-4 plus 4 (zone play) (1)

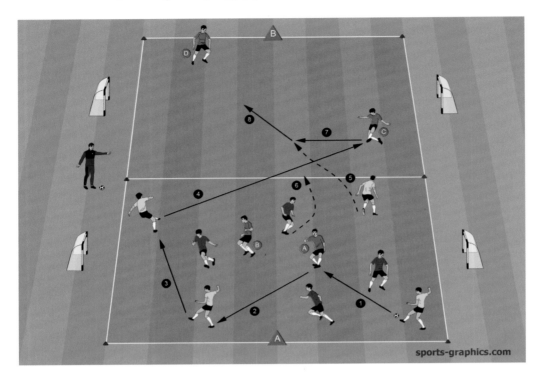

sports-graphics.com

Execution

Players are divided into three teams (see YELLOW, BLUE, and RED teams). The field is divided into two halves (see fields A and B). The RED team players act as neutral players and always support the team in possession. To do so, the RED team players spread out evenly in both halves of the field. Players A and B position themselves in field A and players C and D position themselves in field B. Players A, B, C, and D can only act in their own field and are not allowed to leave the fields. The YELLOW and BLUE teams play 4-on-4 plus 4 for possession and, by involving the neutral players (see 1 and 2), try to keep the ball within their own ranks for as long as possible. The players in possession can play a pass into the opposing field any time they like (see 4). All players from the YELLOW and BLUE teams can also move freely around both fields (see 5 and 6). After a switch of play, the game continues immediately (see 7 and 8). As soon as a ball leaves the field, the coach brings a new ball into the game. The teams regularly switch tasks so all players take a turn as neutral players.

Variations

* Change neutral players after each turnover.
* Change neutral players with each coach's ball.
* Specify passing technique (see 4) for switch of play (direct passes).
* Specify passing technique (see 3 and 7) for neutral players (direct passes).
* Limit touches for superior number players (2/3 touches/1-2-1-2-rhythm).
* Points scored for every eight consecutive passes without the ball being captured.
* Opportunity of finishing on mini goals after predetermined number of passes.
* Specify play on mini goals (direct finish).

3.4.8   4-on-4 plus 4 (zone play) (2)

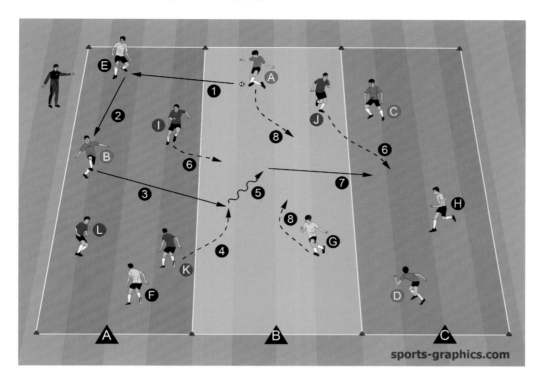

sports-graphics.com

Execution

Players are divided into three teams (see GREEN, YELLOW, and BUE teams) and play 4-on-4 plus 4. Two teams always work together in possession (here GREEN and YELLOW) against one inferior-number team (here BLUE). The field is divided into three areas corresponding to the three teams (see fields A, B, and C). The teams in possession (here GREEN and YELLOW) try to keep the ball within their own ranks for as long as possible without the opposing team capturing the ball (see 1 and 2) and in doing so can move around and play in all three fields. The chasing team (here BLUE) tries to capture the ball (see 4 and 5) and pass it into their own zone (here zone C) (see 6 and 7). As soon as a player has successfully trapped the ball in their own zone, possession immediately changes and the BLUE team works with the YELLOW team in possession. The team that made the previous error (see 3) changes to an inferior number, but first has the opportunity to win back the ball during counter-pressing (see 8) to avoid playing with an inferior number. The assignment of the teams to the three zones must change regularly since the team assigned to the central zone (here YELLOW) has an advantage.

Variation

★   Limit touches for superior number players (2/3 touches/1-2-1-2-rhythm).

3.4.9 5-on-5 plus 5 (compressing and spreading out) (1)

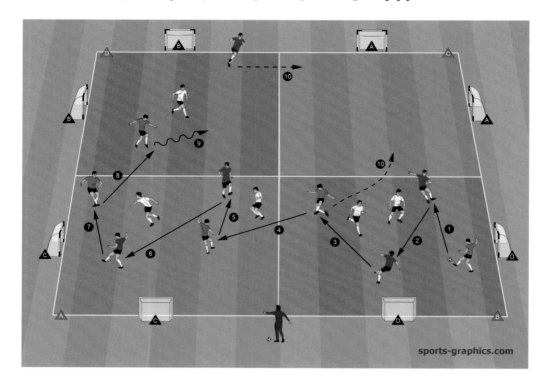

Execution

Players are divided into three teams (see RED, BLUE, and WHITE teams). The playing field is divided into four fields (see fields A, B, C, and D). Each of the four fields is framed by two mini goals that are marked on a diagonal relative to each field (see mini goals A, B, C, and D). Two teams in possession always work together with superior numbers within the entire field (see RED and BLUE teams) against one inferior number and chasing team (here the WHITE team). The superior-number teams in possession must let the ball circulate within their own ranks without the opposing team capturing the ball. In addition the players must try to play three consecutive passes in two fields in a row. The players initially play on field B (see 1, 2, and 3), then switch to field A (see 4) to also play three passes there (see 5, 6, and 7). After two fields have been successfully played on, play on the mini goals begins (see 8). Here the teams in possession play on the mini goals of the previously played-on field (here field A) (see mini goals A) with additional dribbling (see 9) and passing options (see 10). The inferior-number team (here the WHITE team) tries to capture the ball and, after successfully doing so, can directly take a shot on the mini goal of its choice. As soon as a goal has been scored, the superior and inferior-number situation changes. The coach brings a new ball into the game. With each ball the coach plays into the game, the team next in line of a predetermined order becomes the inferior-number team.

Variations

* Ramp up play on fields (4/5/6 consecutive passes).
* Ramp up play on fields (play on 3/4 fields).
* Limit touches for superior number players (2/3 touches/1-2-1-2-rhythm).
* Opportunity to play on several mini goals by playing on additional fields.

3.4.10 5-on-5 plus 5 (compressing and spreading out) (2)

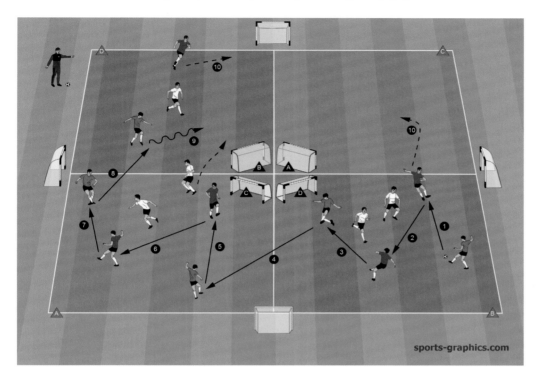

Execution

Players are divided into three teams (see RED, BLUE, and WHITE teams). The playing field is divided into four fields (see fields A, B, C, and D). The entire field is framed by four mini goals. Four additional mini goals marked to correspond to the respective fields are set up in the center (see mini goals A, B, C, and D). Two teams in possession always work together with superior numbers within the entire field (see RED and BLUE teams) against one inferior number and chasing team (here the WHITE team). The superior-number teams in possession must let the ball circulate within their own ranks. In addition·the players must try to play three consecutive passes in two fields in a row. The players initially play on field B (see 1, 2, and 3), and then switch to field A (see 4) to also play three passes there (see 5, 6, and 7). After two fields have been successfully played on, play on the mini goals begins (see 8). Here the teams in possession play on the mini goals with additional dribbling (see 9) and passing options (see 10). The inferior-number team (here the WHITE team) tries to capture the ball and, after successfully doing so, can directly take a shot on the mini goal of its choice. As soon as a goal has been scored, the superior and inferior-number situation changes. The coach brings a new ball into the game. With each ball the coach plays into the game, the team next in line of a predetermined order becomes the inferior-number team.

Variations

* Ramp up play on fields (4/5/6 consecutive passes).
* Ramp up play on fields (play on 3/4 fields).
* Limit touches for superior number players (2/3 touches/1-2-1-2-rhythm).
* Restrict play on mini goals (play on mini goals that match the field).

3.4.11   5-on-5 plus 5 (switch play via goalkeeper)

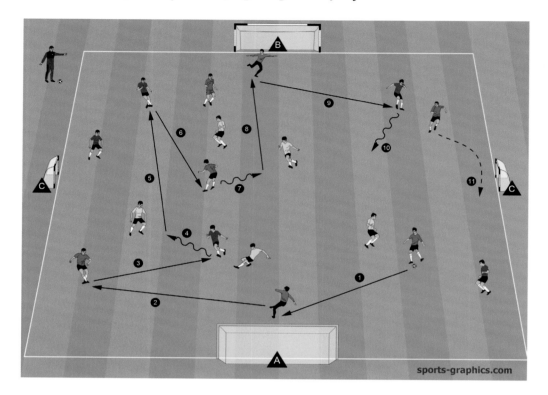

sports-graphics.com

Execution

Players are divided into three teams (see RED, BLUE, and YELLOW teams). Two teams always play together as superior-number teams in possession (see RED and BLUE teams) against one inferior number, chasing team (see YELLOW team). The superior-number teams in possession must circulate the ball within their own ranks. In addition the players must try to involve the goalkeeper as often and as quickly as possible (see 1/2 and 8/9) and to switch play accordingly. After a predetermined number of switches of play or passes via a goalkeeper, play on the goals begins (see 10 and 11). Here the teams in possession attack the goal opposite the goalkeeper (here goalkeeper B) (goal A) who last received a pass. The inferior-number team tries to capture the ball and after successfully doing so, can directly score on the two large goals A and B or the two mini goals (see mini goals C). As soon as a goal has been scored, the superior and inferior-number situation changes. The coach brings a new ball into the game. With each ball the coach plays into the game, the team next in line of a predetermined order becomes the inferior-number team.

Variation

★   Limit touches for superior number players (2/3 touches/1-2-1-2-rhythm).

3.4.12 Double 5-on-3 against 2 (transition after capturing the ball)

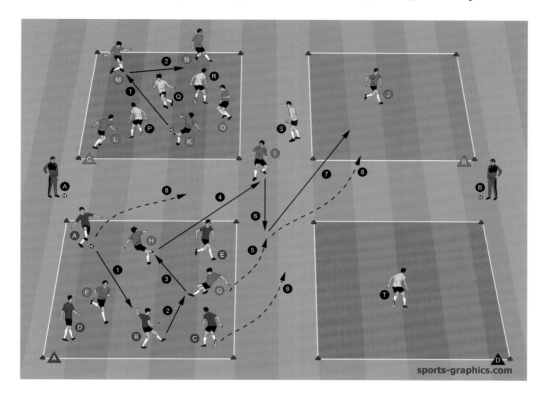

Execution

Players are divided into four teams (see BLUE, RED, GREEN, and YELLOW teams). The BLUE team always plays against the RED team and the GREEN team always plays against the YELLOW team. Each set of two teams plays on two diagonally opposite fields. The BLUE and RED teams play on fields A and B, and the GREEN and YELLOW teams play on fields C and D. In addition, the zone between the fields is manned and used for switches of play after the ball is captured. At the start of the game, the teams play 5-on-3 (see fields A and C). One player from each of the inferior-number teams is positioned in the central area between the fields (see players I and S) and one additional player is positioned in the far fields (see players J and T). The team in possession must keep the ball within their own ranks for as long as possible during 5-on-3 play (see 1 and 2). After a turnover (see 3), the previously chasing team tries to switch play via a center player. To do so, they must pass to the center player (see 4), and a field player must signal (see 5) that he will play a back pass (see 6) and pass the ball into the opposite field (see 7). In a simplified version, the players can pass directly into the opposite field after capturing the ball. After a successful switch of play (see 7), the players (see 8) change to the played-on field, resulting in a new 5-on-3 situation. As soon as a ball has left the field, coach A for the BLUE and RED teams and coach B for the GREEN and YELLOW teams bring a new ball into the game.

Points system

* Passing sequence (8 passes) without opposing touches (1 point)
* Ball capture with subsequent switch of play (1 point)
* Field change even without switch of play after 3 errors by the team in possession

3.4.13   6-on-6 plus 6 (contact rhythm)

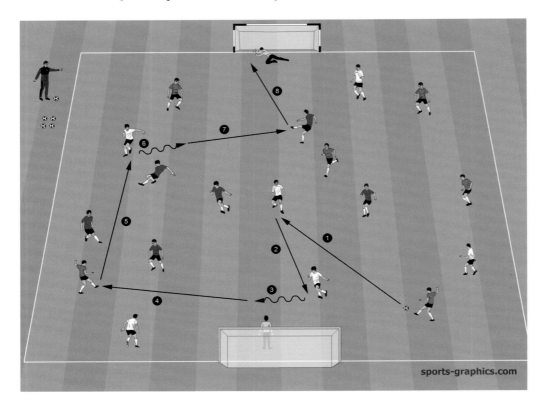

sports-graphics.com

Execution

Players are divided into three teams (see RED, WHITE, and BLUE teams). Two teams always play together as superior-number teams in possession (see RED and WHITE teams) against one inferior-number chasing team (see BLUE team). The superior-number teams in possession must circulate the ball within their own ranks (see 1). In doing so, the touches per player must alternate in a 1-2-1-2-rhythm. A direct pass (see 2) is followed by the next player's action with two touches (see 3 and 4), followed by another direct pass (see 5). The sequence continues in a 1-2-1-2-rhythm (see 6 and 7) until the team in possession has played ten consecutive passes without the opponents capturing the ball, at which point it immediately attacks one of the two large goals manned with goalkeepers (see 8). The inferior-number team tries to capture the ball and, after successfully doing so, can immediately take a shot on the two large goals. As soon as a single player makes a touch error, his team immediately switches to the inferior-number situation. After every goal, the coach brings a new ball into the game.

Game idea

The teams in possession are in a clear superior-number situation. This allows them time to focus and safely implement the predetermined touch rhythm over the entire field. in addition to sensible getting-open behavior, the emphasis is on acting as a unit, and anticipatory playing that aims to fulfill the touch-related task. The actions by the inferior-number team must be coordinated and collaborative as a defensive unit and the ball must be captured by pressing with time pressure.

3.4.14   6-on-6 plus 6 (outside player[s])

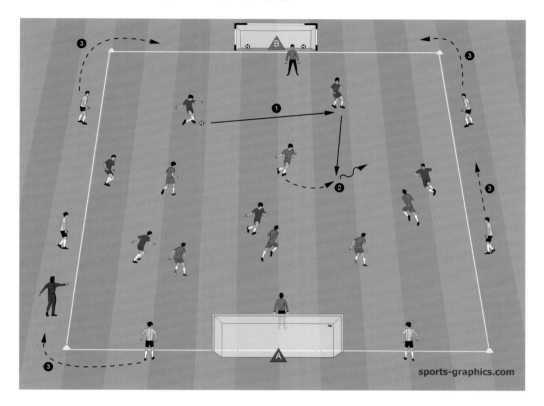

Execution

The BLUE team plays 6-on-6 plus 6 against the RED team. The BLUE team in possession plays on goal A and tries to score (see 1). The RED team tries to prevent the goal and, after successfully capturing the ball (see 2), scores a goal on goal B. The YELLOW team players act as neutral outside players for the team in possession (here the BLUE team). The outside players position themselves in the direction of play of the respective team in possession with two players at each of the sidelines and one player in a deep position on each side of the currently played-on goal (here goal A). After a possession change (see 2) and corresponding change in the direction of play, the outside players take up new positions (see 3). After a goal is scored by one of the teams on the field, the outside players switch to field players. The scored-on team immediately switches to the neutral outside positions. The team that scored the goal remains on the field and now has possession against the new opponent. The goalkeeper brings a new ball into the game for the impending 6-on-6-plus-6 situation.

Variations

* Limit touches for outside players (direct passes).
* Immediate switch after twenty consecutive passes, even without scoring.
* No direct passes between outside players.
* Limit touches for team in possession (2 touches).
* Specify minimum number of touches for team in possession.
* Specify time limit (30 seconds) until shot on goal.

3.4.15 6-on-6 plus 6 (compressing and spreading out)

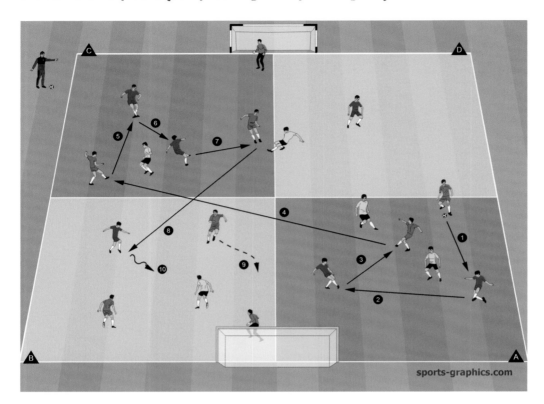

Execution

Players are divided into three teams (see RED, BLUE, and YELLOW teams). The playing field is framed by large goals manned with goalkeepers and is divided into four equal squares (see fields A, B, C, and D). Two teams always play together in possession with a superior number (see RED and BLUE teams) against one inferior-number, chasing team (see YELLOW team). The teams in possession must let the ball circulate within their own ranks. In addition, the players try to play three consecutive passes in two fields in a row (here fields A and C) without the opponents capturing the ball. After the three passes in field A (see 1, 2, and 3), a field change takes place (see 4) to subsequently play three passes in another field (here field C) (see 5, 6, and 7). After two fields have been successfully played in, play on the two large goals immediately begins and the teams in possession try to score on one of the two large goals (see 10) via additional passing options (see 9). The inferior-number team tries to capture the ball and, after successfully doing so, can directly score on one of the two large goals. As soon as a goal has been scored, the superior and inferior-number situations switch. If the inferior-number team scores after capturing the ball, the team that lost the ball becomes the inferior-number team. If the superior-number team scores, the team that did not field the shooter becomes the inferior-number team. After a goal, the coach brings a new ball into the game.

Game idea

This game includes different aspects that require ball holding, getting open in open playing position, sensible spacing of superior number players, integrated shifts in play, switching from short to long passes, and target-oriented transitions toward the goal.

3.4.16   6-on-6 plus 6 (zone play)

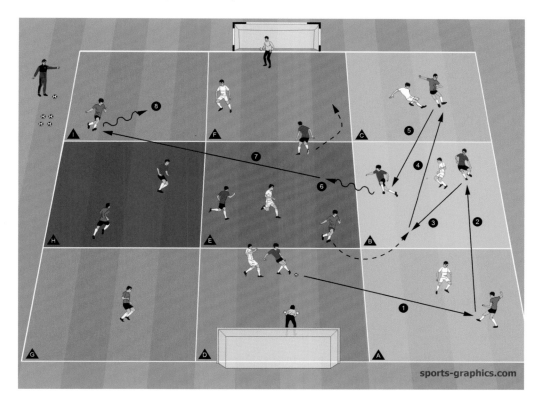

sports-graphics.com

Execution

Players are divided into three teams (see RED, BLUE, and WHITE teams). Two teams always play together in possession with a superior number (see RED and BLUE teams) against one inferior-number, chasing team (see WHITE team). The teams in possession must let the ball circulate within their own ranks (see 1). In addition, the players must try to play at least four consecutive passes (see 2, 3, 4, and 5) in one of the color-coded strips on the field. The teams in possession play the four passes in the YELLOW zone (see fields A, B, and C). After four successful consecutive passes in one strip, play on one of the two large goals via additional possible dribbling (see 6) and passing options (see 7) immediately follows, and the teams try to score a goal (see 8). The inferior-number team tries to capture the ball and, after successfully doing so, can immediately score on the large goals. As soon as a goal has been scored, the superior- and inferior-number situations switch. If the inferior-number team scores after a capturing the ball, the team that lost the ball becomes the inferior-number team. If a superior-number team scores, the team that did not field the shooter becomes the inferior-number team. After a goal, the coach brings a new ball into the game.

Variations

* Facilitate four opening passes within two of the field's strips (see fields A and F).
* Limit touches for superior-number players (2/3 touches/1-2-1-2-rhythm).
* Opportunity to involve both goalkeepers in opening ball holding.

3.4.17   Variable 6-on-6 (opening technique)

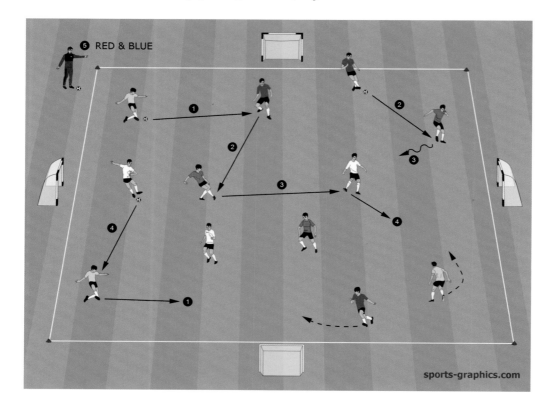

Execution

Players are divided into four teams (see YELLOW, BLUE, RED, and WHITE teams). The field is framed by four mini goals. There are multiple balls in the game and players pass them freely (see 1, 2, 3, and 4). In doing so, players must observe a specific order. The YELLOW team players always pass to the BLUE team players (see 1). The BLUE team players always pass to the RED team players (see 2), and the RED team players always pass to the WHITE team players (see 3). The WHITE team players continue the passing sequence accordingly via a YELLOW team player (see 4). The coach can end the passing order with a coach's signal and initiate 6-on-6 play on the four mini goals. With a signal from the coach (see 5), the players currently in possession of the balls that were previously used for open passing kick them into a mini goal of their choice and all players transition for the ensuing 6-on-6 situation. The coach names two teams (here the RED and BLUE teams) and simultaneously plays a new ball into the game. The named teams (here RED and BLUE) play together against the teams that were not named (here YELLOW and WHITE).

Variations

★ No back-to-back actions with the same ball.

★ Specify number of passes as prerequisite for play on mini goals (2/3/4/5 passes).

★ Use different balls during open passing (tennis balls/futsal balls/foam balls).

★ Use different techniques during open passing (direct passes/left/right).

★ Use different techniques during open passing (throw by hand).

★ Combine different balls and techniques (soccer passes/tennis ball throws).

3.4.18 Variable number ratios (even number, superior number, inferior number)

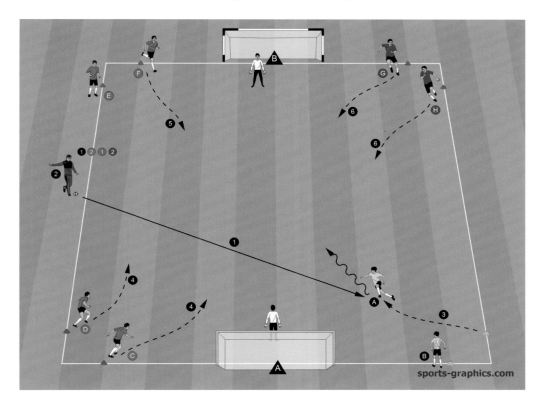

Execution

Players are divided into four teams of two players each (see YELLOW, GREEN, RED, and BLUE teams). Both players from each team position themselves in one of the four corners of the field. The YELLOW team always plays with the GREEN team on the large goal B, and the RED team always plays with the BLUE team on the large goal A. As they play against each other, the number ratio of these teams varies and is determined by the way the coach brings the ball into the game (see 1), as well as a signal (see 2). The coach plays the ball to one of the teams in one of the four corners (here the YELLOW team) and at the same time calls out four numbers (see 2). The numbers (here 1/2/1/2) specify how many players per team can intervene in the current game situation. The first number always applies to the team that has received the coach's ball (here the YELLOW team). The remaining numbers apply to the other teams in a clockwise order. Corresponding to the coach's signal, a player from the YELLOW team (here player A) intervenes in the game (see 3) and works together with two players from the GREEN team (see 4). One of the players from the RED team (see player F) is also allowed to intervene here (see 5) and works with two players from the BLUE team (see 6). As designated by the coach's signal, a 3-on-3 situation ensues. Depending on the specified numerical order, superior- or inferior-number situations can arise. Players coordinate continuously and independently within their own teams as to which player will be first to react to the numbers (see A and B). When the coach calls out "0," none of the players from the respective team is allowed to intervene. As soon as the coach doesn't call out any numbers, all players can intervene in the game situation.

Variations

* Designate players clockwise with uneven first number.
* Designate players counterclockwise with even first number.

3.5   TARGET AREAS AND TARGET ZONES

Target Areas and Target Zones includes games that are geared toward designated target zones and defined spaces to facilitate goal-oriented and promising passes, and a style of play toward the goal or into spaces that threatens the opponent. Here the emphasis is on recognizing, opening up, running into, and playing on target areas and is implemented via passes within a zone, passes through zones, passes across individual marking lines of zones, or first-touch control into zones. Zone play should be prepared via sensible and confident combination play and coordinated efforts for getting open and signaling availability, and should be reinforced by helpful coaching signals from players in possession. The competitive character is defined by different point systems for successful zone play to multi-variant specifications and rewarding follow-up actions with goal orientation. This places special emphasis on group-tactical means of attack that simultaneously address playing intelligence, action speed, and goal orientation in complex ways. The target areas and target zones are marked as lines, triangles, squares, rectangles, and pieces of equipment of various types and sizes, and are geared toward basic offensive playing strategies and realistic competitive play. The games are ramped up via multi-dimensional courses of action for zone play and varying and changing follow-up options for playing on different goals.

PASSING COMBINATIONS
GROUP TACTICS FOLLOW-UP ACTIONS
CLOSE TO THE GOAL PASSING OPPORTUNITIES
SITUATIONAL SPECIFICITY PRE-ORIENTATION
COACHING INTERFERENCE FACTORS
COURSES OF ACTION COACH'S SIGNALS
TIME LIMIT MEANS OF ATTACK
COUNTERPRESSING   FANNING OUT
ACTION SPEED
POINTS SYSTEM TRIANGLES
TARGET ZONES

3.5.1   6-on-6 (spatial behavior)

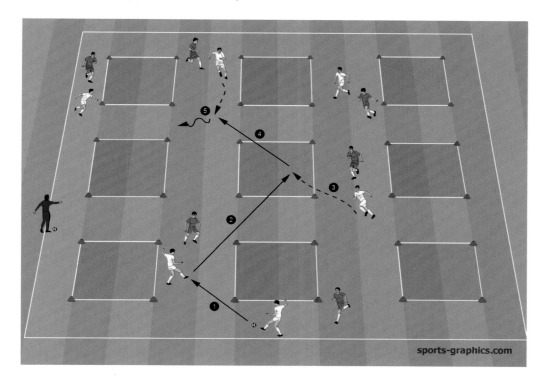

Execution

The WHITE team plays 6-on-6 against the RED team. The team in possession (here the WHITE team) initially tries to play safe passes within their own ranks (see 1). In addition, players have the goal of playing on different target fields. To do so, a player runs toward a pass (see 3) played into the target field (see 2) and passes the ball to the next teammate (see 4). Right after, possession play continues (see 5) and another target field can be played on. The team in possession is awarded a point for each target field it plays into. After a successful turnover, the tasks change.

Game idea

During preparatory ball holding (see 1), the team in possession practices patient goal-oriented possession play. Playing on the target fields requires awareness and recognizing open spaces. Play on target fields must be well-timed and actively demanding (see 3). The subsequent passing play requires pre-orientation and creating additional passing stations. The defending team practices condensing certain field zones and blocking passing lanes.

Variations

* Change fields to play on (BLUE/GREEN).
* Opposing team cannot run through fields.
* Play on target fields by passing across two lines of a field (see 4).
* Play on target fields by dribbling across two lines of a field (see 4).
* Play on target fields by dribbling into the field and pass out of the field (see 4).
* Multiple points for playing on certain target fields (e.g., central target field).

3.5.2   4-on-4 plus 1 (play through the center)

Execution

The RED team plays 4-on-4 plus 1 with one neutral YELLOW player against the GREEN team. The neutral YELLOW player positions himself in the central diamond field. The team in possession (here the RED team) plays for ball holding and tries to keep the ball within their own ranks for as long as possible (see 1). The team in possession must pass to the player positioned in the center (see 2). The opposing team tries to prevent the pass to the neutral player and to capture the ball, and, after gaining possession, tries to involve the neutral player. If a ball leaves the field, the coach has the option of bringing a new ball into the game.

Variations

★ Players may not enter the central BLUE field.

★ Specify passing play for central player (direct passes).

★ Specify minimum number of passes (five passes) prior to pass to central player.

★ Specify passing task (see 2) for central player (simple back pass).

★ Specify passing task (see 3) for central player (third man running).

★ Specify passes (see 2) into diamond (direct play).

★ Specify passes to continue play (see 4) after playing into diamond (direct play).

3.5.3   6-on-6 plus 1 (play through the center) (1)

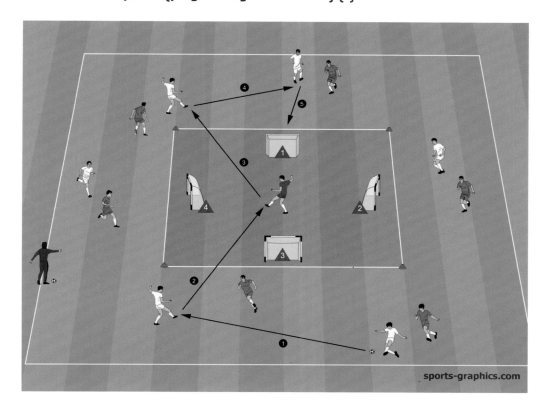

Execution

The WHITE team plays 6-on-6 plus 1 against the RED team. One neutral player is positioned in the central field. The team in possession (here the WHITE team) initially tries to play safe passes within their own ranks (see 1). In addition, they have the goal of involving the teammate in the central target field in the passing sequence (see 2). Afterwards, the central player continues the passing sequence via a teammate who is ready to receive the ball (see 3). Successful play with the central player is immediately followed by the opportunity to play on all four mini goals (see 4 and 5).

Game idea

During preparatory ball holding (see 1), the team in possession practices patient goal-oriented possession and creating additional passing opportunities after a pass into the center. The player in the center practices signaling his readiness and getting open in terms of playing on gaps. The defending team practices condensing in the center and blocking dangerous field zones that provide scoring opportunities for the opposing team.

Variations

* Specify touches for central player (3 touches/2 touches/direct play).
* Specify shooting technique for play on mini goals (direct finish).
* Specify time limit for finish on a mini goal (see 5) after play via central player (see 3).
* Designate mini goals to play on (see mini goals 1, 2, 3, and 4) via coach's signal.

3.5.4   6-on-6 plus 1 (play through the center) (2)

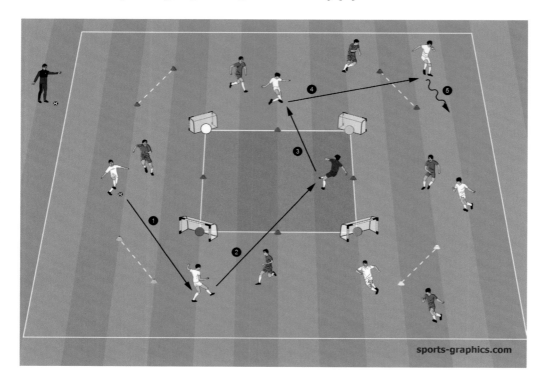

Execution

The WHITE team plays 6-on-6 plus 1 against the RED team. One neutral player is positioned in the central field. The team in possession (here the WHITE team) initially tries to play safe passes within their own ranks (see 1). In addition, players have the goal of involving the teammate in the central field in the passing sequence (see 2). The central player continues the passing sequence via a teammate who is ready to receive the ball (see 3). Successful play with the central player is immediately followed by the opportunity to play on all four mini goals (see 4). The cone goals must be played on with a pass to a teammate (see 4). Immediately after, ball holding (see 5) continues with the targeted involvement of the central player. After successfully playing on the cone goals (see 4) during the game, play on the mini goals of the same color can continue (see 5) as a variation, or after a signal from the coach.

Variations

* Designate mini goal(s) to play on (see WHITE, YELLOW, RED, and GREEN) via coach's signal.
* Designate cone and mini goal(s) for central player (see 3) to play on.
* Time limit for play on cone goals (8 seconds)/time limit for play on mini goals (10 seconds).
* Opportunity to play on all four mini goals after direct pass (see 4) through cone goal.
* Specify touch limit per player (see 1) during ball holding (4/3/2 touches).
* Play on cone goals by dribbling (see 4).

3.5.5   4-on-4 plus 2 (play on the center)

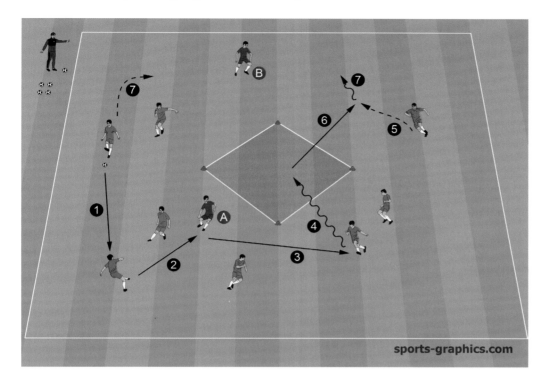

Execution

The RED team plays 4-on-4 plus 2 with the neutral BLUE team players against the GREEN team. The team in possession (here the RED team) plays for ball holding and tries to keep the ball within their own ranks for as long as possible (see 1). In doing so, the team in possession is allowed to involve the two neutral BLUE players in the passing sequence (see 2 and 3). The team in possession tries to play on the central BLUE zone via a specific technical task (here dribble with subsequent pass). In order to successfully play on the central BLUE zone, players must coordinate getting one player open so he can then dribble into the central BLUE zone (see 4). Next, a pass from the central BLUE zone to a teammate (see 5) must follow (see 6). After successfully playing on the central BLUE zone, the game continues without interruption (see 7). The opposing team tries to prevent play on the BLUE zone and to capture the ball to prompt a task change. If a ball leaves the field, the coach has the option of bringing a new ball into the game.

Variations

* Players without a ball cannot enter the central BLUE zone.
* One player from the defending team can enter the central zone.
* Specify play on central BLUE zone (dribble across two lines).
* Specify play on central BLUE zone (pass across two lines).
* Specify passes to continue game (see 7) after play on diamond (direct play).

3.5.6   6-on-6 (play on the center) (1)

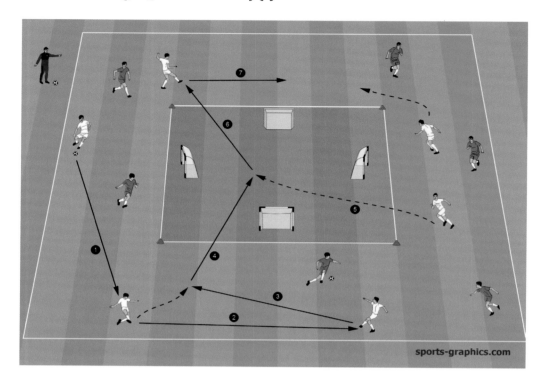

sports-graphics.com

Execution

The WHITE team and the RED team each have a ball. The two teams complete a predetermined number of passes within their own ranks (see 1, 2, and 3). After completing the predetermined number of passes, the subsequent goal is to play on the central field. To do so, one player from each field can run into the central field (see 5) after the predetermined number of passes (see 3) has been completed. The teams now pass to the teammate in the central field (see 4). The receiving player in the central field immediately passes the ball out of the central field (see 6). Right after, the teams begin to play the predetermined passing sequence again (see 7). The mini goals serve as interference factors and imaginary opponents.

Game idea

The team in possession practices fluid ball circulation, preparatory and target-oriented passing for playing on the center, and correspondingly coordinated signaling of availability and efforts to get open in terms of playing on gaps. After the pass into the center, players must signal their readiness and get open to ensure a direct and fluid shot from the center and to subsequently have options for continuing the game.

Variations

* Play on the center with a pass across two lines of the central field (see 4).
* Play on the center by dribbling across two lines of the central field (see 4).
* Play on the center with a double pass around a mini goal.
* Organize as a competition (e.g., Which team is the first to play 10 passes through the center?).

3.5.7   6-on-6 (play on the center) (2)

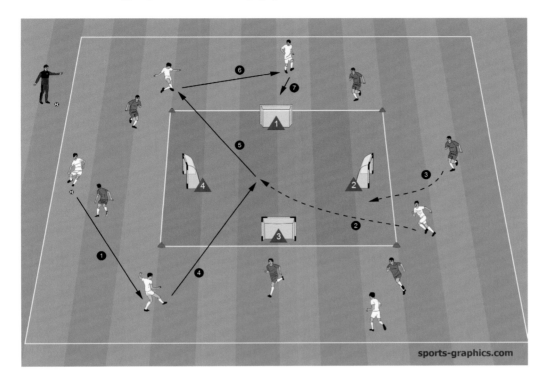

sports-graphics.com

Execution

The WHITE team and the RED team play 6-on-6 against each other. The team in possession (here the WHITE team) initially tries to play safe passes within their own ranks (see 1). After a predetermined number of passes, the subsequent goal is to play on the central field. After completing the predetermined number of passes, teammates and opponents are allowed to run into the central field (see 2 and 3). The team in possession now tries to pass to a teammate in the central field (see 4). The receiving player in the central field passes the ball back to the outer field (see 5). Immediately after, play on the mini goals begins and the team in possession tries to score on one of the mini goals (see 7) via additional passing options (see 6).

Game idea

In preparatory ball holding (see 1), the team in possession practices patient goal-oriented possession, recognizing spaces, and coordinated efforts to signal availability and to get open in terms of playing on gaps. The defending team practices condensing in the center and blocking dangerous field zones with opposing passing and finishing opportunities.

Variations

* Prerequisite for playing on center (2/3/4 passes).
* Opportunity to play on mini goals even without playing on central field.
* Specify shooting technique (see 6) for play on mini goals (direct finish).
* Observe offside rule while playing on central field (see 2 and 3).
* Designate mini goals to play on (see mini goals 1, 2, 3, and 4) via coach's signal.

3.5.8   6-on-6 (play on the center) (3)

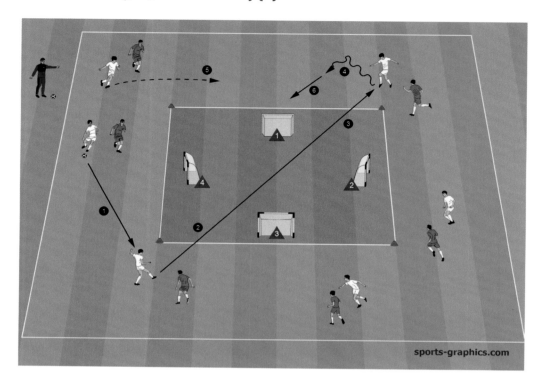

Execution

The WHITE team and the RED team play 6-on-6 against each other. The two teams play a predetermined number of passes within their own ranks (see 1). After completing the predetermined number of passes, the goal is to play on the central field. To do so, a pass must be played to a teammate (see 2 and 3) across two lines of the central field. Right after a complete pass through the field has been played (see 3), play on the mini goals begins (see 4) and the team in possession tries to score on one of the mini goals (see 6) via additional passing options (see 5).

Game idea

Playing on the central field forces slanting and diagonal passes. Here passes that go against the opposing shifting movement are particularly promising. Ball holding, playing on the central field, and playing on mini goals prompt changing game situations and different objectives. Teams are forced to quickly recognize new situations and to make appropriately quick and goal-oriented decisions in order to score a goal.

Variations

* Prerequisite (see 1) for play on center (2/3/4 passes).
* Opportunity to play on mini goals even without playing on central field.
* Specify shooting technique (see 6) for play on mini goals (direct finish).
* Designate mini goals to play on (see mini goals 1, 2, 3, and 4) via coach's signal.
* Specify touch limit per player (see 1) for ball holding (4/3/2 touches).
* Specify passing technique (see 2) for play on central field (direct passes).

3.5.9   6-on-6 (play on the half spaces)

Execution

The WHITE team and the RED team play 6-on-6 for ball holding. The team in possession (here the WHITE team) tries to play as many consecutive passes as possible within their own ranks without the opponents capturing the ball (see 1, 2, and 3). The purpose of this game is to play on (see 1, 2, and 3) the overlapping fields (see fields 1, 2, 3, and 4) and afterwards continue the game for ball holding (see 4 and 5). Players can play on the fields in different ways and with different points systems. After a turnover, the game continues with a different task.

Game idea

In preparatory ball holding (see 1), the team in possession practices patient goal-oriented possession. To play on the fields players practice targeted signaling of availability and getting open in specific and predetermined situations, and using and running into open spaces. The players in possession must continuously facilitate passing options (see 4), particularly after a pass into the critical spaces (see 1). The defending team practices condensing central field zones as a unit, as well as blocking dangerous passing opportunities.

Variations and points system

* Four consecutive passes in YELLOW or BLUE field (1 point)
* Dribble through field 1, 2, 3, or 4 (2 points)
* Pass across two lines of field 1, 2, 3, or 4 (3 points)
* Third man running in field 1, 2, 3, or 4 (4 points)
* Prerequisite for playing on a target zone (four complete passes within own ranks).
* Specify touch limit per player (see 5) for ball holding (4/3/2 touches).

3.5.10   5-on-5 plus 1 (play on athletic equipment) (1)

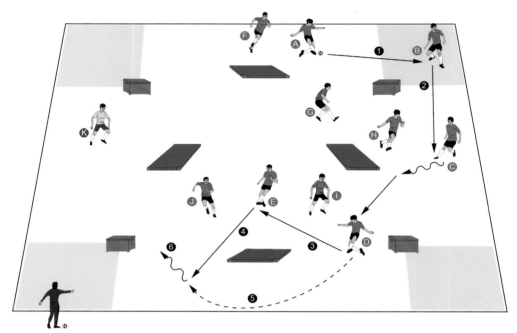

sports-graphics.com

Execution

The GREEN team initially plays 5-on-5 for ball holding against the RED team. Several pieces of equipment are set up on the field. In the center of the field are four mats and in the corners are four vaulting boxes. Each of the boxes marks a YELLOW field directly behind it. The team in possession (here the GREEN team) initially plays for ball holding and tries to keep the ball within their own ranks for as long as possible without the opponents capturing the ball. In addition the team in possession can score points by playing in a predetermined manner on the zones marked by the boxes. The teams in possession score points when they play on the corner zones behind the boxes. To do so, the ball must be passed through the YELLOW zone (see 1 and 2). The teams can also score points by playing on the mats. To do so, players must play a double pass over a mat (see 3, 4, and 5) and afterwards (see 6) play another pass. To simplify, player K can be included in 5-on-5-plus-1 play as an alternative.

Variations

- Modify play on YELLOW zone (double pass).
- Modify play on mats (third man running).
- Modify play on YELLOW zone (pass across 2 lines of the zone).
- Modify play on YELLOW zone (dribble across 2 lines of the zone).
- Specify touch limit (direct passes) for select actions (see 4).

3.5.11   4-on-4 plus 1 (play on athletic equipment) (2)

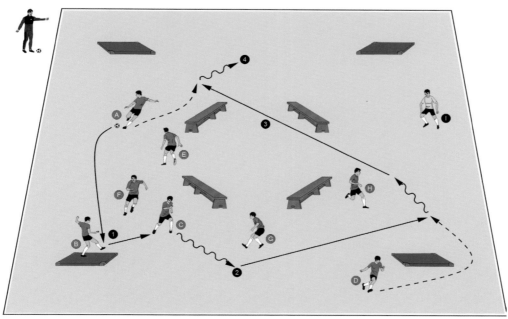

sports-graphics.com

Execution

The GREEN team plays 4-on-4 against the RED team initially for ball holding. Several pieces of equipment are set up on the field. In the center of the field are four benches that represent a central space, and in the corners are four mats. The team in possession (here the GREEN team) initially plays for ball holding and tries to keep the ball within their own ranks for an extended period of time without the opponents capturing the ball. In addition, the team in possession can score points by playing on the pieces of equipment in a predetermined manner. The teams in possession score points by playing on a mat when a teammate, who is positioned on the mat during the game (see player B), receives a high pass and plays it directly out of the air to a teammate (see 1). The action is considered as finished when the receiving player is able to complete a successful follow-up action (see 2). Teams can also score points by playing on the central benches. To do so, a pass must be played between the benches through the central field (see 3). Here, too, a follow-up action by the receiver is necessary (see 4). To simplify, player I can be included in 4-on-4-plus-1-play as an alternative.

Variations

* Modify play on mats (double pass around the mat).
* Modify play on mats (third man running around the mat).
* Modify play on benches in center (dribble through central zone).
* Modify play on benches in center (volley over two benches).
* Specify passing technique for play on mat (inside foot/left/right).
* Specify touch limit (direct passes) for select actions (see 3).

3.5.12 4-on-4 plus 2 (target areas)

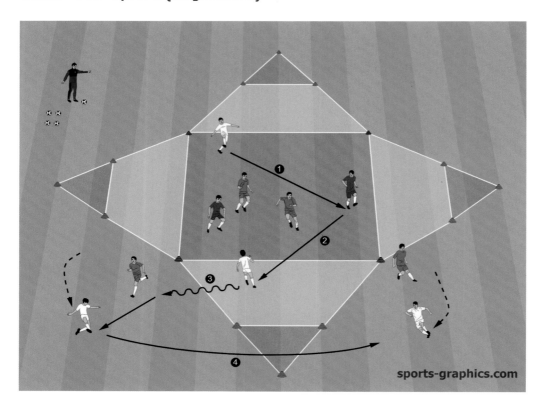

sports-graphics.com

Execution

The WHITE team plays 4-on-4 plus 2 against the RED team. The two BLUE players are neutral teammates for the team in possession. The field is divided into multiple zones. The team in possession (here the WHITE team) plays for ball holding. The opposing team (here the RED team) tries to capture the ball. The team in possession is allowed to involve the neutral players in the game (see 1, 2, 3, and 4) and thereby score points. If a ball leaves the field, the coach has the option of bringing a new ball into the game.

Points system for playing on CENTER zone

★ Three consecutive passes without the opponents capturing the ball (1 point)

★ Ball capture and pass out of field into YELLOW zone (2 points)

Points system for playing on YELLOW zone

★ One-touch ball control, open up and dribble (see 3) out of zone (3 points)

★ Ball control, open up and dribble in BLUE zone (4 points)

Points system for playing on BLUE zone

★ Pass across two lines (see 4) of BLUE zone (5 points)

★ Pass across two lines (see 4) of BLUE zone and receive pass in CENTER zone (5 points)

3.5.13 4-on-4 plus 2 (mini goals)

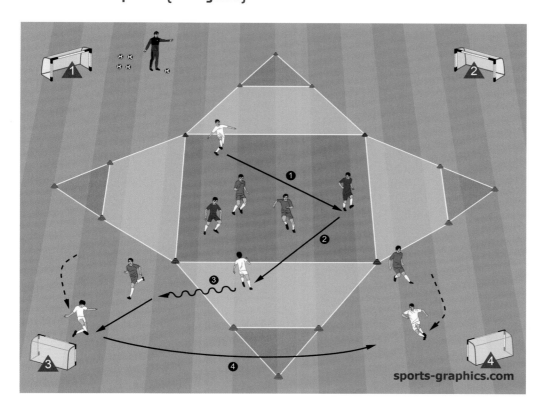

sports-graphics.com

Execution

The WHITE team plays 4-on-4 plus 2 against the RED team. The two BLUE team players are neutral teammates of the team in possession. The field is divided into multiple zones. The team in possession (here the WHITE team) initially plays for ball holding. The opposing team (here the RED team) tries to capture the ball. The team in possession is allowed to include the neutral players (see 1). The team in possession tries to play on the different zones according to specific instructions (see 1, 2, 3, and 4), and by doing so tries to score points and earn the right to finish on the mini goals. If the team in possession has played on the CENTER zone (see 1) all four mini goals 1, 2, 3, and 4 are open. If the team in possession played on a YELLOW or BLUE zone (see 3 and 4), the two weak-side mini goals (here mini goals 1 and 2) are open. If a ball leaves the field or a team scores on a mini goal, the coach has the option of bringing a new ball into the game.

Points system for playing on the zones

- ★ Three consecutive passes (see 1) in CENTER zone without turnover (1 point)
- ★ One-touch ball control, open up and dribble (see 3) out of YELLOW zone (2 points)
- ★ Pass across 2 lines (see 4) of BLUE zone (3 points)

Points system for playing on mini goals

- ★ Goal scored after playing on CENTER zone (1 point)
- ★ Goal scored after playing on YELLOW zone (2 points)
- ★ Goal scored after playing on BLUE zone (3 points)

3.5.14   3-on-3 (target areas and mini goals)

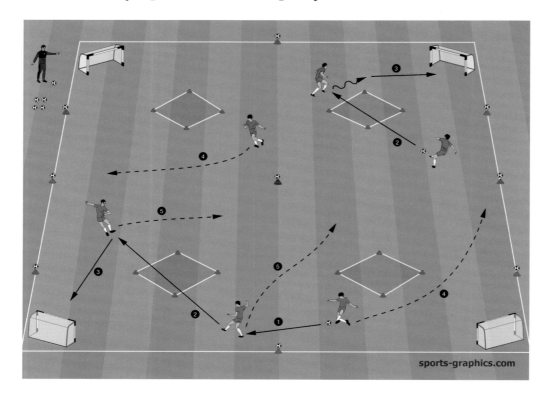

Execution

The RED and GREEN teams initially complete a predetermined passing exercise and immediately afterwards, play 3-on-3 on the target fields and mini goals. Each team starts on the field with its own ball and first has to complete a technical task with a total of five balls, and afterwards must shoot each ball into a mini goal. Passes can be played within the team to quickly solve the task (see 1). The goal is to play a pass across two lines of the four fields (see 2) and afterwards score on one of the mini goals (see 3). After every ball, each team gets another ball (see 4) and all players reorient themselves in the direction of the player currently in possession (see 5) in order to play on a field with the next ball, and finish. Balls for each team marked with the team colors are positioned at the sideline. After each team has played its own balls into the mini goals, 3-on-3 play begins with the ball in the center. A field must be played on again before a final goal can be scored on a mini goal from the 3-on-3.

Game idea

The players must coordinate their runs and the way they signal their availability within their team. Players must work together and position themselves perfectly to quickly continue the game so they can finish the technical task as quickly as possible and thereby earn a promising chance in 3-on-3 play.

Variations

* Prerequisite for finishing on a mini goal (play on multiple target fields).
* Specify touch limit per player (see 1, 2, and 3) during technical task (4/3/2 touches).
* Specify shooting technique (see 3) for finish on mini goals (direct finish).

3.5.15 6-on-6 (target areas and mini goals)

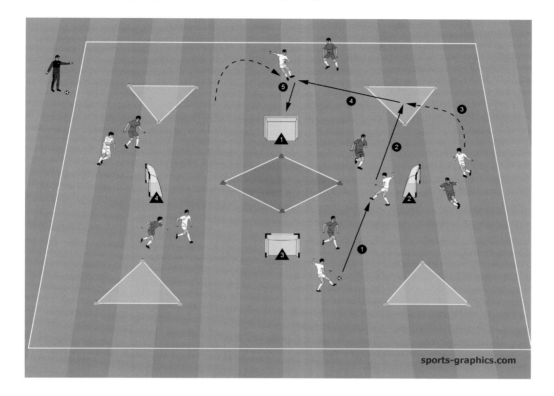

sports-graphics.com

Execution

The WHITE team plays 6-on-6 for ball holding against the RED team. On the field are four mini goals as well as four marked-off triangles (see YELLOW fields) and a central diamond (see BLUE field). The team in possession (here the WHITE team) initially tries to play safe passes within their own ranks (see 1). After playing for ball holding, the goal is to play on the different fields. The fields are successfully played on via a third man running by relaying a pass played into the field (see 2) by a player starting into the field, (see 3) to another teammate (see 4). After successfully playing on a field (see 4), the players purposefully transition toward the goal and try to score (see 5). After successfully playing on a YELLOW field, players can play on both of the mini goals on either side of the field. By playing on different triangles back-to-back, players can play on multiple mini goals. If the central field has been played on, the team in possession can attack all four mini goals.

Game idea

In preparatory ball holding (see 1), the team in possession practices patient goal-oriented possession play. Playing on the target fields requires awareness and recognizing open spaces. Runs into the target fields must be well-timed and actively demanding (see 3). The subsequent passes (see 4) require pre-orientation and creating additional passing stations.

Variations

* Play on target fields via a pass across two lines of the respective field (see 2).
* Play on target fields by dribbling across two lines of the respective field (see 2).
* Designate mini goals to play on (see mini goals 1, 2, 3, and 4) via coach's signal.

3.5.16 4-on-4 plus 2 (target areas and large goals)

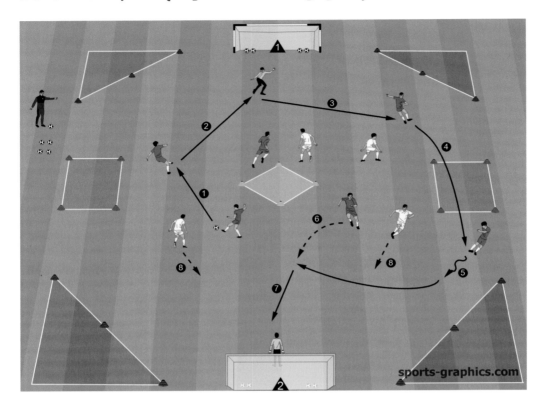

Execution

The RED team plays 4-on-4 plus 2 against the WHITE team. The two green players are neutral teammates of the team in possession. The field is divided into multiple zones. Players are not allowed to run into the four outer zones which narrow play toward the goal. The BLUE and YELLOW zones can be played on during ball holding with specific guidelines. After successfully playing on one of these zones, players can play on the large goals. The team in possession (here the RED team) initially plays for ball holding. The opposing team (here the WHITE team) tries to capture the ball. The team in possession tries to play a pass across two lines of a BLUE zone (see 4). After a successful pass across two lines of a BLUE zone (see 4), 4-on-4-plus-2 play begins (see 5) toward the large goal in playing direction (here goal 2). The players in possession orient themselves according to the new playing direction, transition to offense (see 6), and try to score (see 7). The opposing players transition to defense according to the new playing direction (see 8) and try to prevent the goal from being scored. Next to the BLUE zones, players can also play on the diamond. After successfully playing on the diamond, the team in possession has the opportunity to finish on both large goals 1 and 2. If a ball leaves the field or a team scores on a large goal, the coach has the option of bringing a new ball into the game.

Points system

* Pass across two lines of a BLUE zone and subsequent goal in large goal (1 point)
* Pass across two lines of a YELLOW zone and subsequent goal in a large goal (2 points)
* Play on both BLUE zones back-to-back and subsequent goal in a large goal (3 points)
* Specify shooting technique (direct finish/left/right).

3.5.17   5-on-5 plus 1 (target areas and large goals)

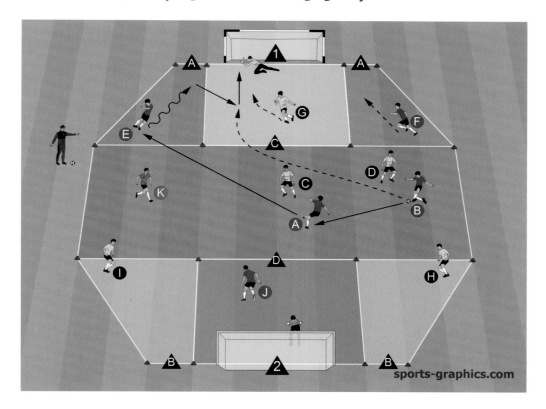

Execution

The BLUE team plays 5-on-5 against the YELLOW team. The field is divided into multiple zones and framed by two large goals (see 1 and 2) manned with goalkeepers. In the center of the field is a wide zone. The field tapers toward the goals and splits into three zones at each end (see BLUE and YELLOW zones). The BLUE team attacks goal 1 and the YELLOW team attacks goal 2. Certain players (see players E/F/J and H/I/G) are positioned in the zones in front of their respective goals. These players can only act inside their zone. The BLUE team positions one player in each of the outside offensive fields A (see players E and F) and one player (see player J) in the central defensive field D. The YELLOW team also positions one player in each of the outside offensive fields B (see players H and I) and one player (see player G) in the central defensive field C. Players A/B and C/D can move freely in all fields.

Points system

*   Goal scored after pass from zone A/B (2 points)
*   Goal scored after direct pass from zone A/B (3 points)

Variations

*   Add a neutral player (see player K) for 5-on-5 plus 1.
*   Specify touches for players in zones A and B (2/3 touches).

3.5.18   4-on-4 (complex zone play)

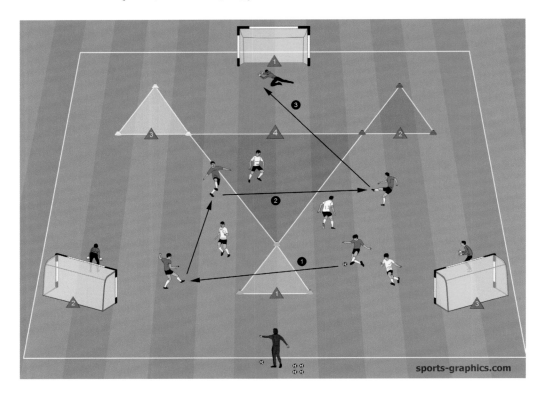

Execution

The GREEN team plays 4-on-4 against the WHITE team on three large goals manned with goalkeepers. In the center of the field are multiple zones marked as triangles. The three fields 1, 2, and 3 in the outer areas are marked with yellow, blue, and white cones. A large field 4 is marked in the center. The teams initially play for ball holding and try to keep possession without the opponents capturing the ball. Here all three of the goalkeepers can be included in 4-on-4 plus 3. The different fields can be played on according to specific guidelines and subsequently facilitate play on the large goals. After successfully playing on field 2, goal 2 must be played on, and goal 3 can be played on after playing on field 3. If multiple fields are played on back-to-back without the opponents capturing the ball, several large goals can also be played on simultaneously. Moreover, after successfully playing on the central field (see field 4), all goals (see goals 1, 2, and 3) can be played on. After a goal is scored or a ball leaves the field, the coach brings a new ball into the game.

Variations

* Play on fields 1, 2, and 3 with pass across two lines of fields (see 1).
* Play on fields 1, 2, and 3 by dribbling across two lines of fields.
* Play on field 4 via pass across two lines of field (see 2).
* Play on field 4 via four touches by a player in the field.
* Flying substitution and independent change of goalkeepers with each new coach's ball.

3.5.19 4-on-4 (complex zone play)

Execution

The RED team plays 4-on-4 against the WHITE team. The field is divided into multiple zones. In the center of the field are four triangles marked with different colors. Additional playing zones are located behind the four mini goals. Initially all players are in the central field. The team in possession plays for ball holding (see 1) and tries to play on a triangle of its choice. To do so, a player in possession must dribble across two lines of a triangle (see 2). After successfully dribbling through a triangle, play on the mini goal of the same color (here WHITE) begins, and players can run into the corresponding field behind the mini goal (see 3). The team in possession tries to lay the groundwork for a finish on the mini goal (see 6) via additional passes (see 4 and 5). After successfully playing on a target field, additional mini goals can be opened up by playing several times on other target fields.

Game idea

Play in the central field is characterized by opponent and time pressure and forces quick recognition of open target fields and courageous dribbling into critical field zones. Fast and purposeful transitions with deep runs and opening passes are promising after playing on the triangles.

Variations

* Observe the offside rule when switching to play on mini goals (see 5).
* Play on target fields via a pass across two lines of a field (see 2).
* Play on target fields via a third man running (see 2).
* Specify shooting technique (see 6) for play on mini goals (direct finish).
* Limit maximum number of advancing offensive players (2 players) and defensive players (1 player).

3.5.20 4-on-4 plus 2 (complex zone play)

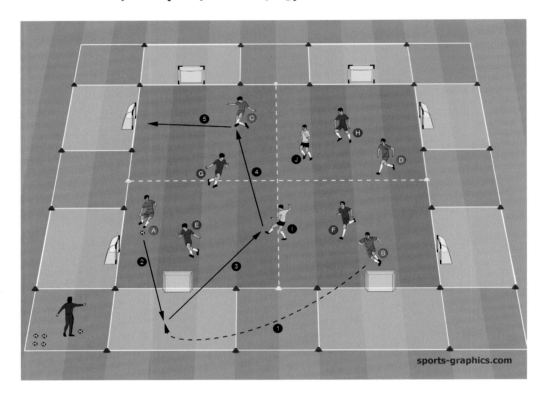

Execution

The RED team and the BLUE team play 4-on-4 plus 2. Two neutral players are positioned in the central field (see I and J). The central field is framed by eight mini goals. Behind each mini goal are marked zones that must be played on before finishing on the mini goals. The team in possession (here the RED team) initially plays for ball holding and tries to keep the ball within their own ranks for as long as possible without the opposition capturing the ball. Both neutral players can be included in the passing sequence (see 3 and 4). The zone behind a mini goal must be played on before scoring on a mini goal. To do so, the players move away from the center (see player B) and run into those zones (see 1). Play on the mini goals starts immediately after a pass into the zone (see 2) and a successful continuation of play out of the zone (see 3). The opposing team tries to prevent play on the zones and a goal. After successfully capturing the ball, the task changes. After a goal has been scored or the ball leaves the field, the coach has the option of bringing a new ball into the game.

Variations

* Limit touches for neutral players (2 touches).
* Prerequisite for the pass out of a zone (see 3) (direct play).
* Specify additional passes (see 4) after playing on a zone (play via neutral player).
* Playing on a zone opens certain goals (mini goals in the opposite half of the field).
* Opportunity to immediately finish on mini goals after capturing the ball.

3.5.21 4-plus-2 against 4-plus-2 (complex zone play)

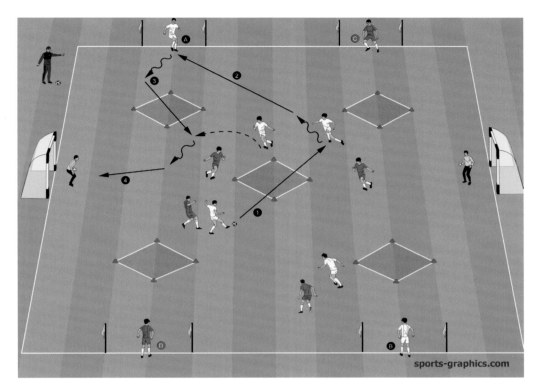

Execution

The WHITE team plays 4-on-4 plus 2 against 4-on-4 plus 2 against the RED team, initially for ball holding (see 1). To do so, four players from each team always operate in the central field and two players from each team are in staggered outside positions (see players A, B, C, and D). The two goalkeepers can initially be included in the play for ball holding. The team in possession (here the WHITE team) tries to keep the ball within their own ranks without the opponents capturing the ball and in addition tries to successfully play on a blue field with a pass across two lines (see 1). After successfully playing on one of the fields of their choice (see 1), an outside player from their own team (here player A) must be included in the game via a pass (see 2) to subsequently score on a large goal (see 4) through additional passing opportunities (see 3). Players in outside positions change regularly.

Game idea

The team in possession practices well-timed signaling of availability and getting open and recognition and purposeful use of promising field zones. Constantly alternating play through the center (see 1) and play on outside zones (see 2) is also prompted.

Variations

* Play on central fields by dribbling across two lines of the respective field (see 1).
* Play on central field with third man running out of the respective field (see 1).
* Prerequisite for play on both large goals (double play on fields (see 3).
* Activate diagonally opposite defender (here player B) after pass to the outside (see 2).
* Specify touch limit per player (see 1 and 2) in play for ball holding (4/3/2 touches).

3.5.22 6-on-6 (complex zone play)

sports-graphics.com

Execution

The WHITE team plays 6-on-6 for ball holding against the RED team. The team in possession (here the WHITE team) initially tries to play safe passes within their own ranks (see 1) and to do so can include both goalkeepers in 6-on-6 plus 2. On the field several target fields are marked with different colors. A central field is marked in the center of the playing field. There are four mini goals positioned around the edges as well as in the center. Next to playing for ball holding the game's objective is to play on the different fields. The fields are played on via a third man running by relaying a pass played into the central field (see 2) by one of the players starting into the field (see 3) to a teammate (see 4). After successfully playing on a field (see 4), the players purposefully transition toward the goal (see 5). After successfully playing on the central field, play on the two large goals (see 6 and 7) begins with additional passing options. If an outside target field (see BLUE and YELLOW fields) was played on, the game moves toward the mini goals of the same color. After successfully playing on these fields, the two goalkeepers can be included once again, and playing multiple times on other target fields can open additional goals.

Variations

* Opportunity to play on central mini goals after playing on multiple target fields in a row.
* Play on target fields with a pass across two lines of the respective field (see 2).
* Play on target fields by dribbling across two lines of the respective field (see 2).

3.5.23 6-on-6 (complex zone play)

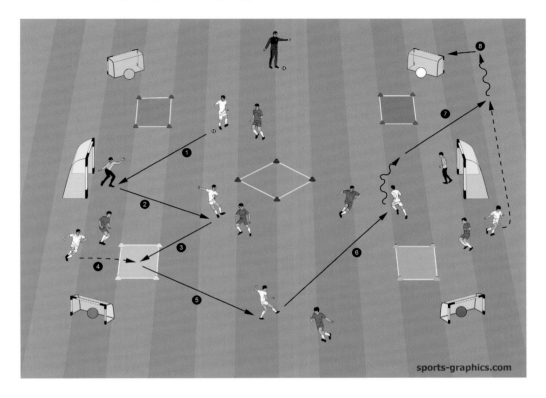

Execution

The WHITE team plays 6-on-6 for ball holding against the RED team. The team in possession (here the WHITE team) initially tries to play safe passes within their own ranks (see 1). Both goalkeepers can be included in 6-on-6 plus 2 (see 2). On the field several target fields are marked with different colors. Next to playing for ball holding the game's objective is to play on the different-colored target fields to subsequently be able to finish on the goals. To do so, a pass played into the target field (see 3) is met with a well-timed run (see 4) and relayed to another teammate (see 5). Depending on the color the played-on target field is marked with (here WHITE), play on the mini goal of the same color directly follows (see 6, 7, and 8). After successfully playing on a target field, the two goalkeepers can be included once more, and playing multiple times on other target fields can open additional mini goals.

Variations

★ Play on target fields with a pass across two lines of a field (see 5).

★ Play on target fields by dribbling across two lines of a field (see 5).

★ Play on target fields by dribbling into the field and pass out of the field (see 5).

★ Opportunity to finish on both large goals after successfully playing on central field.

★ More points awarded for playing multiple times on target fields.

3.5.24 Variable 6-on-6 plus 6 (complex zone play)

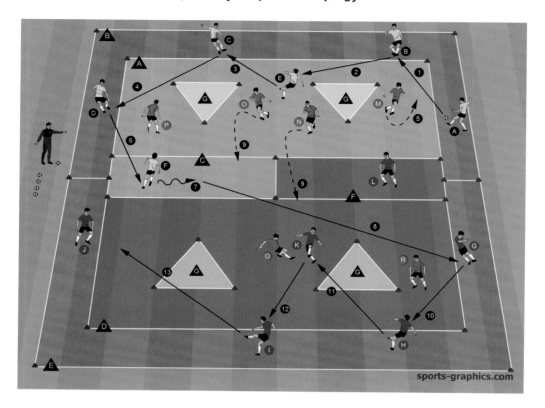

Execution

Players are divided into three teams (see YELLOW, RED, and BLUE teams) of six players each (see players A to R). Players spread out on a field consisting of two outer areas (see fields A and D), a central zone (see fields C and F), and an outer edge for outside players (see fields B and E). Two teams always play together in possession (here the YELLOW and BLUE teams) against an inferior-number, chasing team (see RED team). The players from the team in possession branch out in a specific staggered formation.

The YELLOW team mans the outer zone B with four players (see players A, B, C, and D), field A with one player (see player E) and zone C in the center with one player (see player F). The BLUE team mans zones D, E, and F. The chasing inferior-number RED team branches out in zones A and D. Four players (see players M, N, O, and P) operate in the zone (here zone A) currently played on by the team in possession (see 1, 2, 3, and 4). Two players (see players Q and R) are positioned in the currently not played-on field.

As soon as the ball switches to the opposite field, two players (here players N and O) switch, so the chasing team operates with four players again. The YELLOW team is in possession and plays with two touches (see 1, 2, 3, and 4). The RED team tries to capture the ball (see 5). If the RED team captures the ball and plays three passes within their own ranks, the ball is considered lost. During this time period, the YELLOW team has the opportunity to immediately counter-press and recapture the ball. To do so, the YELLOW team players can operate in field A. To shift the ball to the second field D and get out of a possible pressure situation, the players in the central zone (see players F and L) must always be passed to (see 6). Only these players can switch play (see 7) and pass the ball into the other field (see 8). After a successful switch of play (see 8), two players from the chasing team (here players N and O) switch to the opposite field (see 9). The defending team (here the RED team) is thus always divided in a two-to-four ratio.

It is considered an error if the defending team touches the ball, a bad pass is played, the ball is passed into touch, or a player uses more than two touches. After each error, the coach plays a new ball into the game and prompts a switch of play with each new coach's ball. The defending team (here the RED team) must provoke three errors. After the third turnover, the team trades positions with the team that caused the third error. The two players in the center occupy a special position. They decide whether their own team keeps possession after a back pass or a switch of play will take place. The teams in possession can score points by playing on the fields G and by playing a pass across two lines on these fields (see 11 and 13).

Variations

* Opportunity to shift play exclusively via the own center player.
* Center players move freely around central corridor without field designation.
* Mandatory position change/field change of both center players after switch of play.
* Add mini goals for finishing opportunity after achieving certain playing goals (see 11 and 13).

3.6 SEAMS AND VERTICAL PLAY

Seams and Vertical Play includes games that focus on recognizing and playing on gaps and seams as a defensive chain. Here the emphasis is on opening, deep, and vertical passes into seams initiated via safe combinations and coordinated getting-open efforts. Offering passing options is a prerequisite and is facilitated via space-opening running paths, position changes, cutting, curved runs, and deep sprints. Switching direction of play, targeted play on goals, and supporting play are required follow-up actions and means to continue play. Markers, mini goals, and direct opponents are used to create a realistic representation of defensive chains.

OFFSIDE LINE
PASSING OPTIONS
FOLLOW-UP ACTIONS SPRINTS
DEEP RUNS GETTING OPEN
GOAL ORIENTATION TIMING
SCORING OPPORTUNITIES PROBLEM SOLVING
RUNNING PATHS SUPPORT
CHANGE IN DIRECTION OF PLAY

3.6.1   Open passing (line passes)

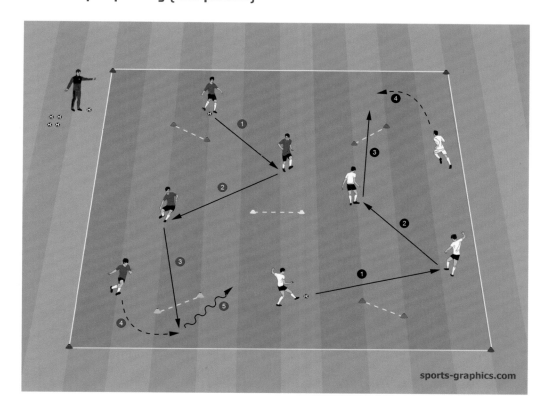

Execution

Players are divided into multiple teams of four players each (see BLUE and WHITE teams). Each of the teams has a ball, and the teams are moving around and passing the balls (see 1) inside the field where several different-colored cone goals are set up. The teams purposefully play on a cone goal of their choice (see 3, 4, and 5) by way of the passing player playing a deep pass (see 3) to a teammate who is getting open (see 4). During the pass, the line marked by the cone goal serves as the offside line. After the pass has been controlled (see 5), the process is repeated with a new passing sequence at a different-colored cone goal.

Basic idea

At the heart of the passing sequences is the coordinated behavior of passer and receiver. An additional requirement for the receiver is the timing for getting open and a deep run.

Variations

* Complete as a competition (e.g., Which team is the first to play ten deep passes through the cone goals?).
* Modify the running and passing paths (run through a mini goal/receive pass next to mini goal).

3.6.2   4-on-4 (line passes)

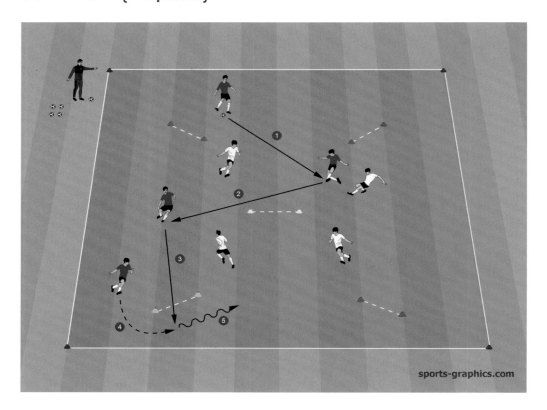

sports-graphics.com

Execution

The BLUE team plays 4-on-4 against the WHITE team. The team in possession (here the BLUE team) initially tries to play several passes within their own ranks without the opponents capturing the ball (see 1 and 2). The subsequent objective is to play on the different-colored cone goals (see 3, 4, and 5). The teams purposefully play on a cone goal of their choice by way of the passing player playing a deep pass (see 3) to a teammate who is getting open (see 4). During the pass, the line marked by the cone goal serves as the offside line. After the pass has been controlled (see 5), the team remains in possession and has the option of playing on another cone goal. The teams score points by correctly playing on the cone goals.

Game idea

At the heart of the passing sequences is the coordinated behavior of passer and receiver under opponent pressure. An additional requirement for the receiver is the timing for getting open and a deep run.

Variations

* Modify running and passing paths (run through mini goal/receive pass next to mini goal).
* More difficult scoring (mandatory follow-up pass after controlling the pass).

3.6.3 4-on-4 on mini goals (same direction of play)

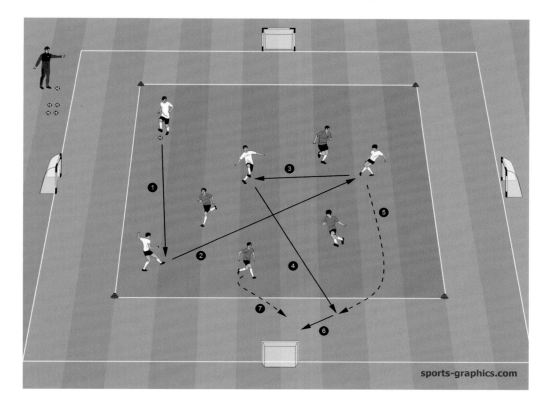

Execution

The WHITE team plays 4-on-4 against the GREEN team. The team in possession initially plays for ball holding (see 1, 2, and 3), and, after three consecutive passes within their own team without the opponents capturing the ball, tries to pass across one of the four lines of the center field (see 4). Teammates are allowed to leave the center field for the deep pass (see 4) and chase it while observing the offside rule, to immediately afterwards play on four mini goals and score (see 6). After a successful pass to a player who is running deep (see 4), an opposing player is allowed to follow to prevent a goal from being scored in 1-on-1 play (see 7) and, after successfully capturing the ball, can also score on a mini goal. In the meantime, the coach brings a new ball into the game.

Game idea

After the opening passes in the center field, the focus is on transitioning to resolve the situation in the center toward the outer mini goals. Timing in getting open and a forward running path as well as coordination between passer and receiver and a purposeful follow-up action are practiced here.

Variations

* Opportunity for all players to move up for support on the entire field.
* Complete passes by hand (deep pass as ground pass).
* Prerequisite for a pass (see 4) into outside zone (2/4/5 consecutive passes).

3.6.4   5-on-5 on mini goals (alternating direction of play)

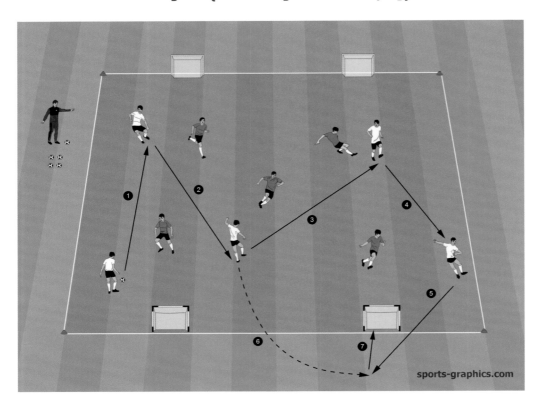

Execution

The WHITE team plays 5-on-5 against the GREEN team. The teams initially play on a field that is framed by four mini goals that are open to the outside. The team in possession (here the WHITE team) initially plays for ball holding (see 1, 2, 3, and 4) and simultaneously tries to play on one of the four mini goals (see 5, 6, and 7) and score. There are two rules for playing on the mini goals. First, the field's boundary lines serve as the offside line, so that a pass receiver must wait to run across the line into the outer field (see 6) until after the pass has been played (see 5). Second, goals must be scored with a direct shot (see 7). After a pass into the outer field (see 5), the defending team can follow into the outer field with all players to prevent a goal from being scored and to possibly capture the ball. If the team in possession is unable to do a direct finish, play must move back to the center field and across another line to finish on a different mini goal. After a turnover, one of the field's boundary lines must also be played on first before a goal can be scored. As soon as the ball leaves the field or a goal is scored, the coach brings a new ball into the game.

Variations

* Modify team sizes (superior- and inferior-number situations).
* Specify mandatory number of passes (2/3/4/5 passes) prior to a deep pass (see 5).

3.6.5   4-on-4 on mini goals (variable direction of play)

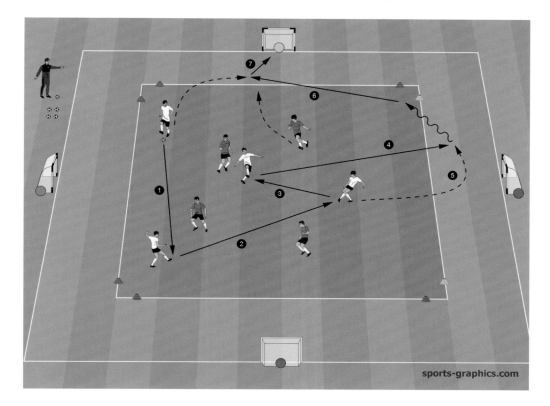

sports-graphics.com

Execution

The WHITE team plays 4-on-4 against the RED team. The team in possession (here the WHITE team) initially plays for ball holding (see 1, 2, and 3) and tries to play a predetermined number of passes within their own ranks without a turnover. Immediately afterwards the objective is to play a pass across a line of the center field (see 4). For the deep pass (see 4), the teammates are allowed to leave the center field and chase the pass (see 5) while observing the offside rule. Immediately afterwards, teammates play on the mini goal of the same color (here the YELLOW mini goal) and, after additional passing options, score a goal (see 7). During play on the mini goal, all players are allowed to follow into the large field (see 5). If multiple sides of the center field were previously played on with a deep pass, the team in possession has the option of attacking several mini goals simultaneously. As soon as the ball leaves the field or a goal is scored, the coach brings a new ball into the game.

Game idea

After the opening passes in the center field, the focus is on transitioning to resolve the situation in the center toward the outer mini goals. Timing in getting open and a forward running path as well as coordination between passer and receiver and a purposeful follow-up action are practiced here.

Variation

* Prerequisite for a pass (see 4) into the outer zone (2/3/4/5/ consecutive passes).

3.6.6   6-on-6 on large goals (alternating direction of play)

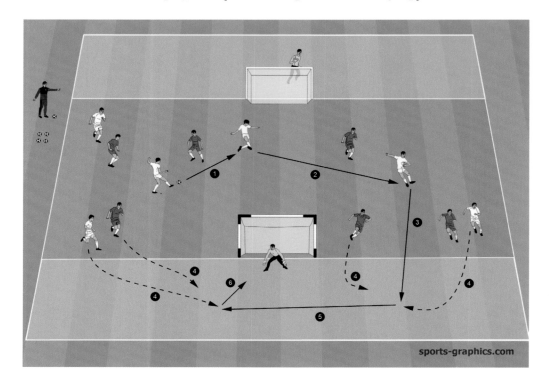

Execution

The WHITE team plays 6-on-6 against the RED team. The team in possession (here the RED team) initially tries to play safe passes within their own ranks (see 1 and 3). All field players are initially in the center field during ball holding. The team in possession must switch play to one of the two yellow target zones via a deep and opening pass (see 3). Play on the large goals begins with a successful pass into the yellow target zone (see 3). At that time, all players are allowed to run into the yellow target zone while observing the offside rule, and then get into offensive or defensive mode (see 4). After additional passing options (see 5), the team in possession tries to score on the large goal (see 6).

Game idea

Observing the offside rule forces active and well-timed deep runs (see 4). Switching play to the yellow zones facilitates controlled passes into the seams of the opposing defensive lines (see 3). The necessary support for the receiving player (see 4) generates quick advances and long deep runs with an open and goal-oriented playing position for the finish.

Variations

* Specify passing technique (see 3) for forward play (direct passes).
* Position cone goals on the offside line for precise forward passes.
* Specify shooting technique (see 6) for play on large goals (direct finish).
* Specify a specific number of passes prior to a possible shift to the yellow zones (3/4/5 passes).

3.6.7   4-on-4 (outside zones) (1)

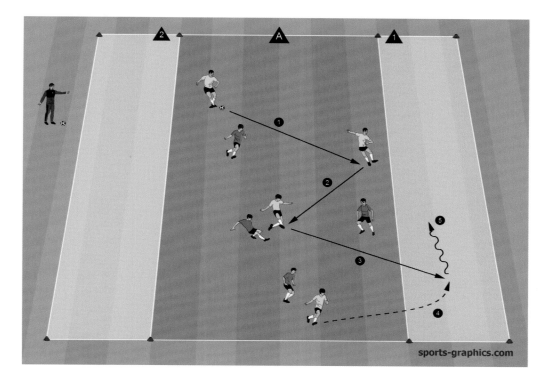

Execution

The YELLOW team plays 4-on-4 against the RED team. The teams initially play for ball holding and try to keep the ball within their own ranks (see 1 and 2) in the center field (see field A) without the opponents capturing the ball. The team in possession (here the YELLOW team) tries to play a pass into one of the end zones (here zone 1) (see 3). A teammate must reach the pass with a deep run (see 4) within the end zone and control the ball there (see 5). The offside rule applies to the pass (see 3) and the run (see 4). The game immediately continues (see 5) with a change in the direction of play. Accordingly the YELLOW team plays on the opposite end zone (here zone 2). The RED team tries to prevent the deep passes and, after successfully capturing the ball, also plays on the end zones.

Game idea

This game focuses on getting open while moving forward. The players anticipating the ball are asked to create deep passing options (see 4). Recognizing and using gaps as well as timing and control in passing all play an important role for the passing players.

Variations

* Complete passes by hand (deep pass as ground pass).
* Players can choose end zone to play on (eliminate direction of play).
* Prerequisite for passing (see 3) into a seam (3/4/5 consecutive passes in field A).

3.6.8   4-on-4 (outside zones) (2)

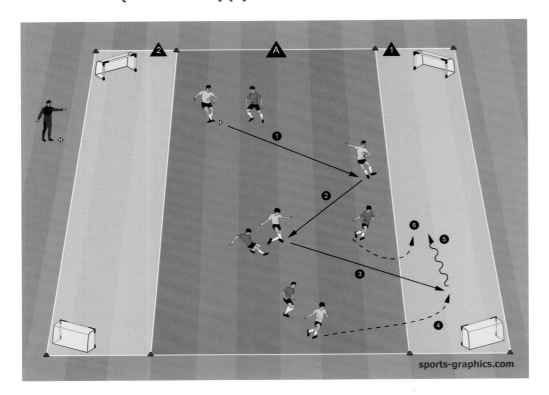

Execution

The YELLOW team plays 4-on-4 against the RED team. The teams initially play for ball holding and try to keep the ball within their own ranks (see 1 and 2) in the center field (see field A) without the opponents capturing the ball. The team in possession (here the YELLOW team) tries to play a pass into the end zones (here zone 1) (see 3). A teammate must reach the pass within the end zone with a deep run (see 4) and control it (see 5). The offside rule applies to the pass (see 3) and the run (see 4). A defender is allowed to follow into the end zone (see 6) with the pass into zone 1. The two players play 1-on-1 in end zone 1 until a goal is scored on the two mini goals or the ball leaves the field. Afterwards the coach brings a new ball into the game.

Game idea

This game focuses on getting open while moving forward. The players anticipating the ball are asked to create deep passing options (see 4). Recognizing and using gaps as well as timing and control in passing all play an important role for the passing players. Further emphasis is placed on a determined follow-up action (see 5) for an advantage in the 1-on-1 situation.

Variations

* Complete passes by hand (deep pass as ground pass).
* Players can choose end zone to play on (eliminate direction of play).
* Prerequisite for pass (see 3) into a seam (3/4/5 consecutive passes in field A).

3.6.9   4-on-4 (passes into the seam)

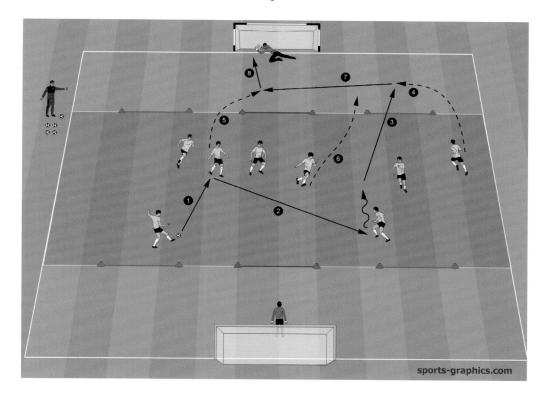

sports-graphics.com

Execution

The GRAY team plays 4-on-4 against the YELLOW team. The team in possession (here the GRAY team) initially plays for ball holding (see 1 and 2) in the center field. After a predetermined number of passes in the center field, the GRAY team tries to play a pass through a cone goal (see 3) and score on the two large goals (see 8) via additional passing options (see 7). Here all players are allowed to run out of the center field (see 4, 5, and 6) and get into offensive and defensive mode. The run out of the center field cannot be made through the cone goals and must be made in observance of the offside rule. After successfully capturing the ball, the defending team (here the YELLOW team) can attack the opposite goal. After a goal has been scored or the ball has left the field, the coach brings a new ball into the game.

Game idea

This game focuses on practicing timing and getting open to create deep passing options (see 4). Players are asked to look for forward running paths and to observe the offside rule (see 4). Additional focus is on improving coordination of passes (see 3) and running path (see 4) to facilitate optimal and goal-oriented continuing play (see 5, 7, and 8).

Variations

* Play on the far large goal after successful pass through a seam.
* Goal scored after outside play (1 point)/goal scored after play through the center (2 points).
* Prerequisite for passing into seams (2/3/4/5 passes within their own ranks without turnover).

3.6.10   5-on-5 (passes into the seam)

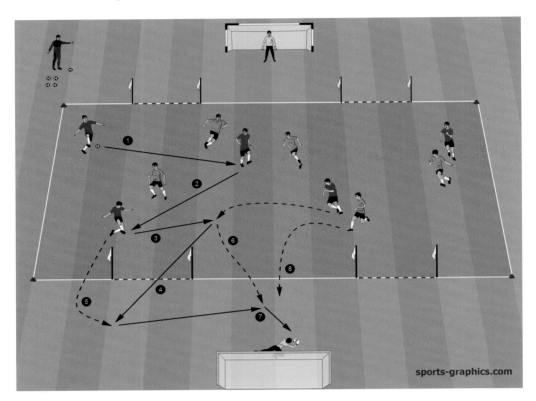

sports-graphics.com

Execution

The BLUE team plays 5-on-5 against the ORANGE team. The teams initially play in a field framed by four pole goals. There are also two goals manned with goal players centered behind the pole goals. The team in possession (here the BLUE team) prepares an opportunity for a deep pass through a pole goal (see 4) by playing passes inside the center field (see 1, 2, and 3). A teammate chases down the deep pass (see 5). The central boundary line serves as the offside line for the deep pass and the pass must be chased through a different gap (see 5). After a successful pass is played (see 4) and has been chased down, the game continues in the direction of the large goal (see 6 and 7). All players can follow into the outer field in front of the large goal (see 8). After possibly capturing the ball, the ORANGE team plays directly on the opposite large goal. As soon as the ball leaves the field or a goal is scored, the coach brings a new ball into the game.

Variations

*   Specify a mandatory number of passes (2/3/4/5 passes) prior to a deep pass (see 4).
*   Specify/choose a designated direction of play for the deep pass.
*   Play on the weak-side large goal after a successful deep pass.

3.6.11   4-on-4 plus 4 (switch of play)

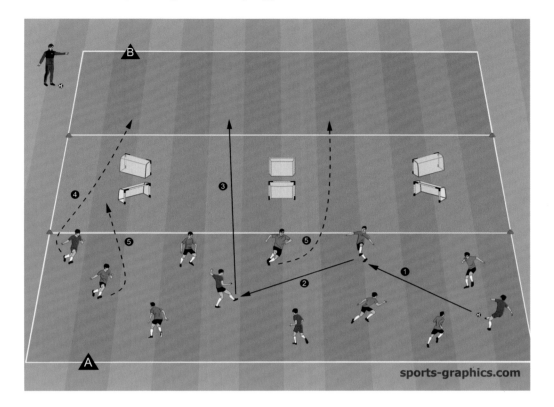

Execution

Players are divided into three teams (see BLUE, RED, and GREEN teams). The teams play 4-plus-4 against 4. Two teams always have possession together (here the BLUE and RED teams). The game begins in one of the outer fields A or B (here field A). A central zone is marked in the center and in it are several mini goals that are open to the sides. The teams in possession initially have the task of keeping the ball within their own ranks without the opponents capturing the ball (see 1 and 2). An additional goal is to play a pass between the mini goals into the opposite field (here field B) (see 3). After the pass has been played, one of the players from the team in possession can chase it down (see 4) while observing the offside rule. All players follow into the opposite field (see 5) and, after another pass in the new field (here field B), play on the three strong-side mini goals is possible. As soon as a team loses the ball in the first field (here field A) or in the second field (here field B), it immediately becomes the inferior-number team and the game continues with the initial goal of achieving the predetermined number of passes for a field change. After a goal is scored, the coach brings a new ball into the game.

Variations

* Complete with neutral players in 4-on-4 plus 4.
* Eliminate offside rule (forward running path is possible [see 4] prior to pass [see 3]).
* Optional opening of weak-side mini goals via additional field changes.

3.6.12   5-on-5 (passes into the seam and switch of play)

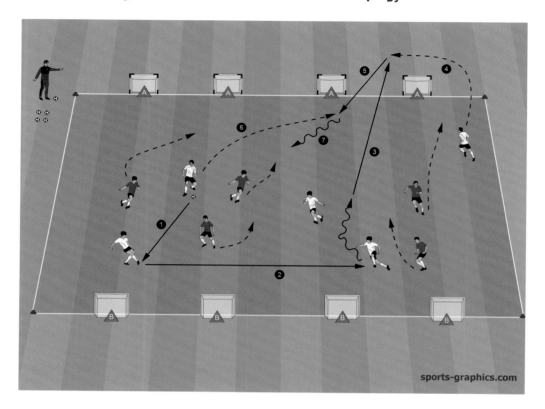

sports-graphics.com

Execution

The WHITE team plays 5-on-5 against the BLUE team. The teams initially play on a field that is framed by eight mini goals that are open to the inside (see mini goals A and B). By playing passes in the center field (see 1 and 2), the team in possession (here the WHITE team) prepares for an opportunity to play a deep pass between the mini goals (see 3). A teammate chases down the deep pass (see 4). The central boundary line serves as the offside line for the pass through the mini goals and the pass must be chased down through a different gap (see 4). After a successful pass has been played (see 3), chased down (see 4), and controlled, the game continues in the direction of the mini goals (see 5, 6, and 7). Here the team in possession attacks the opposite mini goals (here mini goals B). After possibly capturing the ball, the BLUE team attacks the mini goals A. As soon as the ball leaves the field or a goal is scored, the coach brings a new ball into the game.

Game idea

After the opening passes in the center field, the focus is on transitioning to resolve the central game situation toward the outer mini goals. Getting-open efforts and a forward running path along with coordination between passer and receiver and a goal-oriented follow-up action are practiced here.

Variations

★   Specify/choose a designated direction of play for the forward pass.

★   Play on strong-side mini goals after successful forward pass (here mini goals A).

3.6.13 4-on-4 against 3 (passes into the seam and finish)

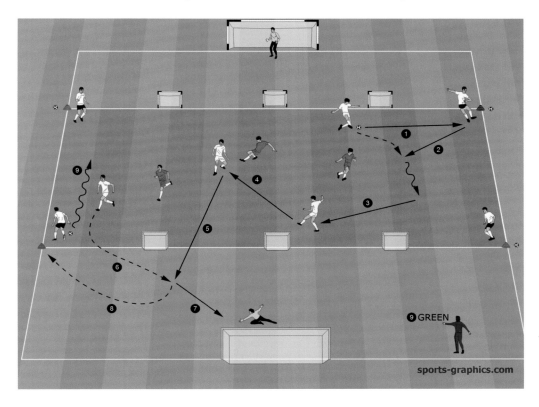

Execution

The WHITE team plays 4-on-4 against 3 inside the center field against the RED team. The WHITE team can include one of the four outside players anytime it wishes (see 1 and 2). The outside players must play direct passes. After an outside player is included in the passing sequence, the WHITE team next tries to play a pass through one of the seams between the mini goals. After including an outside player, the WHITE team can now prepare an optimal moment for a pass into the seam between the mini goals by playing additional passes (see 3 and 4). The pass into the seam (see 5) is chased down by a field player (see 6), controlled, and then exploited for a shot on the large goal (see 7). The shooter is allowed an unimpeded finish on the goal, then retrieves the ball and positions himself back at his starting position (see 8). In doing so, he chooses the position previously vacated by the player (see 9) who now completes the WHITE team in the center and was called by the coach to do so (see colored cone marker). For this purpose, a ball is positioned next to each of the four colored cone markers. After successfully capturing the ball, the RED team plays on the mini goals. After a finish, the coach brings a new ball into the game. The three RED team players change regularly.

Game idea

This game focuses on practicing getting open while moving forward. The players anticipating the ball are asked to create deep passing options (see 6). Recognizing and using gaps as well as timing and control of passes play an important role for the passing players. Further emphasis is placed on a goal-oriented shot on goal (see 7).

3.6.14   3-on-3 plus 2 (deep receivers)

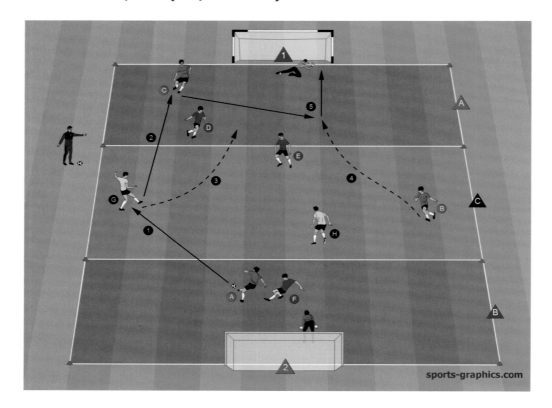

sports-graphics.com

Execution

The RED team plays 3-on-3 plus 2 against the BLUE team. The players from the YELLOW team act as neutral players for the team in possession. The RED team attacks goal 1 and the BLUE team attacks goal 2. The field is divided into three zones (see zones A, B, and C). The team in possession together with the neutral players tries to score a goal (see 1, 2, and 5). Each team must designate a player and permanently position him in the two outer zones A and B for offensive and defensive play. Players A/F can now play in zone B, and players C/D can play in zone A. Players B and E can move freely in all zones (see 4). The neutral players G and H can only move up (see 3) into the offensive zone (here A) if they have first played the pass into this zone (see 2). A goal scored by a neutral player is worth double the points. The permanent players in the outside areas and the two neutral YELLOW players change regularly.

Variations

★   Specify touches for players C and F (direct passes).

★   Prerequisite for passing (see 2) into zones A and B (direct pass).

★   Prerequisite for passing into zones A and B (include one neutral player).

★   Specify shooting technique (direct finish).

3.6.15 4-on-4 (deep receivers)

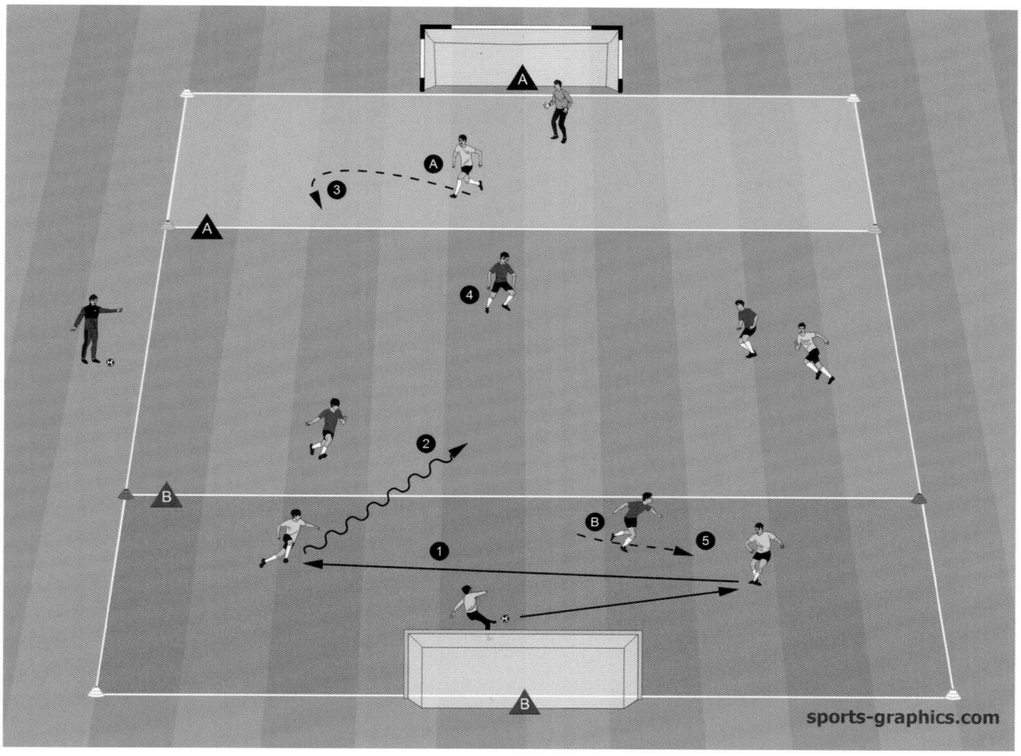

Execution

The YELLOW team plays 4-on-4 against the BLUE team on the large goals with one goalkeeper in each goal. The YELLOW team tries to score on goal A (see 1 and 2) and the BLUE team tries to score on goal B. In front of each goal is a marked zone (see zones A and B). Each team must position a player in one of the zones. The teams position their own player in the offensive zone in front of the opposing goal (see players A and B). Players A and B cannot leave the zones. All other players can run into and play on the zones without guidelines. The deep zone player from the team in possession (see player A) creates depth for his own team and tries to get open in back of the defender (see 3 and 4). When the opposing team has possession, the zone players can interfere with the opposing opening ball (see 5) until the ball leaves the zone (see 2). Zone players change regularly.

Variations

- Zone players are not allowed to finish (need to advance).
- Limit touches for zone players (3/2 touches).
- Opportunity for flying change (change zone players during active play).

3.6.16   4-on-4 plus 4 (deep receivers)

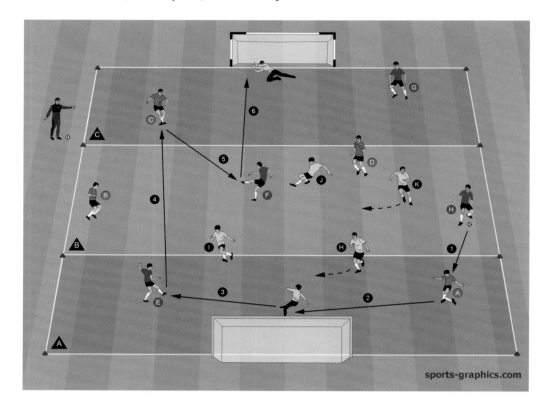

sports-graphics.com

Execution

Players are divided into three teams (see RED, BLUE, and YELLOW). The field is divided into three zones (see zones A, B, and C). Two teams always play together in possession with superior numbers (see RED team and BLUE team) against an inferior-number, chasing team (see YELLOW team). The superior-number teams in possession initially prepare by circulating the ball within their own ranks without the opponents capturing the ball (see 1). During this phase, the teams are able to include the two goalkeepers in the game (see 2 and 3). An additional goal is to play a bridging pass over the central zone (see B) (see 4) from one of the outer zones (see zones A and C). Afterwards the ball must be passed back into the central zone (see 5). Next, the finish is played from the central zone (see 6). After successfully capturing the ball, the YELLOW team can finish directly on one of the two goals. The teams' tasks change as soon as the chasing team (here the YELLOW team) has successfully captured the ball and scored a goal. The team that lost the ball becomes the chasing team.

Variations

* Limit touches (3/2 touches) for teams in possession.
* Limit touches for goalkeepers/no passes to goalkeepers (see 2 and 3).
* Specify shooting technique (see 6) after back pass (direct finish).
* Specify passing technique (see 4) for pass to switch play (direct pass).
* Opportunity to play on both goals after back pass into central zone (see 6).
* Opportunity to shoot on goal from all zones (see 6).

3.6.17 5-on-3 plus 2 (playing deep after transition)

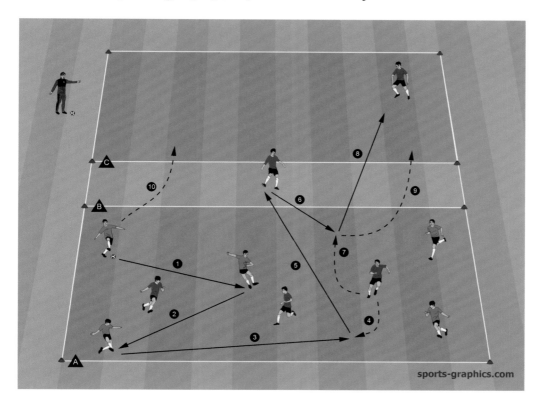

Execution

Players are divided into two teams (see BLUE and GREEN teams). One team (here the BLUE team) positions itself in field A at the beginning of the game and plays 5-on-3 for ball holding against three players from the BLUE team. The opposing team (here the BLUE team) positions itself in field A with three players and an additional player in fields B and C. The superior-number team (here the GREEN team) tries to keep the ball within their own ranks for as long as possible without the opposing team capturing the ball (see 1 and 2). After eight consecutive passes, the team in possession scores a point. The inferior-number team tries to chase and capture the ball as a team (see 4). After capturing the ball, it must be played into the opposite field C (see 8) via a forward-bounce combination (see 5, 6, and 7). After a successful pass into the opposite field (see 8), the game continues as 5-on-3 in field C. All players from the BLUE team (see 9) and three players from the GREEN team (see 10) switch to field C. Two players from the GREEN team position themselves in fields A and B. The coach brings new balls into the game for quick continuation of play. After three bad passes by the GREEN team, the coach plays a new ball into field C and prompts a field change even without a successful forward-bounce combination.

Points system

★ Complete as a competition (e.g., Which team scores the most points?).

3.6.18   4-on-4 plus 2 (play through the center)

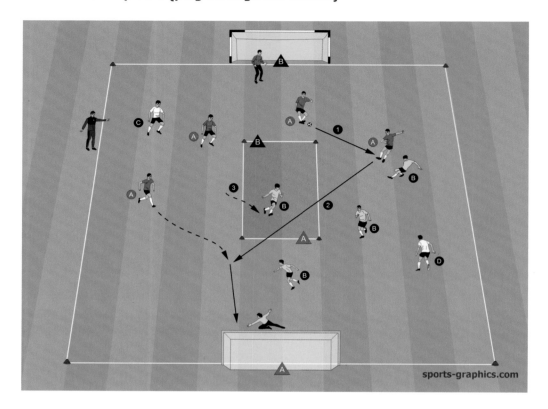

Execution

The RED team plays 4-on-4 against the YELLOW team. The RED team attacks the large goal A, and the YELLOW team attacks the large goal B. A rectangular zone is marked in the center of the field. Players can include the zone as they play on the goal and score double points, but the goal can also be played on without first playing on the zone. The zone is correctly played on when a pass is played across two lines (see 2). Here it is the far line in the direction of play that must be crossed (see lines A and B). So the RED team always plays across line A, and the YELLOW team always plays across line B. Only one player from the defending team (here the YELLOW team) can play in the zone (see 3) and run into it to prevent passes.

Variations

* Add neutral players (see players C and D) for team in possession.
* Limit touches for team in possession (4/3/2 touches).
* Limit touches for possible neutral players (direct play).

Points system

* Simple goal without playing on central zone (1 point)
* Goal after successful pass through central zone (2 points)
* Goal (direct finish) after pass (direct pass) through central zone (3 points)

3.6.19   5-on-5 (play through the center)

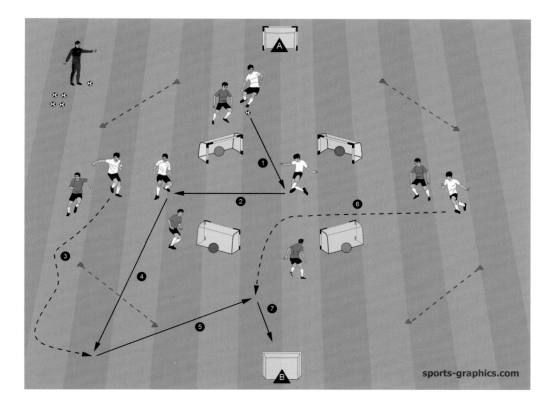

Execution

The WHITE team plays 5-on-5 against the GREEN team. Four color-coded mini goals are set up in the center of the field. In addition to the mini goals, cone goals and two additional mini goals (see mini goals A and B) in corresponding colors are set up in the outer area. The team in possession initially plays for ball holding (see 1 and 2) and tries to keep the ball within their own ranks without the opponents capturing the ball. The team in possession has the additional goal of playing on the space between the mini goals positioned in the center. The center has been successfully played on as soon as a pass is played between two mini goals or the center is bridged via a third man running (see 1 and 2). During play for ball holding, the defending team is not allowed to run through the center between the mini goals. After successfully playing on the center, the team in possession tries to play on a cone goal. The teams purposefully play on a cone goal of their choice by means of the passers playing a deep pass (see 4) to a teammate who is getting open (see 3). During the pass, the line marked by the cone goal serves as the offside line. After successfully playing on the cone goal, the game finishes on the mini goals. The team in possession can score either on the strong-side mini goal (here mini goal B) or the mini goals in the center that match the color of the cone goal (here RED). After the goal, the coach brings new balls into the game.

Variations

- ⁎ Opportunity to play on weak-side mini goal (here mini goal A).
- ⁎ Opportunity to play on both mini goals (see mini goals A and B).
- ⁎ Opportunity to play on cone goals without first playing on center.

3.6.20 4-plus-2 against 4-plus-2 (play through the center)

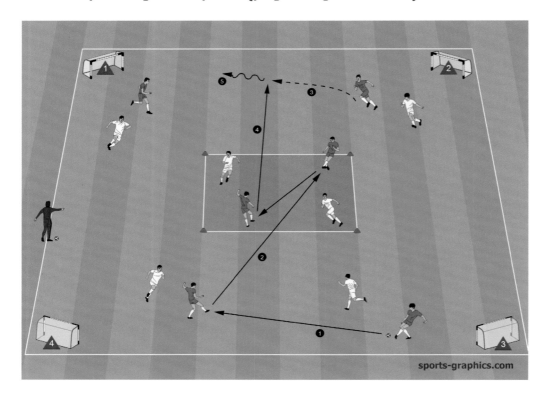

Execution

The RED team plays 4-plus-2 against 4-plus-2 against the WHITE team. Two players from each team are positioned in the center field. The players in the center field cannot be attacked. The team in possession (here the RED team) initially tries to play safe passes within their own ranks (see 1). An additional goal is to include the teammates in the center field in the passing sequence (see 2). In doing so, the two players in the center continue the passing sequence via a teammate (see 3) who makes a well-timed run to get open (see 4). The pass to the center can either be continued directly with a double pass back to the outer field or via the second center player.

Game idea

The team in possession practices patient goal-oriented possession play via the preparatory play for ball holding. The players in the center practice signaling their availability and getting open in terms of a staggered and open playing position. Diagonally staggered and deep spacing is promising for forward-bounce combinations with respect to play in the center field. The defending team practices condensing and blocking passing paths to the center as a unit.

Variations

* Preparing for tasks by passing in groups.
* Broadening via a neutral player in the center field.
* Both center defenders actively play to capture the ball.
* Opportunity to finish on mini goals after successful play on center field (see 5).
* Designate mini goals to play on (see mini goals 1, 2, 3, and 4) via coach's signal.

3.6.21 4-on-4 plus 4 (outside play)

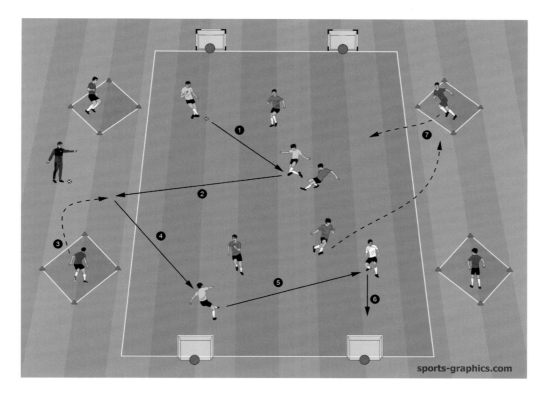

Execution

The GRAY team plays against the RED team in the center field. The center field is framed by four color-coded mini goals. Outside the field are four fields that correspond to the colors of the mini goals, and each field is manned with a player from the BLUE team. The team in possession (here the GRAY team) tries to keep the ball within their own ranks without the opposing team capturing the ball (see 1). An additional goal is to include one of the outside players in the passing sequence (see 2). The outside player must offer himself in a curved run across one of his field's back lines and can only use one touch. The outside player plays the ball directly back into the center field (see 4). Afterwards play continues on the matching-color mini goals. The GRAY team tries to score on the mini goal of the same color as the previously played-on field (see RED mini goal) via additional passing options. The team in possession also has the option of including additional outside players to facilitate play on multiple mini goals. After scoring a goal, the team that scored remains in the field (here the GRAY team) and the opposing team changes (see 7) to the outside positions (here the RED team). The coach brings a new ball into the game to the outside players who are switching to the field (see BLUE team).

Game idea

At the heart of this game is the continued play after a forward pass. The player anticipating the ball moves into an open playing position with a well-timed curved run and has the opportunity to optimally initiate a goal-oriented continuation of play.

3.6.22 4-on-4 (outside play)

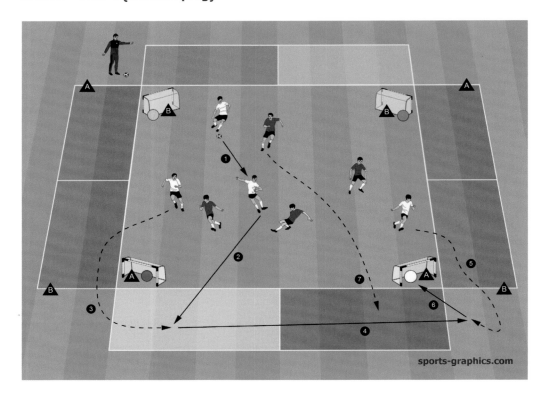

Execution

The WHITE team plays against the BLUE team initially for ball holding in the center field (see 1). In each corner of the field is a mini goal that is open to the outside. These four mini goals are marked with a letter (see mini goals A and B) as well as a color (see GREEN, WHITE, and YELLOW mini goals). Multiple marked fields (see fields A, B, WHITE, GREEN, YELLOW, and BLUE) surround the center field. The team in possession tries to play on the outer fields, thereby facilitating play on the mini goals. As soon as a field is played on, play on the corresponding color mini goals can begin. A field is successfully played on when a deep pass into a field (here the WHITE field) is played (see 2) and a teammate chases down and controls the pass with a running path through another field (see 3). Afterwards the finish on the mini goal that corresponds to the field (here the WHITE mini goal) (see 6) becomes feasible via additional passing (see 4) and running paths (see 5). After a field has been successfully played on (see 2 and 3), all players can leave the center field (see 5 and 7) and get into offensive and defensive mode. The team in possession is allowed to play on multiple fields back-to-back at any time and can facilitate play on additional mini goals. After a goal is scored, the coach brings a new ball into the game.

Variations

* Specify shooting technique (see 6) for play on mini goals (direct finish).
* Prerequisite for play (see 2) on fields (2/3/4/5 passes within the own ranks).

3.6.23 4-on-4 (handball)

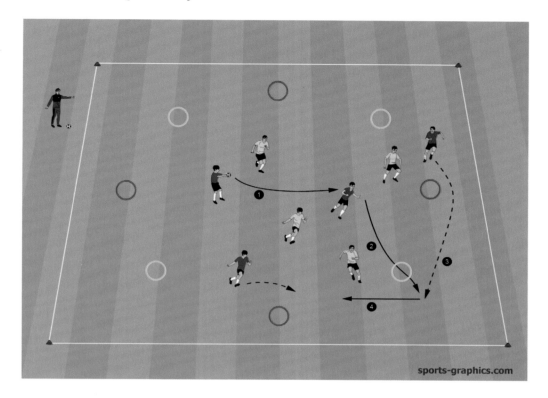

Execution

The GRAY team plays 4-on-4 against the BLUE team. The ball is played only by hand. The two teams in the field initially play for ball holding (see 1). The game's objective is to play a two-handed pass over a hoop (see 2) to an approaching teammate (see 3). Only after the subsequent pass back into the field marked by the hoops (see 4) does the team in possession score a point. If a player in possession is touched by another player's hand or the ball touches the ground, possession immediately changes.

Basic idea

This game requires the players in possession to exhibit well-timed and situation-appropriate getting-open behavior. The scoring requirements prompt forward runs. The additional rules regarding change of possession generate distinct and cross-space getting-open and breaking efforts and quick continuation of play after each received pass.

Variations

* Specify technique for ball holding (bounce/dropkick/volley/play by foot).
* Modify task with hoop (double pass around hoop/lob over hoop).
* Alternating play on hoops (RED/YELLOW).

3.6.24 5-on-5 (Frisbee)

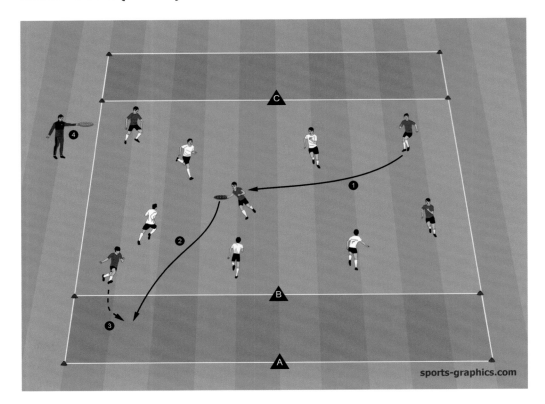

Execution

The BLUE team plays against the WHITE team. The field is divided into three fields (fields A, B, and C). The game begins in the central field B. The outer areas are divided into fields A and C. The teams play Frisbee. The teams initially keep the Frisbee purposefully within their own ranks (see 1). An additional goal for the team in possession of the Frisbee is to play on the outer fields (see fields A and C). The teams try to throw the Frisbee into one of these zones (see 2) and a teammate tries to chase it down and catch it before it touches the ground (see 3). Possession of the Frisbee changes as soon as an opposing player tags the player holding the Frisbee by hand or the Frisbee touches the ground.

Basic idea

This game requires the players in possession to exhibit well-timed and well-coordinated getting-open behavior and quick continuation of play after each received pass.

Variations

* Permanent allocation of end zones (BLUE team/field A and WHITE team/field C).
* Change direction of play after each point scored.

3.7   ACTION SPEED AND PLAYING ABILITY

Action Speed and Playing Ability includes games with complex tasks. Here the emphasis is on improving action speed and playing ability. Players learn creative playing solutions via action alternatives and practice the elements of perception, reaction, anticipation, and decision making. Games include different subtasks and playing goals with different superior- and inferior-number ratios, the use of neutral players, and changing team combinations through color-coding and changing team affiliation and orientation during offense and defense while the game is in play. Moreover, elements of spatial awareness in playing, executing follow-up actions after a signal, recognizing color signals, goal-oriented transitioning, and playing on different fields and goals are integrated with changing shooting options.

COLOR SIGNALS
ACTION ALTERNATIVES
REACTING   DECISION MAKING
PLAYING SOLUTIONS ANTICIPATING
CHANGES IN DIRECTION OF PLAY
TRANSITIONING
COLORED MARKERS ZONES
ACTION SPEED
RECOGNIZING

3.7.1 4-on-4 (lines) (1)

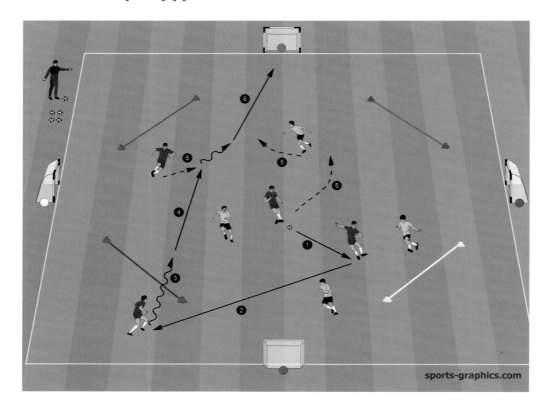

Execution

The BLUE team plays 4-on-4 against the GRAY team. On the field are four different-colored cone goals. Four corresponding-color mini goals that match the cone goals are set up in the outer playing area. The team in possession (here the BLUE team) tries to keep the ball within their own ranks for as long as possible (see 1 and 2). The team in possession must play on one of the cone goals at a dribble (see 3). After a successful dribble over a marked cone goal (here the BLUE cone goal), the team in possession must play another pass (see 4). After a successful pass following the dribble, play on the corresponding-color mini goal begins (see BLUE mini goal). All players transition for play on the mini goal (see 5). The team in possession now tries to score on the corresponding-color mini goal (see 6). The opposing players try to capture the ball so once in possession they will be able to open a mini goal after successfully dribbling through a cone goal. If the ball leaves the field or a goal is scored, the coach has the option of directly bringing a new ball into the game.

Variations

* Specify dribbling through cone goals (from outside to inside/from inside to outside).
* Raise number of mandatory passes after dribbling (see 4) for play on mini goals.
* Specify number of passes needed for play on cone goals (see 1 and 2).
* Double point score for dribbling across different lines multiple times.
* Opportunity to play on multiple mini goals simultaneously after dribbling through multiple cone goals.
* Specify shooting technique (see 6) for play on mini goals (direct finish).

3.7.2   4-on-4 (lines) (2)

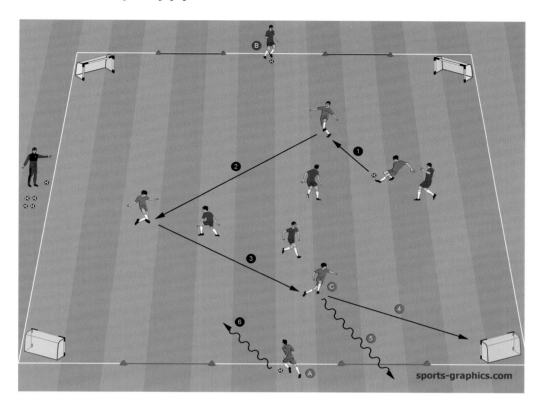

Execution

The RED team plays 4-on-4 against the BLUE team. The field is framed by four mini goals positioned in the corners. Between the mini goals to be played on are two additional cone goals marked with the same colors. A player from each team is positioned between the cone goals to be played on, with his own ball at his foot (see players A and B). The RED team in possession always plays on the two dribble and mini goals in the direction of its own outside player (see player A). The opposing team defends the four named goals and, after successfully capturing the ball, plays on the dribble and mini goals positioned next to its outside player (see player B). The task of the team in possession (here the RED team) is to keep the ball within their own ranks for as long as possible without the opponents capturing the ball (see 1, 2, and 3) and to play a predetermined number of passes. After the predetermined passes have been played (see 3), the team in possession can immediately finish on the mini goals (see 4) or dribble across a cone goal (see 5). After a team in possession has scored a point (see 4 or 5), their own outside player (here player C) starts into the field with his ball (see 6). The game immediately continues. The shooter (see player C) retrieves his ball and repositions himself at the outside position A. If a ball leaves the field or a shot on a mini goal goes wide, the coach has the option of bringing a new ball into the game. In this case, the outside players remain in their positions and don't change into the field.

Points system

* Dribble through a cone goal (1 point)/score on a mini goal (2 points)
* Back-to-back double point score without turnover (3 points)

3.7.3   4-on-4 (lines and zones) (1)

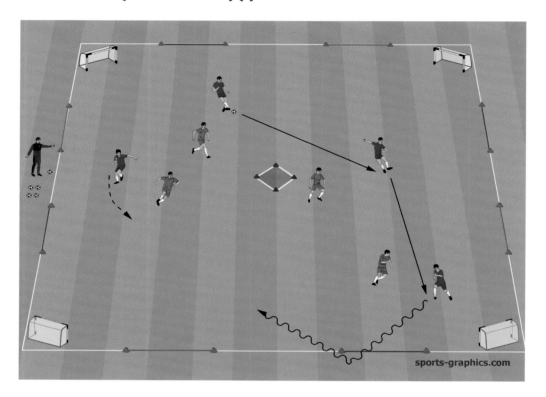

Execution

The BLUE team plays 4-on-4 against the RED team. The field is framed by four mini goals positioned in the corners. There are also cone goals that match the team colors positioned at the sidelines. The team in possession must dribble through one of the corresponding-color cone goals. After successfully dribbling through a cone goal, the dribbling player immediately returns to the field with the ball at his foot. The game continues with two new tasks. After successfully dribbling through a cone goal, the team in possession (here the BLUE team) has the option of finishing on the four mini goals. To do so, the team in possession must either play five follow-up passes within their own ranks without the opponents capturing the ball, or play on the center diamond by dribbling or with a pass. The opposing team tries to capture the ball. After successfully capturing the ball, the tasks change. If a ball leaves the field or a goal is scored on the mini goals, the coach has the option of bringing a new ball into the game.

Points system

★ Dribble through a corresponding-color cone goal with subsequent pass (1 point)

★ Score on a cone goal after five consecutive follow-up passes (2 points)

★ Score on a mini goal after follow-up play on center diamond (3 points)

Variation

★ Broaden/simplify by adding two neutral players to 4-on-4 plus 2.

3.7.4   4-on-4 (lines and zones) (2)

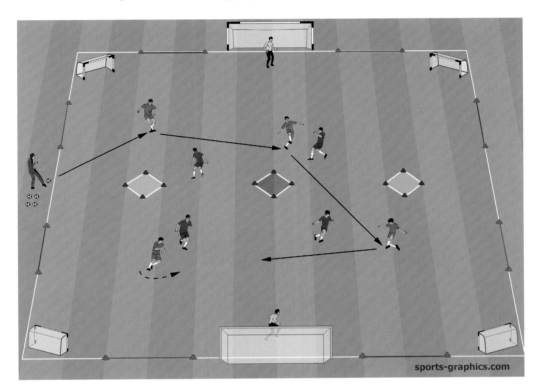

Execution

The RED team plays the BLUE team. The field is framed by two large goals manned with goalkeepers and four mini goals positioned in the corners. Positioned at the sidelines are additional cone goals that match the team colors. The coach alternates passing several balls, one by one, into the game to each team. With each new coach's ball the playing goal changes.

★   Playing goal 1: Three passes within their own ranks and subsequent play on both large goals.

★   Playing goal 2: Three passes within their own ranks and subsequent play on mini goals.

★   Playing goal 3: Three passes and play on corresponding-color dribble goals.

★   Playing goal 4: Three passes and subsequent play on center diamond fields.

Variations in play on center diamond fields

★   Dribble through the yellow diamond fields and dribble on the dribble goals of the same color.

★   Pass through the yellow diamond field and finish on mini goals.

★   Dribble through center diamond field and play on all dribble and mini goals.

★   Pass through the center diamond field and play on both large goals.

Variations

★   Include the two goalkeepers as neutral players in 4-on-4 plus 2.

★   Specify play on large and mini goals (direct finish).

3.7.5   4-on-4 plus 2 (zones and fields)

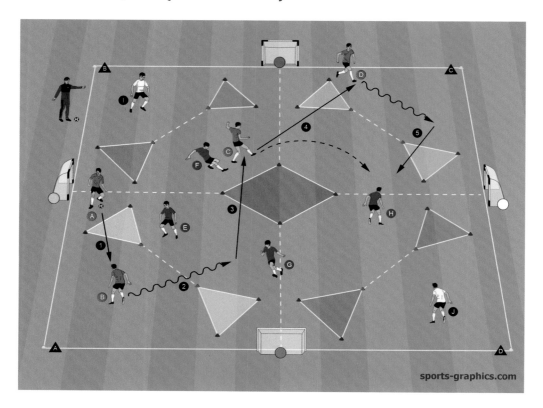

Execution

The RED team plays 4-on-4 against the BLUE team. The field is divided into four sections (see fields A, B, C, and D) and framed by four mini goals. In the center of the field is a central diamond field. In each of the four sections are two triangles that are connected by an imaginary dribble line. There are always two triangles of the same color. The far mini goals match the colors of the triangles. The team in possession tries to play on the different fields and dribble lines. In doing so, individual triangles can be played on with a pass (see 1) and individual dribble lines can be dribbled across (see 2). In addition, the teams try to play combinations on two connected triangles. Here a pass through a triangle (see 1) can be followed by dribbling across the line (see 2) or a pass through a triangle (see 4) can be followed by another pass through the second triangle of the same color (see 5). After a team has successfully played on the fields (see field A), it must next head for another field (here field C). The center diamond field can also be played on via a pass (see 3) or by dribbling. To simplify, additional players can be added as neutral players (see players I and J). Allowing play on the mini goals can modify the game. After successfully playing on the ngles, the far mini goal of the same color opens up. The players can open multiple mini goals by playing on triangles back-to-back.

Points system

* Basic play on triangles/diamond via passes (see 1 and 3) or by dribbling (see 2) (1 point)
* Combination play on triangles (see 1/2 and 4/5) via passes/dribbling (2 points)
* Goal scored on mini goal (1 point)

3.7.6   4-on-4 plus 4 (center players) (1)

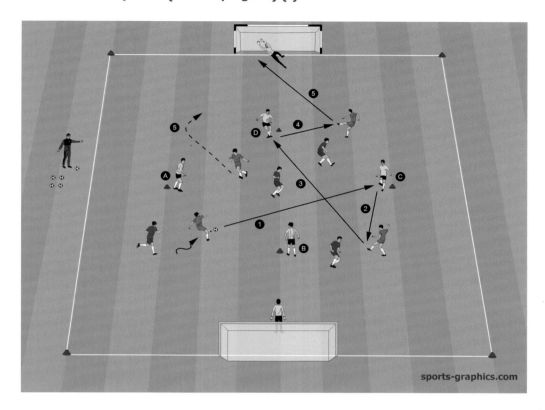

Execution

The RED team plays 4-on-4 plus 4 against the BLUE team, initially for ball holding, and then against the two large goals. To do so, the four neutral players (see players A, B, C, and D) position themselves at the four cone markers in the center. The team in possession (here the RED team) initially plays for ball holding and tries to keep the ball within their own ranks for as long as possible without the opponents capturing the ball. The team in possession has the task of including the neutral players in the passing sequence (see 1 and 2). After the team in possession has managed to involve two neutral players (see 3 and 4), play on the two large goals begins immediately. To do so, the players from the team in possession transition and try to score (see 5). The opposing team (here the BLUE team) tries to capture the ball. After successfully capturing the ball, the tasks change. If the ball leaves the field or a goal is scored, the coach has the option of immediately bringing a new ball into the game. After a goal has been scored, the team that was scored on changes to the neutral positions in the center and the four neutral players receive a new coach's ball.

Variations

* Play on large goals already after pass to first neutral player (see 1 and 2).
* Limit touches for team in possession (two touches).
* Limit touches for neutral players (direct passes).
* Specify shooting technique (see 5) for play on large goals (direct finish).

3.7.7 4-on-4 plus 5 (center players) (2)

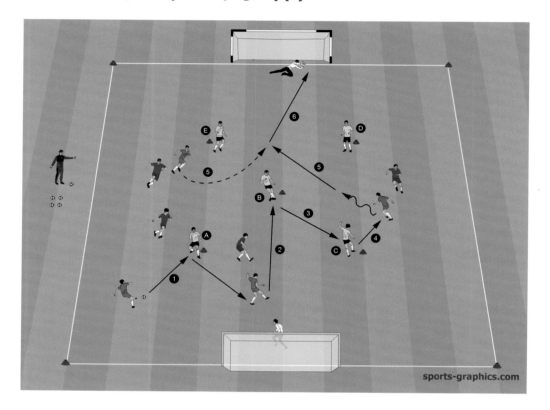

Execution

The RED team plays 4-on-4 plus 5 against the BLUE team, initially for ball holding, and then on the two large goals. To do so, five neutral players (here players A, B, C, D, and E) position themselves at the five cone markers in the center. The team in possession (here the RED team) initially plays for ball holding and tries to keep the ball within their own ranks without the opponents capturing the ball. To do so, the team in possession can include a neutral player at any time (see 1). The team in possession has the goal of including two neutral players in a row in the passing sequence (see 2, 3, and 4). After the team in possession has managed to involve two neutral players in a row, play on the two large goals begins immediately. To do so, players from the team in possession transition to offense (see 5) and try to score (see 6). The opposing team (here the BLUE team) tries to capture the ball. After successfully capturing the ball, tasks change. If the ball leaves the field or a goal is scored, the coach has the option of immediately bringing a new ball into the game. The players in the center change regularly.

Variations

✶ Additional passes within the team in possession (see 5) after the pass to the center player.

✶ Limit touches for players in possession (two touches).

✶ Limit touches for neutral players (direct passes).

✶ Specify shooting technique (see 5) for play on large goals (direct finish).

✶ Option to include both goalkeepers in ball holding for 4-on-4 plus 7.

3.7.8   4-plus-2 against 4-plus-2 (center players)

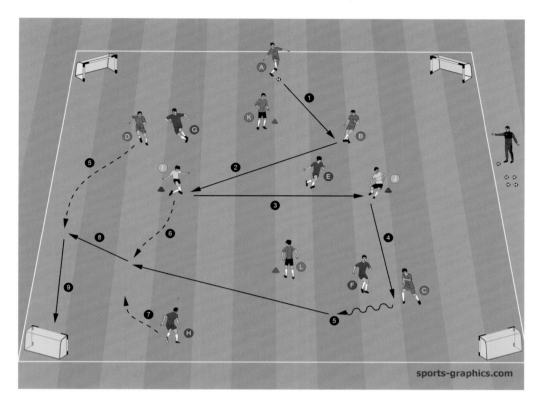

sports-graphics.com

Execution

The RED team plays 4-plus-2 against 4-plus-2 against the BLUE team, initially for ball holding (see 1). Two neutral players (see players I and J) from the RED team position themselves in the center at the black cone markers. While in possession, the teams are allowed to involve their own neutral players. For ball holding, a back pass can be played from one of the center players to one of the field players. The goal of the team in possession is to play a combination with the two center players (see 2 and 3) to one of the field players (see 4). This passing sequence involving both center players facilitates play on the mini goals (see 5). After successfully passing via the two center players, the center player who was first passed to (here player I) can join in 5-on-4 on the mini goals (see 6) and be involved in subsequent play (see 8). All players from the team in possession (here the RED team) switch to offense (see 5). Players from the BLUE team switch to defense (see 7), try to prevent a goal, and, after successfully winning the ball with their own center players (see players K and L), try to play combinations to subsequently be able to play on the mini goals. In case of a turnover, the active center player (here player I) in the 5-on-4 resumes his starting position at the cone marker. The coach brings new balls into the game and players in the center positions switch regularly.

Variations

★ Play on mini goals in 4-plus-1 against 4 already begins after pass to a player (see 2).

★ Activate the weak-side opposing pass receiver (here player K).

3.7.9   4-plus-2 against 4-plus-2 (center players)

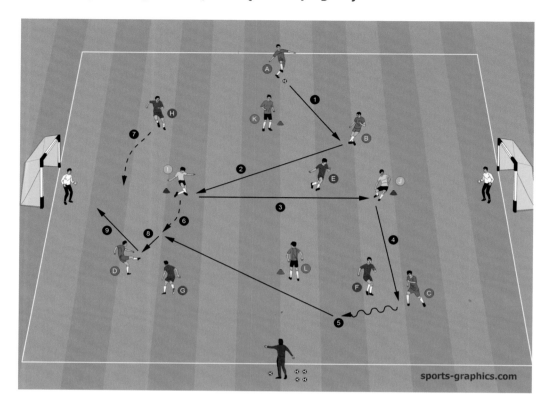

Execution

The RED team plays 4-plus-2 against 4-plus-2 against the BLUE team, initially for ball holding (see 1). Two neutral players (see players I and J) from the RED team position themselves in the center at the black cone markers. The two neutral players for the BLUE team (see players K and L) position themselves at the green cone markers. While in possession, the teams are allowed to involve their own neutral players. For ball holding, a back pass can be played from one of the center players to one of the field players. The goal of the team in possession is to play a combination with the two center players (see 2 and 3) to one of the field players (see 4). This passing sequence involving both center players facilitates play on the large goals (see 5). After successfully passing via the two center players, the center player who was first passed to (here player I) can join in 5-on-4 on the large goals (see 6) and be involved in subsequent play (see 8). The players from the BLUE team switch to defense (see 7), try to prevent a goal, and, after successfully capturing the ball with their own center players (see players K and L), try to play combinations to subsequently be able to play on the large goals. In case of a turnover, the active central player in the 5-on-4 (here player I) resumes his starting position at the cone marker. The coach brings new balls into the game and players in the center positions switch regularly.

Variations

* Play on mini goals in 4-plus-1 against 4 already begins after pass to a player (see 2).
* Activate the weak-side opposing pass receiver (here player K).
* Start a 6-on-6 situation and activate all players after ten consecutive passes.

3.7.10   4-plus-3 against 4-plus-3 (outside players)

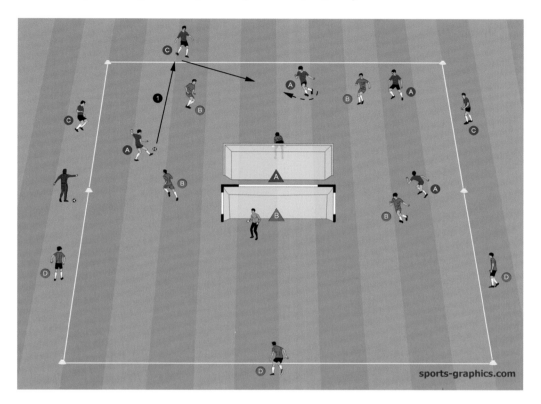

Execution

The BLUE team (see players A and C) plays 4-plus-3 against 4-plus-3 against the RED team. Two large goals are set up back-to-back in the center of the field, each manned with a goalkeeper. The BLUE team tries to score on goal A, and, after successfully capturing the ball, the RED team tries to prevent the goal and counter on goal B. The teams play 4-on-4 in the field (see players A and B). Each team has three outside players (see players C and D) in the half around the opposing goal. These outside players can be included any time in the game (see 1). The field players can use no more than three touches per action. The outside players must play direct passes. Outside players change regularly.

Variations

★   Modify guidelines for passes (open passing).

★   Prerequisite for finishing on large goals (direct pass).

★   Prerequisite for finishing on large goals (direct finish).

★   Prerequisite for pass (see 1) to an outside player (direct pass).

3.7.11   5-on-5 (outside zones)

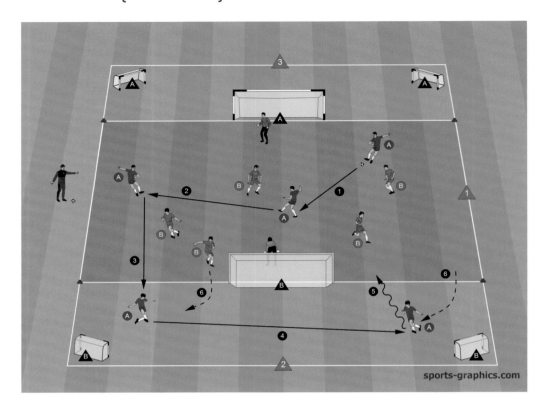

Execution

The BLUE team plays 5-on-5 against the RED team (see players A and B). The playing field consists of a central field (see field 1) with two large goals. Behind each large goal is an additional space with two mini goals (see fields 2 and 3). The teams initially play for ball holding and, after successfully completing a passing task, they have the opportunity to play on the large goals as well as the mini goals. The team in possession (here the BLUE team) tries to play six consecutive passes within their own ranks in field 1 without the opponents capturing the ball (see 1 and 2). After the team in possession has played the six passes, it can finish on both large goals A and B. During ball-holding play, players can also play any time on fields 2 and 3 behind the large goals (see 3). As soon as passes have been played all the way around a large goal outside the center field (here field 2) (see 4 and 5), players can immediately start play on the three opposite goals (here large goal A and mini goals A). All players can run into the spaces behind the large goals at any time (see 6) to play on and defend them. After a goal is scored or the ball leaves the field, the coach brings a new ball into the game.

Variations

* Only 1/2 players from defending team can run into fields 2/3.
* Prerequisite for pass (see 3) into fields 2 and 3 (direct passes).
* Prerequisite for finish on large goals/mini goals (direct finish).

3.7.12 From 2-on-2 plus 2 to double 4-on-2

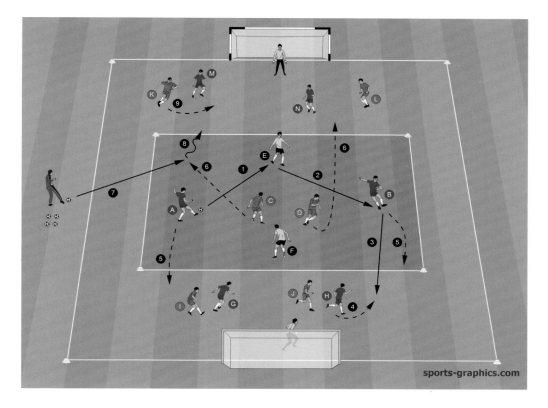

sports-graphics.com

Execution

The BLUE team plays 2-on-2 plus 2 to 2-on-2 against the RED team. Two players from each the BLUE (see players A and B) and RED team (see players C and D) position themselves in the center field. Two neutral players (see players E and F) are also positioned in the center field. The team in possession initially plays 2-on-2 plus 2 for ball holding and tries to play a predetermined number of passes without the opponents capturing the ball (see 1 and 2). As soon as the predetermined number has been reached (see 2), the team in possession (here the BLUE team) can choose a side and begins play on a large goal. To do so, the team in possession plays one of their own outside players (see 4) in front of the chosen goal (see 3). The two players from the center field move up for the 4-on-2 (see 5). After a team has played a successful pass out of the center field, the team previously playing defense (here the RED team) transitions toward the other goal (see 6) and receives a second ball from the coach (see 7). With the coach's ball, another 4-on-2 situation now starts against the other goal (see 8 and 9). After both 4-on-2 situations have ended, the coach has the option of bringing a third ball into the game for 6-on-6 plus 2. The positions of the individual teams and positions change regularly.

Variations

- Limit touches for the team in possession during opening 2-on-2 plus 2 (two touches).
- Specify passing technique (see 3) for certain passes (direct passes).
- Offensive team can move up neutral players for 5-on-2.
- Defensive team can move up neutral players for 4-on-3.

3.7.13   From 3-on-3 plus 1 to 5-on-5 plus 1

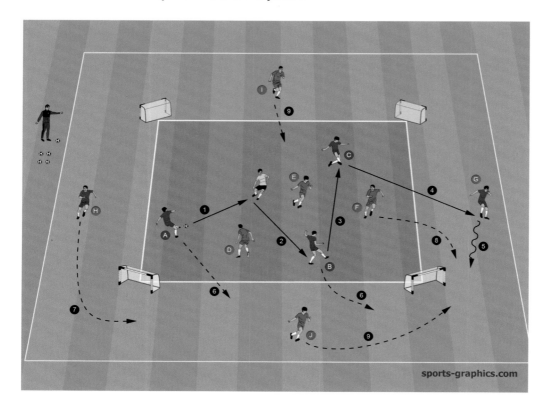

sports-graphics.com

Execution

The BLUE team initially plays 3-on-1 for ball holding against the RED team in the center field. The center field is framed by four mini goals that are open to the outside and that both teams can play on after completing a predetermined task. One neutral player positioned in the center field can be included in the passing sequence by the team in possession (see 1 and 2). The team in possession (here the BLUE team) must play three consecutive passes without the opponents capturing the ball (see 1, 2, and 3). The opposing team (here the RED team) tries to interrupt the passing sequence and capture the ball. Play on the mini goals begins immediately after the mandatory three consecutive passes by the team in possession or after the ball is captured. First a pass must be played to an outside player (here player G) (see 4). After a successful pass to an outside player, play on the mini goals begins (see 5) on the large field. The possession team's players in the center transition to offense (see 6) and the far outside player (here player H) also gets into offensive mode for play on the mini goals (see 7). The opposing team's players in the center transition to defense (see 8) and both outside players (see players I and J) also get into defensive mode (see 9). The neutral player remains in the center and can continue to be included in the game in 5-on-5 plus 1. If the ball leaves the field or a goal is scored, the coach has the option of bringing a new ball into the game. If the coach initiates a new game situation, all players return to their starting positions.

Variation

★   Modify the task in 3-on-3 plus 1 (4/5 consecutive passes/include both outside players).

3.7.14   From 3-plus-4 against 3-plus-4 to 7-on-7

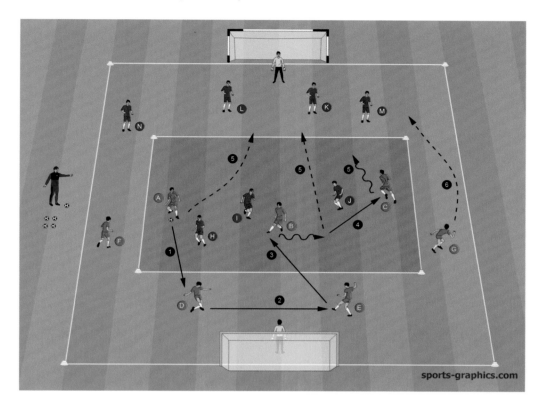

Execution

The RED team plays 3-plus-4 against 3-plus-4 against the BLUE team, initially for ball holding. Three players from each team are positioned in the center field (see A/B/C and H/I/J). Four additional players are positioned in front of their own goal (see players D/E/F/G and K/L/M/N) and occupy the positions of center backs (see players D/E and L/K) and wingbacks (see players F/G and N/M). While playing for ball holding, the team in possession (here the RED team) can include their own four defensive chain players in their own passing sequence (see 1, 2, and 3). After the team in possession has played the predetermined number of passes without the opponents capturing the ball (see 4), 4-on-4 play on the large goal begins (see 5). One wingback (here player C) from their own chain can get involved in the game (see 6). The RED team tries to push past the opposing chain and score on the large goal. The three opposing players in the center (see players H/I/J) remain in the center field and intermittently are not allowed to intervene in the playing action. As soon as the BLUE team (see players H/I/J) captures the ball in the center field, the tasks change. As soon as the defending chain captures the ball during play on the large goals, a 7-on-7 situation ensues and all players are involved. If a ball leaves the field or a team scores a goal, the coach has the option of bringing a new ball into the game. To do so, all players assume their starting positions. The positions of individual teams and players change regularly.

Variations

* Weak-side fullback (see player N) cannot intervene in 4-on-3 play.
* Option for weak-side fullback to move up for 5-on-4.

3.7.15   From 4-on-4 to 4-plus-1 against 4

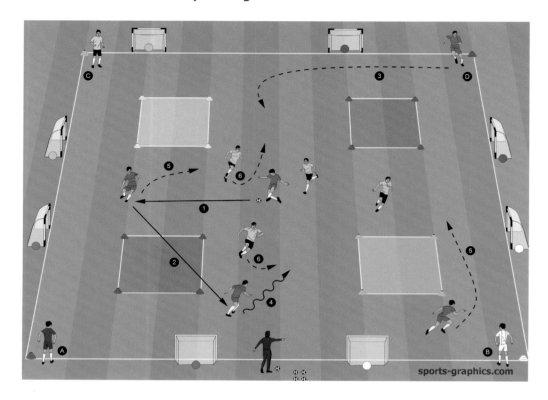

Execution

The RED team plays 4-on-4 against the GRAY team. Four different-colored fields are marked inside the playing field. Two mini goals that match the colors of the four fields are set up along each field boundary line. The corresponding color mini goals are set up diagonally across and on the far side of the fields. Four outside players that match the colors of the fields (see players A, B, C, and D) are also in position. The outside players are also positioned diagonally across and on the far side of the respective fields. The team in possession (here the RED team) tries to keep the ball within their own ranks for as long as possible without the opponents capturing the ball (see 1). The team in possession has the task of playing on a field of its choice by playing a successful pass to a teammate across two lines through a field (here the GREEN field). After a successful pass (see 2), the outside player of the same color as the played-on field (see player D) is activated and can participate in the subsequent 4-plus-1 against 4 on the mini goals (see 3). During the now ensuing 4-plus-1 against 4, the team in possession can score with a goal on the mini goals of the same color as the played-on field (here the GREEN mini goals). The player who receives the ball after the pass through the GREEN field controls the ball in the direction of play toward the mini goals to be played on (see 4). The players from the team in possession transition to offense (see 5). The opposing GRAY team tries to capture the ball in order to open two mini goals in possession after a successful pass through a field, and activate the respective outside player of the same color. After a change in possession, the outside player (here player D) resumes his starting position. If the ball leaves the field or a goal is scored, the coach has the option of immediately bringing a new ball into the game.

3.7.16   From 5-on-3 to 5-on-5

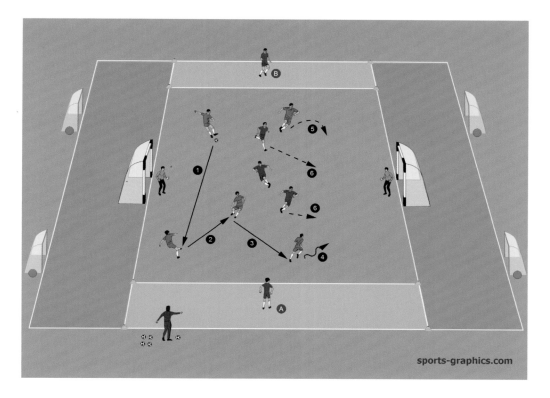

Execution

The RED team plays 5-on-3 against the BLUE team, initially for ball holding, and only in the center field between two large goals manned with goalkeepers. The team in possession (here the RED team) tries to keep the ball within their own ranks for as long as possible without the opponents capturing the ball (see 1 and 2). After a predetermined number of passes has been played (see 3), play on the two large goals begins (see 4). To do so, the offensive team players transition to offense (see 5) and try to score a goal. The BLUE team tries to interrupt the passing sequence to prevent a goal from being scored and to capture the ball. After successfully capturing the ball, the BLUE outside players (see players A and B) are activated and can intervene in the playing action and receive passes from the BLUE team. After successfully capturing the ball, play now continues also on the four mini goals behind the two large goals in an enlarged field. The BLUE team tries to score on the four mini goals in 5-on-5 play. After the RED team successfully captures the ball, the RED team again plays on both large goals. Players regularly alternate manning the outside positions (see A and B).

Variations

* Prerequisite for playing on large goals in 5-on-3 (three passes with right/left).
* Prerequisite for playing on large goals in 5-on-3 (involve all five players).
* Opportunity to include both goalkeepers in 5-on-5 plus 2 after capturing the ball.
* Continue play with same tasks after coach's ball to RED team.
* Continue play with changing tasks after coach's ball to BLUE team.

3.7.17   From 5-on-3 to 8-on-5

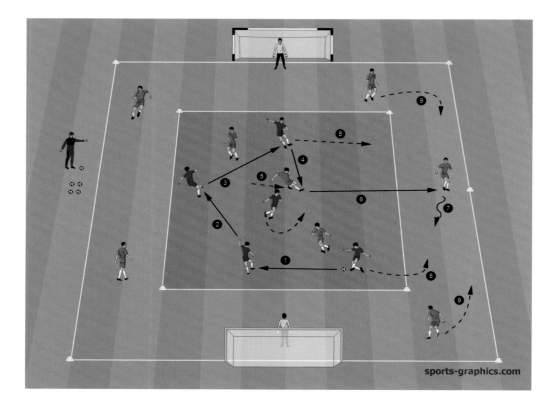

sports-graphics.com

Execution

The BLUE team plays 5-on-3-on-5 against the RED team. All five of the BLUE team players position themselves in the center field. Three of the RED team players position themselves in the center field and five other players are positioned in the large field outside the center. The game begins in the center with the BLUE team in possession. During 5-on-3 play the BLUE team tries to play as many consecutive passes as possible without the opponents capturing the ball (see 1, 2, and 3). The RED team tries to capture the ball (see 5) and play a pass out of the center field to one of their own outside players (see 6). After a pass out of the center field (see 6), 8-on-5 play on the two large goals begins. The ensuing 8-on-5 is played in the large field. To do so, the BLUE team players immediately transition to defense (see 8) and try to prevent a goal from being scored, and, after possibly capturing the ball, score a goal on the large goals. The players from the RED team now in possession transition to offense to play on the large goals (see 9), but, before they can finish, must play at least four additional passes without the opponents capturing the ball. If the ball leaves the field or a goal is scored, the coach has the option of immediately bringing a new ball into the game.

Variations

* Limit maximum number of touches for respective player in possession during 5-on-4 (two touches).
* Limit maximum number of touches for respective receiver in 8-on-5 (two touches).
* BLUE team starts play on large goals after eight consecutive passes in 5-on-3 play.

3.7.18   From quadruple 2-on-1 to 6-on-6

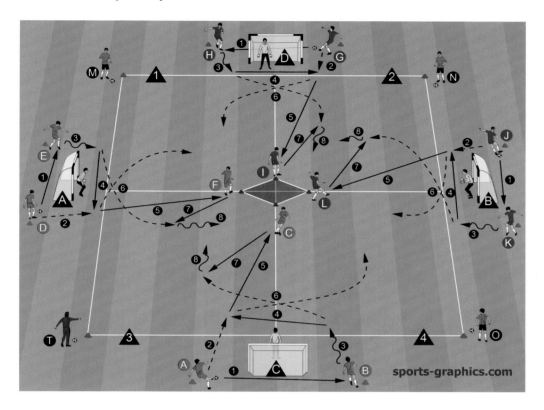

Execution

After a starting signal, four passing sequences begin. The players positioned behind the goals play combinations with the players positioned in the field. Player A plays a square pass to player B (see 1) and runs into the field (see 2). Player B controls the ball in the field (see 3) and passes to player A (see 4). Player A passes to player C (see 5). Players A and B cross running paths (see 6) and player C lets the ball bounce off into B's running path (see 7). Players A and B attack the opposite goal D in 2-on-1 play against the BLUE player I. Player C turns and becomes the defender against the BLUE players G and H, who have played through the opposite sequence. The simultaneous execution that begins at the four starting positions behind the goals creates four 2-on-1 situations. The players A and B play on goal D against player I. Players D and E play on goal B against player L. Players G and H play on goal C against player C. Players J and K play on goal A against player F. The four 2-on-1 situations end with a goal or with a defender clearing a ball into touch. After the 2-on-1-situation ends, three balls are brought into the game one after the other. Here the players M, N, and O bring their balls into the game, but remain in their wing positions and do not intervene in the game. After the end of the 2-on-1 situation, all players have the opportunity to ask for a new ball from the outside players in the order listed. In the subsequent game situation, all of the RED team players play against all of the BLUE team players and have the option of finishing on all four goals. The prerequisite is a pass across two lines of the central diamond field or four consecutive passes within their own ranks. Depending on which and how many players are involved in the new game situation after the 2-on-1 situations, different superior- and inferior-number situations will intermittently result. Finally the coach (see C) brings a last ball into the game. After each round, the outside players M, N, and O switch with another group of three.

3.8   GAME IDEAS AND RULE VARIATIONS

Game Ideas and Rule Variations introduces different game ideas and rules. This overview should be seen as separate from any particular training topic and primarily serves as a pool of ideas. The implementation of creative playing ideas and the use of different rule variations in practice games can bring variety and diversion to everyday training and can make playing and competing pleasurable.

POSITION CHANGES
GAMES OF CATCH MOVEMENT TASKS
VARIETY CHAOS GAMES
INFERIOR NUMBER SPECIALIZED PLAYERS
SUPERIOR NUMBER DIFFERENT SPORTS
CAPTURING THE BALL COMPETITIONS
NUMBERS SOCCER POSSESSION
ZONE PLAY PROVOCATION RULES
TRANSITION MOMENTS

3.8.1   Quick continuation of play

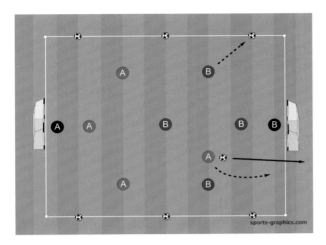

Game idea

Teams A and B play 4-on-4 on the large goals in the field. At the edge of the field are several game balls. After a finish, the game immediately continues with a new ball. To do so, one player from the previously defensive team can choose one of the balls from the edge of the field. The shooter from the previously offensive team must retrieve the used ball and place it in the now open outside position before he can come back into the game.

3.8.2   Switching players (1)

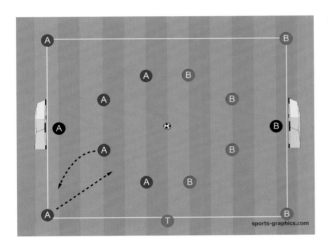

Game idea

Teams A and B play 4-on-4 on the large goals. Two other players from each team position themselves next to their own goal, but do not participate in the game. After each goal, the coach brings a new ball into the game. During the game, the coach chooses a player who must immediately trade places with one of their own outside players.

3.8.3   Switching players (2)

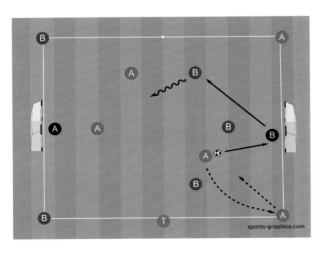

Game idea

Teams A and B play 4-on-4 in the field. Two additional players from each team position themselves next to the opposing goal, but do not participate in the game. After each finish, the shooter must immediately trade places with an outside player from their own team. The game immediately continues with the opposing goalkeeper. The team in possession after a finish can strategically use their temporary advantage.

3.8.4   Back-pass rule

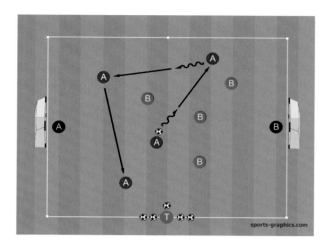

Game idea

Team A plays 4-on-4 against team B. The teams play freely without a touch limit. But after a back pass, the receiving player can use only one touch and must therefore play a direct pass. Should the receiving player use more than one touch after the back pass, possession changes immediately.

3.8.5   Possession vs. goal hunt

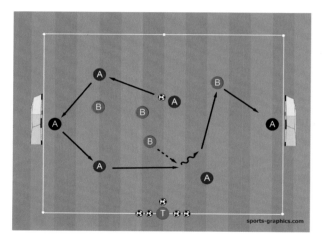

Game idea

Team A plays with the goalkeeper A against team B. Team A together with the two goalkeepers tries to keep possession for as long as possible without the opponents capturing the ball. After team B successfully captures the ball, team B can score on the goals. After team A possibly captures the ball, team A continues to play for ball holding.

3.8.6   Special tasks

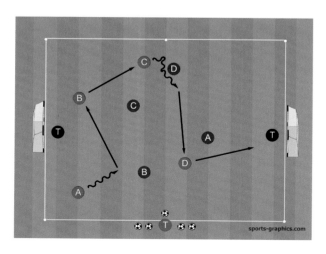

Game idea

The RED team plays 4-on-4 on the large goals against the BLUE team. Each player is given an individual task as a specialized player. Player A (dribble player) must always use three touches, player B (passing player) can only play direct passes, player C (tackling player) can score an additional point by beating an opponent in 1-on-1, and any possible goals by player D (shooter) earn double points.

3.8.7   Switching teams

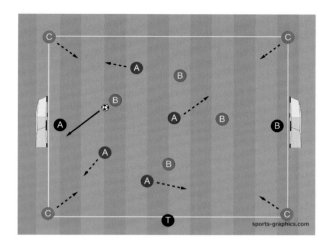

Game idea

Players are divided into three teams (see teams A, B, and C). Two teams play in the field and can include the neutral players of the third team in 4-on-4 plus 4 on the large goals. As soon as a team scores a goal (here team B), the team that was scored on (here team A) is eliminated and takes over the outside positions. The team in the outside positions switches to the field. The previously successful team remains in the field.

3.8.8   Changing teams

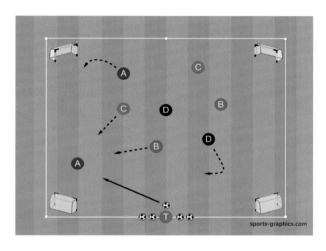

Game idea

Players are divided into four teams (see BLUE, RED, GREEN, and BLACK teams). With each new coach's ball the coach chooses two teams (here teams B/RED and C/GREEN). The chosen teams play 4-on-4 together on the four mini goals against the teams not chosen. The coach's ball always goes to the player who transitions quickest or who offers himself intelligently with a curved run or in a gap.

3.8.9   Headers

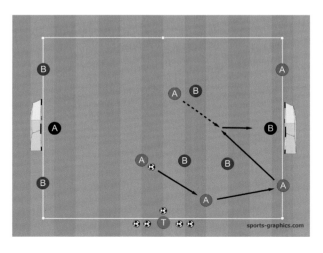

Game idea

Team A plays 3-plus-2 against 3-plus-2 against team B. To do so, two outside players from each team position themselves to the left and right of the opposing goal. The teams circulate the ball by hand, can only take three steps with the ball in hand, and can involve the outside players at any time. A goal can only be scored with the head and after a pass from an outside player. As soon as the ball has touched the ground, possession changes.

3.8.10 Netballs

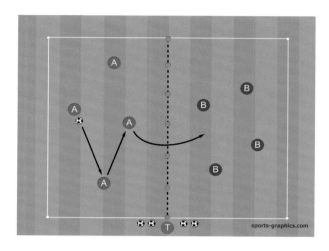

Game idea

Team A plays against team B. Each team positions itself in their own half. The halves are divided with a net. Players pass each other the ball by hand and finally throw the ball into the opposing half. The ball should make contact with the ground more than once in the opposing half. The team anticipating the ball tries to avoid a second ground contact and to catch the ball directly, or after the first time it touches the ground.

3.8.11 Passing vs. center

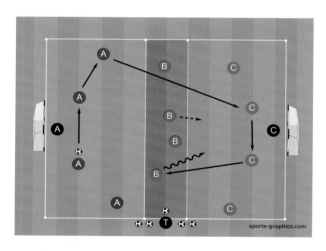

Game idea

Team A plays with team C against team B. In doing so, team A tries to play the ball through the central zone to a player from team C. Afterwards, team C tries to play the ball back to team A. As soon as a player from team B is able to intercept a pass, team B attacks on the large goal (here goal C) against the team that lost the ball (here team C). After scoring a goal, the team in the center can switch to an outside field.

3.8.12 Dribbling vs. center

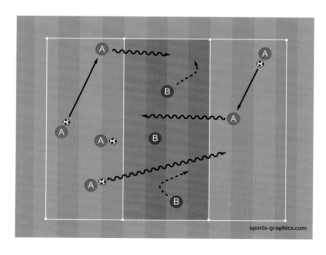

Game idea

The RED team plays against the BLUE team. The BLUE team positions itself in the central zone and tries to touch the players from the RED team with their hands. The RED team possesses several balls. Players from the RED team can pass each other their own balls in the outside zones and try to run through the central field dribbling the ball without being touched by one of the BLUE players. After a predetermined amount of time, the teams switch.

3.8.13 Number ratios (1)

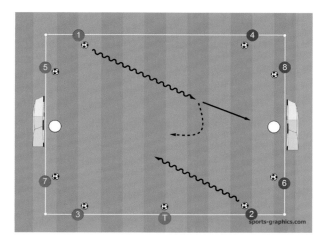

Game idea

Players from both teams are numbered consecutively. After a starting signal, the first player starts on the opposing goal with a ball at his foot for the 1-on-0. With his finish, the next player also starts with a ball at his foot to engage the previously active shooter in 1-on-1. With each subsequent finish, another player starts, so that each time a new game situation and number ratio is created all the way to 4-on-4.

3.8.14 Number ratios (2)

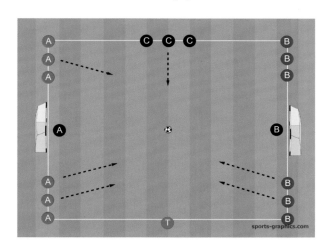

Game idea

The two teams A and B position themselves next to their own large goal. Two additional neutral players C are positioned at the edge of the field. After a starting signal from the coach, play on the large goals begins. The coach calls out three numbers at the start of each game (example: 3/2/1):

First number: Number of players team A.
Second number: Number of players team B.
Third number: Number of neutral players.

3.8.15 Number ratios (3)

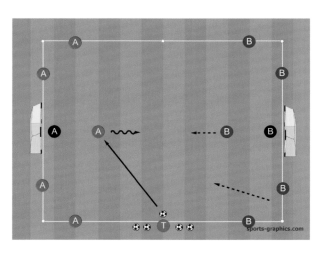

Game idea

The game begins with a 1-on-1 situation. With each finish, the coach brings a new ball into the game for either outside player A or B. With each new coach's ball, one player from each team starts into the center. After the 1-on-1, a 2-on-2 situation begins. Finally, 4-on-4 follows the 3-on-3 situation. With each coach's ball, the active players must quickly transition and, depending on possession, must get into offensive or defensive mode.

3.8.16 Game changes

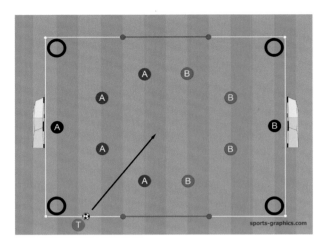

Game idea

After each goal the coach brings a new ball into the game. The game changes with each new ball:

First ball: Soccer on the large goals.
Second ball: Soccer on the dribble goals.
Third ball: Rugby on the hoops.
Fourth ball: Handball on the large goals.
Fifth ball: Soccer on the large goals and the dribble goals.

3.8.17 Obstacles

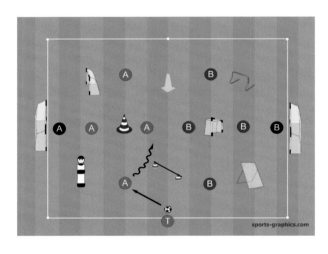

Game idea

The teams A and B play 4-on-4 in the field on the large goals. After each goal, the coach brings a new ball into the game. There are multiple obstacles in the field. Players must make clever runs around the obstacles and can use them strategically to their advantage. Obstacles can be large pieces of training equipment (e.g., rebounders) or can be marked as zones that cannot be entered.

3.8.18 Movement tasks

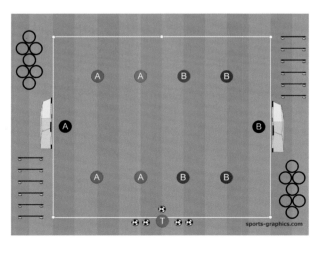

Game idea

Team A plays team B in 4-on-4 on the large goals. After each finish/goal, the goalkeeper from the team previously in possession immediately brings a new ball into the game. Depending on the finish/goal, certain players must complete movement tasks at the pieces of equipment and only afterwards can they get back into the game. When a goal is scored, an opposing player must complete a movement task, and the shooter of a missed shot must be active.

3.8.19 Training with hoops (1)

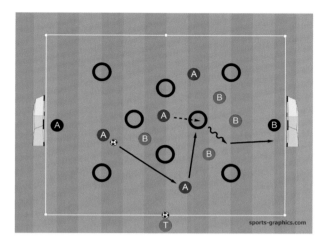

Game idea

The BLUE team plays on both large goals against the RED team. The team in possession (here the BLUE team) must have played on a hoop in order to finish on a goal. After capturing the ball, the RED team must also play on a hoop. When playing by hand, a hoop is considered played on when a player has caught the ball in a hoop, and when playing by foot, a double pass must be played over a hoop.

3.8.20 Training with hoops (2)

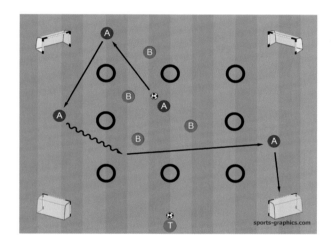

Game idea

The BLUE team plays on four mini goals against the RED team. The team in possession (here the BLUE team) must have played on the hoops in order to finish on a goal. The hoops can be played on in different ways (play from the center to the outside/play into the center to the inside/dribble to the inside/dribble to the outside/ pass across two lines/dribble across two lines).

3.8.21 Training with poles

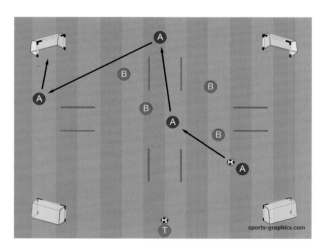

Game idea

The BLUE team plays on four mini goals against the RED team. The team in possession (here the BLUE team) must have played on the slalom poles arranged in a tube shape, before they can finish on a goal. The poles can be played on in different ways (play from the center to the outside/play into the center to the inside/dribble to the inside/dribble to the outside).

3.8.22 Target shooting

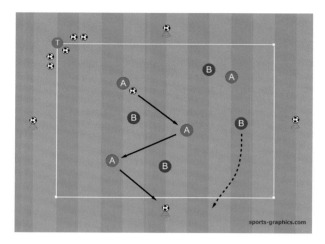

Game idea

The RED team plays 4-on-4 against the BLUE team. Next to the field are several cones, each with a ball placed on top. The teams must initially play three consecutive passes for ball holding and immediately afterwards can finish by shooting a ball off one of the outer cones with one shot (one point). The coach immediately brings a new ball into the game and after a successful shot, an opposing team player must place the ball back on the cone.

3.8.23 Play on training equipment (1)

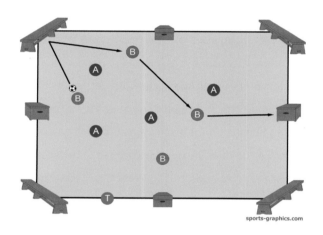

Game idea

Players are divided into two teams (see BLUE team and RED team) and play on the turned over benches in the corners or on the vaulting boxes. The pieces of equipment can be played on in different ways (double pass with a bench, play over a bench, double pass with a vaulting box, play over a vaulting box, or lob over a vaulting box to a teammate). The team in possession scores points by successfully and accurately playing on the equipment.

3.8.24 Play on training equipment (2)

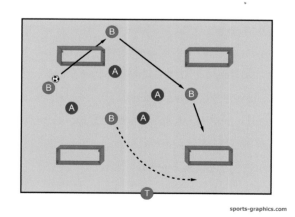

Game idea

Players are divided into two teams (see BLUE and RED teams) and play on the boxes that are positioned away from the boards. The boxes can be played on in different ways (pass through a box, lob over a box, or play a double pass off the box). The team in possession scores points by successfully and accurately playing on the boxes.

3.8.25 Handball vs. football (1)

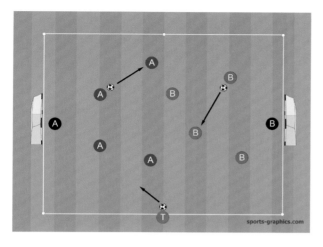

Game idea

The BLUE team plays 4-on-4 against the RED team. Each team circulates their own ball by hand within their own ranks. The coach brings a game ball into the game. The teams try to score on the opposing goal with the coach's ball. In doing so, only the player who simultaneously holds their own ball in his hand is allowed to finish. Any shooter must simultaneously have a ball in his hand and possess the game ball for the finish.

3.8.26 Handball vs. football (2)

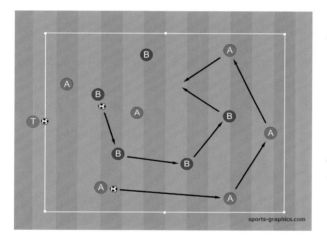

Game idea

The BLUE team plays 4-on-4 against the RED team. The RED team plays for ball holding with their own ball. The BLUE team plays with their own ball with both hands. Players from the BLUE let their own ball circulate by hand so they can bring down the RED team's game ball. As soon as the balls touch, the tasks change. The players from the BLUE team can only take three steps while in possession of their own ball.

3.8.27 Seeking the ball vs. stealing the ball

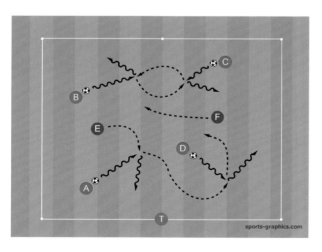

Game idea

Players play individually and freely in a field. At first several players have a ball (see players A, B, C, and D) and some players do not have a ball (see players E and F). The players with a ball dribble openly around the field. At a signal from the coach, all players leave their balls. Now all players try to pick up and take possession of a now open ball. For the new action, two players will not possess a ball (see players D and F).

3.8.28 Superior-number game of catch (1)

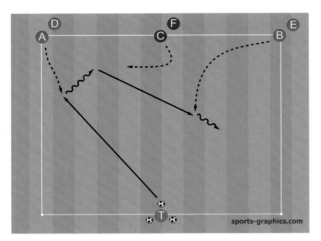

Game idea

The game starts with a ball from the coach to player A or B (here player A). All three players run into the field. The team in possession (here players A and B) tries to play a pass. The receiving player must control the ball and get another touch on the ball. The opposing player (see player C) ends the game with a simple touch. After a touch on the ball by player C or two touches by player B, a new action begins immediately.

3.8.29 Superior-number game of catch (2)

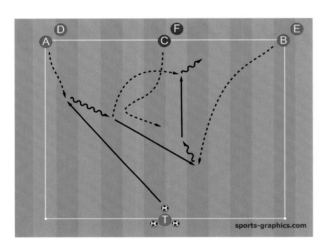

Game idea

The game starts with a ball from the coach to player A or B (here player A). All three players run into the field. The team in possession (here players A and B) tries to play two passes. The opposing player (here player C) ends the game with a simple touch. To modify, the sequence can start with a player already in possession.

3.8.30 Superior-number game of catch (3)

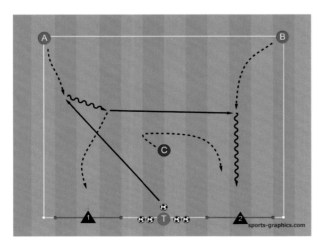

Game idea

The coach brings a ball into the game for player A or B (here A). Players A and B try to run into the cone goals 1 and 2 (one point) without getting tagged by central player C's hand. Players A and B can play passes to each other. Player C can tag the player in possession (two points) or the player without a ball (one point). Starting positions change regularly.

3.8.31 Chaos

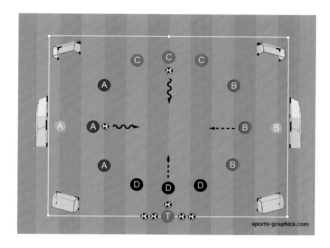

Game idea

Team A plays against team B on the large goals manned with goalkeepers. At the same time, team C plays against team D on the mini goals in the same field. After a goal is scored or a ball leaves the field, the coach brings in new balls for both games and the players transition accordingly.

3.8.32 Goal change

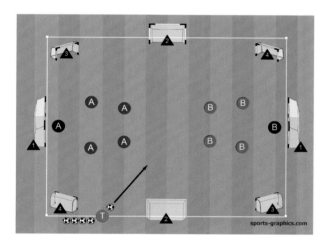

Game idea

The BLUE team plays on different goals (see goals 1, 2, 3, and 4) against the RED team. With each new ball the coach plays into the game, he designates the goals to be played on with that ball. By designating other goals during active play, the coach has the option of prompting a transition. To modify, the goalkeeper can defend the respective goals to be played on and as a result must also transition.

3.8.33 Staggered goals

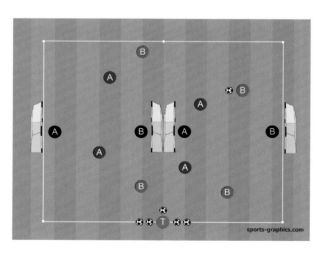

Game idea

Team A plays against team B. Each team attacks two goals and must defend two goals. Team A attacks both goals B and team B attacks both goals A. The teams try to score on the outside goals (one point) or the central goals (two points). After a goal is scored or a ball leaves the field, the coach brings a new ball into the game.

3.8.34 Hexagonal game (1)

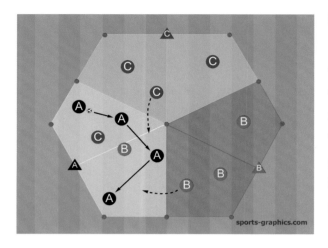

Game idea

Players are divided into three teams of four players each (see teams A, B, and C). The field is divided into different areas. Each team is assigned a field with the same name. Two players from each team must remain in their own field (see teams B and C). Each team has the goal of keeping the ball within their own ranks for as long as possible and to play as many passes as possible in their own field (see team A in field A).

3.8.35 Hexagonal game (2)

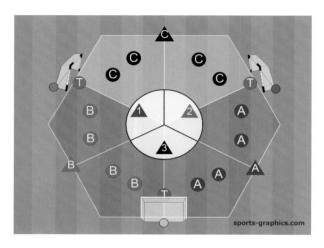

Game idea

Players are divided into three teams of four players each (see teams A, B, and C). The coach brings a ball into the game and picks two teams who will play against each other in 4-on-4 plus three goalkeepers. After three passes in their own field, the team in possession can attack the corresponding-color large goals in the own field. Goals scored after dribbling through their own center field score double points.

3.8.36 Hexagonal game (3)

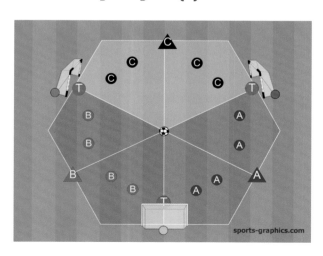

Game idea

Players are divided into three teams of four players each (see teams A, B, and C). Each team is assigned a field (see fields A, B, and C). A large goal of the same color as the field is set up on the opposite side of each field. The coach brings a ball into the game and picks two teams who will play against each other in 4-on-4 plus three goalkeepers. After three passes in their own field, the respective team in possession can attack the large goal that matches the color of their own field.

3.9 PLAYING FIELDS AND ZONE RULES

Playing Fields and Zone Rules introduces different game ideas and rules of play geared toward realistic playing field zones. Games are characterized by the marking of different fields and zones. The arrangement of the zones and the partitioning of the fields are based on the different technical and tactical training goals. The key training aspects are differentiated and enhanced in conjunction with the rules for playing on these zones.

DRIBBLE LINES
GOAL ARRANGEMENT PLAYING FIELD ZONES
ZONE RULES PROVOCATION RULES
LARGE GOALS FIELD MARKINGS
MINI GOALS POINTS SYSTEM
FINISHES POSSESSION
PASSING FIELDS

3.9.1   Hexagon (1)

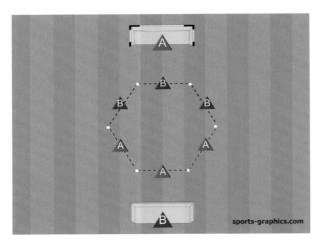

Game idea

A hexagon is marked in the center of the field. In the outer area are two large goals (see goals A and B) that match the colors of the connecting lines of the hexagon. By playing on the hexagon's lines (dribble or pass), players can subsequently play on the large goals of the same color. After correctly playing on a red/blue line, players can then play on the appropriate far large goal A/B.

3.9.2   Hexagon (2)

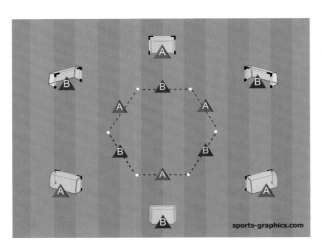

Game idea

A hexagon is marked in the center of the field. In the outer area are six mini goals (see mini goals A and B) that match the colors of the connecting lines of the hexagon. By playing on the hexagon's lines (dribble or pass), players can subsequently play on the mini goals of the same color. After correctly playing on a red/blue line, players can then play on one of the mini goals A/B.

3.9.3   Hexagon (3)

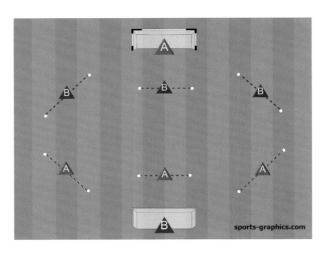

Game idea

Two sets of three color-coded cone goals are set up in the center of the field. Two large goals (see goals A and B) that match the colors of the cone goals (see lines A and B) are set up in the outer area. By playing on the individual lines (dribble or pass), players can subsequently play on the large goals of the same color. After correctly playing on a red/blue line, players can then play on the far large goal A/B.

3.9.4   Hunt for points (1)

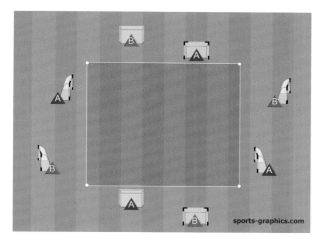

Game idea

Several mini goals are set up around a central field. The mini goals open in different directions. Two teams play for ball holding in the central field and try to play a predetermined number of passes. Afterwards players can finish on the mini goals A and B. Shots can be taken on the mini goals A that open to the inside (1 point) or the mini goals B that open to the outside (2 points).

3.9.5   Hunt for points (2)

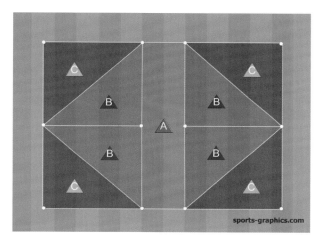

Game idea

The field is divided into several zones (see zones A, B, C, and D). Two teams play for ball holding on the same field while trying to prevent the opponents from capturing the ball. In addition, the teams play freely on the different zones. A player can score a point by playing four touches back-to-back. Teams score points for successfully playing on the zones: zone A (3 points), zone B (2 points), zone C (1 point).

3.9.6   Hunt for points (3)

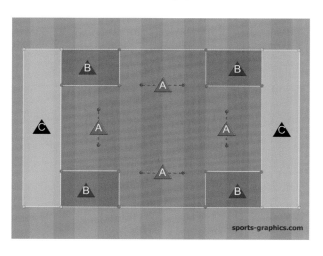

Game idea

The field is divided into several zones and dribble lines (see lines A and zones B and C). Two teams play on the entire field with the goal of holding on to the ball without the opponents capturing it. In addition, the teams play freely on different zones and lines. A player scores a point by crossing a dribble line A (1 point) with the ball at his foot, by playing two passes in zones B (2 points) or three passes in zones C (3 points).

3.9.7 Playing deep (1)

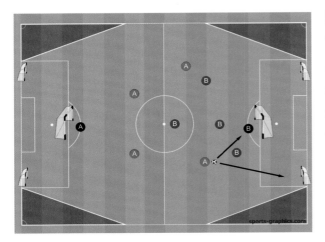

Game idea

Teams A and B have the option of attacking a large goal and two mini goals positioned farther back and to the sides. All players can run into and play on the playing zones behind the large goals on both sides. This applies to offensive play as well as the game start in their own half.

3.9.8 Playing deep (2)

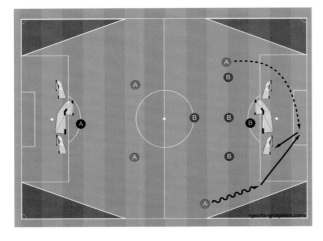

Game idea

Teams A and B have the option of attacking a large goal and two mini goals on either side that are open to the back. All players can run into and play on the playing zones behind the large goals on both sides. This applies to offensive play as well as the game start in their own half.

3.9.9 Time limit

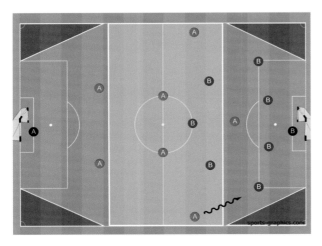

Game idea

Teams A and B play on the large goals. A zone is marked in the center of the field. As soon as a player from the team in possession has offensively played across that zone by dribbling or passing in the direction of play, the shot on goal must be taken within the next five seconds. If the attacking team does not finish within five seconds, possession changes immediately.

3.9.10 Realistic zones (1)

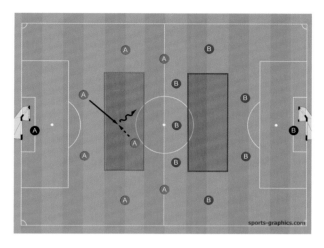

Game idea

Teams A and B play on the large goals. A central zone is marked in each half. By having a player from the team in possession receive a pass inside the zone, control the ball in the zone, open up, and continue play, the teams can successfully play on this zone during offensive play. A goal scored after a play during which the zone was successfully played on scores double points.

3.9.11 Realistic zones (2)

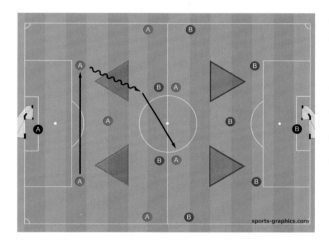

Game idea

Teams A and B play on the large goals. Two zones are marked in each half. The teams can successfully play on these zones as part of the game start by having a player from the team in possession dribble through the zone and subsequently continue the game. A goal scored after a play during which the zone was successfully played on scores double points.

3.9.12 Realistic zones (3)

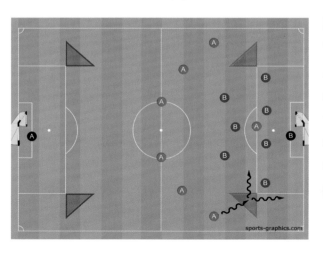

Game idea

Teams A and B play on the large goals. Two zones are marked in each half. The teams can successfully play on these zones during offensive play by having a player from the team in possession dribble through the field and subsequently continue the game. A goal scored after a play during which the zone was successfully played on scores double points.

3.9.13 Playing via outside players (1)

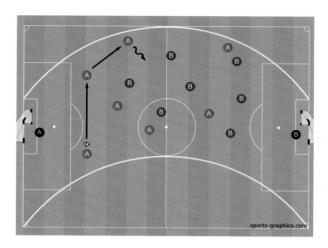

Game idea

Teams A and B play on the large goals. The playing field is bent and excludes the central area on one side and the corners on the other side. For the teams, the game switches accordingly to one side. In possession, team A is forced to play on the left side, and defends against the ball on the left. Team B in possession plays on the right and also defends to the right.

3.9.14 Playing via outside players (2)

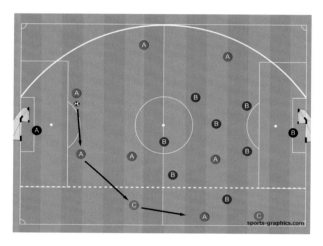

Game idea

Teams A and B play on the large goals. The field is bent on one side and the corners are cut off accordingly. There are two neutral players (see players C) in the outer area on the other sides that can be included in play by both teams. The system allows the team in possession to create a major advantage in the outside lane without giving up passing opportunities for a switch of play to the weak side.

3.9.15 Playing via outside players (3)

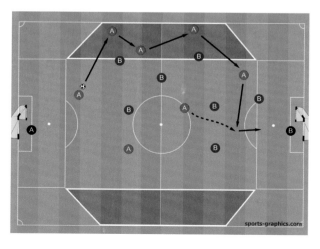

Game idea

Teams A and B play on the large goals. There are two marked zones in the outer areas of the field. The teams in possession can successfully play on these zones during build-up by playing two (3/4) passes in this zone. A goal scored after a play during which the zone was successfully played on scores double points. Triple points are awarded to the team that plays on both zones during an attack (switch of play).

4 COMPETITIVE GAMES

Competitive Games includes the key subjects of 1-on-1, 2-on-2, and team against team, and comprises many different games, relays, and technical contests with a competitive character. Here the focus is on building a fundamentally performance-oriented training and playing attitude and developing a success-oriented competitive mindset. Depending on its direction and support, the direct athletic competition with teammates aims to generate increased motivation, dedication, a willingness to take risks, self-confidence, accountability, perseverance, success orientation, a winning mentality, and team spirit.

OFFENSIVE BEHAVIOR
GAME SITUATIONS **TACKLES**
GROUP TACTICS TRANSITIONS
INDIVIDUAL TACTICS LOSING COMPETITIONS
DEDICATION OPPONENT PRESSURE COURSES OF ACTION
TECHNICAL COMPETITIONS ACHIEVEMENT ORIENTATION
WINNING TIME PRESSURE DEFENSIVE BEHAVIOR
POINTS SYSTEMS MOVEMENT COMPETITIONS
PERSEVERANCE

4.1 1-ON-1

1-on-1 includes competitive games to improve tackling skills in defensive and offensive play. The players are supposed to develop a responsible attitude, perseverance, and passion. A defensive role requires steadiness, fair toughness, and physical play. An offensive role requires courage, a willingness to take risks, and creativity. Moreover, the training exercises are specifically geared toward coaching defensive and offensive behaviors in 1-on-1 play. While defensive actions include elements such as a lateral defensive position, low center of gravity, decreasing distance, picking up the pace, and capturing the ball, offensive play focuses on using feints, increasing tempo, changing direction, and purposefully moving toward the goal.

CENTER OF GRAVITY
PASSING TASKS REORIENTATION
STANDING UP TO THE OPPONENT TACKLING
OPPONENT PRESSURE PLAYING SOLUTIONS
INDIVIDUAL TACTICS DEFENSIVE ACTIONS
CONTROLING THE OPPONENT CAPTURING THE BALL
OFFENSIVE ACTIONS RUNNING TASKS
RUN UP POINTS SYSTEM
TRANSITIONING
FINISHING ABILITY TIME PRESSURE
OPPONENT DISTANCE LATERAL POSITION

4.1.1   1-on-1 after running path

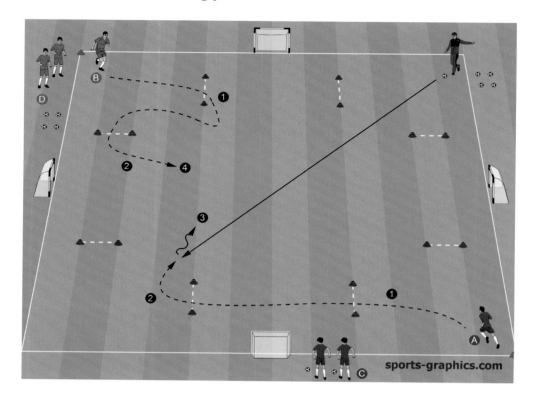

Execution

A 1-on-1 situation ensues in a field bounded by four mini goals. The goal of every 1-on-1 is to score on one of the mini goals. To do so, both players must first complete a running task through the cone goals set up in the field before they can receive the coach's pass for the 1-on-1. After a starting signal, players A and B simultaneously run into the field and through two cone goals of their choice (see 1). Once the players have run through the second cone goal (see 2), the coach brings a ball into the game, which will start the immediately following 1-on-1 situation. In doing so, the coach has the option of varying the passes. The pass receiver settles the pass (see player A and 3). The player who did not receive the pass reacts and gets into defensive mode (see player B and 4). Before the players can finish on a mini goal from 1-on-1, they must dribble through a mini goal. After that they can finish on one of the four mini goals. Player B tries to capture the ball and, after successfully doing so, tries to also dribble through a mini goal and finish. Whenever a 1-on-1 ends with a goal in one of the mini goals, two new players start (see players C and D).

Variations

* Lengthen the running path prior to receiving the ball (3/4 cone goals).
* Ramp up the task before the finish (dribble through 2/3 cone goals).
* Modify the running tasks (backwards/skip/180° pivot in cone goal).
* Start by dribbling the ball and finish on a mini goal before the coach's ball.
* Specify player A's running path (mirror-reverse execution of running path by player B).
* Modify coach's ball (pass to the faster player/hip-high pass.

4.1.2   1-on-1 after dribbling (1)

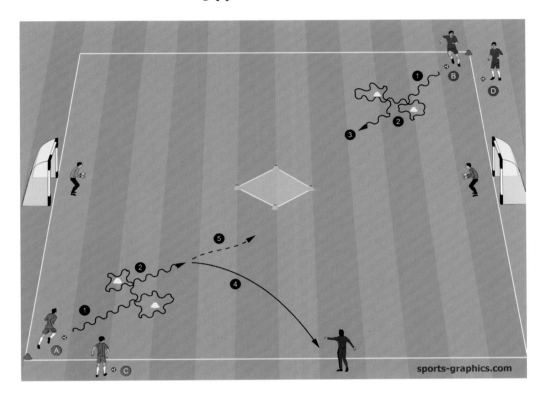

Execution

After a predetermined opening technique in the form of a dribbling and passing task, a 1-on-1 situation on both large goals ensues. At a signal from the coach, players A and B simultaneously start their actions. Players A and B dribble into the field (see 1) and must dribble a figure eight around the two cone goals directly in front of them (see 2). The coach names the faster player (here player B), who dribbles further into the field (see 3) and remains in possession for the subsequent 1-on-1. The slower player (here player A) passes his ball outside to the coach (see 4) and runs into the field without a ball for the 1-on-1 (see 5). Player B now tries to score on the large goal. Player A tries to prevent the goal from being scored. As soon as a player in possession dribbles through the central diamond field, he has the opportunity to finish on both goals. After the 1-on-1 situation ends, the coach plays the second ball into the field for another 1-on-1. Next, players C and D start a new action.

Points system

* Goal scored on large goal by opponent (1 point)
* Goal scored on large goal after turnover (2 points)
* Goal scored on large goal after dribbling through the central diamond field (3 points)

Variations

* Specify playing leg for dribble task (left/right/strictly alternate).
* Modify dribble task (change cone arrangement to slalom).
* Modify coach's ball (hip-high/high/hard pass).

4.1.3   1-on-1 after dribbling (2)

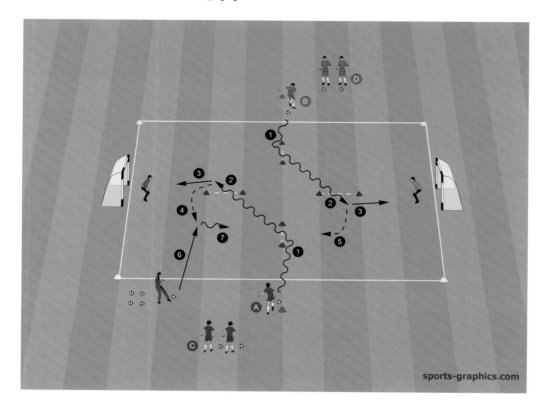

Execution

After a predetermined opening technique in the form of a dribbling and passing task, a 1-on-1 situation on the large goals ensues. After a signal from the coach, players A and B simultaneously start their actions. Players A and B dribble into the field (see 1) and must dribble through two cone goals in a row with the ball at their foot (see 1 and 2). After players A and B have dribbled through the two cone goals (see 2), both players finish on the large goal and try to score (see 3). The faster player (here player A) transitions right after his shot and runs into position for a subsequent pass from the coach (see 4). The slower player (here player B) also transitions after his shot (see 5) and gets into defensive mode for the subsequent 1-on-1. The coach passes a new ball to the faster player (see 6). The faster player (here player A) controls the ball (see 7) and tries to score on the large goal from 1-on-1 play. Player B tries to prevent a goal from being scored and, after possibly capturing the ball, also tries to score on the opposite large goal. After the 1-on-1 ends, players C and D start a new action.

Variations

★   Ramp up task prior to finish (dribble through 3/4 cone goals).

★   Specify a technical task after receiving the ball (see 7) prior to 1-on-1 (dribble through cone goal).

★   Specify dribbling (see 1 and 2) prior to finish (left/right/strictly alternate).

★   Ramp up technical task (see 1 and 2) prior to finish (feint at cone goal).

★   Modify coach's ball (hip-high/high/hard pass).

4.1.4   1-on-1 after running path and dribbling (1)

Execution

A 1-on-1 situation ensues in a field bounded by four mini goals. The goal of every 1-on-1 is to score on one of the mini goals. In doing so, the shooters can only finish on certain mini goals. The RED players (see players A) can only finish on the two RED mini goals and the BLUE players (see players B) can only finish on the two BLUE mini goals. Player A begins with the ball at his foot and dribbles through the cone goal marked directly in front of him (see 1), and afterwards dribbles into the field for the 1-on-1 situation (see 2). Player B starts with A's first touch and does a curved run through the cone goal marked in front of him (see 3), and then on into the field (see 4). Player A tries to score on the two RED mini goals. Player B tries to prevent a goal from being scored and, after possibly capturing the ball, plays on the BLUE mini goals. Whenever a 1-on-1 situation ends with a goal in one of the mini goals, two new players start (see players C and D). After a while the teams switch starting positions to play offense as well as defense.

Variations

* Opportunity to finish on all four mini goals after dribbling through the center field.
* Modify opening run (180° turn/forward roll/backwards run/cross running paths).
* Modify opening technique (180° turn/feint/switch feet/fake pass).

4.1.5   1-on-1 after running path and dribbling (2)

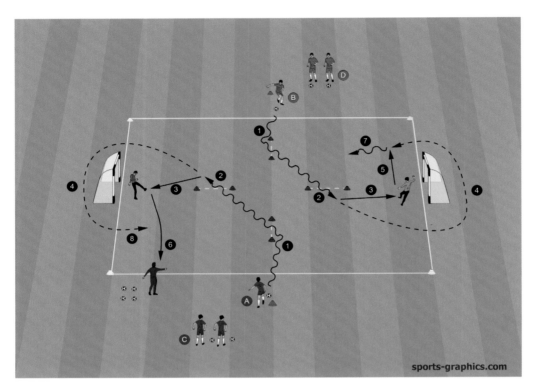

Execution

After a predetermined opening technique in the form of a dribble task and specific running paths, a 1-on-1 situation on the large goals ensues. With a signal from the coach, players A and B simultaneously start their actions. Players A and B dribble into the field (see 1) and must dribble through two cone goals in a row with the ball at their foot (see 1 and 2). After players A and B have dribbled through two cone goals (see 2), they pass their ball to their own goalkeeper (see 3). Then they immediately run around their own large goal (see 4). The faster player (here player B) is now in possession for the subsequent 1-on-1 and receives the pass from the coach (see 5). The slower player's (here player A) goalkeeper passes his ball outside to the coach (see 6). Player B controls the ball (see 7) and tries to score on the opposite large goal during the subsequent 1-on-1. Player A runs farther into the field (see 8) and tries to prevent a goal from being scored and, after possibly capturing the ball, also tries to score on the opposite large goal. After the 1-on-1 situation ends, both players again transition toward the coach and receive the second ball (see 6) for another 1-on-1. After the second 1-on-1 ends, players C and D start a new action.

Variations

* Ramp up task prior to finish (dribble though 3/4 cone goals).
* Specify technical task after receiving the ball (see 5) prior to 1-on-1 (dribble through cone goal).
* Specify dribble (see 1 and 2) prior to finish (left/right/strictly alternate).
* Ramp up technical task (see 1 and 2) prior to finish (feint at cone goal).

4.1.6   1-on-1 after passing sequence

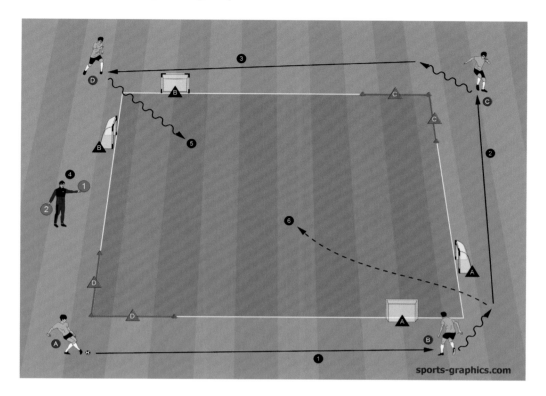

Execution

Players A, B, C, and D complete a predetermined passing sequence around a central field. After a signal from the coach, a situation-dependent 1-on-1 situation ensues. The center field is framed by two mini goals at two corners (see mini goals A and B). There are also dribble goals marked at the remaining two corners (see dribble goals C and D). The players start with the passing sequence and player A passes to player B (see 1), and player B passes to player C (see 2). The passing sequence continues via players C and D (see 3) and back to player A. The players circulate the ball continuously around the central field for as long as there is no signal from the coach, and in doing so remain in their positions behind the mini and dribble goals. With a signal from the coach, a 1-on-1 situation begins. The player in possession or the player receiving the ball competes against the player diagonally opposite him. Player A always plays against player C and player B always plays against player D. After the coach's signal (see 4) during player C's pass to player D (see 3), the receiving player (here player D) settles the ball toward the central field and tries to score on the opposite goals (here mini goals A) (see 5). Player B reacts and runs into the field (see 6) to prevent a goal from being scored and, after possibly capturing the ball, counters on the mini goals B.

Variations and coach's signals

* Complete an opening pass prior to 1-on-1 (player D passes to player B).
* Opportunity to play on goals on opposite side and the two side goals.
* Complete as 2-on-2 (passes as prerequisite for finish on goals).
* Complete as 1-on-1 plus 2 (inactive players as neutral teammates for player in possession).

4.1.7   Double 1-on-1 after passing sequence

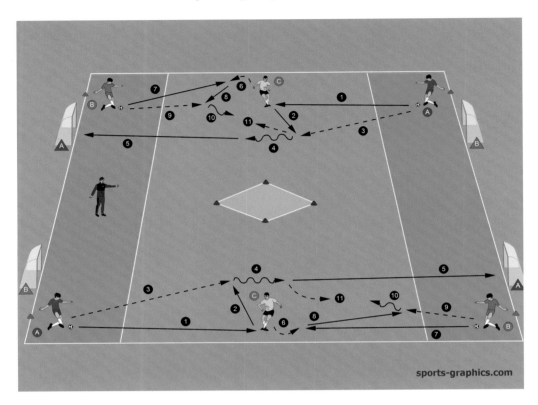

sports-graphics.com

Execution

After a predetermined passing sequence and a shot on goal, two 1-on-1 situations begin, each on two goals. Player A begins the action and passes to the neutral receiver C in the center (see 1). The neutral player C passes the ball right back (see 2). Player A follows his pass (see 3), controls the ball (see 4), and finishes on the opposite mini goal A (see 5). Right after his first pass, the neutral player C turns (see 6) and receives a second pass from player B (see 7). The neutral player C also plays this ball directly to the passing player (see 8). Player B follows his pass (see 9) and controls the ball for the ensuing 1-on-1 situation (see 10). After his finish, player A immediately transitions (see 11) and gets into defensive mode. Player B in possession now tries to win the 1-on-1 and score on the opposite mini goal (see mini goal B). Player A tries to prevent a goal from being scored and, after possibly capturing the ball, counters on mini goal A.

Points system

* Goal scored without the opponent capturing the ball (1 point)
* Goal scored after capturing the ball (2 points)

Variations

* Opportunity to play on both mini goals (see mini goal A and B) after dribbling through diamond.
* Complete predetermined feints prior to certain passes and shots (see 1, 5, and 7).
* Specify shot on goal (see 5) prior to 1-on-1 (direct finish/left/right).

4.1.8   1-on-1 (speed dribbling)

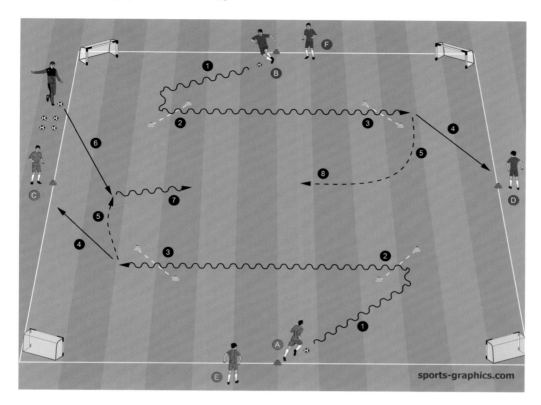

Execution

After a predetermined opening technique in the form of a dribbling and passing task, a 1-on-1 situation on four mini goals ensues. With a signal from the coach, players A and B simultaneously start their actions. Players A and B dribble into the field (see 1) and must dribble through two cone goals in a row with the ball at their foot (see 2 and 3). After players A and B have dribbled through the two cone goals (see 3), they pass their ball outside to a teammate (see 4) and transition without a ball for the imminent 1-on-1 (see 5). The faster player (here player A) has possession in 1-on-1 and receives the pass from the coach (see 6). Player A settles the ball (see 7) and player B gets into defensive mode (see 8). Player A now tries to score on a mini goal from 1-on-1 play. Before a possible finish on a mini goal, the player in possession must dribble through another mini goal. Player B tries to prevent a goal from being scored and, after possibly capturing the ball and subsequently playing on a cone goal, also tries to score on a mini goal. After the 1-on-1 situation ends, players C and D immediately start a new action with their balls (see 4) and, prior to the coach's ball, pass their balls to players E and F. A goal scored on a mini goal without the opponent capturing the ball (1 point). A goal scored after capturing the ball (2 points). Dribbling through two cone goals during 1-on-1 (3 points).

Variations

* Finish on mini goal after a technical task (see 4).
* Ramp up technical task (see 2 and 3) prior to finish (feint at cone goal).
* Opportunity for a pass to own outside player for 1-on-1 plus 1.

4.1.9   1-on-1 (line dribbling) (1)

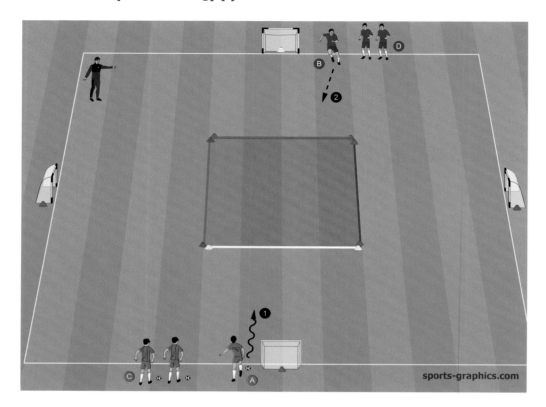

Execution

A 1-on-1 situation is under way in a field bounded by four mini goals. The goal of each 1-on-1 is to score on one of the mini goals. To do so, the players in possession must first dribble across a line of the central field and then play on the mini goal of the same color. Player A begins with the ball at his foot and dribbles into the field (see 1) for the 1-on-1 situation. Player B starts with A's first touch and also runs into the field (see 2). Player A tries to dribble into the center field to then leave the field again at a dribble across another line, and thereby have the opportunity to finish. Player B tries to prevent a goal from being scored and, after possibly capturing the ball, also tries to play across a line and score a goal. After a 1-on-1 ends with a goal, two new players (see players C and D) start. After a while, the teams change positions so they will play in offensive as well as defensive positions.

Variations

* Modify color arrangement of lines and mini goals.
* Opportunity to finish on all four mini goals after dribbling across two lines.
* Opportunity to finish on far mini goal without first playing across a line.

4.1.10 1-on-1 (line dribbling) (2)

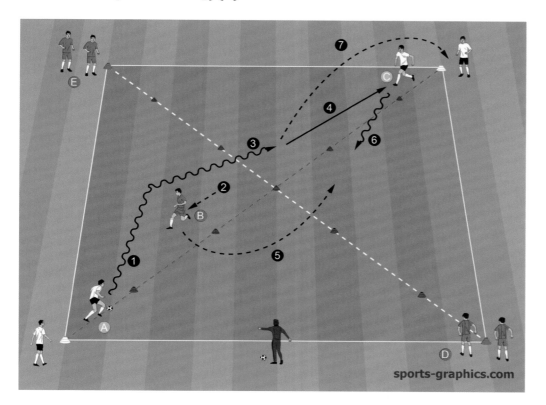

Execution

Player A begins the 1-on-1 in possession against player B. To do so, player A dribbles into the field (see 1) and player B confronts the attacker in front of the WHITE line (see 2). Player A has the goal of dribbling across the white line without player B capturing the ball. After successfully crossing the white line (see 3), player A passes to player C (see 4). Player B remains in the game as the defender, quickly transitions, and again competes in the 1-on-1. Player C dribbles into the field (see 6) and now tries to cross the WHITE line from the other side. Player A lines up at position C (see 7). After capturing the ball in 1-on-1, player B passes the ball to one of the outside players D or E and after the pass, takes over the outside position he passed to. The receiving player D or E becomes the attacker and now tries to cross the red line against the defender from the WHITE team (see player A). The 1-on-1 situations continue indefinitely.

Variations

* Specify minimum number of touches prior to crossing the centerline (3/4/5/6 touches).
* Specify minimum number of touches with weak foot (2/3/4 touches).
* Specify passing leg (left/right) for final pass (see 4).
* Complete predetermined feint prior to crossing the centerline.
* Specify minimum number of touches after crossing the centerline.
* Defender switches independently after four actions without capturing the ball.

4.1.11   Double 1-on-1 (zone dribbling) (1)

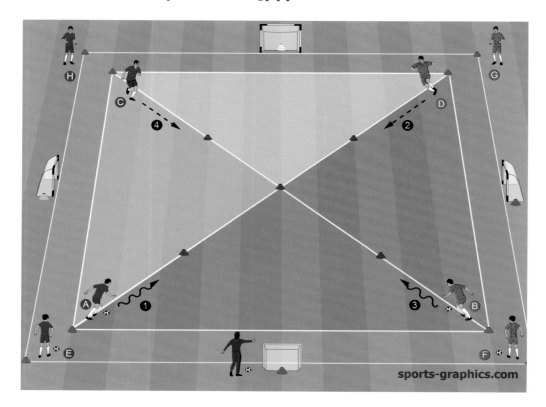

Execution

Two simultaneous 1-on-1 situations are under way in a square diagonally divided playing field. The goal of each 1-on-1 is to score on one of the mini goals. In doing so, the shooters can shoot only from the field marked directly in front of the mini goal. For example, the lower BLUE mini goal can only be shot on from the lower BLUE field. First the respective opponent must be outplayed in 1-on-1 and a target zone must be reached. Player A begins with the ball at his foot (see 1) and attacks player D (see 2). At the same time, player B begins with the ball at his foot (see 3) and plays against player C (see 4). After the ball is captured, the 1-on-1 continues until a goal is scored. If a 1-on-1 ends with a goal in one of the mini goals, two diagonally opposite players start a new action (see players E and G or players F and H). Each player can shoot on two predetermined mini goals. Players A and E can finish on the GREEN and WHITE mini goals. Players B and F can finish on the white and yellow mini goals. Players D and G can finish on the YELLOW and BLUE mini goals. Players C and H can finish on the BLUE and GREEN mini goals. After a while the players change positions so they will play in offensive as well as defensive positions.

Points system

★   Goal scored on a mini goal without the opponent capturing the ball (1 point)

★   Goal scored on a mini goal after capturing the ball (2 points)

★   Goal scored on a mini goal after losing the ball and capturing the ball (3 points)

4.1.12   Double 1-on-1 (zone dribbling) (2)

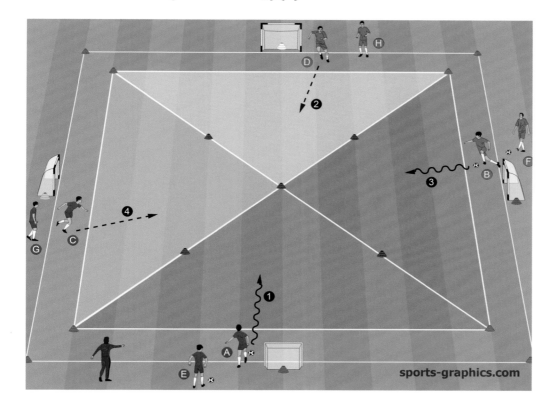

Execution

Two simultaneous 1-on-1 situations are underway in a square field divided into quarters with cone markers. The goal of each 1-on-1 is to score on one of the mini goals. The shooters can always attack the three far mini goals. For example, player A can finish on the YELLOW, WHITE, and GREEN mini goals, but first the respective opposing player must be outplayed in 1-on-1 and a target zone must be reached. Player A begins with the ball at his foot (see 1) and attacks player D (see 2). At the same time, player B begins with the ball at his foot (see 3) and plays against player C (see 4). After the ball is captured, 1-on-1 play continues until a goal is scored. If a 1-on-1 ended with a goal scored on a mini goal, two diagonally opposite players start a new action (here players E and H or F and G). Each player can finish on three designated mini goals. Players A and E can finish on the YELLOW, WHITE, and GREEN mini goals. Players B and F can finish on the BLUE, YELLOW, and WHITE mini goals, Players D and H can finish on the GREEN, BLUE, and YELLOW mini goals. Players C and G can finish on the WHITE, GREEN, and BLUE mini goals. After a while the players change positions so they will play in offensive as well as defensive positions.

Points system

* Goal scored in a near (see player A in the YELLOW or GREEN mini goal) mini goal (1 point)
* Goal scored in the far (see player A in the WHITE mini goal) mini goal (2 points)
* Goal scored after capturing the ball (3 points)
* Goal scored after losing and capturing the ball (4 points)

4.1.13   1-on-1 (transition)

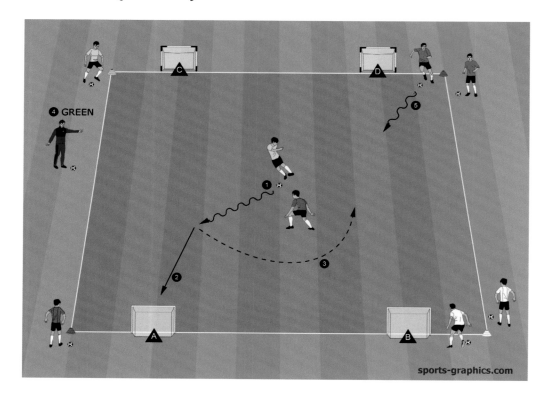

Execution

The field is framed by four mini goals (see mini goals A, B, C, and D). Players compete in 1-on-1 play. To do so, the YELLOW and GREEN team players always attack mini goals A and B and the RED and WHITE team players always attack mini goals C and D. The player in possession (here the YELLOW player) tries to score a goal (see 2) in 1-on-1 play (see 1) against the defender (here the RED player). If the RED player captures the ball, he will counter on goals C and D. After a goal is scored, the shooter remains on the field and plays as the defender (see 3) in the next and immediately following 1-on-1 situation. The coach chooses the next player (see 4). The respective shooter always determines the continuation of the game (here the YELLOW player). After his action, the previously inferior player (here the RED player) takes over his team's starting position.

Basic idea

Next to the basic elements of 1-on-1 play (lateral position, low center of gravity, decreasing distances, controlling the attacker, stripping the opponent of the ball, capturing the ball), particular emphasis is placed on transitioning after a finish. After transitioning and reorienting, the defender must adapt his behavior to the new situation.

Variations

* Coach's signal (see 3) as visual command (show team color).
* Specify time limit (second rule) until finish for player in possession.
* Eliminate player in possession for failure to adhere to time limit (second rule).
* Modify game continuation in 2-on-2 (optional activation of all teams).

4.1.14   1-on-1 (goal hunt)

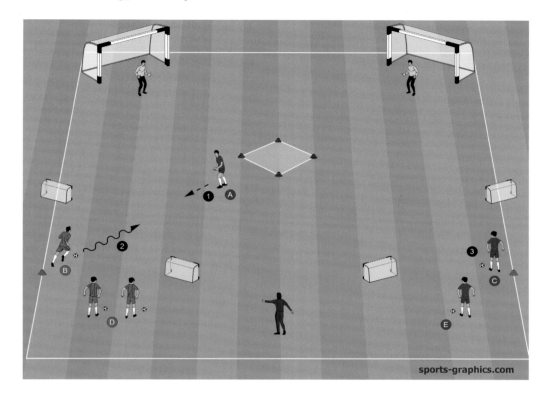

Execution

Continuous 1-on-1 situations are underway in a field bounded by multiple goals. The attackers in possession can attack the two large goals manned with goal players, and after successfully capturing the ball, the defenders can attack the four mini goals. To start, player A positions himself in the center as a defender without a ball (see 1). Player B begins with the ball at his foot and dribbles into the field for 1-on-1 play (see 2). In doing so, player B tries to attack the far large goal and score. As soon as player B has dribbled across two lines of the central diamond field, he has an additional opportunity to attack the second large goal. Player A tries to prevent a goal and the dribbling through the central diamond field and, after possibly capturing the ball, to counter on the four mini goals. After player A or B finishes, player C immediately starts the new action (see 3) and plays against player B, who immediately gets into defensive mode after the 1-on-1 ends.

Points system

★ Goal scored on large goal without the opponents capturing the ball (1 point)

★ Goal scored on large goal after dribbling through the central diamond field (2 points)

★ Goal scored on mini goal after capturing the ball (3 points)

Variations

★ Opportunity for attacker to finish on mini goals after twice dribbling through the diamond.

★ Opportunity for defender to include goalkeeper for 1-on-1 plus 2.

4.1.15   1-on-1 after opening technique and transition (1)

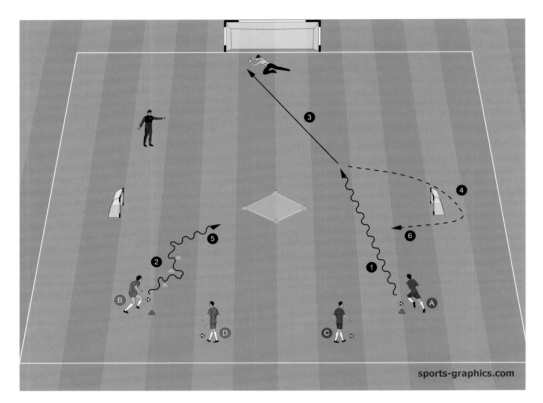

Execution

After a predetermined opening technique in the form of dribbling and a shot on goal (see player A), a 1-on-1 situation ensues. Player A begins his action and dribbles into the field (see 1). Player B reacts and starts at his opponents' first touch (see 2). After dribbling, player A finishes with a shot on the large goal (see 3), transitions and runs around the near mini goal (see 4). Player B completes a dribble task (see 2) and afterwards guides his ball into the field for the subsequent 1-on-1 (see 5). Player B tries to score on the far mini goal. Player A runs into the field for the 1-on-1 (see 6), tries to prevent a goal from being scored, and after possibly capturing the ball, tries to score on the opposite mini goal. As soon as a player in possession has dribbled across two lines of the central diamond field, he has the opportunity to score on the large goal. After the 1-on-1 situation ends, players C and D immediately start a new action with their balls. Players regularly change positions.

Points system

- ★ Goal scored from shot on goal (see 3) during opening technique (1 point)
- ★ Goal scored on mini goal without the opponents capturing the ball (2 points)
- ★ Goal scored on mini goal after capturing the ball (3 points)
- ★ Goal scored on large goal after dribbling through central diamond field (4 points)
- ★ Goal scored on large goal after capturing the ball and dribbling through central diamond field (5 points)

4.1.16   1-on-1 after opening technique and transition (2)

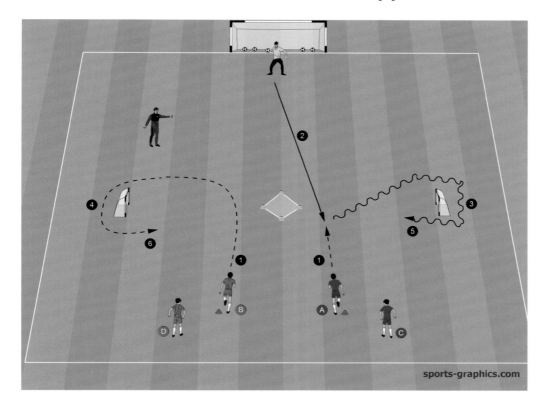

Execution

After the throw-out by the goalkeeper and a predetermined running and dribbling task for players A and B, a 1-on-1 situation ensues. Players A and B run straight into the field (see 1). The goalkeeper throws the ball out (see 2) to a player of his choice (here player A). Player A settles the throw-out and dribbles around the near mini goal (see 3). Player B reacts and runs around the other mini goal without a ball (see 4). Player A dribbles on into the field for the subsequent 1-on-1 and tries to score on the opposite mini goal (see 5). Player B also runs into the field (see 6) and tries to prevent a goal from being scored, and after possibly capturing the ball, tries to score on the opposite mini goal. As soon as a player in possession has dribbled across two lines of the central diamond field he has the opportunity to score on the large goal. After the 1-on-1 situation has ended, the goalkeeper immediately starts a new action with players C and D. Players regularly change positions.

Points system

- ★ Goal scored on mini goal without the opponents capturing the ball (1 points)
- ★ Goal scored on mini goal after capturing the ball (2 points)
- ★ Goal scored on large goal after dribbling through central diamond field (3 points)
- ★ Goal scored on large goal after capturing the ball and dribbling through central diamond field (4 points)

4.1.17   Double 1-on-1 after opening technique

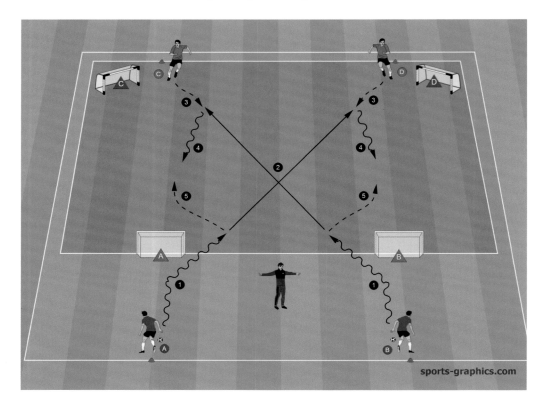

Execution

After a brief opening technique in the form of dribbling and a feint, two 1-on-1 situations ensue. Players A and B position themselves with a ball at two outside positions off the field. Players C and D position themselves on the opposite side of the field. The field is framed by four mini goals (see mini goals A, B, C, and D). After a signal from the coach, players A and B simultaneously start the opening technique, briefly dribble and execute a feint in front of the mini goal (see 1), and then play a diagonal pass to players C and D (see 2). Players C and D start toward the pass (see 3) and control the ball toward the opposite mini goals (see 4). After their passes, players A and B run into the field (see 5) for the subsequent 1-on-1 situations. Player C plays against player A and tries to score on mini goal A (two points). Player D plays against player B and tries to score on mini goal B (one point). After successfully capturing the ball, player B tries to score on mini goal D (two points). Player C competes for time against player D and tries to score faster than his opponent. Player A competes for time against player B and tries to capture the ball faster than his opponent and score a goal. After each round, players switch their offensive and defensive positions.

Variations

★   Opportunity to play on both mini goals C and D after successfully capturing the ball.

★   Opportunity to play on both mini goals A and B.

4.1.18   From 1-on-1 to 1-on-1 plus 2 after a passing sequence and shot on goal

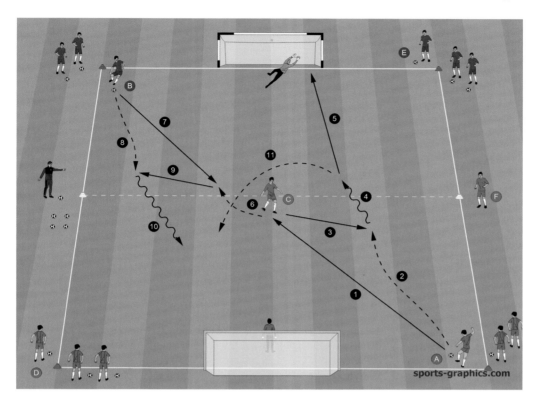

Execution

After a predetermined passing combination and a shot on goal, a 1-on-1 situation ensues. Player A begins the action and passes to the neutral receiver C in the center (see 1). Player A follows his pass (see 2) and receives the back pass (see 3). Player A controls the pass toward the goal (see 4) and finishes (see 5). After his first pass (see 3), the neutral receiver C immediately turns (see 6) and receives a pass from player B (see 7). Player B follows his pass (see 8) and receives the back pass from player C (see 9). Player B controls the pass toward the goal (see 10). After his shot on goal (see 5), player A transitions (see 11) and tries to prevent player B from scoring a goal. After successfully capturing the ball, player A can also attack the opposite large goal. Right after the 1-on-1 ends with a goal scored on a large goal, the coach brings another ball into the game for 1-on-1 plus 1. Here player C acts as a neutral teammate of the player currently in possession. Players A and B transition and try to score in this next 1-on-1-plus-1 situation. After the 1-on-1 plus 1 ends, players D and E start a new action. The neutral player C changes in regular intervals (see player F).

Variations

* Change direction of play after coach's ball.
* Specify minimum number of touches prior to a possible finish by player B (see 10).
* Opportunity to include player F after player A captures the ball.

4.2 2-ON-2

2-on-2 includes competition formats for improving group-tactical tackling behavior in groups of two. The players essentially learn to develop a joint problem-solving approach and coordinated behaviors. Playing defense requires players to safeguard each other and encourages double-teaming or concise coaching amongst themselves. Playing offense requires coordinated running paths, joint target focusing, or creating passing lanes via running paths. In addition, these drills include lots of transitioning. This places particular emphasis on joint perception, orienting, and acting.

SLALOM COURSE
OPENING TECHNIQUE SAFEGUARDING
DRIBBLE TASKS
COUNTERS GRADUATED DEPTH
GROUP TACTICS DOUBLE-TEAMING
DRIBBLE TASKS FINISHING ABILITY
COURSES OF ACTION SCORING OPPORTUNITIES
CAPTURING THE BALL TRANSITIONS
PROBLEM SOLVING
ORIENTATION

4.2.1   2-on-2 (opening technique) (1)

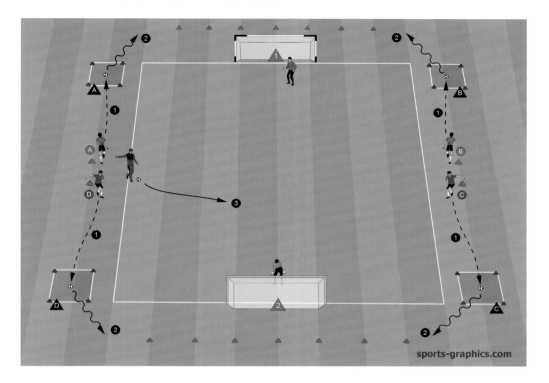

Execution

After a predetermined opening technique via a slalom course, a 2-on-2 situation on the large goals 1 and 2 ensues. The RED team players (see players A and B) and the BLUE team players (see players C and D) position themselves on the start markers at a level with the centerline. In front of the players, next to each corner of the playing field, is a marked-off field (see fields A, B, C, and D) with a ball in it. Behind each of the large goals 1 and 2 is a marked slalom course. With a signal from the coach, all four players start toward the field marked in front of them (see 1) and take the ball positioned there along toward the slalom course (see 2). The players dribble through the slalom course and deposit the ball in the teammate's field on the opposite side of the field. Player A places his ball in field B. Player B places his ball in field A. Player C places his ball in field D. Player D places his ball in field C. Afterwards all four players run into the field for the subsequent 2-on-2 situation. The coach brings a ball into the game (see 3), and the BLUE team attacks goal 1 and the RED team attacks goal 2. After a goal has been scored or the ball leaves the field, the players begin again with an opening technique.

Variations

* Run through the slalom course without a ball (run backwards/hobble/left/right).
* Specify dribbling technique on slalom course (strictly alternate/left/right).
* Deposit ball in own field (complete slalom course out and back).
* Modify starting action (double pass with own goalkeeper prior to slalom course).

4.2.2   2-on-2 (opening technique) (2)

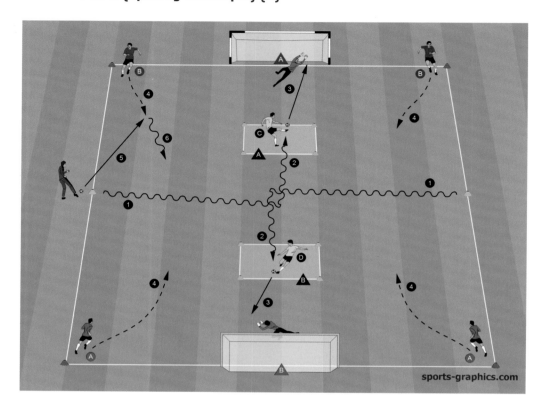

Execution

After a starting action by players C and D with subsequent shot on goal, a 2-on-2 situation ensues between the RED team (see players A) and the BLUE team (see players B). Players C and D start the action and each dribbles from the starting cone toward the center with a ball at his foot (see 1). The players dribble past each other and turn toward the large goals A and B. Player C dribbles into field A (see 2) and finishes on goal A (see 3). Player D dribbles into field B (see 2) and finishes on goal B (see 3). After their shots, players C and D remain in fields A and B and act as neutral players for the team in possession in the subsequent game situation. As players C and D finish (see 3), teams A and B start toward the center (see 4) for the 2-on-2. One player (here player B) receives a ball from the coach (see 5) and is in possession for the subsequent 2-on-2 situation (see 6). Team B attacks goal B and team A attacks goal A. The respective team in possession can include players C and D for 2-on-2 plus 2. Players change starting positions for the next action.

Variations

* Specify passing technique for players C and D (direct passes).
* Limit one neutral player per team (team A/player C and team B/player D).
* Prerequisite for possible play on both goals (include both players C and D one after the other).
* Prerequisite for possible play on both goals (eight consecutive passes without turnover).
* Specify shooting technique (see 3) for players C and D (laces/inside foot/outside foot).
* Complete a predetermined feint prior to shot on goal (see 3) in fields A and B.

4.2.3 2-on-2 (opening technique) (3)

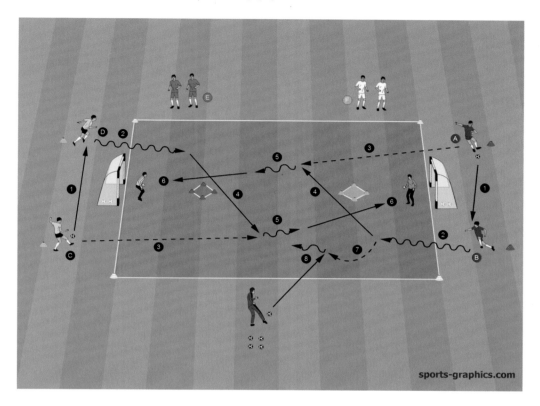

sports-graphics.com

Execution

Players are divided into multiple teams of two. After a predetermined opening technique in the form of a passing sequence with shot on goal, a 2-on-2 situation on both large goals ensues. The two teams of two (see BLUE and YELLOW teams) simultaneously start the opening technique behind the own goal. Player A passes to player B (see 1). Player B settles the ball and dribbles into the field (see 2). Player A follows his pass, runs into the field (see 3), and receives the back pass from player B (see 4). Player A controls the ball (see 5) and finishes on the opposing large goal (see 6). Now the 2-on-2 follows. All four players transition (see 7) and the coach brings a ball into the game. The teams of two now play on the opposing goal until a goal is scored or the ball leaves the field. As soon as a team has dribbled through the diamond field of the same color near the opposing goal, both large goals are open and the team in possession can attack two goals. After the 2-on-2 situation ends, two new teams immediately start (see teams E and F).

Points system

* Goal scored (see 6) after opening technique (1 point)
* Goal scored in 2-on-2 (2 points)

Variations

* Expand opening technique (back pass after pass 2/overlap after pass 4).
* Specify certain feints prior to select actions (see passes 1 and 4, and shot 6).

4.2.4 2-on-2 (opening technique) (4)

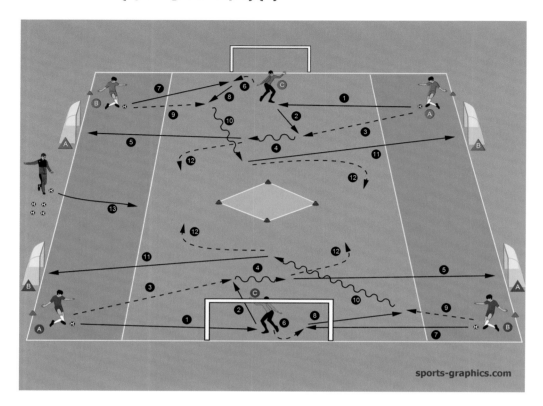

sports-graphics.com

Execution

After a predetermined passing combination and two shots on the mini goals, a 2-on-2 situation on the two large goals ensues. The BLUE team and the RED team simultaneously start the opening technique. Player A begins the action and passes to their own goalkeeper C (see 1). Goalkeeper C passes the ball right back (see 2). Player A follows his pass (see 3), controls the ball (see 4), and finishes on the opposite mini goal A (see 5). Right after his first pass (see 6), goalkeeper C turns and receives a second pass from player B (see 7). Goalkeeper C plays this pass right back to the passing player (see 8). Player B follows his pass (see 9), controls the ball (see 10), and finishes on the opposite mini goal B (see 11). After their actions, both players A and B transition and orient themselves for the subsequent 2-on-2 on the two large goals (see 12). The coach brings a ball into the game for the 2-on-2 (see 13). The faster team gets possession.

Points system

★ Goal scored on a mini goal during opening technique (1 point)

★ Goal scored on a large goal in 2-on-2 (2 points)

Variations

★ Opportunity to play on all six goals after dribbling through the diamond.

★ Complete predetermined feint prior to certain passes and shots (see 1/7 and 5/11).

★ Specify shot on goal (see 5/11) prior to 2-on-2 (direct finish/left/right).

4.2.5 2-on-2 (transition) (1)

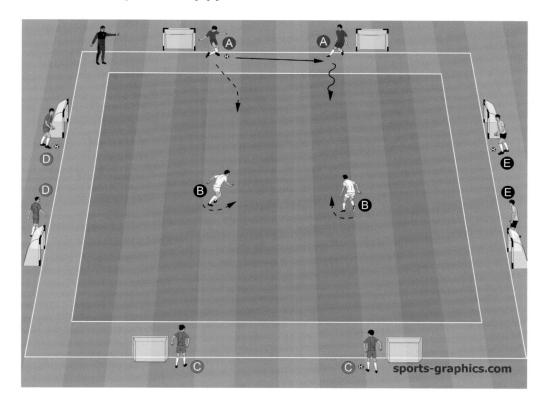

Execution

Players are divided into five teams of two (see team A, team B, team C, team D, and team E). The direction of play is specified at the beginning of the drill. The BLUE team A plays on the lower mini goals, the WHITE team B plays on the upper mini goals, the GREEN team C plays on the upper mini goals, the RED team D plays on the mini goals on the right, and the YELLOW team E plays on the mini goals on the left. The game starts with the BLUE team A in possession against the WHITE team B on defense. After a goal has been scored or the ball is off the field, the coach names another team, which immediately dribbles into the field with a ball of their own. The team that has played longer is eliminated and takes over the open positions outside. The team that has played for a shorter period of time remains on the field and transitions into defensive mode against the newly starting team. After each coach's signal, the named team starts with a square pass (see team A).

Variations

★ Change team composition (players switch to other teams).

★ Change size of goals (play on four large goals manned by goalkeepers).

★ Add a neutral player (2-on-2 plus 1).

★ Prerequisite for playing on goals (specify minimum number of passes).

★ Specify shooting technique for finish on mini goals (left/right/direct finish).

★ Modify opening technique (double pass/overlap/double double-pass).

4.2.6   2-on-2 (transition) (2)

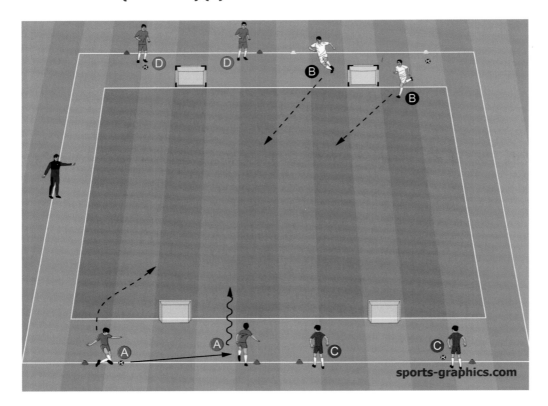

sports-graphics.com

Execution

Players are divided into four teams of two players each (see team A, team B, team C, and team D). The direction of play is predetermined and remains the same. The RED team A and the BLUE team C always attack the two upper mini goals and the WHITE team B and the GREEN team D always attack the two lower mini goals. All four teams position themselves at the cone markers behind a mini goal with one ball per team. The coach designates two teams at the start (here team A and team B). The first 2-on-2 situation begins with the RED team in possession. As soon as a team scores a goal or the ball leaves the field, the coach immediately names a new team. The named team plays a square pass and starts with their own ball for the 2-on-2. The team that has played longer is eliminated and takes over the open positions outside. The team that has played for a shorter period of time remains on the field and immediately gets into defensive mode against the newly starting team.

Variations

★ Change team composition (players switch to other teams).

★ Change size of goals (play on two large goals manned by goalkeepers).

★ Add a neutral player (2-on-2 plus 1).

★ Specify shooting technique for finish on mini goals (left/right/direct finish).

★ Modify opening technique (double pass/overlap/double double-pass).

4.2.7 2-on-2 (transition) (3)

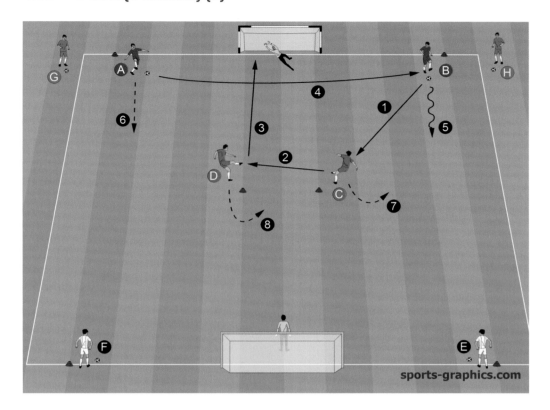

Execution

Players are divided into several teams of two and position themselves to the sides of the large goals. Each player has a ball. After situational opening techniques in the form of short passing sequences and a shot on goal, several 2-on-2 situations ensue. A team of two (see the RED team) positions itself at the starting position at the two cone markers in the center. The BLUE team starts the action. Player B begins and passes a ball to player C (see 1). Player C quickly passes to player D (see 2). Player D finishes on the large goal (see 3). After the first pass from player B, player A can immediately play the square pass to player B (see 4), and the BLUE team start as attackers into the 2-on-2 against the RED team. Player B takes the ball into the field (see 5) and after his pass, player A moves into an offensive position (see 6). Player C transitions right after his square pass (see 7), and player D also immediately transitions (see 8) after his shot on goal (see 3) and gets into a defensive position. After the RED team possibly captures the ball, the RED team counterattacks on the opposite large goal. The subsequent 2-on-2 continues until a goal is scored or the ball leaves the field. If a goal is scored, the team that scored remains on the field. If the ball leaves the field without a goal, the team that has been on the field for a shorter amount of time stays. In both cases the still-active team immediately transitions and runs straight to the cone markers or around the two starting positions, so that the next team (here the WHITE team, see players E and F) can quickly initiate a new action.

Variation

★ Shooter intervenes in 2-on-2 (here player D) only after scoring (see 3).

4.2.8 2-on-2 (goal hunt)

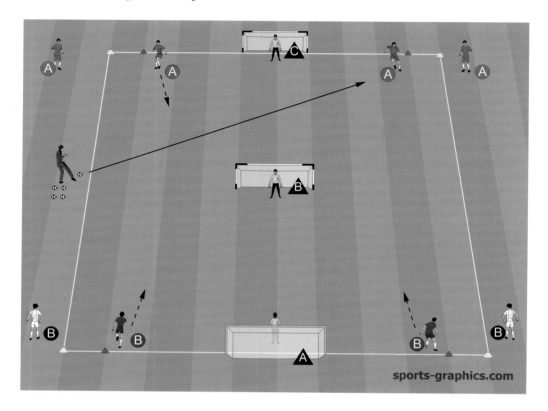

sports-graphics.com

Execution

Players are divided into several teams of two and are positioned on the baseline next to the two large goals. The direction of play and the respective large goals to be played on are predetermined for the teams. The teams in position A (see the RED team and the GREEN team) always play on goal A. The teams in position B (see the BLUE team and the WHITE team) always play on goals B and C. The 2-on-2 situations always start with a ball from the coach. The coach passes the ball to the RED team. The players A start in possession against the players B. Team A tries to score on goal A. After possibly capturing the ball, team B tries to score on goal B or C. During play on goal C, the goalkeeper in goal B can be passed to as a neutral player for a 3-on-2 superior-number situation. As soon as a goal is scored or the ball leaves the field, the coach brings a new ball into the game and passes the ball to a team positioned outside (see the WHITE team and the GREEN team). For the next 2-on-2 situation, one previously active team is always eliminated and one previously active team remains on the field, immediately transitions, and gets into defensive mode for the next 2-on-2 situation. Which team remains on the field is determined by the coach's ball, namely which starting position (see position A and B) the coach plays the ball to. After a coach's ball to position A, the previously active team B (here the BLUE team) remains on the field. After a coach's ball to position B, the previously active team A (here the RED team) remains on the field.

Points system

* Goal scored on goal B without the opponents capturing the ball (1 point) and on goal A/C (2 points)
* Goal scored on goal B after capturing the ball (3 points) and on goal A/C (4 points)

4.2.9   Variable 2-on-2 (goal hunt)

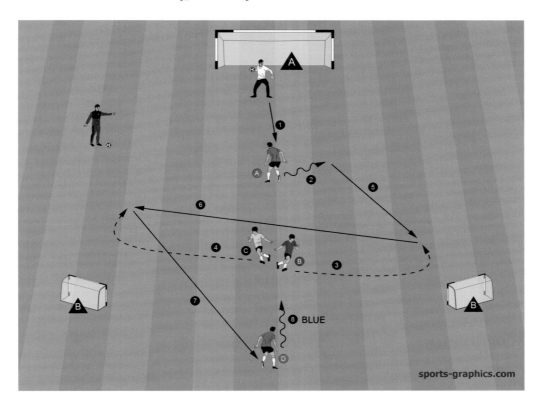

Execution

After a predetermined passing combination, a 2-on-2 situation on the large goal A and the mini goals B ensues. Players A, B, C, and D each wear a colored bib (see RED, BLUE, YELLOW, and GREEN players). The players position themselves in a row in front of the goal. Player A takes a position close to the goal. Players B and C stand close together in the center and player D stands farther away between the mini goals B. The goalkeeper begins the action and rolls the ball to player A (see 1). Player A opens up with the ball (see 2). While player A turns, players B and C get open with an outside running path (see 3 and 4). Player A passes to one of the two players (see 5). The player receiving the ball (here player B) passes to the second center player (see 6). The player receiving the ball (here player C) passes the ball on to player D (see 7). Player D settles the ball toward the large goal A and at the same time names a teammate (here the BLUE player) for the subsequent 2-on-2 (see 8). Players D and B in possession attack the large goal A and try to score (1 point). Players A and C switch to defense, defend, and, after possibly capturing the ball, can counter on the mini goals B (two points). Players change starting positions for a new action.

Variations

* Coach names a color (see 8) and designates teams for 2-on-2.
* Coach names receiving player (player B/C) for pass from A (see 5).
* Specify passing technique (direct passes).

4.2.10   Double 2-on-2 (timed play)

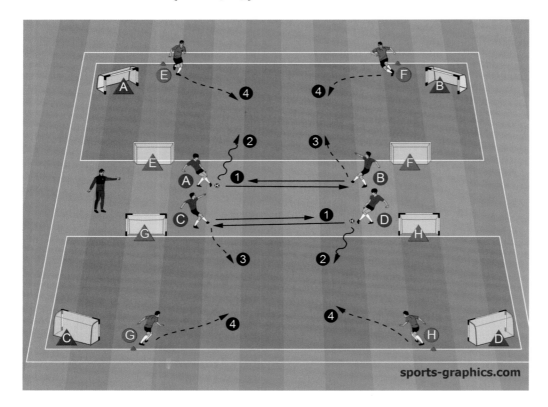

Execution

After a simple and brief opening in the form of direct passes, two 2-on-2 situations begin with a signal from the coach. The players spread out on different starting positions. Players A/B and C/D play direct passes to each other (see 1). At a starting signal from the coach, the 2-on-2 situations begin and the respective players in possession (here players A and D) move the ball in the direction of the outer fields (see 2). The respective teammate without a ball (see players B/C) follows into the field (see 3). At a signal from the coach, the defenders also start into the field (see 4). Players A and B attack mini goals A and B and play against defenders E and F. After successfully capturing the ball, players E and F attack the mini goals E and F. Players C and D attack mini goals C and D and play against the defenders G and H. After successfully capturing the ball, players G and H attack the mini goals G and H. Team A/B plays for time against team G/H and tries to prevent a goal from being scored and to launch a counter more quickly than the opposing team. Next a new round begins with changing playing positions. Players E/F and G/H get possession.

Points system

* First goal scored during competition between team A/B and team C/D (1 point)
* First goal scored during competition between team E/F and team G/H (2 points)

4.2.11   Double 2-on-2 (chaos)

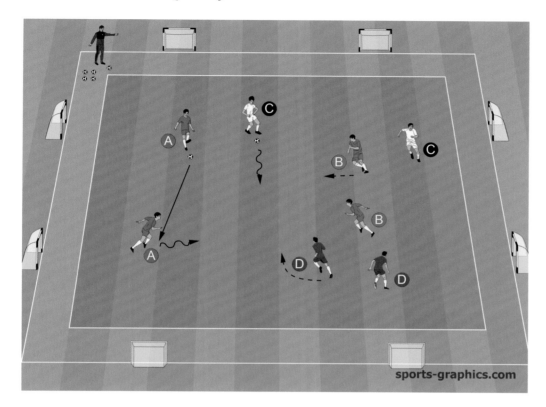

Execution

Players are divided into four teams of two players each (see team A, team B, team C, and team D). The RED team A plays with a ball against the GREEN team B. At the same time in the same field and with a second ball, the WHITE team C plays against the BLUE team D. The direction of play is specified at the beginning of the two 2-on-2 situations. The RED team A attacks the two mini goals on the right and the WHITE team C attacks the two mini goals at the bottom. After possibly capturing the ball, the GREEN team B attacks the mini goals on the left and the BLUE team D attacks the mini goals at the top. As soon as a team scores a goal or the ball is out of the game, the coach plays a new ball into the game. The direction of play changes with each new coach's ball. After team A scores a goal or finishes on the mini goals on the right, the coach brings a new ball into the game for teams A and B. Afterwards team A attacks the mini goals on the left and team B attacks the mini goals on the right.

Variations

* Change opponents (team A against team C and team B against team D).
* Change size of goals (play on four large goals manned with goalkeepers).
* Change the direction of play by 90° after each coach's ball.
* Add neutral players (double 2-on-2 plus 1).
* Prerequisite for play on goals (specify minimum number of passes).
* Specify shooting technique for finish on mini goals (left/right/direct finish).

4.2.12 Variable 2-on-2 (chaos)

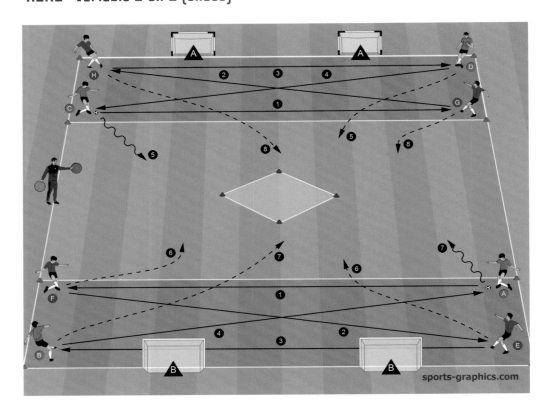

Execution

After two predetermined passing combinations, two 2-on-2 situations begin with a signal from the coach. Players spread out on different starting positions and circulate two balls in a predetermined passing sequence. Player A/C passes to player F/G (see 1). Player F/G passes to player E/H (see 2). Player E/H passes to player B/D (see 3), and player B/D passes to player A/C (see 4). The players continuously circulate the ball and after each pass stay in their positions. Next, the coach names a team color (here the RED team) and thereby determines possession for the 2-on-2 situations. Within the group one of the players on the named team (here player A/C) now gets the ball and dribbles into the center for the subsequent 2-on-2 situations. Players C/D attack the opposite mini goals B (see 5) and play against players E/F (see 6). After successfully capturing the ball, players E/F attack the mini goals A. At the same time, players A/B attack the mini goals A (see 7) and play against players G/H (see 8). After successfully capturing the ball, players G/H attack the mini goals B. If a team plays on the center diamond by dribbling or with a pass, all four mini goals can be attacked. Team A/B plays for time against team G/H and tries to score first. Team E/F plays for time against team G/H and tries to prevent a goal from being scored and to launch a counter-attack more quickly than the opposing team. Afterwards a new round begins with the same positions. The coach varies the coach's signal so all teams have equal possession.

Points system

* First goal scored in competition between team A/B and team C/D (1 point)
* First goal scored in competition between team E/F and team G/H (2 points)

4.2.13 2-on-2 plus 1 (zone play)

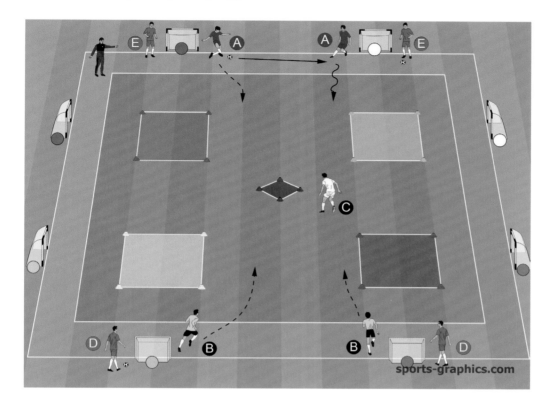

Execution

Players are divided into four teams of two players each (see team A, team B, team D, and team E). There is always one neutral player (see player C) in the center who can be passed to by the team in possession, creating a 2-on-2-plus-1 situation. Several color-coded fields are marked off on the playing field. The teams initially have the task of playing for ball holding in these fields. As soon as a field has been played on, the two mini goals of the same color open up for subsequent finishing opportunities. The game begins with the BLUE team A in possession plus player C against the YELLOW team B in 2-on-2 plus 1. After a goal is scored or the ball is out of the game, the coach names the next team, which immediately dribbles into the field with their own ball. The team that has played longer is eliminated and takes over the open outside positions. The team that played the shorter amount of time remains on the field and immediately gets into defensive mode against the new starting team.

Points system

* Play on 1/2/3/4 squares plus score on a mini goal (1/2/3/4 point(s))
* Play on the diamond plus score on a mini goal (5 points)

Variations

* Modify play on fields (dribble across two lines/pass across two lines).
* Opportunity to play on multiple fields in a row to open up several mini goals.
* Opportunity to play on center diamond to open up all mini goals.
* Modify playing rights (a longer-playing team also remains on the field after scoring a goal).

4.2.14   2-on-2 plus 2 (outside zones)

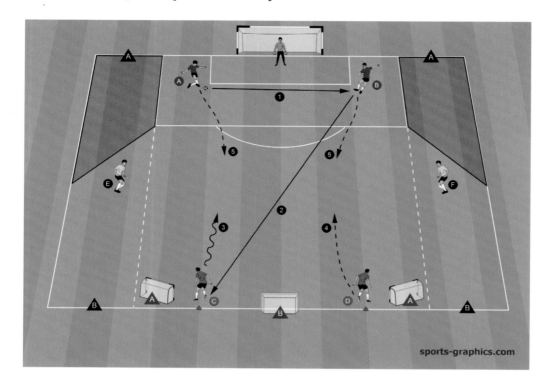

Execution

Players spread out in different starting positions. Players A and B from the BLUE team position themselves with a ball at the six-yard box and act as defenders. Players C and D from the RED team position themselves in the center between the mini goals A and B and act as attackers. Players E and F position themselves in the outside zones B and act as neutral receivers. Players cannot run into or play on zones A. Player A begins with a pass to player B (see 1). Player B passes to one of the RED team players (see 2). The receiving player (here player C) controls the ball and dribbles into the field (see 3). The teammate (here player D) also runs into the field (see 4). After the opening passes, players A and B move up (see 5) and out of the penalty box to act as defenders. Players C and D try to score on the large goal. Players A and B try to prevent a goal from being scored and, after successfully capturing the ball, counter on mini goals A and B. The penalty box serves as the offside line. The offside line can only be crossed by dribbling or with a long pass and a receiving player. The team in possession can involve the outside players E and F. The outside players E and F can only play direct passes and, in doing so, can also play a long pass into the penalty box. Positions change after each round.

Points system

* Goal scored on large goal by attacker (1 point for RED team)
* Goal scored on mini goal A by defender (1 point for BLUE team)
* Goal scored on mini goal B by defender (2 points for BLUE team)
* Deep pass from an outside player (1 point for YELLOW team)

4.3   TEAM AGAINST TEAM

Team against Team includes drills with varying training content. Teams face off in a competitive setting and measure each other's performance. The competitive character emphasizes superior and competition-oriented qualities and behaviors. The competitive drills allow the focus to be placed on developing team spirit and performance-oriented handling of wins and losses. Moreover, the training intensity and training load can be increased via the competitive drills, and elements such as precision, effectiveness, and goal orientation are addressed.

TEAM SPIRIT RELAYS
MOVEMENT DRILLS
WINNING GAMES OF CATCH
LOSING COORDINATION TASKS
PASSING SHOT ON GOAL
DRIBBLING FEINTS JUGGLING
TECHNICAL COMPETITIONS
PASSING COMPETITONS POINTS SYSTEM
CHALLENGE

4.3.1 Game of catch

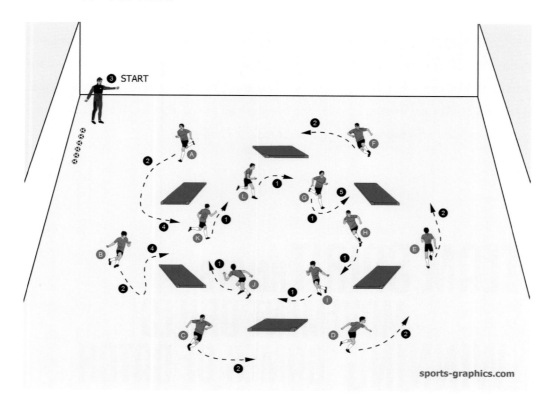

Execution

Players are divided into two teams (see GREEN and RED teams). A circle is formed using several mats with even gaps in between. The GREEN team positions itself around the outside of the mat circle and the RED team positions itself in a circle inside the mat circle. The teams simultaneously run in circles. In doing so, the RED team runs clockwise inside the mat circle (see 1) and the GREEN team runs counterclockwise outside the mat circle (see 2). With a signal (see 3), the coach initiates a game of catch. After the coach's signal, the GREEN team players try to chase the RED team players and tag them by hand (see 4). To do so, they run through the gaps into the mat circle. The RED team players try to avoid getting tagged and save themselves by getting on a mat (see 5). As soon as a RED team player has been tagged, he is eliminated and sits down on the ground. The GREEN team players can chase and eliminate several opponents in a row. The tasks change for the next round.

Variations

- ★ Complete with ball (all players dribble their own ball).
- ★ Complete with ball for the RED team (player in possession cannot be caught).
- ★ Modify RED team's objective (tag a gym wall).
- ★ Modify RED team's objective (tag the gym wall on the opposite side).

4.3.2   Running competition

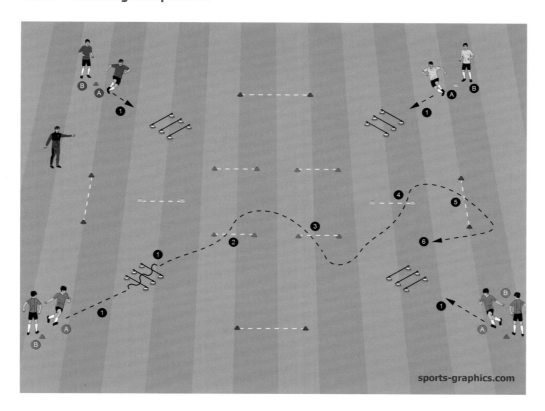

sports-graphics.com

Execution

Players are divided into four teams (see RED, GREEN, YELLOW, and BLUE teams) and spread out in the corners of the field. The teams consist of at least two players (see players A and B) and face off in a running and moving competition. On the field is one group of hurdles per team as well as different-colored cone goals. After a starting signal from the coach, the first player from each team (see player A) begins and runs into the field (see 1). He has the task of running through four different cone goals (see 2, 3, 4, and 5). Afterwards he returns to his team and activates the next player (see 6). During each run the players must run through the group of hurdles positioned directly in front of the starting position (see 1) and complete a predetermined coordination task as an opening coordination exercise. The cone goals the next player (here player B) runs through must be a different color than those the previous player ran through. The competition ends as soon as a team has completed 20 runs.

Variations

* Specify movement task at the group of cone goals (standing jump/one-legged jump).
* Specify running through cone goals (180° turn).
* Modify running style (backwards/sidestep).
* Complete competition with jump rope (run through cone goals at skipping run).
* Complete movement tasks while dribbling with the ball at the foot.

4.3.3   Movement competition

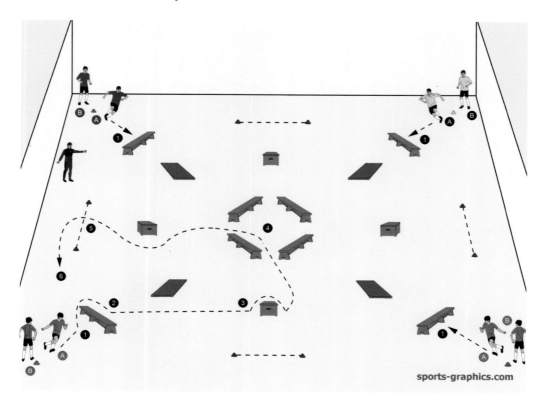

Execution

Players are divided into four teams (see RED, GREEN, YELLOW, and BLUE teams) and spread out in the corners of the field. The teams consist of at least two players (see players A and B) and face off in a running and moving competition. On the field are several pieces of exercise equipment (see mats, vaulting boxes, and benches) and four cone goals. After a starting signal from the coach, the first player from each team (see player A) begins and runs into the field (see 1). He has the task of completing two actions at the pieces of equipment or the cone goals. Afterwards he returns to his team and activates the next player (see 6). During each run the players must jump over the bench positioned directly in front of the starting position (see 2) and run through the center (see 4). For his two actions, player A chooses a vaulting box (see 3) and a cone goal (see 5). The next player (here player B) must choose different apparatuses. The competition ends as soon as a team has completed 20 runs.

Variations

★ Specify movement task at vaulting box (standing jump/one-legged jump).

★ Specify movement task at bench (standing jump/one-legged jump/side vault).

★ Specify movement task at mat (forward roll/backwards roll/cartwheel).

★ Complete competition with jump rope (run around apparatuses at skipping run).

★ Complete movement tasks while dribbling with the ball at the foot.

4.3.4   Coordination competition

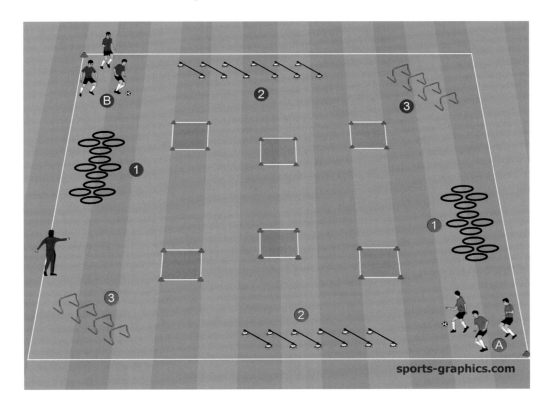

sports-graphics.com

Execution

The RED team competes against the BUE team. To do so, players position themselves at two starting positions of the same color. Each team has a ball and three different coordination stations (see 1, 2, and 3) where the teams must intermittently complete predetermined movement sequences. Beginning at the starting positions, all players dribble and run into the field together and perform certain tasks at the fields marked off in the center. The predetermined tasks for playing on the fields must be completed at ten fields. After the predetermined task has been competed, each player runs to a coordination station and completes the predetermined task there before all three players run back into the field to again play on the fields with their own ball. After repeating the sequence three times and after each player has completed each coordination station, the group returns to the starting position with the ball. The first team to return to the starting position wins. Movement tasks at the coordination stations change regularly.

Variations for playing on fields

* Complete a feint in the field/pass to a teammate.
* Dribble into a field/right-foot pass out of the field to a teammate.
* Dribble into a field/left-foot pass out of the field to a teammate.
* Pass across two lines of a field to a teammate.
* Pass to a teammate/first-touch ball control into a field/pass to the next teammate.
* Pass as lob to a teammate across a field.

4.3.5   Running relay

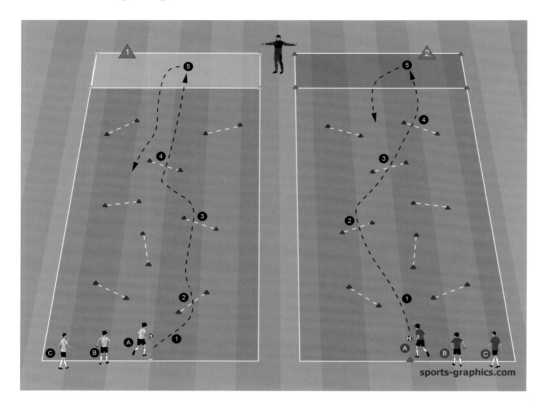

Execution

The YELLOW team competes against the BLUE team. Each team has its own playing field with a target zone (see zones 1 and 2). On the field are several cone goals. To compete, all players position themselves at the start marker (see players A, B, and C). The beginning player (here player A) is in possession and holds the ball in his hand. After a coach's signal, the competition begins and one player from each team runs into the field with the ball (see 1). The players A now must run through three different cone goals (see 2, 3, and 4). Afterwards the players A run into the target zone and deposit the ball there (see 5). The players A then transition and run back to their own team's start marker to activate the next player. The next player (here player B) also starts through three different cone goals and retrieves the ball placed in the target zone by the previous player and brings it back to their own team. He hands the ball off to the next player (here player C). To win, the teams must complete 20 actions in the target zone and must do so faster than the opposing team.

Variations

* Complete competition by dribbling with ball at foot (inside foot/outside foot/left/right).
* Complete predetermined feint at each cone goal.
* Modify running path (run through different cone goals than previous player).
* Modify running path (return run through cone goals).

4.3.6 Passing relay

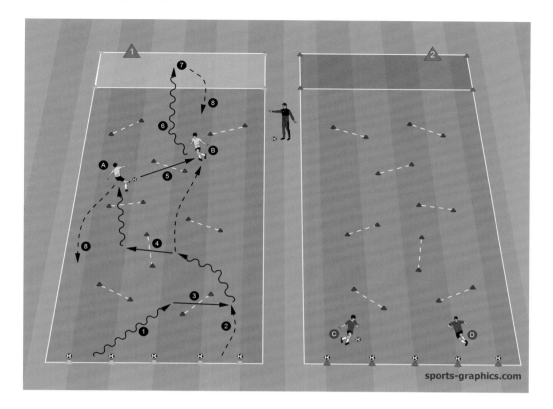

Execution

The YELLOW team competes against the BLUE team. Each team has its own playing field with a target zone (see zones 1 and 2). There are several cone goals on the field. There are several game balls at the starting position. To compete, two players from each team position themselves at the lower end of the field (see players C and D). The two players play together and one after the other play on the cone goals with the game balls and deposit the balls in the target zones. After a coach's signal, players A/B and C/D start simultaneously. One player (here player A) runs into the field with the ball at his foot (see 1) and his partner (here player B) follows without a ball (see 2). Players A and B play on three different cone goals one after the other in passing play (see 3, 4, and 5). Afterwards one player dribbles (here player B) the used ball toward the target zone (see 6) and deposits the ball in the target zone (see 7). Then the two players A and B immediately transition and run back to the starting position (see 8) to start the sequence over from there with the next ball. Players A/B and C/D now successively use all of the balls positioned at their own starting position. The first team to deposit all game balls in the target zone wins.

Variations

* Complete the competition with the ball in hand (throw through cone goals to partner).
* Complete predetermined feint prior to each pass through a cone goal.
* Modify passing paths (play on different cone goals than previous round).
* Specify passing and receiving leg (left/right).

4.3.7   Dribbling (follow-up action)

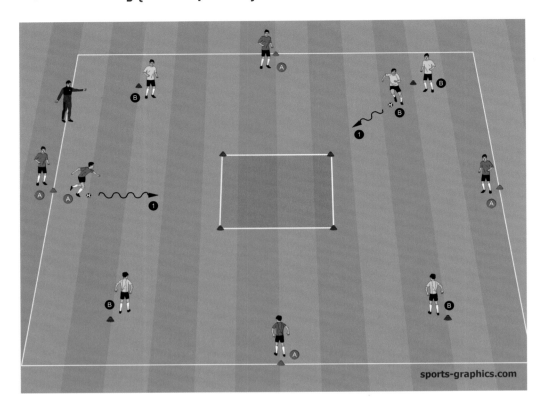

Execution

The RED team competes against the YELLOW team. To do so, players position themselves at starting positions of the same color. The starting positions are double-manned. Beginning just before the starting position, the first player dribbles into the center field, performs a predetermined action, passes the ball on to an outside position of his choice, and takes over the position of the player he passed to. The player now in possession starts a new action to another outside player via the center field. To win, teams must complete 20 actions in the center field and do so faster than the opposing team.

Variations for playing on the center

* Dribble/feint/right-foot pass/position change.
* Dribble/feint/left-foot pass/position change.
* Dribble/feint/double double-pass/position change.
* Dribble/feint/pass across two lines of center field/position change.
* Dribble/feint/pass across two lines of center field/double pass/position change.
* Dribble/six touches by juggling in center field/position change.
* Dribble/six touches by juggling/double double-pass/position change.
* Dribble/pass as lob across field/position change.
* Dribble/pass as lob across field/double pass/position change.

4.3.8   Opening up (follow-up action)

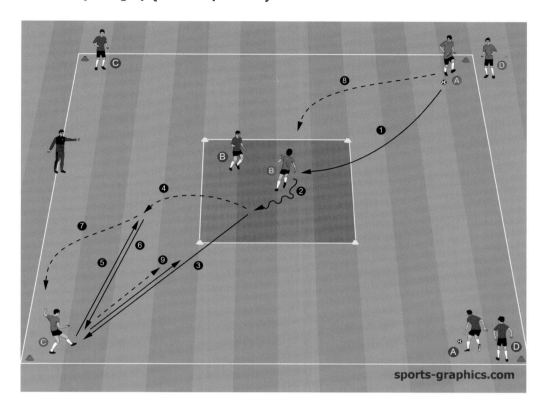

sports-graphics.com

Execution

The RED team competes against the BLUE team. To do so, players position themselves at the two outside positions (see players A, C, and D). The starting position is double-manned (see players A and D). Another player from each team positions himself in the center field (see player B). Each team has a ball. The players must complete a predetermined passing sequence. For a countable valuation, the respective task must be comprised of a total of 20 complete actions. The team that completes the 20 actions faster than the opposing team wins the competition. The passing sequence begins at position A. Player A passes the ball to player B in the center (see 1). Player B opens up (see 2) and passes the ball from the center field to player B at the opposite position (see 3). Player B runs sideways out of the center field (see 4) and receives the back pass from player C (see 5). Player B plays the ball to player C again (see 6) and takes over player C's position (see 7). The predetermined passing sequence is now finished and player C begins a new action. For that, player A moves directly to player B's position in the center field (see 8) after his first pass. The new action begins with player C to player D via player A (see 9).

Variations for playing on the center

* Open up (see 2) with the right/left inside leg.
* Open up (see 2) with the right/left outside leg.
* Open up (see 2) with the right inside leg behind the left supporting leg.
* Open up (see 2) with the left inside foot behind the right supporting leg.
* Open up (see 2) to a side specified with a call from the passing player.

4.3.9   Passing sequence (movement task)

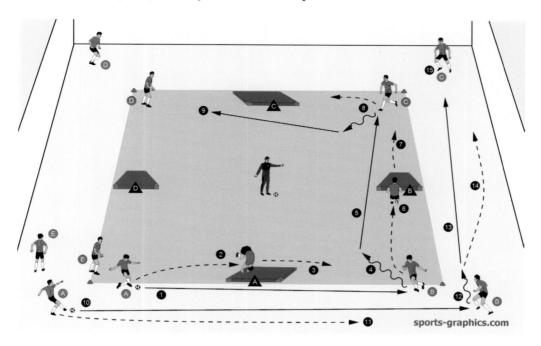

Execution

The RED team competes against the GREEN team. Each team must complete a predetermined passing sequence. The teams play separately and complete different tasks. The RED team plays in the center field and at the mats. The GREEN team plays outside around the center field. The RED team circulates the ball in a predetermined order. Player A passes to player B (see 1), runs to the mat and completes a predetermined movement task (see 2), and then takes over player B's position (see 3). Player B controls the ball (see 4) and passes to player C (see 5). Player B also runs to the mat to complete a movement task (see 6) and then takes over player C's position (see 7). Player C continues the passing sequence (see 8 and 9). Finally the ball travels to player E via player D, and player E continues the combination via player A. Both teams start their passing sequences at the same time. The GREEN team lets their own ball circulate around the center field. The GREEN team does not have to complete any movement tasks. Player A passes to player B (see 10) and takes over player B's position (see 11). Player B controls the ball (see 12) and passes to player C (see 13) to take over player C's position (see 14). Player C (see 15) continues the GREEN team's passing sequence via players D and E. The GREEN team must execute 20 complete passing rounds. The GREEN team's ball must therefore reach the starting position A/E 20 times. While the GREEN team works to complete this task, the RED team has the same amount of time to keep up its own passing sequence and collect points. Points are awarded for each completed movement task at the mats. Afterwards the tasks change. Now the GREEN team tries to exceed the previous score by the RED team.

Variations

⚬ Vary movement task at the mats (forward roll/backwards roll/pushups/cartwheel).

⚬ Specify number of touches per player (2/3/4 touches).

⚬ Vary the passing sequence (double double-pass) or specify passing leg (left/right).

4.3.10 Passing sequence (follow-up action)

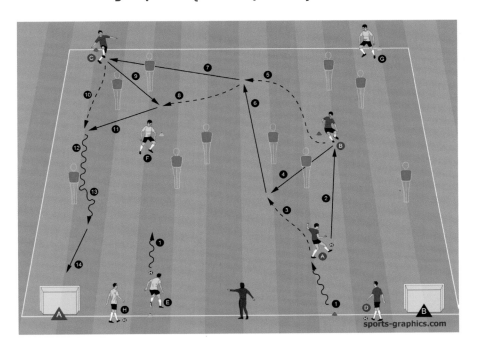

Execution

The BLUE team competes against the YELLOW team. After a predetermined passing sequence, each team tries to score on a mini goal (see mini goals A and B) (1 point). To do so, players position themselves at the cone markers. The first position is double-manned (see players A/D and E/H) and each of the players positioned there has a ball. The first players at the starting positions start their actions simultaneously (see players A and E). Player A briefly dribbles (see 1) and plays a pass to player B (see 2). Player A follows his pass toward the center (see 3) and receives the back pass from player B (see 4). Here a dummy is outplayed with a double pass (see 2, 3, and 4). Right after his pass, player B breaks away (see 5) and receives the pass from player A (see 6). Here, too, a dummy is outplayed with a double pass (see 4, 5, and 6). Player B passes to player C (see 7), follows his pass (see 8), and receives a back pass (see 9). After the pass, player C breaks away toward the dummy positioned in front of the mini goal (see 10) and receives the final pass of the passing sequence (see 11). The double double-pass by players B and C (see 7, 8, 9, 10, and 11) outplays two dummies. Player C controls the pass (see 12), performs a feint at the dummy (see 13), and finishes on mini goal A (see 14). Afterwards, player C takes over the starting position A/D. The players involved in the passing sequence move up one position. The next player D starts a new round with the last pass from player C (see 12). The competition ends as soon as a team has scored the predetermined number of goals.

Variations

* Specify passing technique (direct passes or play with two touches).
* Specify shooting technique (laces/inside foot/left/right).

4.3.11   Passing sequence (breaking away)

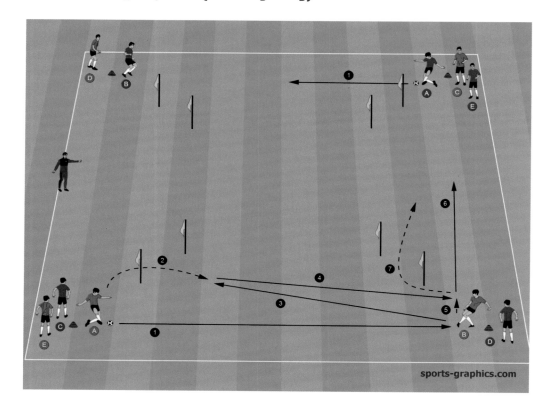

Execution

The RED team competes against the BLUE team. To do so, players position themselves at four starting positions of the same color. The starting positions are double-manned. At the starting position, the first player A plays a pass to player B (see 1). Afterwards, player A runs through the pole goal (see 2), receives the back pass (see 3), and plays the ball again (see 4) to the next player (see 5). The next player B repeats the described sequence (see 6 and 7) via the player on the next position (see player C). The teams circulate their own ball around the pole goals in the described order. The teams must play 20 complete rounds and the faster team wins the competition. The direction of play changes regularly.

Variations

* Dribble and feint prior to first pass/position change.
* Dribble and pass (see 1) with right foot/position change.
* Dribble and pass (see 1) with left foot/position change.
* Dribble and pass (see 1) as laces instep kick/position change.
* Running path (see 2) run backwards/position change.
* Dribble through pole goal/pass/position change.

4.3.12 Passing sequence (third man running)

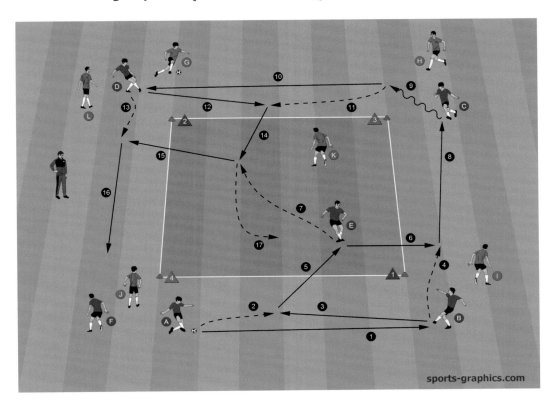

sports-graphics.com

Execution

The BLUE team competes against the RED team. The teams consist of at least six players each and position themselves around a center field. The players spread out evenly at the four cone markers, whereby the starting position is always double-manned and has a ball (see players A/F and G/H). In addition, one player from each team is positioned inside the center field (see players E and K). The teams simultaneously circulate their own ball around the center field and repeatedly include the center player. The BLUE team plays counterclockwise and the RED team plays clockwise. After a signal from the coach, both teams simultaneously start their passing sequences. Player A passes to player B (see 1) and follows his pass (see 2). Player B plays a back pass (see 3) and breaks away to the outside around cone marker 1 in the direction of play (see 4). The ball comes back to player B via the center player E (see 5 and 6), and B continues the passing sequence with a pass to player C (see 8). Right after his pass, the center player transitions toward cone marker 2 (see 7). Player C controls the ball in the direction of play (see 9) and plays to player D (see 10). Player C follows his pass (see 11) and receives a back pass from player D (see 12). Player D breaks away from cone marker 2 in the direction of play (see 13) and the ball travels around cone marker 2 (see 14 and 15) via player E (see 7), who has run into position. Player D plays to player F. All of the players involved in the passing sequence move up one position. The center player (here player E) remains in the center position and transitions toward cone marker 1 for the next round. Player F immediately starts a new round. During the passing sequence the BLUE team outplays cone markers 1 and 2 with a third man running. The RED team outplays cone markers 3 and 4 with a third man running. The teams must play 20 complete rounds and the faster team wins.

4.3.13 Open passing (movement tasks)

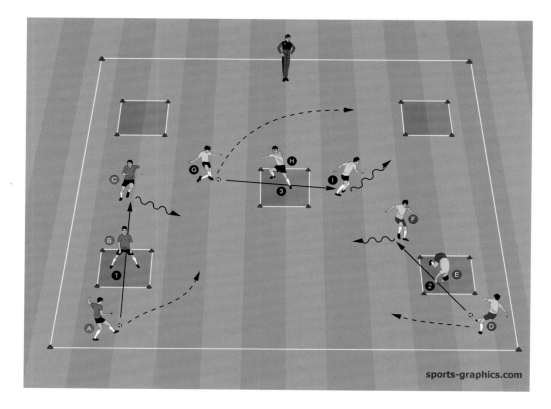

sports-graphics.com

Execution

Players are divided into multiple teams of three players each (see RED, BLUE, and YELLOW teams) and face off in a passing and technical competition. On the playing field are several marked fields that the teams must play on one after the other. Each team has one ball and plays on the fields in an arbitrary order and according to certain guidelines. The competition ends as soon as a team has successfully played on a predetermined number of fields and has gathered in one field with their own ball.

Tunneling variation (see RED team)

The player in possession dribbles toward a field. A teammate (here player B) runs into the chosen field and stands in a straddle position (see 1). The passing player (here player A) plays the ball to the third player on the team (here player C) through the legs of the player positioned in the field.

Forward roll variation (see BLUE team)

The player with the ball dribbles toward a field. A teammate (here player E) runs into the chosen field. The passing player (here player D) passes to the team's third player (here player C) so the ball passes close to the player running into the field. Player E dives over the played ball and does a forward roll (see 2).

Leap variation (see YELLOW team)

The player in possession dribbles toward a field. A teammate (here player H) runs into the chosen field. The passing player (here player G) passes to the team's third player (here player I) so the ball passes close to the player running into the field. Player H leaps over the played ball.

4.3.14 Open passing (follow-up action)

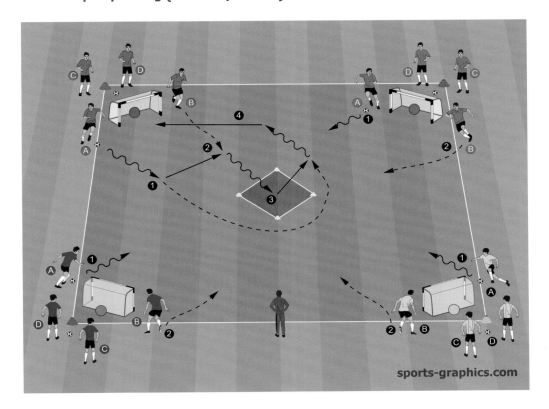

sports-graphics.com

Execution

The BLUE, YELLOW, RED, and GREEN teams compete against each other and position themselves in the corners of the field. In each corner is a mini goal that matches the color of the respective team. In the center of the field is a diamond. After a signal from the coach, two players from each team start into the field with a ball (see players A and B) (see 1 and 2), play on the diamond field with a predetermined technical task (see 3), and finish on their own mini goal (see 4). The shot is the starting signal for the team's next set of players (see players C and D). The teams try to take the predetermined number of shots as quickly as possible.

Variations of technical tasks

* Pass and one-touch ball control into diamond field.
* Pass into diamond and dribble out of diamond
* Pass across two lines of diamond.
* Pass in front of and behind diamond.
* Pass behind diamond and dribble through diamond.
* Dribble through diamond and pass behind diamond.
* Pass (hip-high/high) over diamond.

4.3.15 Open passing (play on athletic equipment and spaces)

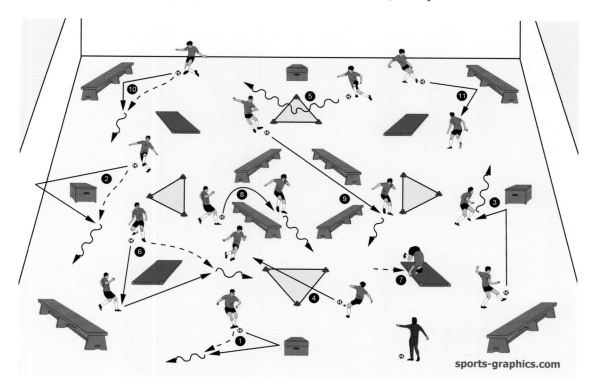

Execution

Several teams compete against each other. Teams can consist of two, three, or four players. After a starting signal, each team plays with their own ball on the different pieces of equipment (vaulting box, mat, and bench) or zones with predetermined techniques or passing sequences. Teams start simultaneously after a signal from the coach and the first team to have played on the predetermined number of apparatuses wins.

Variations and tasks

* Player A passes against the vaulting box, controls the ball, and plays to player B (see 1).
* Player A passes behind a box via the boards, controls the ball, and plays to player B (see 2).
* Player A passes against the box, player B controls the rebound (see 3).
* Player A juggles the ball, crosses over the box, and plays to player B.
* Player A lobs the ball over the box to player B.
* Player A passes across two lines of the field to player B (see 4).
* Player A dribbles into the field, performs a feint, and passes to player B (see 5).
* Player A passes into the field and player B plays a direct pass out of the field to player C.
* Players A and B play a double pass over a mat (see 6).
* Player A passes to player B and does a forward roll/backwards roll on the mat (see 7).
* Player A lobs the ball over the bench into the center to player B (see 8).
* Player A passes to player B through the center between the benches (see 9).
* Player A passes against the bench, controls the ball, and passes to player B (see 10).
* Player A passes against the box and player B controls the rebound (see 11).

4.3.16 Juggling (finish)

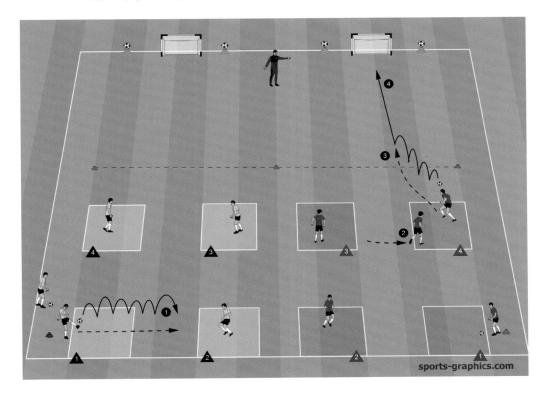

sports-graphics.com

Execution

The YELLOW team competes against the BLUE team. After completing a predetermined juggling task, each team tries to score on a mini goal (one point) or hit a ball placed on top of a cone (two points). One player from each team begins the action at a start marker. The other players position themselves in fields 1, 2, 3, and 4. Each field is manned with a player. The starting player begins with his own ball and tries to juggle the ball into field 2 without it touching the ground and pass it off to the next player. As soon as a player has passed off the ball without making an error, the passing player takes over the position in the receiving player's field (see 2). The pass receiver continues the juggling task and tries to juggle into the next field. As soon as a player makes an error and the ball touches the ground, the player must return with his ball to the starting position and start over. Finally the teams try to juggle the ball into field 4 and the last player juggles out of field 4 across a finish line (see 3). After the finish line has been crossed players can finish on the target (see 4). After his finish, the shooter starts again at the starting position.

Variations

* Specify juggling technique (strictly alternating/left/right/head).
* Specify shooting technique (see 4) for finish (volley/dropkick/header).
* Specify receiving technique after ball handoff (inside foot/thigh/head/left/right).

4.3.17 Juggling (soccer tennis)

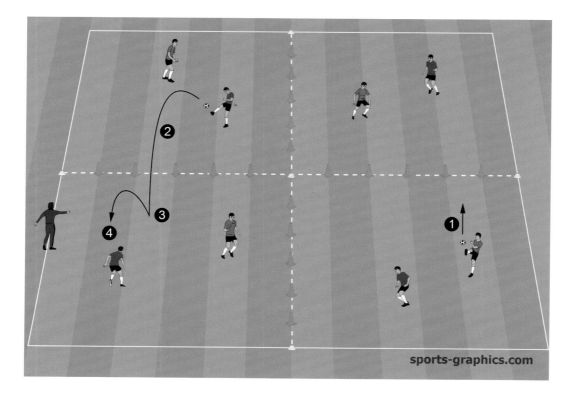

Execution

The RED team competes against the BLUE team. To do so, one player from each team is positioned in one of the four halves. Each team has a ball. Players must complete a predetermined juggling task (see 1). To score points, the respective task must be completed correctly. After successfully completing the juggling task or after a failed attempt, the ball is passed to a teammate in an adjacent field (see 2). To do so, the ball is played high over the cone markers and can make contact with the ground no more than once in the adjacent field (see 3) before the next player begins the juggling task (see 4). Here the correct pass over the cone markers (see 2) counts as part of the passing player's juggling task. The predetermined ground contact (see 3) and the correct receiving of the ball count as part of the receiving player's juggling task (see 4). The teams must complete 20 correct actions in the form of the predetermined juggling task and the faster team wins.

Variations

★ Five juggling touches with right/left foot.

★ Five juggling touches with right/left knee.

★ Five juggling touches with the head.

★ Ten strictly alternating juggling touches w/left and right foot.

★ One juggling touch with outside foot for maximum of 5 juggling touches total.

★ One juggling touch with the heel for maximum of 5 juggling touches total.

★ One juggling touch with the shoulder for maximum of 5 juggling touches total.

4.3.18 Crosses

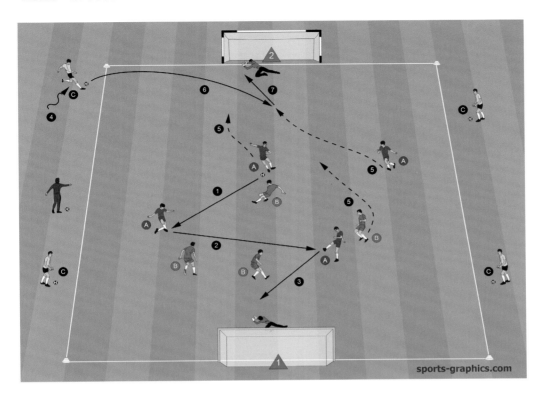

sports-graphics.com

Execution

The BLUE team competes against the RED team and plays 4-on-4 on the large goals 1 and 2, each manned with a goalkeeper. The teams initially play freely on both goals (see 1 and 2). The game begins with ball holding and, after three successful passes in a row without the opponents capturing the ball, the team in possession can finish on the two large goals (see 3). Each finish is followed by another action in which the outside players (see players C) are involved. The outside player positioned diagonally across from the shooter briefly dribbles (see 4) to play a cross in front of the previously not played-on goal (here goal 2). All players immediately transition for the cross (see 5) and get into offensive and defensive mode. The team previously in possession (here the BLUE team) tries to exploit (see 7) the cross (see 6). If the attackers manage to score (see 7) or a defender is able to clear the cross with a volley, another action follows in the form of a second cross on the opposite goal (here goal 1). Depending on whether or not a goal was scored after the first cross or the defending team cleared the ball, the players get into defensive or offensive mode to exploit and defend the second cross accordingly. Increasing points can be scored based on the chronological order of the three possible finishes per action. The successful team is awarded points for a goal during the game (one point), a goal scored after the first cross (two points), or a goal after the third cross (three points). The team in the outside positions (see players C) also gets points with each exploited cross (one point). After a predetermined period of play, the teams switch positions and four new crossing players take over the outside positions.

4.3.19 Headers

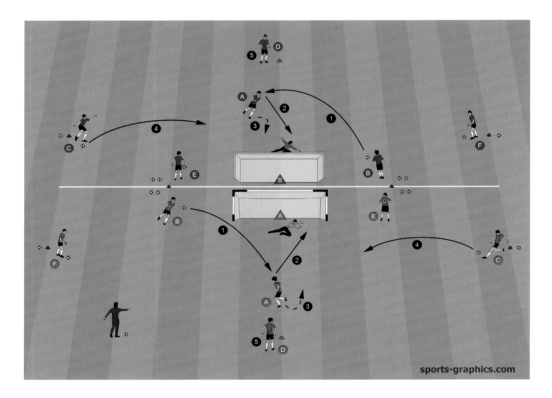

sports-graphics.com

Execution

The RED team competes against the BLUE team. Each team plays on an own goal, which is manned by an opposing goalkeeper. Each team tries to score more goals from headers more quickly than the opposing team. To do so, two players position themselves at a starting cone in the center (see players A and D). Two other players with balls position themselves next to the goal as throwers (see players B and E) and in the outside positions as cross players (see players C and F). After a starting signal from the coach, the teams start simultaneously. Player A runs toward the goal, receives a high throw from player B (see 1), and tries to score with a header (see 2). After the finish, player A immediately transitions (see 3), reorients himself, and receives a cross from player C (see 4). Player A tries to also score with his second header. With the second header from player A, the next player D starts his new action (see 5) and also gets to finish twice via players E and F.

Variations

★ Specify jumping technique for header (jump forward/to the side/two legs/one leg).

★ Exploit as a group of two (throw to player A/cross to player D).

★ Immediate position change after each action (position A to position B to position C).

★ Double points for certain techniques (diving header/bouncing shot).

★ Opportunity for varying finishing techniques (sideways scissor-kicks/volleys).

4.3.20 Shot on goal

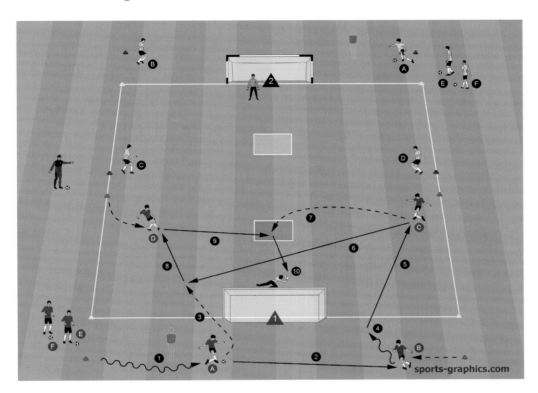

Execution

The BLUE team competes against the YELLOW team. After a repeating and predetermined passing sequence, the teams try to score as many goals as possible on the large goals manned by goalkeepers. After a signal from the coach, the competition starts and the first player from each team (see player A) begins the action. Player A briefly dribbles and does a feint at the dummy (see 1), then plays a pass to player B (see 2) behind the goal, and immediately orients himself toward the center (see 3). Player B moves toward the pass and controls the ball toward the center (see 4). Player B plays a pass to player C (see 5). Player C plays a diagonal pass to player A (see 6) and does a curved run toward the center field (see 7). Player A passes to the approaching player D (see 8). Player D plays a precision assist into the center field for player C (see 9). Player C takes a shot on goal 1 from the center field (see 10). The shot (see 10) is also the starting signal for the next player (here player E), who immediately starts a next action with his own ball. The previously active players each move up one position according to the passing order. Each team has the goal of scoring as often as possible and wins after scoring ten goals.

Variations

* Specify touches (see 9) for certain actions (direct play).
* Specify technique (see 10) for shot on goal (direct finish/laces kick/inside foot/left/right).

4.3.21   1-on-1

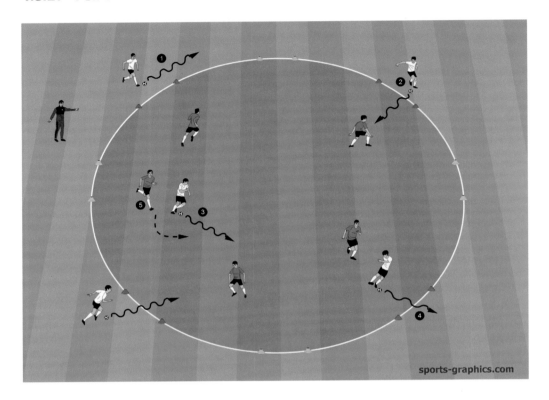

sports-graphics.com

Execution

Players are divided into two teams (see GREEN and WHITE teams). The WHITE team players each have a ball, spread out outside the center circle, and dribble around the center (see 1). In the center circle are several different-colored cone goals. The opposing team (here the GREEN team) positions itself inside the circle and gets into defensive mode. At a signal from the coach, the WHITE players have two minutes to score as many points as possible. A point is scored when a player dribbles into the circle (see 2), dribbles through the circle (see 3), and dribbles out through another cone goal (see 4). The GREEN team players try to prevent this from happening (see 5). After two minutes, the tasks change.

Variations

* ★ Complete as competition (e.g., Which team gets the highest score?).
* ★ Complete as competition (e.g., Which player scores the most points?).
* ★ Vary the task (enter through the YELLOW goal/exit through the RED goal).

4.3.22 2-on-2

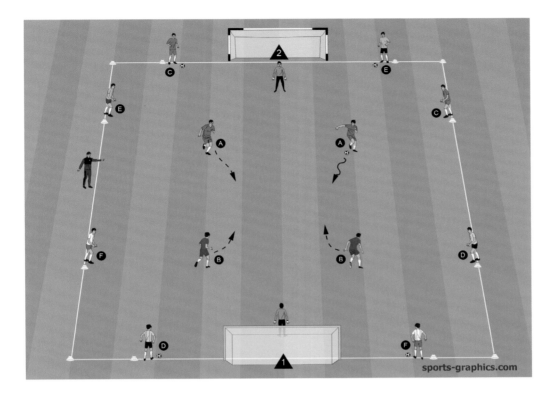

Execution

Teams consist of two players each (see teams A, B, C, D, and E) and compete against each other. Consecutive 2-on-2 game situations are created in the process. In the beginning, two teams (see teams A and B) are positioned in the center of the field. The other teams (see teams C, D, E, and F) are positioned in the outside positions. A 2-on-2 situation ends when a goal is scored or a shot misses the goal. If the goalkeeper deflects a shot, he brings the saved ball back into the game until the 2-on-2 situation ends. The team that scored or missed the goal remains in the field for the next 2-on-2 situation. The other team is eliminated and takes over one of the four outside positions. The drill starts with 2-on-2 play between team A and team B. Team A plays on goal 1 and team B plays on goal 2. As soon as team A scores a goal or misses the goal, team B is eliminated. Now team A defends goal 1 in the subsequent 2-on-2 situation and attacks goal 2. Next, a team in possession (see teams C and E) dribbles into the field from the opposite side for the subsequent 2-on-2 situation. If team B captures the ball during the first round and scores a goal or misses the goal, team A is eliminated. Team B remains in the field to defend goal 2 in a subsequent 2-on-2 situation, and a team from the opposite side (see teams D and F) dribbles a ball into the field and attacks goal 2. The teams in the outside positions (see teams C/E and F/D) previously coordinated which team intervenes in the next action. The 2-on-2 situations continue indefinitely.

Variation

* Entry from outside positions via diagonal pass.

4.3.23 Double 2-on-2

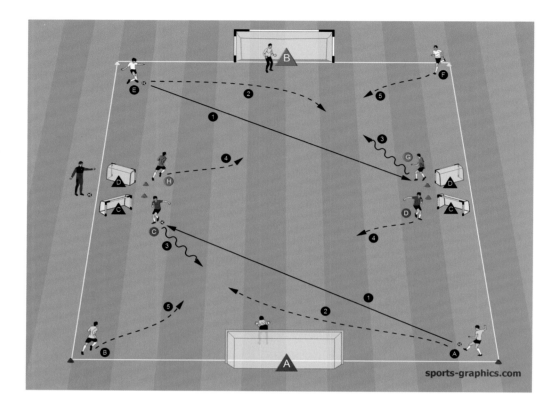

sports-graphics.com

Execution

Players are divided into four teams of two (see YELLOW, BLUE, WHITE, and RED teams). The teams compete against each other in the two halves of the field. The YELLOW team plays against the BLUE team on goals A and C and the WHITE team plays against the RED team on goals B and D. All four teams play against each other, resulting in a total points system. At a signal from the coach, player A plays his ball to player C (see 1) and follows his pass (see 2). Player C controls the ball (see 3) and together with player D (see 4) attacks the large goal A in 2-on-2 play. Player B completes the YELLOW team (see 5). After the YELLOW team possibly captures the ball, they can counter on the two mini goals C. After a goal is scored in 2-on-2 play, the teams change starting positions. In a subsequent action, the BLUE team defends the large goal A and the YELLOW team attacks the large goal A. In the other half, the WHITE and RED teams face off in analogous order. Due to the total points system, the teams must quickly initiate a new action after a 2-on-2 situation ends so they can score as many points as possible. The competition ends when a team has scored 20 goals.

Points system

* Goal scored on large goals A/B (1 point)
* Goal scored on goals C/D after capturing the ball (2 points)
* Goal scored on goals A/B after capturing the ball (3 points)
* Goal scored after direct shot (2 points)

4.3.24 4-plus-1 against 4-plus-1

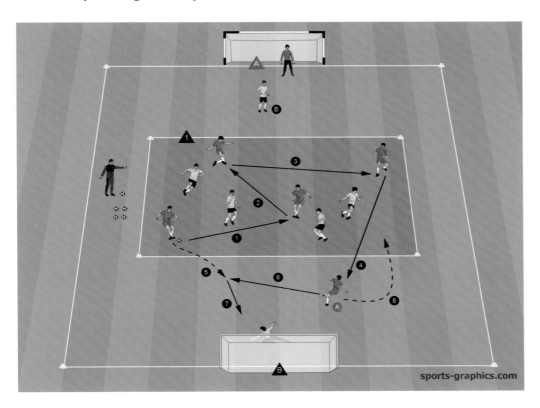

Execution

The RED team competes against the YELLOW team. To do so, four players from each team position themselves in the center field (see field 1). Another player from each team is positioned in front of the large goals (see players A and B). The competition begins with a 4-on-4 game in the center field. The team in possession (here the RED team) tries to play three consecutive passes without the opponents capturing the ball (see 1, 2, and 3). After three successful passes, their own outside player (see player A) can be passed to (see 4). With the opening pass (see 4), one player from the team in possession can run out of the center field (see 5), receive a pass from player A (see 6), and finish on the large goal (see 7). The passing player (see player A) immediately switches to the center field (see 8). The coach brings a new ball into the game for the next 4-on-4 situation. The shooter takes over player A's position. The teams try to score as many goals as possible.

Variations

* Shot on goal (see 7) as direct finish.
* Shot on goal (see 7) with right/left inside foot.
* Shot on goal (see 7) with right/left outside foot.
* Shot on goal (see 7) with right/left instep.
* Coach's ball for inferior-number team (here the RED team).
* Coach's ball for superior-number team (here the YELLOW team).
* Specify passing technique (see 4) for opening pass (direct pass).
* Prerequisite for opening pass (see 1, 2, and 3): 2/3/4 passes within own ranks.

4.3.25 Increasing player ratio

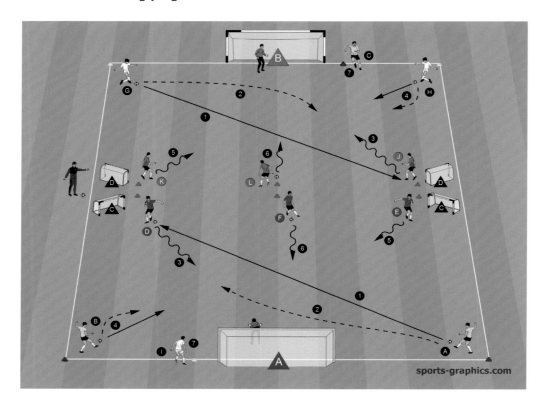

sports-graphics.com

Execution

Players are divided into four teams of three (see YELLOW, BLUE, WHITE, and RED teams). The teams compete against each other in two halves of the field. The YELLOW team plays against the BLUE team on goals A and C, and the WHITE team plays against the RED team on goals B and D. All four teams play against each other, resulting in a total points system. At a signal from the coach, player A plays his ball to player D (see 1) and follows his pass (see 2). Player D controls the ball (see 3) and tries to score on the large goal A in 1-on-1 play. After the finish in the 1-on-1 situation, player B plays a diagonal pass to player E (see 4). Player E controls the ball and together with player D tries to score on the large goal A in 2-on-2 play against players A and B (see 5). After the finish in the 2-on-2 situation, player F dribbles his ball into the field (see 6) and together with players D and E tries to score a goal on the large goal A against players A and B plus C. With the first touch by player F, player C starts to quickly balance the advantage. After successfully capturing the ball in 1-on-1, 2-on-2, or 3-on-3, the YELLOW team players counter on mini goals C. With the coach's starting signal, the WHITE and RED teams begin an identical sequence in the opposite half of the field. After all six balls are out of the game, the teams change positions. The individual players also change starting positions within the own team. The BLUE team now defends against the YELLOW team and the RED team now defends against the WHITE team. The competition ends as soon as a team has scored 20 goals.

Points system

* Goal scored on large goals A/B (1 point)
* Goal scored on goals C/D in 1-on-1/2-on-2 after capturing the ball (1 point)/3-on-3 (2 points)

5 ATHLETIC TRAINING

Athletic Training emphasizes functional training. The term *functional training* refers to a training methodology in the areas of fitness, athletics, and rehab. Functional training is geared toward creating healthy and high-performing athletes. Here a foundation for improved performance development in a sport is created In accordance with individual requirements. In doing so, the objective is to increase movement quality and quantity by improving coordination, adaptability, balance, mobility, stability, strength, endurance, and speed. The conventional fitness industry is primarily focused on bodybuilding and muscle-building systems built on isolation exercises. By contrast, the athletic requirements and objectives in soccer require sport-specific differentiated strength training. Functional training forgoes the emphasis on individual muscles and meets the soccer-specific requirements by comprehensively promoting and demanding movements. The following training content attempts to highlight central and important elements of soccer-specific athletic training, and to offer a sensible balance from the extensive and complex scope of functional training. At the center of the drills is the correction of muscular imbalance and improving soccer-specific mobility and stability, as well as good activation as preparation for a training unit. In addition, training content with the sling trainer as a training aid is introduced as part of a holistic training program.

HOLISM SLING TRAINER ENDURANCE SELF-MASSAGE STRENGTH
FASCIA TRAINING FUN SELF-RESPONSIBILITY STABILITY BALANCE
PERFORMANCE DEVELOPMENT FUNCTIONAL TRAINING COORDINATION
PROMOTE MOVEMENT CORRECT IMBALANCES MOBILITY

5.1 ACTIVATION

Activation exercises optimize training preparation via complex movement patterns. In doing so, the central nervous system and the muscles are prepared for traction, tension, and momentum. The soccer-specific approach focuses on gluteal and trunk activation. Strength development in these areas of the body is fundamental and affects the extremities. Here the use of mini bands as a useful training tool achieves optimal activation of the crucial muscles. In the starting position of the standing mini band exercises, emphasis must be placed on an upright trunk position, the head as an extension of the spine, toes pointing forward, and the pelvis tilting forward. The knees are only slightly bent, and movement originates primarily in the hip and gluteal muscles. There is tension on the mini band during the entire exercise.

TRUNK ACTIVATION
COMPLEX MOVEMENT PATTERNS
MOBILITY CENTRAL NERVOUS SYSTEM
JOINT PREPARATION
TRAINING PREPARATION SOCCER-SPECIFIC
MINI BANDS PREPARATORY TENSION
CORRECTION OF IMBALANCES
MOMENTUM STABILITY

5.1.1   5.1.1   Standard

Opening up

The athlete starts in a lunge position. Both hands press into the floor, the right knee is stacked over the foot, and the left leg is fully extended. Next, the athlete twists his body to the left with his arm extended. His eyes follow his right hand. The exercise ends by moving the right elbow toward the right ankle.

Walking hands

In the starting position, the athlete folds his upper body toward the floor. Next, the athlete takes small forward steps with his hands. The exercise ends by taking small steps with the feet toward the hands. The legs are always fully extended.

Adductor seesaw

To start, the athlete kneels on the floor on his left leg with the right leg extended to the side with the foot on the floor. Next, he twists his upper body to the right. His gaze follows his right hand. The exercise ends with the upper body twisting to the left. In doing so, the right hand moves between the left knee and left arm.

Hip rotation

In the starting position, the athlete internally rotates the left hip and externally rotates the right hip. In doing so, the left knee touches the right heel. The hands are balled into fists in front of the body. Next, the athlete moves into a neutral seated posture in which his knees point to the ceiling. The exercise ends with the athlete returning to the starting position in the opposite direction.

Lunge

The athlete starts in a high lunge. His hands are on his hips, his gaze is directed forward, and the upper body is erect. Next the athlete drops the left knee toward the floor. The knee is stacked over the foot. The exercise ends with a forward arm movement.

Quadruped walk, straight

In the starting position, the athlete is on all fours. The knees are slightly raised, the shoulders are stacked over the hands, and the back is straight. Next, the left leg and right arm simultaneously move forward. There should be as little upper body movement as possible during the execution of this movement. The athlete slowly moves forward with the same movement on the other side.

Quadruped walk, sideways

In the starting position, the athlete is on all fours. The knees are slightly raised, the shoulders are stacked over the hands and the back is straight. Next, legs and hands simultaneously move sideways with a controlled movement. There should be as little upper body movement as possible during the execution of this movement.

5.1.2   5.1.2 Mini bands

Straight steps (forward and backwards)

Lateral steps (knees)

Lateral steps (knees and ankles)

Lateral steps (knees and feet)

Lateral steps (straight legs)

Internal rotation

Squat

Pelvic lift

Shoulder clock

5.2 CORRECTING EXERCISES

Correcting Exercises counteract limitations in mobility and stability, and are geared toward avoiding imbalances, correcting movement patterns, and establishing an improved function status for stresses and strains. The ultimate goal is to minimize the risk of injury to ensure optimal performance development. Here the *functional movement screen (FMS)* is a field-tested analysis system for detecting imbalances and asymmetries. Training exercises to counteract the individual weak spots are chosen based on the FMS.

MOBILITY
INDIVIDUAL WEAK SPOTS
STABILITY IMBALANCES
CORRECTION OF LIMITATIONS
FUNCTIONAL MOVEMENT SCREEN
LOWERING RISK OF INJURY
HIP MOBILITY FUNCTION STATUS
MOVEMENT PATTERN BREATHING
MOVEMENT ANALYSIS

5.2.1   Breathing

Deep belly breathing with band

The athlete is in a prone position on the floor with the band around his trunk. His head rests on his hands and his toes are tucked. Next, he takes a deep breath through the nose. In doing so, the band should expand sideways as well as upward. The exercise ends with a long slow exhale through the mouth.

Deep belly breathing with a balloon (1)

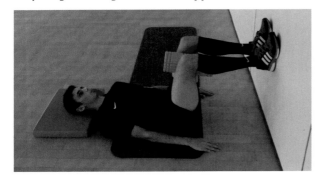

The athlete lies on his back with the head slightly elevated and the legs at a 90° angle with the feet resting against the wall. The arms rest alongside the body. The athlete holds a balloon in his mouth and has a foam roller between his knees. Next, the athlete takes a deep breath through the nose. The exercise ends with a long slow exhale through the mouth into the balloon.

Deep belly breathing with a balloon (2)

The athlete starts on all fours. The hips are stacked over the knees and the shoulders are stacked over the hands. The back is straight and the head is an extension of the spine. The athlete holds a balloon in his mouth. Next, he takes a deep breath through the nose into the belly. The exercise ends with a long slow exhale through the mouth into the balloon.

5.2.2 Hip mobility

Hip stretch

The athlete begins by lying on his right side. The head is slightly elevated. The right knee is bent and pushed back, the left hand holds on to the right leg. The left knee is bent and moves forward at a 90° angle. The right hand grips the inside of the left thigh. Next, the upper body and head turn to the left. In doing so, both knees are separated as much as possible, supported by deep belly breaths.

Bent-knee pelvic lift

The athlete lies on his back. He pulls one knee into the chest and holds it there with his hands. The other foot is planted with the knee bent. Next, he raises his hips toward the ceiling, supported by deep belly breaths. The heel of the planted foot presses into the floor.

Leg extension

In the starting position, the athlete lies on his back. Both legs are extended toward the ceiling. The band is placed around the right foot and pulled tight with the hands. Next, the extended left leg is raised off the floor. The right leg also remains extended during the exercise. As he lowers the left leg, the athlete actively pulls the right leg closer to his body with the band.

Leg extension with a band

In the starting position, the athlete lies on his back. Both legs are extended toward the ceiling. The band is placed around the right foot and pulled tight with the hands. Next, the extended left leg is raised off the floor. The right leg also remains extended during the exercise. As he lowers the left leg, the athlete actively pulls the right leg closer to his body with the band.

5.2.3 Thoracic spine mobility

Thoracic spine opener with a foam roller

In the starting position, the athlete lies on his right side. The head is slightly elevated. The right leg is extended. The left knee is bent at a 90° angle and rests on the foam roller. The elbows are also bent and the palms touch. Next, the upper body twists to the left. The gaze follows the left hand and the inside of the left thigh actively presses into the roller.

Thoracic spine rotation

The athlete kneels, sitting back on his heels with his upper body lowered to the floor. In doing so, his posterior touches his feet, the left hand touches the back of the neck, and the right forearm rests on the floor. Next, the upper body rotates to the left. The gaze follows the left elbow and his posterior continues to touch his feet.

5.2.4 Core stability

Leg extension with mini band

In the starting position, the athlete lies on his back with his head slightly elevated. The mini band is placed around the feet. The knees are bent at a 90° angle and the shins face the ceiling. Next, the right leg extends forward while the left leg remains at a 90° angle. The exercise ends with the same movement in the opposite direction. The athlete exhales deeply while lowering the leg.

Clamp the roller

The athlete lies on his back with his head slightly elevated. The knees are bent at a 90° angle and the shins face the ceiling. The athlete holds a foam roller between his left elbow and left thigh. Next, the right leg is extended forward while the left leg remains at a 90° angle. There is constant pressure on the roller. The athlete exhales deeply while lowering the leg.

5.3 SELF-MASSAGE

A *massage* that targets specific body tissue is a way to optimally prepare for the physical exertion of training, and improves the ability to regenerate after a training unit. The rolling technique primarily targets stiff or shortened muscles with increased muscle tension (trigger points). Self-massage techniques as preparation for physical exertion decrease muscle tension, and post-exertion use promotes quick regeneration. Prior to physical exertion, the length of treatment per muscle group should be approximately 10-30 seconds at a rather rapid pace. After exertion, the length of treatment per muscle group should be approximately 60 seconds at a slow pace. While administering a self-massage, the athletes should be made aware of the following training guidelines. Movements should be controlled while breathing regularly. The massage should be comprehensive and from all directions and combined with joint movements. When introducing massage techniques, it is important to overcome the initial discomfort, and massage techniques should not be used at all in cases of acute injuries.

FASCIAE
MASSAGE ROLLING
BREATHING BALL ROLLER
PRESSURE POINTS REGENERATION
INJURY PREVENTION
PREPARATION MOBILITY
MUSCLE TENSION

5.3.1 Ball

Bottom of the foot

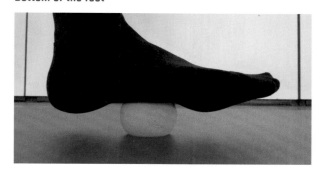

Calf

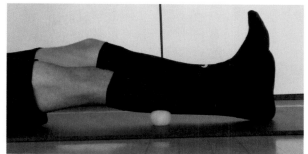

Piriformis muscle

Gluteal

Hip

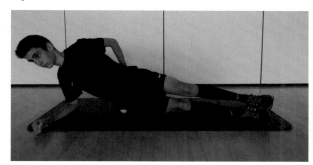

Thoracic spine

5.3.2 Roller

Calf

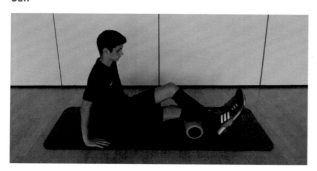

Hamstring

Thoracic spine

Latissimus dorsi muscle

Tibialis anterior muscle

Quadriceps

Iliotibial band

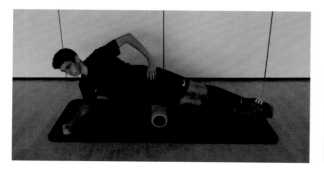

Hip flexors

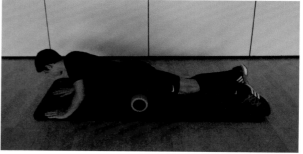

5.4   SLING TRAINING

Sling Training is geared toward an improved functional performance and works with bodyweight resistance. The intentional instability of the sling trainer affects and works strength development, coordination, deep muscles, stability, and balance. Due to its unstable position, the body is constantly forced to work against gravity. Training exercises are ramped up or made easier via angles and distances to the attachment point and should be guided by integrated movement patterns to cover all muscle groups. When working with the sling trainer, it is important to maintain good body tension. In doing so the head, hips, and feet should be lined up. It is important to breathe regularly while moving.

GRAVITY
COORDINATION INSTABILITY
BALANCE MOVEMENT PATTERNS
FUN CHALLENGE
HOLISM VARIABILITY
FUNCTIONAL PERFORMANCE
BODY TENSION TRUNK CORE
DEEP MUSCLES
STRENGTH

5.4.1   Trunk

Bicycle

Dynamic forearm plank

Pike

Roll out (kneeling)

Roll out (standing)

Side crunch

Side plank

Anti-rotation

Rotation

5.4.2 Hip dominance

Pulling knees to chest

Hip raise

Standing back scale

5.4.3 Knee dominance

Deep squat

One-legged squat

Squat with rotation

Supported lunge

Stable lunge with foot in sling trainer

Unstable lunge with foot in sling trainer

Burpee

5.4.4 Chest and shoulder

Push-up (hands in sling trainer)

Push-up (feet in sling trainer)

T-position

5.4.5 Back

Row

Intense row

W-position

6 CREATIVE COACHING TIPS

Creative Coaching Tips includes an illustrated list of various tips and assists for training, competitions, and support for their own team. The individual coaching tips are intended to simplify organization, planning, and implementation of training and running a competition. Moreover, easily implementable training tools are introduced.

SCREEN SHOTS BALL DEPOTS
COACHING ZONE SET PIECES
PLAYING POSITIONS PLAYER MAGNETS
FIELD MARKERS
TACTICAL TOOLS COACH'S SIGNALS
TRAINING PLANNING COLOR SIGNALS
TRAINING TOOLS HAND SIGNALS

6.1 TRAINING PLANNING

Field markers (1)

Use the existing lines on the field to designate zones and fields for easier orientation.

Field markers (2)

Avoid interfering cones inside the field by marking off fields to be played on with discs or shims.

Field markers (3)

Bibs placed in advance make getting in position and formations easier.

Goal markers

Use a combination of caution tape or streamers and slalom poles to easily mark a goal.

Cone markers

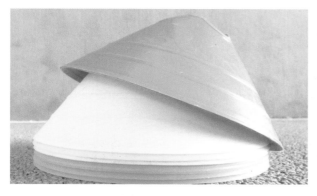

Simplify converting playing fields or zones by stacking multiple cone markers in advance.

Cooler and doctor's kit

Have a cooler and a doctor's kit at the ready at practice and during competitions.

6.2 BALL DEPOTS

Goals

Store and keep replacement balls in goals for a quick continuation of play.

Cones

Place balls on cones as a ball depot or starting position.

Field

Store and keep replacement balls in a depot marked with cones.

Mini goals

Store and keep replacement balls in a depot marked with a mini goal.

Box

Use a gymnastics box to store balls.

Bench

Use a bleacher bench to store balls.

6.3 TRAINING TOOLS

Hand pump

Always keep a hand pump on the field in the ball bag.

Types of balls

Use and integrate different types of balls or sports for diverse training.

Goal markers (1)

Divide the goal space with different targets and sub-areas.

Goal markers (2)

Use colored bibs or cone markers to mark the goal.

Instability

Use unstable surfaces as a substitute for expensive training materials for coordination training.

Shoe hockey

Use soccer shoes and a ball to play the game shoe hockey.

6.4 COACH'S SIGNALS

Whistle

Always carry one and keep it on your key ring.

Hand signals

Reaction to a coach's signal with a hand motion or prompt.

Cone marker

Reaction to a coach's color signal in the form of a colored cone marker.

Color swatches

Reaction to a coach's color signal (color swatches) in the form of a card of different-colored swatches.

Number

Reaction to a visual coach's signal in the form of different number cards.

Letter

Reaction to a visual coach's signal in the form of different letter cards.

6.5 TACTICAL TOOLS

Magnets

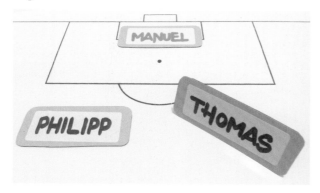

Write players' names on magnetic boards for changes in the order.

Didactics

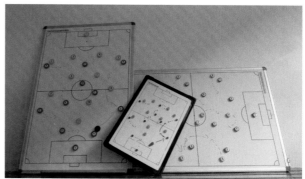

Standardization of the direction of play (players' view) for all tactical discussions to simplify recognition or comprehensibility.

Templates

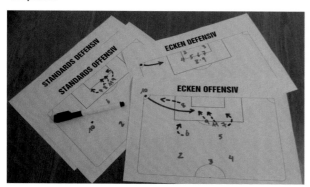

Write player numbers for current game day on standard templates to bring along and for visualization in the locker room.

Coaching zone

Prepare substitutes' bench with templates and tactical charts for half-time meeting and prior to substitutions.

Playing positions

Prepare for tactical drills by placing colored bibs in specific playing positions on the field.

Screenshot

Prepare and use screenshots from tactical videos for better explanations with a still frame.

APPENDIX

Photo Credits

Cover design: Claudia Sakyi

Cover photos: @Thinkstockphotos/iStock/jessicahyde

Interior layout: Andreas Reuel

Jacket photos: Author photo: Norbert Gettschat (www.foto-gettschat.de).
                   Background graphics: @Thinkstockphotos/iStock/jessicahyde

Interior photos: Fabian Seeger & Loïc Favé

Graphics: All graphics for games and drills were created with easy
                   Sports-Graphics (www.easy-sport-software.com).

Typesetting: Guido Maetzing

Editing: Anne Rumery, Kristina Oltrogge

Acknowledgments

Loïc Favé

I would like to dedicate this book to my grandfather, who passed away last year, and to my grandmother. I learned so much from you and you always supported me. Merci beaucoup, je vous aime très fort. I want to thank my parents, my girlfriend Lincy, my friends, and my extended family.

I would also like to thank Stephan, Lewe, and Fabian for their enormous soccer support, my team (Eimsbütteler TV year 2000), and my coaching team Jasper, Paddy, and Jonas, as well as Steffi, and the entire ETV team.

Fabian Seeger

I would like to thank my colleagues at the association, base camp, and club level for the continuous exchange and successful collaboration. I dedicate this book to my parents, my brother Alexander, and my girlfriend Annika.

SOCCER –
TECHNIQUES & TACTICS

ISBN: 9781782551041
$ 32.00/£ 24.00

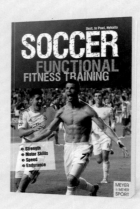

ISBN: 9781782550907
$ 34.95/£ 23.95

ISBN: 9781782550723
$ 19.95/£ 12.95

ISBN: 9781782550624
$ 16.95/£ 12.95

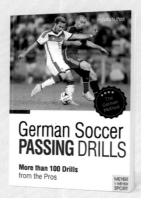

ISBN: 9781782550488
$ 17.95/£ 12.95

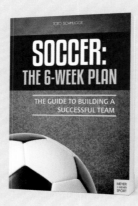

ISBN: 9781782550921
$ 16.95/£ 11.95

All information subject to change. © Thinkstockphotos/photodisc_Ryan McVay

MEYER & MEYER Sport
Von-Coels-Str. 390
52080 Aachen
Germany

Phone   +49 (0) 2 41 - 9 58 10 - 13
Fax   +49 (0) 2 41 - 9 58 10 - 10
Email   sales@m-m-sports.com
Website   www.m-m-sports.com

All books available as e-books.